Joe Gorman was born in Brisbane, raised in the Blue Mountains, and has lived in Sydney and Melbourne. He has written for the *Guardian*, the *Sydney Morning Herald*, the *Age*, the *Courier-Mail*, *Overland*, *New Matilda*, *Sports Illustrated*, *Penthouse* and SBS. He has appeared on ABC television and radio, and on Al Jazeera. *The Death and Life of Australian Soccer* is his first book.

THE
DEATH
& LIFE OF
AUSTRALIAN
SOCCER

JOE GORMAN

First published 2017 by University of Queensland Press
PO Box 6042, St Lucia, Queensland 4067 Australia

www.uqp.com.au
uqp@uqp.uq.edu.au

Cover design by Josh Durham, Design by Committee
Cover images: Front cover, centre: Mark Viduka © Penny Stephens/Fairfax Syndication.
Front cover, clockwise from top: John Kosmina scores © Les Shorrock; St George Stadium
© Calistemon/Wikimedia Commons; Socceroos World Cup 1974 qualification squad,
courtesy of the National Archives of Australia (NAA), A6180, 18/12/73/53; Attila Abonyi
leaps © Les Shorrock; Socceroos World Cup 1974 squad, courtesy of the NAA, A6135,
K22/5/74/14; Charles Perkins, courtesy of Colin and Paul Tatz/*Australian Soccer Weekly*;
Perth Glory fans, courtesy of Perth Glory Football Club. Back cover photographs ©
Les Shorrock. From top to bottom: John Kosmina; Attila Abonyi 1969; Malcolm Fraser and
Frank Lowy prior to NSL Grand Final. Les Shorrock photographs reproduced courtesy of the
Les Shorrock Collection, Deakin University Library; reproduction fees waived in favour of a
donation to the Cancer Council.

Typeset in 11.5/16 pt Bembo Std by Post Pre-press Group, Brisbane
Index by Puddingburn Publishing Services
Printed in Australia by McPherson's Printing Group

  The University of Queensland Press is assisted by
the Australian Government through the Australia
Council, its arts funding and advisory body.

National Library of Australia
Cataloguing-in-Publication data is available at http://catalogue.nla.gov.au

ISBN
978 0 7022 5968 5 (pbk)
978 0 7022 5925 8 (ePDF)
978 0 7022 5926 5 (ePub)
978 0 7022 5927 2 (Kindle)

University of Queensland Press uses papers that are natural, renewable and recyclable products
made from wood grown in sustainable forests. The logging and manufacturing processes conform
to the environmental regulations of the country of origin.

For Dad, who taught me how to hit the white dot.

CONTENTS

AUTHOR'S NOTE

Researching a book of this scope presented several challenges. For this reason, the quotes are drawn from a mix of archival research and from interviews I conducted between 2013 and 2016. All quotes from the archives have an endnote. Those without an endnote are from the interviews. Other sources without an endnote include off-the-record interviews and confidential documents which cannot be acknowledged.

The translations from the Croatian newspapers in the 1983–1985 chapter are thanks to Dario Brentin. All diacritics have been eliminated for consistency.

The research for this book has been funded in part thanks to scholarships from Macquarie University and Victoria University. Sections of the book have also been published by the *Guardian* and Fairfax Media.

THE WORLD IS FOR THEM

Introduction

As you approach Fairfield and Bossley Park, on the western fringes of Sydney, the closer you get to the stadium and clubhouse the more impressive the new subdivisions look: splendid, if a trifle over-ornate brick palazzos with big terraces or balconies, Spanish hacienda-type villas, with lots of grotesque garden gnomes or white marble lions guarding the entrance, like modern-day Cerberuses [...]

Marconi, it seems, has everything: the perfect set-up to create and run a highly successful soccer organisation, perennially vying for top honors, a sort of Inter Milan or Juventus in the bush. They have what we used to say was needed to make a go of soccer in this country, all in one spot [...]

Andrew Dettre

Soccer Action, 1985[1]

In the Marconi directors' box, Sutherland's winning goal was met with anguish and despair. The president of Marconi, Vince Foti, threw his hands in the air and turned his back on the action. An elderly man to my left, who had been whimpering for most of the match, let out a long, exasperated groan. Behind him sat Ray Richards, a former Marconi captain, Les Scheinflug, a former Marconi coach, and Klaus Okon Snr, the father of Paul Okon, perhaps the greatest Marconi player.

Together they formed a council of Australian soccer elders. This was not a performance befitting of their presence.

Scheinflug stood up, looked around theatrically, winked, and announced his farewell to Australian soccer. Richards just shook his head forlornly. Throughout the evening Okon Snr had pointed proudly to the spot behind the goals where he first met his wife. Now, as the final minutes approached, he grimaced.

'Never before have Marconi finished last, not even when we played in the Southern Districts competition,' he said, staring into the middle distance. 'This lot have made history.'

It was the first day of August 2015, Round 20 of the New South Wales National Premier Leagues season, and the final home game for Marconi. Don't let the embellished title fool you – the NPL is simply a rebadged version of the NSW state league.

Marconi was first promoted to the top echelon of this league in 1970, and by 1977 was a founding member of the National Soccer League (NSL). In 2015, Marconi was one of only three clubs in Australia, along with South Melbourne Hellas and Hakoah, to have four national league titles to its name.

But the lustre had well and truly worn off. Marconi would finish on just seven points for the season, a whopping 13 points below the second-last placed Parramatta FC. And for the first time, Marconi would be relegated to the second division.

Soccer people know Marconi. Often referred to as 'the Palace', the club is such a landmark in south-west Sydney that it even has its own Marconi Road. It has been frequented by local mayors, state politicians, prime ministers, pop stars, the great Juventus club from Turin, and received accolades from the ambassador of Italy, the Patriarch of Venice and the Queen of England.

Marconi has helped produce generations of great soccer players, from Ray Richards to Rene Colusso, Mark Jankovics to Mark Schwarzer, Christian Vieri to Paul Okon. The grounds have been host to bocce tournaments, entertained its members at Easter chestnut picnics and Blue Light Discos, and provided a home for generations of Italian families.

On the wall inside the social club there is a series of photos that charts Marconi's rise from a tin shed in a paddock to a glittering empire in a rapidly expanding suburb of south-west Sydney. For decades, the stadium had grown to match the suburb. At its peak, Marconi Stadium had three comfortable grandstands, private boxes for media and corporate types, and room to fit more than 10,000 supporters. Yet on this particular evening there were more players, staff and club officials in attendance than paying spectators. A lonely smattering of people sat in the main grandstand.

Running adjacent to the car park, to the right of the directors' box, used to be a grandstand that boxed in the pitch from all sides. It has since been demolished, leaving behind a disused tower and an artificial incline where they buried landfill in the early 1970s. The famous giant Marconi soccer ball, which rises majestically above the arena, looks like a relic of a bygone era, similar to one of those dusty old silos on stilts from a long-forgotten rural town.

As the referee blew her whistle for full-time – Sutherland 2, Marconi 1 – this once-loved stadium stood forlorn at the unhappy spectacle playing out below. A single beam of light from an empty canteen shone through the cold Saturday-night gloom.

It's the same wherever you go, whether it's Lakeside Stadium in South Melbourne, Knights Stadium in Sunshine or St George Stadium next to Sydney Airport. Excluded from the A-League, Australia's premier soccer competition, the game's pioneer clubs have been locked in the torpor of their local state leagues, living off old glories and fading dreams. This is the death and life of Australian soccer.

★

Six months prior to the match between Marconi and Sutherland, in February 2015, I was in Melbourne to watch the grand final of the Palestinian Community Association (PCA) Futsal League. It is a recreational competition in which each of the teams takes its name from a lost or occupied Palestinian town. I was there at the invitation of Ghassan Zakaria and Mohammad Othman, two young Australians of Palestinian heritage.

'The idea was to reintroduce the youth to Palestinian culture,' Zakaria told me. 'The names are to get players thinking of where they come from.'

Zakaria, like most of the players and organisers, is heavily involved in Melbourne's Palestinian community. The competition's best player, Ahmed Azzam, alone raised more than $25,000 to rebuild infrastructure in Gaza in the months leading up to the match. Othman, the league's photographer and videographer, is a board member of the Olive Kids Foundation, which sponsors Palestinian children in Gaza and the West Bank. Others teach at Arabic Sunday schools.

On centre court at Olympic Village, eight young dancers performed the *dabke* before kick-off. They smiled as they hopped, skipped and jumped to the beat of their homeland. Dressed in black, the women wrapped the Palestinian *keffiyeh* around their waists while the men draped it over their shoulders and around their necks.

Gaza FC demolished Gaza Warriors 7–3, with Azzam the standout performer. A Victorian state league player of considerable talent, he told me after the match that it was his dream to represent Palestine. He'd seen them in the flesh just a month earlier during the 2015 Asian Cup.

These young Palestinians initially thought to form a soccer team in the Victorian state leagues, but the cost was too great and the entry conditions too stringent. Football Federation Victoria, under directives from the national federation, requires all teams to have junior sides, a home ground and to drop any 'foreign' or ethnic references in their team name and logos.

Naturally, these rules ran counter to the whole point of the exercise. There is no geographic location in Melbourne that this team represents – they are an imagined, inherently political community bound by memory, song, dance, food, resistance and soccer.

'These youngsters, this generation, is probably more Australian than any of us,' explained Imad Sukkar, an elder statesman of the PCA. 'They know the culture and they can communicate effectively. I want them to hold the flag and take over the responsibility. The world is for them.'

A few generations ago, the PCA Futsal League would likely have taken form as a united state league club, probably called Melbourne Palestine. Now it is hidden away in its own league, playing a compressed, indoor version of soccer, unrecognised by state or national federations.

The social conditions that led to this futsal league, and the decline of clubs like Marconi, prompted me to write this book. Why have Australia's great migrant soccer clubs been mostly cleansed of their names, their flags and their symbols? Why are many Asian, African and Arab migrants playing outside soccer's existing structures in order to retain a piece of their identity? In a so-called multicultural society, how did ethnicity become a dirty word in Australia's most diverse sport?

For most of its history, soccer in Australia has been an incongruous proposition. Soccer is the most popular sport in the world, yet it is often regarded as a third-rate game in Australia. Soccer has more participants than Australian Rules football and rugby league, yet its professional competition lags behind the AFL and the NRL. In terms of age, gender and cultural diversity, soccer has long been the most democratic sport in Australia, yet it has also been the most despised.

Australian soccer's great national question is whether immigrants and ethnic communities should have the right to run their own affairs, rather than assimilating into pre-existing district clubs and institutions. For this reason, the game has always been pegged to debates around citizenship, identity and multiculturalism. Soccer in Australia is never just soccer. Soccer's national question is Australia's national question.

This book is an argument about soccer's social and cultural role in Australia. It may frustrate some fans and a few historians – particularly in this current era where soccer is trying to move away from its ethnic image – that the multicultural aspect of the game is such a focus here. There are indeed many other Australian soccer stories to tell, but without properly recognising the diversity, nationalism and politics that successive migrant communities have brought to soccer, the account would be woefully incomplete.

For generations, Australian soccer has been characterised by its vibrant, passionate and sometimes difficult ethnic communities. This has been the principal source of its survival and also the reason that it has never truly been accepted as an Australian pursuit. Soccer has been side-eyed, only occasionally thrust into the national conversation. At times scorned, and always distrusted, soccer in Australia has provided a unique space for almost every conceivable ethnic group, each representing a shard in a messy, incomplete mosaic known as soccer, football or 'wogball'.

I use the word 'soccer' deliberately. Of all the things this book seeks to do, understanding the past is the most important. The lexical shift from soccer to football that occurred in 2004 might have brought us in line with the rest of the world, but it betrays our own history.

Australians of all backgrounds have long called the game soccer, whether they loved it, hated it or took no interest in it at all. The men's national team is nicknamed the 'Socceroos'. The specialist newspapers have been called *Soccer World*, *Soccer Action* and *Australian Soccer Weekly*. And when the anarchist Greek-Australian poet πO (pronounced Pi-O) wrote about the game, he titled the poem 'Soccor'.

While πO is mostly uninterested in sport, and certainly not hung up on the etymological debate of 'soccer' versus 'football', he is known for his mastery of language and phonetics and for expressing truthfully the sounds and lived experience of Australia's ethnic communities. So if πO remembers a game called soccer, then so do I.[2]

★

I believe soccer to be a game of love, expressed through the relationship between friends, communities, fathers and sons. This is not to devalue the role of women in soccer; however, the period of history that I am concerned with in this book was a heavily male-dominated environment, and so this is the basis from which I have gathered the stories.

I remember little of attending my first soccer match, but the brief flashes of memory are reflective of my current interest in the game. It was 1998, I was eight years old and, like many young Australian boys, I was obsessed with sport. Growing up two hours west of Sydney in Katoomba, I played soccer in winter, cricket in summer, basketball and soccer at school, and watched whatever sport was on television. My father encouraged these interests with a fanaticism that caused our family weekends to be completely given over to sport.

I remember Harry Kewell, for reasons that puzzled me for years, during the opening game of the 23rd season of the NSL. The golden boy of Australian soccer wasn't playing that day, nor was he even in the stadium. But Northern Spirit used his face, his image and his credibility as a marketing ploy.

Kewell grew up in Smithfield in Sydney's western suburbs, and although Northern Spirit represented Sydney's north, Kewell's image lured middle Australia to one of Sydney's first non-ethnic NSL clubs.

I also remember approaching Robbie Slater just outside North Sydney Oval and requesting an autograph. Slater was an Australian international, part of the Blackburn Rovers side that won the English Premier League in 1995, and one of the stars of Northern Spirit. Slater obliged, scrawling his mark on my tattered soccer ball. Against my wishes, a tall, darkly handsome man who walked beside Slater did the same. Years later, it just so happened that my first major interview as a soccer journalist was with Mark Rudan, that same man. I mentioned to him that he had signed my ball all those years ago, though I decided not to admit that I hadn't the faintest clue who he was.

It was the first and last NSL game Dad and I attended. This book, in many ways, tries to find out why.

Why did Dad and I go along at all? Well, we loved soccer. I started playing before I learned to walk – Dad would hold my arms and swing me at the ball, probably for his own delight more than mine. When jumpsuit gave way to soccer kit, Dad became my first coach, and before long he was hooked and started playing in the over-35 competition.

The skills he learned as a kid in Brisbane's working-class suburbs had never left him. He was good – really good – and when I was 15 we won the Lithgow all-age competition together. I delivered the free-kick, he scored the goal, we won the final, and he retired soon after. I suspect that was the pinnacle of his career, and, to be honest, it was probably mine too.

I loved watching him play, even though I was frequently embarrassed at his excesses. A striker, he was the top goal-scorer at every club he played for, often by a wide margin, but every season the team would retire the prize so they wouldn't have to award it to him.

Nearly every season Dad would sign on for a new club, such was his volatile relationship with his teammates. One season, after his hard-as-nails prison-guard teammate requested their team be called 'The Black Adders', Dad named the team 'The Marshmallows' and ordered a full set of pink jerseys. Another memory has him winding up a rival defender for an entire match, scoring a late winner, and then blowing a kiss in the defender's direction. The defender was an ugly, pig-headed thug, and I was thrilled by the outcome, but Dad was lucky not to be punched in the face.

My favourite memory, however – and probably Dad's finest moment – was when he caused a Buddhist from his own team to be sent off. This poor man cracked under Dad's relentless instruction of 'pass the ball to my feet', abandoned his faith, and screamed obscenities at Dad until the referee ordered him from the field.

Dad, by the way, is a poet.

He gave me soccer, forced me to appreciate character, and encouraged me to write. Most of all, he made me realise that sport is an intellectual pursuit and a way of understanding the world around me. He would tell me stories about his childhood at Souths United in Brisbane, of games against opponents with names such as Azzurri, Polonia, Germania, Coalstars, Hollandia and Grange Thistle. On long car trips he would pepper me with questions about geography, history and politics. I knew the answers mostly from soccer. Describe the flag of Argentina? Easy – I'd seen it at the World Cup.

I loved the World Cup, and went to great lengths to learn about the competing nations. Several months before our first NSL match, I saw Dad cry for the first time when Iran beat the Socceroos in a vital World Cup qualifier at the Melbourne Cricket Ground. That image of him crying at the door, staring out beyond the fly-screen and into the night, has never left me.

I was 14 years old when the NSL collapsed, and 15 when the A-League began in 2005. The new competition arrived at a perfect time for both Dad and me. In 2007 I finished high school and we bought season tickets to Sydney FC. In 2008 I moved out of home. Although I did not fully realise it at the time, I know now that the A-League enabled Dad and me to spend every other weekend during the summer together, at least for a few hours. More than anything else, the A-League enabled us to become mates.

The game's uniquely Australian story soon made me want to know more. I knew that the A-League wasn't an immaculate conception, but there was little talk about what came before it. So, armed with many questions, I went looking.

The following is the product of several years of research and writing, tens of thousands of kilometres of travel, a forensic scanning of fading old newspapers, countless hours of interviews and an almost obsessive desire to answer these questions. They are questions, I learned, that have been asked by many other Australians. I hope this book goes some way to explaining their conclusions, and my own.

Joe Gorman
May 2017

PART I

THE NATIONAL INTEREST

'This goes further than soccer; this is also our national interest.'

Sir Arthur George, 1971

THEY SPEAK WITH A SOCCER ACCENT

1950–1966

And it came to pass, that a small band of strangers who had journied from far-distant lands did play amongst themselves a strange game called Soc, which was unknown to the natives of Aus. And after a space of time, many who lived in Southlands, did also play Soc with great skill [...]

Now came one of great wisdom, beloved by the people, And they cried to him saying, 'What thinkest thou oh Fatchen?' And he replied saying, 'What manner of men are these of Soc? Are they stricken with plague, that they have not the strength to pick up the ball?'

After these words, many people spake saying, 'It is true, should the Game of Soc sweep through the land, the habits of our people will change. Is it the wish of our brethren that their children lose the use of their hands?'

And a great fear gripped the multitude lest their offspring eat with their feet.

'The Gospel According to Trevor Jones'
Soccer Mirror, 1953[1]

On a warm summer day in December 1949, four weeks after it set sail from Naples, the USAT *General WM Black* sailed purposefully into Sydney Harbour. It had been a comfortable trip for Andrew Dettre, a bright-eyed 23-year-old Hungarian refugee. He was all alone, thousands of kilometres from home, with no money and no idea what to expect from this new land. But he took comfort from the rolling green of the governor-general's lawn, the majesty of the Sydney Harbour Bridge and an inviting city skyline.

Dettre had left behind family and friends and a continent ravaged by war, political upheaval and acute poverty. He got out of Hungary in 1948 after the communists shut down *Szegedi Nepszava*, the newspaper he had worked for. His tearful father, also a writer, had begged him to stay, but his mother scolded her husband. 'We can't guarantee his safety in Hungary. Let him find his luck in the West.'

His father relented and handed Dettre a collection of precious belongings to exchange for money and food. A young journalist on the run, Dettre worked the land in Vienna and dreamed of the United States of America. In The Hague he had tried to find a place at university, but without papers or a passport he had been deported by the Dutch authorities to Germany. From there, he had gone from one refugee camp to another, thieving chickens and trading the fruit given to him by British soldiers for solid food.

'It was a ruined land,' he later remembered. 'You had to survive in that atmosphere, you didn't have any lofty ideas or plans. It was just the next meal.'

As Europe recovered from World War II, more than two million migrants would arrive in Australia between 1945 and 1965, christened as 'New Australians'. Wary of economic downturn and Australia's geographic vulnerability, the postwar Labor government packaged the mass immigration program as a means of survival, and as the nation committed to a steady increase in its population, migrants from all over Britain and continental Europe settled in the vast landmass. These were the golden years of Australia's immigration program.

Upon arrival, Dettre was interned at a migrant camp in Bathurst, 200 kilometres west of Sydney. He was one of the hundreds of thousands of migrants who came with hope in their hearts and with soccer in their souls. These people weren't interested in horseracing or cricket or Australian Rules football or rugby league, and just as their churches, social clubs and cafes became a link to the homeland, soccer was a bridge between the old world and the new. This golden age of Australian immigration laid the foundation for a golden age of soccer.

Across the country soccer clubs with exotic names sprouted without warning over social kickabouts. Hakoah was one of the first, born at Rushcutters Bay in Sydney in 1939. Juventus was established by the Italians in Melbourne in 1948, while Napredak, a club formed by Yugoslavs, recruited players from the mines of Broken Hill.

Dettre's team, Ferencvaros, named after the famous Hungarian club, was formed in the Bathurst migrant camp. 'It was here,' wrote Dettre, 'on the large, sunburned open spaces of this huge, desolate camp, that a few young migrants laid the foundations for what was soon to form the nucleus of Hungarian soccer in Australia.'[2]

Ferencvaros would eventually migrate to the city, while Dettre worked in factories and as a cleaner in order to save enough money to get out. Nobody wanted to stay in Bathurst.

In Sydney Dettre found an Australian girlfriend whom he would later marry, and a job as an interpreter. Yet he wanted more. Like many other soccer-loving immigrants, he was continually baffled by Australia but determined that the game's acceptance in this strange land would precipitate his own.

While most of these men raised money, tended to the soccer fields and concreted the clubhouses, Dettre wrote. And he wrote beautifully. His reportage would show the influence of Evelyn Waugh's elegant prose and the dark, political literature of Aleksandr Solzhenitsyn and Boris Pasternak. He was a soccer intellectual.

Yet as an immigrant Dettre had to be twice as good as the next journalist, and he had to take the jobs that nobody else wanted. He sent resumes to newspapers and magazines throughout the country, was granted just one interview, and was told that he would never make it.

Nursing an espresso and his disappointment, he spotted a small advertisement for a reporter at the Bathurst *National Advocate*. He rushed to the airport, hopped on a plane, flew back to Bathurst and secured the job. Under the editorial supervision of a wretched alcoholic, in a sleepy town not fit for an urbane young reporter, Dettre worked in what he would later describe as 'the worst English-language newspaper in the Southern Hemisphere'.

The 'New Australians', although they perhaps were not aware at the time, were settling on stolen country with a dark, hidden past. Bathurst was on Wiradjuri land and its Indigenous people had fought a long war of resistance against the white settlers, culminating in the Bathurst War of 1824 that had wiped out much of the Wiradjuri population.

Since the British invasion in 1788, these First Nations had been broken up and the Indigenous people massacred, wiped out by foreign diseases, herded onto repressive reserves called 'missions' and ordered to act white. The tribal laws and boundaries that had existed since time immemorial were disregarded and replaced by colonial institutions named after white settlers and British landmarks. This was the tyranny upon which Australia was founded.

The White Australia policy, which had been passed upon Federation in 1901, would fortify the disgrace for generations. White Australia rested upon twin pillars of exclusion and assimilation. Asian immigration was severely restricted, and just as the Indigenous people were ordered to stop speaking their native languages and practising their culture, the immigrants who arrived from Europe were on a program of rapid acculturation into the so-called Australian way of life.

It was soccer, the universal language, that would present the greatest threat to assimilation. The migrant soccer club, later to be called the ethnic club, would reimagine the way in which Australians organised themselves, ignoring the district and suburban lines of demarcation in favour of their own ancestral loyalties, cultural pride and community self-determination.

Since the late 1800s soccer had grown in the cities and in the bush, enjoyed by craggy coalminers and rugged factory workers and happy school children. By the early 1950s, however, the game was run by a monocultural, unimaginative and largely amateur group of men. There was no life in the game, no colour, and any ambition was betrayed by a lack of direction and professionalism. And when the new migrant clubs started to pop up, many saw them as a threat rather than as an opportunity.

'The whole question of these new Australians being allowed to form National clubs should be the subject of special investigation,' concluded the *Sporting Globe* in 1950, 'and although one does not advocate a boycott of these recent arrivals from the playing fields it certainly would be much better if they were assimilated into the ranks of teams mainly of British stock and thus become better "mixers" instead of keeping to themselves and in some cases endeavouring to settle political differences on the football field.'[3]

Yet many of the established teams closed their ranks to the new immigrants, while many fans of other sports, particularly the native Australian Rules football, adopted an unofficial policy of containment.

'People who come to this country and accept all the advantages should support Australian Rules football instead of furthering their own code,' said one committeeman in 1951.[4] 'There must be a united front from all Australian football clubs to halt the soccer movement,' said another.[5]

In South Australia, after a small newspaper named *Soccer Mirror* was established in 1953 to 'help to hasten the onward march of soccer in South Australia', three Adelaide soccer grounds were vandalised. Amid the wreckage were large signs that proclaimed: 'Down with the soccer. Play Australian Rules you bastards.'[6]

Soon after, a stone crashed through the window of *Soccer Mirror*'s office. In the shattered glass, a note was found wrapped around the stone: 'Stop printing *Soccer Mirror*, or else ...'

The editor of the newspaper, a moustachioed Serbian immigrant named Dragisa J Braunovic, told his readers that the newspaper was 'At War with a Sadist' and labelled the attacks 'organised outrages'.[7] Yet within weeks he had relented. The newspaper was rebadged as *Sporting Mirror*, and articles on Australian Rules football were included for the first time.

This was a proxy war for the soul of modern Australia. The fight was to lay claim over its land, its people and its institutions. In 1953, Australian Rules officials quietly prevented a Chinese soccer side from playing at the Melbourne Cricket Ground, and in 1954 the Prahran Council leased Toorak Park to a local Australian Rules football club for a peppercorn rent of £25. Jugoslav United Soccer Team (JUST), which had offered the council £800, was told to play elsewhere.

The message was clear. Assimilation meant speaking English, anglicising the family name, getting a job, and dropping soccer for Australian Rules football, cricket or rugby league.

'Nothing can draw them away from their national games,' the Melbourne *Argus* once concluded. 'What they do has no effect upon Australian Rules. What does matter, however, is what their children do.'[8]

★

The soccer revolution began in Sydney and spread like wildfire around the country. In 1954, Hakoah entered the NSW second division and finished second behind Dutch club Sydney Austral. Controversially, neither side was promoted, despite North Shore and Balgownie Rangers languishing at the bottom of the first division.

Everywhere else in the world, promotion and relegation was the lifeblood of soccer. Traditionally, at the end of every season there would be a reshuffling of the deck, allowing successful clubs to realise their ambitions while punishing the weaker teams. Not so in Australia.

Next season, the first division was expanded from ten to 12 teams, and Prague and Sydney Austral were promoted. But when Hakoah finished top of the second division in 1956 it was again denied a place in the top tier. As unhappy rumblings turned to conspiratorial rumours, the Hakoah president, Walter Sternberg, called a meeting of club executives to his home in Sydney's eastern suburbs.

The group took drastic action and broke away from the old, staid NSW Soccer Association to form the NSW Federation of Soccer Clubs. Their resolution, signed on 5 January 1957, was framed in the grandest terms, urging the 'immediate affiliation of all soccer bodies in NSW [...] in this democratic movement to establish soccer as a major football code in this State, and to be officially affiliated with all recognised interstate, national and international soccer organisations'.[9]

This standoff between old and new would spread across the country, threatening the authority of the Australian Soccer Association and its state affiliates. The new federations were headed by men of different faiths and nationalities: Jews and Christians, Scots and Italians, Greeks and Hungarians and Australians.

One of the NSW federation's first initiatives was a knockout cup competition, held under floodlights at Lidcombe Oval in Sydney's inner west. The first Kennard Cup, named after its brainchild, William Kennard, was won by Hakoah in March 1957. 'Nearly 4500 people last night saw the Federation of Soccer clubs successfully present its first soccer matches,' reported the *Sydney Morning Herald*. 'The standard of the play and the presentation of the matches left little to be desired. Federation officials were delighted with the attendance and the gate was nearly £300.'[10]

The director of the Ampol petroleum company, William Walkley, soon came on board as a major sponsor. 'Soccer,' said Walkley, 'is one way of bringing new Australians into our community life and making them feel at home.'[11]

In the newspapers that chronicled the rise of soccer, there was proud and prolific use of the phrases 'our game' and 'our code'. Immigrants did not assimilate into soccer, as they did in rugby league, Australian Rules or cricket. They rebuilt the game in their own image and began to dictate its culture and its conversations.

'The old football clubs formed an integral part of the social and cultural life of their communities,' wrote Lex Marinos, the famous Greek-Australian actor, in his autobiography. 'They were also evidence of the great commitment the migrants had made to their new country; and they were places where people could relax, sing their songs, dance their dances and be treated with respect and dignity. A refuge from the other world.'[12]

Into this milieu arrived Leopold Baumgartner, a striker for FK Austria. During the club's 1957 tour he marvelled at the beautiful scenery in Manly and lunched at a restaurant called Prague in Sydney. He took those memories back to Vienna and, over a meal with team-mate Karl Jaros, hatched a plan to return to Australia. Their wives agreed, fascinated by the prospect of white-sand beaches. The pair were signed by Prague, one of the NSW federation's more glamorous migrant clubs, in 1958.

Prague did not pay FK Austria a transfer fee for either Baumgartner or Jaros, breaking the laws of the Federation Internationale de Football Association (FIFA). Instead Prague claimed they were immigrants, and as more unauthorised players followed from Malta, Austria and Holland, FIFA began to field complaints from European clubs.

Still, these internationally recognised players made Australian soccer seem stylish and its possibilities endless. Baumgartner's arrival was a harbinger for a new style of play. Blond and balletic, with neat foot-work and an eye for goal, he was the gold standard to which future generations of Australian players were compared. Nicknamed the 'Little Professor', he moved the supporters' minds as well as their emotions.

In one match, he would score an incredible last-gasp winner by curling the ball into the net from a corner-kick. In another, he would waltz around two defenders, skip past the advancing goalkeeper and casually dribble towards goal. Instead of simply side-footing the ball into the net, however, he would kneel down, pause for theatrical effect, and push the ball over the line with his forehead.

Almost every section of Australian society found a place in soccer. By 1958, around the country there were Italian teams called Juventus and APIA, Dutch clubs such as Hollandia, Wilhelmina and Windmills, the Greeks of Pan Hellenic, and Czech clubs named Prague and Slavia. The Scots supported Caledonians and Rangers, the Yugoslavs cheered for Yugal and JUST, the Croatians for Croatia, the Hungarians for Budapest, and the Maltese for Melita and George Cross.

In Sydney, an all-Asian side named 'Wings' played in the Metropolitan League. It was made up of mostly Chinese students on study visas, and its star player was a strapping young Malaysian inter-national named Wong Leong Kong.

Nicknamed 'the Golden Boy' by his teammates, Wong was born in Ipoh, Malaysia, to Chinese parents in 1936. He had made his inter-national debut at 19 years of age, and was then sent to Australia by his father to study accountancy. By 1959, he was snapped up by North Side United and finished third in the *Sydney Morning Herald* best and fairest award. He was one of the few Asians in the country, and the only Asian in top-flight sport.

'Because of Australia's great migrant intake,' reported *Soccer World*, 'the population has now become very cosmopolitan. The success of the Federation has been due to the fact that they have catered for that type of fan.'[13]

Soccer World was first published as *Soccer and Other Sports* on 12 July 1958. From the beginning the newspaper suited Andrew Dettre's style of writing and his disposition. Its editor-in-chief was Marcel Nagy, a bespectacled senior who had once served as the president of the Hungarian Football Association, and the green newsprint – which gave it the nickname 'the Green Paper' – was an homage to the colours of Ferencvaros and *Nemzeti Sport*, the most famous sports daily in Hungary.

The newspaper was passionate about Australian soccer, sensitive towards the needs of migrants and their clubs, and critical where it was necessary to improve the standard of the game. From the outset it promised to 'act as a link between Australians and New Australians in bringing them together on the field of sport'.[14] At soccer grounds it would be advertised by an enthusiastic Hungarian salesman whose catchcry, *Soccer Vorld! Get your Soccer Vorld!* became the defining sound of Sydney soccer.

Having moved from Bathurst to work for Sydney's *Daily Telegraph*, in August 1960 Dettre made his first foray into the newspaper that he would later edit and own. 'The term "Australian" and "New Australian" club can no longer apply,' he wrote in a thoughtful letter to the editor of *Soccer World*. 'Where is the borderline, what is the number of players that qualifies a team to be called old or new Australian? The question cannot be properly answered; any attempt is absurd [...] Born Australians and migrants are hopelessly intermingled in just about every club's management.'[15]

This letter marked the beginning of Dettre's attempt to resolve Australian soccer's great national question. During a period of more than two decades, he would use *Soccer World* to report all the paradoxes, the characters, the identities and the nationalisms that pervaded the game in the postwar period. His own writing formed the first draft of the most decisive period of Australia's soccer history. He wrote about soccer with intensity, passion and verve, each article forming a piece of his own biography.

In a deeply conservative society where the journalists had names like McNicoll or Walker or Hughes, *Soccer World* immediately gave immigrants a unique platform. This was a time when *They're a Weird Mob*, a novel about the travails of an Italian migrant trying to fit in, was published by an Australian named John O'Grady under the pseudonym Nino Culotta. In *Soccer World*, the writers were actual recent immigrants, not Anglo-Celts with pseudonyms and affected accents. But *Soccer World* was much more than an ethnic newspaper – it was printed in English rather than a foreign language and was read by every national group that followed the game. This made it a forum for ideas, a conduit for cultural exchange and a place of lively self-determination.

'All right, so we are one of the weird mob,' read one of *Soccer World*'s very first editorials, 'but if doing something for Australian soccer comes under that heading, then we are happy to be one of the mob and to keep on being that way.'[16]

As soccer grew more diverse, and its participants grew confident in their place in the new society, a debate grew about the role and scope of Australia's assimilation policy. *Soccer World* dismissed assimilation as 'an ugly word' and praised the NSW federation for having 'many overseas members in its ranks, both on and off the field'.[17]

Yet in April 1960, as *Soccer World* was discussing how best to promote the domestic game, FIFA suspended Australia's membership.

'The Austrian and Dutch players did not immigrate to Australia and incidentally become members of a soccer club,' concluded Helmut Kaiser, the FIFA secretary general. 'On the contrary, you wanted to recruit good footballers from Europe and make them look like immigrants.'[18]

This was an intensely complicated issue. Australian clubs certainly owed the European clubs transfer fees, but at the same time many players had grown to love Australia and intended to stay. Leopold Baumgartner, for example, announced after just six months that 'Australia is an ideal country for soccer', and began planning for a new life. His younger brother joined him and his wife in Sydney, a new line of Baumgartner soccer boots was launched, he urged clubs to develop their own junior players, and recommended that Australia unite behind a single, national 'super league'. This, he wrote for *Sport* magazine, 'would give our soccer its greatest ever shot in the arm and put Australia closer than ever to international status'.[19]

★

'We have heard quite a lot recently about nasty soccer clubs preventing boys from playing the great Australian football game,' joked the South Australian *Soccer News* in 1960. 'It has been pointed out to us that the principal culprits are a class of people known as "International Footballers" who, instead of allowing themselves to be duly assimilated, persist in eating garlic, spaghetti, wiener schnitzel, paprika and, what's worst, in playing an outlandish game known as soccer.'[20]

A few months later, *Soccer News* was fronted by the headline 'A Real Australian Boy Makes Good'. On the cover were three pictures of Charles Perkins. As a young Indigenous man, Perkins was not yet counted as part of the national census. Yet while the state did not recognise him as a citizen, *Soccer News* explained that he was 'a real dinky-di Australian boy' and that he 'deserved to win the Popular Players Competition'.[21]

Charles Nelson Perkins was born in Alice Springs in 1936. His ticket out of Australia arrived through soccer. In June 1957, in a letter from the Everton Football Club, Perkins had been promised £60 to book a passage to England. He had arrived in London soon after, wearing a shirt with one sleeve and with just a few shillings in his pocket.

In Liverpool, Perkins had worked on the shipyards of the River Mersey and learned how to play tough, hard soccer on miserable, mud-heaped pitches. He wasn't immediately popular. The Everton players hadn't taken kindly to an outsider competing for a place in the first XI, while the union members didn't appreciate being taken to task by Perkins – a black man – for their attitude towards a fellow West Indian worker.

'I stood up for myself,' Perkins later recalled. 'I wouldn't call any of the bosses "Sir" in soccer or the shipyards or anywhere else.'[22]

Further north, Perkins found a home away from home at the great amateur side Bishop Auckland. After one match against Oxford University, he reflected on the lot of his people back home, and thought: 'I must go to university. I've got to prepare myself educationally.'[23]

Despite an offer to trial with Manchester United in the English first division, in 1959 Perkins had returned to the South Australian second division. 'Charles would have stayed in England longer,' noted one reporter, 'but the un-Australian world of soccer called him back to become captain-coach of a Croatian team in Adelaide.'[24]

The president of Adelaide Croatia, Branko Filipi, sponsored Perkins' return. Filipi had arrived in Australia with Andrew Dettre on the USAT *General WM Black* in 1949. He respected Perkins not just for his playing ability but also for his leadership and his intellect. In Perkins' first season with the club in 1959, Adelaide Croatia was promoted to the first division. In 1960, with another Indigenous man, Gordon Briscoe, on the team, Adelaide Croatia won the Advertiser Cup.

'Our first choice for the year 1960 is Charlie Perkins,' reported the *South Australian Soccer Year Book*. 'Charlie is a fair dinkum Aussie if there ever was one. He is known among all soccer lovers in the state [...] For his club, Croatia, Charlie was a tower of strength on the field of play, and as such, an inspiration to his side.'[25]

John Moriarty, an Indigenous man who played for Port Adelaide, Adelaide Juventus and Adelaide Croatia, looked to Perkins as a 'big brother'. When the pair were selected to play for the South Australian state team, Moriarty was asked to speak to the local news reporters. Shy and quiet, he requested that Perkins accompany him. 'Charlie was a good talker on the field and off it,' remembered Moriarty. 'He was about three years older and we used him as a role model.'

Perkins, Briscoe and Moriarty first played soccer together as children at the St Francis Boys Home in Semaphore, a coastal suburb of Adelaide. They had good times at St Francis, but nothing could hide the fact that the boarding house was designed to remove them from their families, their country and their traditions. The boys' upbringing was one of strict assimilation into white Australian life.

If assimilation was an inconvenience for immigrants, it was a matter of life and death in Indigenous communities. After Federation, Australia had gradually stopped slaughtering its Indigenous people and began a new policy of cultural genocide. By order of the Commonwealth, Indigenous children like Moriarty were forcibly split from their parents, taught to be white, and disconnected from land, language and culture. Between 1910 and 1970, between one in three and one in ten Indigenous children would be forcibly removed from their families and their communities.

In soccer, the migrant institution, Perkins, Briscoe and Moriarty were treated with respect and their ambitions were encouraged. Soccer gave these young Indigenous men a platform, a chance to lift their gaze, an opportunity to reach for new horizons and to develop a public profile. As a soccer-playing threesome they would form relations with the press, find access to the institutions, and be held in an esteem not usually afforded to Indigenous people.

'We were accepted as equals,' remembered Moriarty. 'Being Aboriginals we didn't have the chance to vote, and we were still second-class citizens in those days. I think the soccer fraternity embraced us, no questions asked.'

★

By 1961, Asian and Indigenous people formed less than 2 per cent of the Australian population. They were not liked, not wanted, denied the same rights as their fellow man and sometimes jeered in the streets.

But in soccer, Charles Perkins became 'Charlie', John Moriarty became 'Giovanni', and Wong Leong Kong, Polonia-North Side's winger, had earned the nickname 'Johnny Wong'. The NSW selectors picked him for a state match against Queensland, and *Soccer World* reported: 'Off the field Johnny Wong is a most shy and unassuming fellow. On the field he is a perfect gentleman, whom no referee has ever cautioned.'[26]

Soccer had become a truly radical game. It was the most progressive sport and one of the most culturally democratic institutions in Australian society. In the soccer newspapers and the park grounds, Asians, Indigenous Australians and Europeans were mingling as equals; *Soccer World* confidently declared that 'There is no such thing as assimilation of migrants'; while in the boardrooms, the migrant-backed Australian Soccer Federation challenged the authority of the old, Anglo-dominated Australian Soccer Association.[27]

'As far as soccer is concerned, the stage is set for a complete breakaway from the old, parochial way of life, from narrow-minded and limited vision,' announced *Soccer World*'s first editorial of 1962. '*Soccer World* is the first football publication on a national scale and soccer itself will soon be the first code played nationally. And, we hope, one will help the other.'[28]

To prove the commitment, *Soccer World*'s 'Star Parade' column was relaunched as 'Australian Star Parade'. Charles Perkins, who was born in the Northern Territory, raised in South Australia and christened 'Sydney's most "dinki-di" soccer star', was the first to be featured.[29]

Perkins had moved from captain-coach of Adelaide Croatia to captain-coach of Pan Hellenic in Sydney. Pan Hellenic helped finance his first home and his university studies, and in 1962 he was named in the NSW state squad alongside teammates of German, Austrian, Hungarian, Greek, Scottish, Dutch, Spanish, Argentinian, South African and Israeli background.

Andrew Dettre once called this 'the Baumgartner era' – a golden age where foreign players arrived, crowds flocked to support their teams and people started to seriously wonder if soccer would become Australia's number-one sport. Immigrants flooded the local market as every club in Sydney tried to find their own Leopold Baumgartner.

Dettre was enlisted by the Budapest club, which grew out of Ferencvaros, to find high-quality, Hungarian-speaking imports. He penned a letter to *Magyar Szo*, the Hungarian-language newspaper in Yugoslavia, and sent it away with a copy of *Soccer World* enclosed. In Vojvodina, a reporter by the name of Frank Arok opened the envelope. This was the beginning of Arok's lifelong love affair with Australia. Over the next three decades, he would become one of the nation's best-loved coaches.

At Arok's suggestion, Petar Banicevic and Mladen Krgin – two Hungarian-speaking Yugoslavs – arrived at Sydney's Budapest club in 1962. They were soon followed by Argentinians Eduardo Massey and Miguel Mazzina, and within seven years there would be 22 Argentinians playing top-flight soccer in Sydney. At the centre of it all was Dettre, acting as a journalist, a clubman and a part-time immigration agent.

The European immigrants had brought theatre, professionalism and an entrepreneurial spirit to soccer, accelerating the game's transformation from a quaint participatory pursuit to a thriving spectator sport. They took to the soccer fields, staffed the offices of the clubs and federations, and spoke their own language on the sidelines.

The Australia Cup, a new national competition, was established to unify the states behind the Australian Soccer Federation. A Hungarian poet from Melbourne named David Martin published *The Young Wife*, the first novel to be set around a migrant soccer club, which the *Sydney Morning Herald* declared to be a 'milestone on Australia's road to literary maturity'.[30] And in December, a record crowd of 26,770 spectators crammed into the Sydney Sports Ground to watch the grand final between Budapest and Hakoah. Represented in the match were nine different nationalities from four continents – eight Austrians, seven Hungarians, an Englishman, a Yugoslav, a Spaniard, a Scot, a Kiwi, an Argentinian and an Israeli. There wasn't a single player born in Australia.

In *Soccer World*, a column titled 'Language of the Future?' confirmed the game's foreignness to the Australian public.

> A nine-year old first generation Aussie, brought up in our code by virtue of his parents' influence, came home to announce excitedly that new people had taken over the local cake shop.
>
> 'Who are they' asked Dad.
>
> 'I don't know,' said the little fellow, 'but they speak with a soccer accent.'[31]

On 17 February 1963, Australian Soccer Federation chairman Dr Henry Seamonds walked out of a tempestuous meeting at Soccer House in St Kilda, suffered a heart attack and died. The subject of the meeting, which lasted for many hours, had been Australia's ban from FIFA. Dr Seamonds complained of chest pains, but stayed until the end. 'I feel that he gave too much of himself to soccer,' lamented Walter Sternberg, the president of Hakoah. 'This may have aggravated his illness.'[32]

Seamonds was replaced by Theo Marmaras, a Greek from South Melbourne Hellas, while William Walkley took over as president of the ASF. Within one month, the old Australian Soccer Association was wound up and replaced by the Australian Soccer Federation. Finally soccer would be run by a single, unified governing body.

By this time Dettre was working for the *Daily Telegraph* in Sydney, was contributing to the English magazine *World Soccer* and had taken over the editorship of *Soccer World*. Already endowed with a huge sense of self-assurance, he immediately made *Soccer World* an organ for his opinions and a place of lively debate.

He took the pseudonym 'Paul Dean' to disguise his role at *Soccer World* from the *Daily Telegraph* and, when the *Telegraph* accused soccer of fostering violent fans, Dettre valiantly defended his sport. And in

June, as *Soccer World* celebrated its fifth birthday, Dettre wrote a long article on the pros and cons of rejoining FIFA. He pointed out that Australian clubs had improperly recruited European players under the guise of migration, but also admitted that this had been the cause of Australia's biggest soccer boom.

Within a month a negotiated settlement was paid by the ASF for the imports that Australian clubs had signed from Europe, and Australia was readmitted to FIFA. This allowed the ASF to form a national team, enter the World Cup, and invite touring teams down under. Crowds were at an all-time high, the game had rejoined the world unified behind a single national body, and discussions were now being held to start a national league.

The 1964 NSW first division grand final between APIA and Budapest highlighted the rapid transformation that soccer had experienced over the last decade and a half. There were players from all walks of life: the oldest was APIA's goalkeeper Adauto Iglesias, a Spaniard who had played with Real Madrid, and the youngest was Budapest's German-born 21-year-old defender, Manfred Schaefer. The coaches were both Hungarian, while John Watkiss, born in England but raised in Sydney, scored five goals in a romping 7–2 victory to APIA.

Watching on from the stands was an Asian referee, the Nigerian Olympic team and a host of newspapermen from both the mainstream and ethnic press. Johnny Wong, APIA's winger, was the best man on ground. He created four of APIA's seven goals, was singled out by the headline 'Budapest Had the Wong-complex during Big Game', and was described by one reporter as the 'brain' behind the victory.[33]

★

Two months after Charles Perkins led a group of university students on an historic Freedom Ride to protest racial segregation in rural NSW towns, on Sunday 25 April 1965, thousands of straight-backed ex-soldiers marched on Sydney streets to commemorate Anzac Day. As the convoy moved along George Street, cheers and flowers were tossed in the direction of the old diggers, and medals of war shone brightly from proud chests. The 100,000 people who lined the streets of Sydney mourned the 50th anniversary of the bloody Gallipoli campaign and harked back to the birth of what war historian Charles Bean labelled 'an Australian character' – a monocultural society bound by mateship, service and a tough brand of tenderness. As the crowd moved to the Domain, a speaker announced: 'As a nation we hate war; we are not a militarist people.'[34]

Later that afternoon, just down the road from the Anzac Day ceremony, more than 8000 people crowded into Wentworth Park for a Federation Cup double-header. In the first match APIA beat St George-Budapest 4–2, with two goals to APIA's Johnny Wong. An hour into the second match, a crazed Pan Hellenic supporter jumped the boundary fence, raced across the field and punched South Coast United's Jim Kelly in the face.

As Kelly's teammates rushed to his aid and savagely kicked his assailant, supporters whooped and hollered and transformed a soccer match into a riot. A few uprooted the corner flags for weapons, while others used feet and fists to maim their enemies. Kelly left the field with a face full of blood while the referee nursed broken ribs, busted teeth and a bump on the head. The match was soon abandoned.

A life ban was handed to Jim Condos, the 27-year-old Pan Hellenic fan who started the brawl. At his home in Leichhardt in Sydney's inner west, one reporter noted that he was a music lover and a ballet enthusiast. 'The Federation has not heard my side of the story,' he told the reporter. 'I only wanted to talk to my friend Jim Kelly.'[35]

The match was immediately christened 'The Battle of Wentworth Park', and 'the Anzac Day riot'. The *Daily Telegraph* called the soccer violence 'alien and unwanted',[36] while the *Sydney Morning Herald* decreed that 'Sunday's incident was the worst exhibition this State has seen of the mass hysteria and rioting which Soccer provokes overseas'. In between reverential Anzac Day coverage, the editor warned that soccer was engendering violence unfamiliar to 'Australian sports crowds', and that 'Australians' would not attend a sport that allowed hooligans to assault players and referees.[37]

The readers of *Soccer World*, meanwhile, were given a more nuanced explanation of the events. Andrew Dettre published letters from the general public, club officials and players. What emerged from the debate was that the European migrants, including Dettre, were dismayed by South Coast United players charging opposition goalkeepers. This was technically within FIFA rules, but its interpretation divided Britain from the rest of the world. The British regularly charged goalkeepers, while the Europeans and the South Americans deplored it.

'Don't believe for one moment the cheap advice that you are reviving the "lost art of charging goalkeepers",' wrote Dettre in an open letter to Max Tolson, a young forward from South Coast United. 'You're not charging them: you're putting them out of the game.'[38]

Ian O'Toole, a resident of Croydon, wrote to *Soccer World* to accuse South Coast United of confusing 'toughness' with 'roughness' and of using 'illegal tackles, hands, arms and fists to inflict injuries on their opponents'. 'Although I do condemn the behaviour of fans in the incident which is now known as the "Anzac Day Battle of Wentworth Park",' he wrote, 'I can fully understand the reasons which made some Pan Hellenic supporters do what they did.'[39]

This was a localised version of the debate between continental Europe and Britain, a cultural exchange between 'old' and 'new' Australians at its most elemental level.

The world rushed in on Australia, arriving first from the immigrant ships and then on the soccer fields. All the incidents of violence were laced with national feeling and cultural suspicion.

At one lower-league match, a Greek player named Doulaveros was sent off and suspended for grabbing a referee in a headlock. Doulaveros claimed it had been a terrible misunderstanding, and that in fact he was simply trying to demonstrate to the referee how he had been manhandled by an opponent. 'I don't speak good English,' he lamented, 'so I thought I better show him.'[40]

Referees complained of being used as political footballs and in Melbourne vandals chopped down the goalposts at Middle Park, one of Victoria's most revered soccer grounds. Before the bandits stole away into the night, they attempted to set fire to the grandstand. Those who made the grim discovery were greeted with two notices, daubed in 18-inch letters on the walls. 'Down with soccer' read one. 'Go Home Wogs' read the other.

Five months after the Anzac Day riot, soccer's most tempestuous season concluded with a grand final rematch between St George–Budapest and APIA. The match finished 2–0 to APIA, with Johnny Wong scoring the final goal of the season. 'This delicate, elusive and clever player was the star of the forward line,' wrote Andrew Dettre. 'When in form, Wong is a sheer pleasure to watch as he speeds along the wing, cuts in and out and sets up goals for the others.'[41]

By the end of 1965, Australia was a member of several treaties and pacts with Asian nations. The Menzies Liberal government had sent troops to fight communism in Malaysia and Indonesia, and stepped up Australia's commitment to the American war in Vietnam. There were many Asian students, including Wong, studying in Australian institutions, but there was still no formal method for them to seek permanent residence or citizenship. Australia's alliances with Asian nations were not complemented by true integration in the region.

'If the impression has been given that no one in Australia ever thinks of Asia, it should be pointed out that this is now far from true,' wrote Donald Horne in *The Lucky Country*, published in 1964. 'Over the last ten years or so there has been a huge shift in attitudes. Sensations burst into the newspapers, seminars are held, articles are written. But the interest is sometimes that of someone momentarily attracted to an idea: *Fascinating stuff I must find out what it's all about sometime.* There is not very much real *feel* for Asia.'[42]

Soccer World sought to change this attitude. Since as early as 1960, Dettre had advocated that Australia join the Asian Football Confederation (AFC), while his colleague Lou Gautier went on several tours of Asia to check the pulse of soccer in the region. There was no other newspaper like it in the country. And it was owned, staffed and read by refugees and immigrants – the people that the

Australians looked down on as 'wogs', 'reffos' and 'DPs' (displaced persons).

In November 1965, as Australia embarked on its first ever World Cup qualification campaign with a tour of Cambodia, Hong Kong and Malaysia, Dettre wrote an editorial hoping that it would 'create an atmosphere of friendship and goodwill' and 'open a new era in sporting relations between Australia and her neighbours'.[43]

In the end, Australia lost its matches against North Korea, and was crucified by an ignorant media bred on the parochial sports of Australian Rules, rugby and horseracing. But at *Soccer World*, there was high praise for the skill of the Koreans and a warning that the loss was 'a first-class lesson for the future'.[44]

When one sportswriter from the *Daily Telegraph* noted that most of the squad were 'New Australians', Dettre responded angrily: 'ALL members of the Australian World Cup party are Australians. NONE is New Australian. If neither the legal process of naturalisation or long residence in this country qualifies a man to be regarded and recognised as an Australian, our entire immigration scheme must be considered a huge flop'.[45]

Soccer was still treated by many Australians as too foreign, too slow, too effeminate or too violent. It was the invader and the corrupter of youth. To be a soccer fan was to negotiate Australia's immigration program, the demands of state, national and international federations, the local resistance from a largely backward, insular population, three other competing codes of football, and the politics of the various immigrant communities. This made soccer a stressful sport to be involved in, yet it was also the most important social leveller. Whether it was the role of immigrants in Australian life, the possibility of starting a national league or relations with Asia, soccer was the first sport to start having a national conversation.

Not long after the Australian team returned from its tour of Asia, APIA faced Hakoah in an all-Sydney Australia Cup final. The match finished 1–1, and was taken to a penalty shootout. After ten attempts, the scores remained locked at 8–8, and the players wanted to share the trophy and the prize money. Instead, another set of penalties was ordered, and by the end of 30 attempts, the scores remained level at 13–13. As dusk turned to night and the players struggled to see through the darkness, a replay was convened, which Hakoah won 2–1. APIA's only goal came from Johnny Wong.

It would be his last goal in Australia. By the end of 1965, after seven years in Sydney, Wong was ordered to leave the country by the Immigration Department.[46] He had overstayed his student visa, and failed in many of his subjects. 'I had to work during the day and study at night, I played soccer as well,' he lamented. 'It was too much.'[47]

'He was a very quiet sort of boy, unassuming,' once recalled John Roberts, a teammate of Wong's at APIA. 'Everyone liked him. He was a lovely fella, you know, very quiet. He spoke English pretty well, but mind you, every player at APIA was a different nationality, so it wasn't a problem. He was on a study visa, but he overstayed it by double the length of time. They were trying to throw him out for a long time. He would have stayed if he could.'

Wong joined a mass departure of players from the Sydney soccer scene. The withdrawal started at the end of 1965, intensified over the Christmas period, and became a hot topic for soccer writers in early 1966. Roberts himself joined Chelsea in England. It was, as *Soccer World* explained, 'a far cry indeed from the late 1950s and early sixties when overseas players by the score were arriving in Sydney monthly'.[48]

Leopold Baumgartner, the man who began this influx back in 1958, soon joined the exodus. He had played for Prague, Canterbury, APIA, Hakoah and NSW; coached juniors at Sutherland; opened a restaurant that cost him a small fortune; and coached Sydney Croatia in the NSW first division. But after losing a match to Yugal, Croatia's fiercest rival, he was sacked. Sick of the politics, he would leave top-flight soccer and turn his focus to junior coaching. 'The game has no personalities, no attractions, no magic,' he told Andrew Dettre before leaving. 'It's gone flat, like old beer.'[49]

Charles Perkins also retired from the game, and in 1966 became the first Indigenous man to graduate from university. Both John Moriarty and Gordon Briscoe were there for his graduation, and later completed their own degrees.

Perkins and Baumgartner implored soccer officials to broaden the base of support to the Australian-born spectators and sharpen their focus on the development of junior players. Andrew Dettre, who now had an Australian wife and two young children, agreed. Baumgartner, he wrote, was 'the kingpin of many stars, the chief attraction wherever he appeared'. Next to a picture of Baumgartner in full stride, Dettre slapped the headline: 'Leo's Exit Spells End of Our Greatest Era'.[50]

IT'S TIME

1967–1976

They were just a band of brothers, from all corners of the globe.
Facing all adversaries, as across the world they strode.
From the war-torn fields of Vietnam, training fields lined with mines.
Machine guns at world airports, were merely signs of the time.
They stood together in Asia, the Middle East and Europe too.
They were reaching for impossibles only they knew they could do.
In Sydney, Tehran and Hong Kong, they wore the green and gold.
Standing side by side in Hamburg, is the memory that we hold.
They will never be forgotten, endeared like none since or afore.
The first to tackle FIFA's best, were Rale's boys of '74.

Ray Richards
The Birth of the Socceroos[1]

One Sunday afternoon in March, in the first half of the first Victorian State League match of 1967, Attila Abonyi raced over to Cedo Cirkovic and kicked him in the shin.

Cirkovic, JUST's left-half, collapsed to the ground and needed to be carried from the field. He lost the physical contest but won the psychological battle: for ten minutes straight, Cirkovic had ankle-tapped Abonyi repeatedly, never going so far as to warrant caution from the referee but just enough to excite the temper of Melbourne Hungaria's impetuous inside-right.

As the crowd cried out in protest, the referee ordered Abonyi from the field. Handed a lengthy ban by the disciplinary committee, 20-year-old Abonyi sulked for three weeks and then burst back on the scene in Round 5, scoring the opening goal in a 3–0 victory over Polonia at the St Kilda Cricket Ground.

By Round 12 he had notched ten goals; by Round 16 his tally was 14. In Round 19, a top-of-the-table clash against Melbourne Juventus, he scored his 18th of the season to secure a 1–0 win. Three weeks later, in the final round, Melbourne Hungaria beat Melbourne Hakoah 1–0 at Middle Park to secure the 1967 Victorian first division title. It was Melbourne Hungaria's first ever trophy and the winning goal came from Abonyi – his 20th of the season.

Whippet-thin with pale, pointed cheekbones, a mop of unruly hair and crooked teeth, Abonyi darted across soccer fields with the dexterity and cunning of a man accustomed to being on the run. In the late winter cold of 1956, two months after Soviet tanks crushed the Hungarian uprising, the Abonyis – Joseph, Helen, Attila and Joseph Jnr – had caught a train from Budapest to a border town with nine others. From there, they marched for hours through dense forests and waded across shallow creeks to their freedom. Their excitement was overshadowed by genuine paranoia – at one point the entire group stood frozen still for 20 minutes when they spotted a figure in the distance. The guard turned out to be a tree stump.

Young Atti was just ten years old at the time. His father Joseph, a fitter and turner by trade, was determined to find a new home as far away as possible. All he knew of Australia was sport.

As the Abonyi family were plotting their escape, news filtered through about a fiery, politically charged water polo match between Hungary and the Soviet Union at the 1956 Melbourne Olympics. In the stands, Andrew Dettre had been commentating for Radio Free Europe and working on his first major assignment as a sports reporter with the *Daily Telegraph*. He had noted that the Hungarian athletes were 'edgy and depressed', and that one of the water polo players had 'joined the Olympic team at the very last minute still carrying his machine gun'.[2]

By virtue of his arrival in 1949, Dettre was part of a group of Hungarian migrants known as the '49ers'. They had watched the convulsions in Budapest from afar, and were soon joined in Australia by a new wave of Hungarians called the '56ers'. When the first 56ers arrived in Australia, the federal minister for immigration, Athol Townley, delayed his trip to New Zealand to receive them, while the 49ers dressed in traditional garb and held placards that read *Isten Hozott* (Welcome).

The influx of 56ers increased the Hungarian population to 30,000 and led to the emergence of 'Little Budapests' in Melbourne and Sydney. Hungarian businesses began trading, cafes – called *espressos* – were opened, and the newspaper *Fuggetlen Magyarorszag* (Free Hungary) started circulating. Dettre had taken a second job at the outwardly anti-communist newspaper, and many of his articles railed against assimilation and explored the trials and tribulations of being a migrant in a strange land.

Melbourne Hungaria Soccer Club was born in 1957, and by 1960 the side had been promoted to the Victorian first division. To satisfy the requirements of the Victorian Soccer Federation, the committee created the club's first junior team. Melbourne Hungaria took out advertisements in Hungarian-language newspapers and approached Joseph Abonyi, who promptly enrolled his boys in the new side.

The club gave Attila Abonyi a platform to further his ambitions and his parents a social outlet. Never a God-fearing family, Abonyi's parents found community through soccer rather than the weekend church service. Here they could mingle with their people, speak their native tongue and enjoy a game that connected them to worlds new and old. When he played as a junior at St Kilda, Abonyi never once saw his father at a game, but at Melbourne Hungaria both his parents were there more or less every weekend, munching happily on *virsli* and *langos* and mixing with new friends.

When Leopold Baumgartner, Charles Perkins and Andrew Dettre talked of Australia's need to nurture its junior players, Attila Abonyi was the kind of young man they had in mind. He was part of a new generation; a group that spoke English perfectly, grew up in Australian schools, were nurtured at migrant clubs and often acted as intermediaries between their parents and the new society.

'Soccer was more enjoyable as a child,' Abonyi once remembered. 'Having grown up in Melbourne, I used to always look up to Sydney. I used to buy the Green Paper, *Soccer World*. As a kid I would buy it at Flinders Street railway station, under the clocks, on the way home from training at Melbourne Hungaria.'

In October 1967, not long after Melbourne Hungaria won its first title, *Soccer World* labelled Abonyi 'one of the best-ever locally produced players'.[3] He was in career-best form, had been selected for the national side, and had led Melbourne Hungaria to the final of the Australia Cup. Between 1963 and 1965, Melbourne Hungaria had never finished better than eighth in the Victorian first division. It was a humble outfit that lived in the shadow of St George-Budapest, a fraternal Hungarian club in Sydney. But with Abonyi scoring at a rate of a goal per game, an unlikely league–cup double loomed.

When the Australia Cup first began in 1962, Cliff Connolly, the chairman of the South Australian Soccer Federation, had predicted that it would lead to the creation of a national league within five years. He was wrong. Yet by 1967, the tournament had expanded to include teams from every state.

From NSW there was APIA, St George-Budapest, South Sydney Croatia, Lake Macquarie, Newcastle Austral and Pan Hellenic; from Victoria there was Melbourne Hungaria, Melbourne Juventus, Melbourne Croatia and Footscray JUST. West Adelaide Hellas and Adelaide Juventus qualified from South Australia, while Tasmania provided Launceston United, Western Australia contributed Perth Azzurri, Latrobe-Western Suburbs represented Queensland and Canberra Juventus came from the ACT. It was the most geographically and ethnically diverse tournament in the country.

Since 1962, the Australia Cup had been won by five different migrant clubs – Yugal, Hakoah, APIA, George Cross and Slavia. Never before had the winners of the NSW and Victorian state leagues met in a Cup final, and in 1967 Melbourne Hungaria was seen as a rank outsider against the glamorous APIA. Abonyi's opposite number, John Watkiss, was named as the man to watch.

The match was held on the afternoon of 29 October 1967. Abonyi scored the first goal after just 19 minutes, but APIA equalised soon after. Abonyi scored again on 53 minutes, but again the opposition cancelled it out. On 74 minutes Melbourne Hungaria went 3–2 ahead, before Watkiss levelled scores with a 30-yard screamer. Momentum swung to APIA, but there was still more left in Abonyi. Five minutes into extra time, he completed his hat-trick. 4–3.

Melbourne Hungaria, the champions of Victoria, were now the champions of Australia. It would stand as one of the most brilliant individual grand final performances, and perhaps Australian soccer's greatest underdog upset.

Next day, Abonyi was the sole representative from Melbourne Hungaria to depart for Vietnam with the Australian national team. In Saigon the players ate with Australian soldiers, witnessed a car explode in the street and, after dodging landmines on the training fields, warmed up on the roof of their four-storey hotel.

In the first game against New Zealand at Cong Hoa Stadium, Abonyi's first international hat-trick was soundtracked by distant artillery fire. The Australian team had entered the Vietnam War, sent into battle on a propaganda mission at the behest of the conservative prime minister, Harold Holt.

'I doubt if any other sport could boast of a tour that will do so much to promote goodwill and increase Australian prestige in Asia,' wrote Johnny Warren, the captain of Australia, in his regular column for the *Leader* newspaper.[4] Dettre wrote that the tour would 'indicate to the people of Vietnam that Australia is keen to participate in their sporting life, not just their war'.[5]

The Quoc Khanh Cup included South Vietnam, New Zealand,

Singapore, South Korea, Malaysia, Thailand and Hong Kong. Abonyi started in the forward line in place of Watkiss, whom he had injured in an accidental collision during the Australia Cup final. The coach of Australia, Joe Vlasits, later admitted that if it hadn't been for Watkiss' injury he would have started ahead of Abonyi.

Grateful for the opportunity, Abonyi scored seven goals in five matches, including one in the 3–2 grand final win over South Korea. It was Australia's first international trophy, and as top goal-scorer Abonyi was awarded the Golden Boot.

After receiving the trophy, Australia played three more friendly matches in Indonesia, Singapore and Malaysia. Naturally, Abonyi continued his goal-a-game scoring rate. He finished the year with state, national and international titles, and 38 goals.

The Hungarians in Australian soccer were men of the balance sheet and boardroom, of clipboard and instruction, and of pen and prose. They were a highly erudite, thoughtful group of bohemian intellectuals. 'The well-educated were over-represented,' wrote Frank Kunz, author of *The Hungarians in Australia*, 'and there was an absence of peasants.'[6]

Attila Abonyi was a rare flash of instinct and daring – the finest Hungarian-born player ever to play soccer in Australia. Andrew Dettre likened him both in appearance and style to the Soviet ballet dancer Rudolf Nureyev.

In Vietnam, Abonyi had roomed with the St George-Budapest and Australian captain Johnny Warren, who also had a breakthrough season in 1967. Warren was the best-known player in the country, the Aussie kid who grew up playing high-level rugby and cricket but chose instead to pursue a soccer career. He was good-looking, articulate, intense and serious, and in 1967 was awarded McDowell's Sportstar of the Year.

'I'd heard of him before I met him,' Abonyi later recalled. 'I was in Melbourne, he was in Sydney. He was only three or four years older than me, but to me he was like God. We became extremely good mates.'

By 1969 Abonyi and Warren were key members of the Australian team that embarked on a string of World Cup qualifying matches in South Korea, Israel and Mozambique. The tour started with a win over Greece – the first Australian victory against European opposition – in which Abonyi scored the only goal of the game.

Australia then beat both South Korea and Japan in Seoul. Andrew Dettre used the opportunity to make friends with the Japanese manager Shun-ichiro Okano, write feature articles about his impressions of Korean society, and even arrange for a column written by a Japanese journalist to be printed in *Soccer World*.

This was the way Dettre operated. He used *Soccer World* to broaden his own mind, extend his network and spark the imagination of his readers. Yet the tour did not end in success. Australia struggled past Rhodesia in Mozambique but lost the decisive qualifying match against Israel. 'The big question which must be decided is this,' concluded Dettre in *Soccer World*. 'Are we to continue our international expansion policy or will Australia retreat into its old isolationist stance.'[7]

On a personal level, at least, he had already settled on the former. By 1971 he was convinced that Australia needed to leave the Oceania Football Confederation and apply for membership of the Asian Football Confederation. He complemented words with actions, travelling to Tokyo and, with the help of his new friend Okano, organising for St George-Budapest to play at the Tokyo International tournament.

The tour began well, with St George-Budapest cruising to a 6–1 victory over a Macao XI. In Hong Kong, the team defeated Jardines, and took the time to reunite with Johnny Wong, who was working for the British Trade Commission.

This was just one part of their ambassadorial role. In Tokyo the hotel manager told Dettre that St George-Budapest were the best behaved team they had ever hosted, while Okano admitted that it had been 'a masterstroke' to invite the Australians and said he looked forward to hosting them again. And in Omiya, a city to the north of Tokyo, Mrs Hiroko Yamada, who had previously worked with Hungarian businessmen in Japan, approached the players and, in perfect Hungarian, asked: 'Good evening. Does anybody here speak Hungarian?'[8] The Hungarians could hardly believe their ears.

St George-Budapest finished the tournament on five points, one clear of Danish side Boldklubben Frem. Japan 'A' and 'B' finished with three points and zero points respectively. In the final match at Tokyo's Olympic Stadium, St George-Budapest trounced Japan 'B' 6–2. Harry Williams opened the scoring, Warren, Mike Denton and Adrian Alston each found the back of the net, while Abonyi bagged a double.

As the referee blew his whistle for full-time, Mrs Yamada was one of the first people the players embraced. The door to Asia was nudged ever so slightly ajar. 'The significance of the St George tour,' predicted Dettre, 'may only be realised in years to come.'[9]

The task of getting Australia into the Asian Football Confederation fell to Arthur George, the president of the Australian Soccer Federation. Born Athanasios Theodore Tzortzatos to Greek immigrant parents in 1915, George became involved in soccer by way of Pan Hellenic in Sydney. He was a lawyer and an Anglophile, a staunch Liberal Party man and a generous benefactor to the game.

'I became interested in soccer because I saw it as a challenge,' he once told Andrew Dettre. 'For one thing, it's a good way to get the migrants on common ground with the Australians. Secondly, I think it fits in well with our national aspirations. All our neighbours in Asia have one sport in common with us, played by the masses, and that is soccer. Thirdly, it's an international sport and I really think Australia can do just as well in soccer as they do in other sports.'[10]

It was a time of great social and cultural progress. Australians had voted overwhelmingly to include Indigenous people in the census; thousands of immigrants had taken on Australian citizenship, bought homes and established successful businesses; and the racial immigration restrictions had been eased to allow entry to some skilled Asian workers.

In 1971, Gough Whitlam, leader of the opposition Labor Party, became the first Australian leader to visit communist China. In a column for the *Australian* newspaper, he wrote that he had embarked upon the diplomatic mission 'so that the Australian people should come to terms with the realities of our situation and our future in this region'.[11]

Yet in both practice and philosophy, soccer remained ahead of the curve. The tours of Asia by the Australian national team and St George-Budapest had built a reservoir of confidence both on and off the field, and many soccer officials, journalists and supporters began to see their future as intertwined with Asia.

Not long after St George-Budapest returned to Sydney, the ASF dramatically pulled out of the Oceania Cup. Arthur George lamented the lack of international matches of competitive interest, questioned the efficacy of the organisation and recommended that Australia join the Asian Football Confederation. 'This goes further than soccer,' he told Dettre, 'this is also our national interest.'[12]

By December 1971 Dettre was on a flight back to Asia, this time joined by Tibor Kalman, a prominent Jewish businessman and official at the Hakoah Club. Together the pair travelled for 16 days on behalf of the ASF. From Japan to Korea to Hong Kong, Malaysia and Indonesia, they asked questions, took notes and probed Asian officials for their attitude towards Australia. Dettre reported positively about matches they saw in Jakarta and Seoul, and in Kuala Lumpur Kalman presented a large silver trophy at the Southeast Asian Peninsular Games as a token of Australia's friendship.

Soccer's immersion with Asia was happening at a personal and institutional level. In Sydney, a South Korean player named Kim Jung-nam made his debut for Sutherland in the NSW first division. In Malaysia, Johnny Warren undertook a FIFA coaching course alongside several high-profile players from Japan, South Korea, India, Iran and Thailand. He arranged for *Soccer World* to be airmailed to him each week, and shared the newspaper with his colleagues. And at a glittering function at Sydney's Tatts Hotel, on 3 May 1972, Australia's 1974 World Cup mission was launched. Australia would need to beat Asian nations to qualify.

In front of an esteemed audience of politicians, soccer officials and fellow sportsmen, the ASF unveiled a new national team logo. It was a little cartoon kangaroo dressed in soccer boots, shrouded by green and gold with the name 'Socceroo'.

The word had first entered the Australian lexicon in 1967, after the tour of Vietnam, during a *Daily Mirror* naming competition.[13] Emus had in fact been the most popular suggestion, ahead of Wattles, Jackaroos, Wombats, Bandicoots, Boomerangs, Baddawalers, Wallaroos, Merinos, Koalas, Woomeras and Sharks. But after the launch in 1972, the *Daily Mirror* began using the term Socceroos to describe the team. The nickname stuck, and Australia's route to the 1974 World Cup was officially underway.

Several companies pitched in for a $100,000 World Cup fund and in June the Socceroos defeated Wolverhampton Wanderers at Olympic Park in Melbourne. After 83 minutes of stoic Australian defending, Attila Abonyi pounced on an errant back-pass to score the winner, creating history as the first Australian team to beat an English side.

One month later in Sydney, Australia held Brazilian side Santos to a 2–2 draw. Ray Richards, an English-born naturalised Australian, had for weeks pestered coach Rale Rasic to give him the job of marking Pele, a three-time World Cup winner with Brazil and scorer of over 1000 goals.

Richards wore a bushy moustache and was built, as Abonyi once described in impeccable Australian, 'like a brick shithouse'. Pele tried to evade him like a man trying to outrun his own shadow. Incredibly, Richards fouled Pele just once and limited him to two shots on goal from open play. With scores locked at 2–2, Pele – who usually exited the field five minutes before full-time in exhibition matches – stayed on until the final whistle. Richards, said Pele after the match, 'is easily one of the best and certainly the fairest I have ever played against'.[14]

The victory over Wolverhampton and the draw against Santos ushered in a new Australian confidence free from the pangs of past failure. Within weeks, Australia departed the Oceania Football Confederation and looked to Asia for its future.

★

Andrew Dettre had never lived under a progressive government. Just three days before he arrived in Sydney, on 10 December 1949, the Liberal Party came to power and held on to it for 23 long years. The party had been built in the image of Robert Menzies, a thin-lipped conservative who served two prime ministerial terms, the first from 1939 to 1941, the second from 1949 to 1966. Menzies was known for his loyal dotage to the monarchy and his pride in being 'British to the bootstraps'.

In stark contrast stood Gough Whitlam, the stately, internationalist leader of the Labor Party. Whitlam had narrowly lost the federal election in 1969, but was elected to office on 2 December 1972.

'I believe exciting months and years are ahead for all of us,' he told the nation. 'Abroad I believe we are already forging a new style and image for Australia – nothing raucous or rash or abrasive – but Australia is speaking with a firm, clear and independent voice and I believe we are being heard with a new respect.'[15]

In Whitlam, Dettre saw a kindred spirit and an historic opportunity; a man who included soccer as part of his vision for a new Australia. As deputy leader of the opposition, Whitlam had once written a long feature article for the *Sun*, predicting that by 1986 Australia would fly its own national flag, Indigenous people would have achieved full equality, fees would be abolished in educational institutions, Australia would have closer ties with Asia, and soccer 'will have become the most popular winter sport'.[16]

His government immediately set out to achieve these aims, sweeping away the last remnants of an old, stale Australia. It abolished the final vestiges of the White Australia policy, university fees and conscription, and freed from prison those who had resisted the draft. Australia established official relations with China, ended them with apartheid South Africa and Rhodesia, and strengthened the Department of Aboriginal Affairs and the case for equal pay for women. Whitlam exalted the role of immigrants in Australian life, and appointed Al Grassby, a man with suits as colourful as his ideas, as the minister for immigration.

At the same time, Dettre left his day job at the *Daily Telegraph* to work as a special adviser, speechwriter and press secretary to Frank Stewart in the Ministry of Tourism and Recreation. It was the first federal ministry to deal with sport.

With the ear of the government, Dettre pushed for better outcomes for soccer and, under the pseudonym Mike Renwick, mischievously reported the results in the pages of *Soccer World*. The Green Paper carried little sidebars about the Labor government's funding for an under-23 national team to visit Indonesia, and tidbits on the financial support for an Australian junior championship to be held in 1973. Not long after Whitlam came to power, Dettre wrote, '[A]t least he [Whitlam] knows we exist, we have hopes and aspirations and, more importantly, we offer Australia a vehicle which few other sports do: a common ground with our Asian neighbours.'[17]

Determined to assert a new Australian identity, Whitlam directed financial support to the arts and on Australia Day 1973 announced that a new national anthem would be decided by the Australian public to replace the imperial 'God Save the Queen'.

No other sports newspaper watched the anthem debate as closely as *Soccer World*; but, then again, no other sports newspaper had Dettre lurking in Canberra's corridors of power. Initially, *Soccer World* reported that 'Waltzing Matilda' would be the official national anthem, before informing readers that the Department of Foreign Affairs had confirmed the team would sing 'Advance Australia Fair'. 'This will be the first time, to our knowledge, that "God Save The Queen" will not be played as the home team's anthem at an international football match in any code in Australia,' announced one proud editorial. 'This should please the prime minister, Mr Whitlam.'[18]

In March, the Socceroos began a long and arduous World Cup qualification campaign. Placed in a group with New Zealand, Iraq and Indonesia, the Socceroos played the latter two nations in Sydney and New Zealand in a home-and-away series.

A 1–1 draw in the first game against New Zealand put Australia in a perilous situation – lose against Iraq and the series would be effectively over. In front of Gough Whitlam, who gave a rousing speech before the game, the Socceroos proceeded to play one of their best matches on home soil, beating Iraq 3–1. The Socceroos then beat Indonesia twice, drew with both Iraq and New Zealand, and finished the series on top of Group A.

Before the next round of qualifying matches against Iran and South Korea, Al Grassby released a paper titled *A Multi-cultural Society for the Future*. He spoke of the growing desire 'to see things re-ordered as they could be or should be, rather than simply retained as they have always been'.

'Where is the Maltese process worker, the Finnish carpenter, the Italian concrete layer, the Yugoslav miner or – dare I say it – the Indian scientist?' he asked. 'Where do these people belong, in all honesty, if not in today's composite Australian image?'

Grassby dismissed terms such as assimilation and integration, instead using the friendlier 'Family of the Nation'.

'In a family,' he said, 'the overall attachment to the common good need not impose a sameness on the outlook or activity of each member, nor need these members deny their individuality and distinctiveness in order to seek a superficial and unnatural conformity.'

He used soccer, not Australian Rules or rugby or cricket, to illustrate his point, noting happily that '[o]ur bid for inclusion among the final contenders for the World Cup soccer championship has set tingling a nerve of patriotism that has run right through our ethnic communities'.[19]

The Indigenous and ethnic communities had already established many institutions that would symbolise multicultural Australia. There were ethnic social clubs, restaurants, newspapers, soccer teams and houses of worship. In Sydney, the former Adelaide Croatia star Gordon Briscoe had played a crucial role in setting up the Aboriginal Medical Service and the National Tribal Council, and in 1972 both he and Charles Perkins had helped establish the Aboriginal Embassy on the lawns of Parliament House in Canberra. Much like the ethnic soccer clubs that Perkins and Briscoe had once played for, these were pillars of self-determination.

The Socceroos were one of the most potent symbols of the new Australia, with a squad of players who had been born in six different nations – Scotland, England, Yugoslavia, Germany, Hungary and Australia. Migrants such as Peter Wilson, Ray Richards, Adrian Alston, Doug Utjesenovic and Branko Buljevic blended seamlessly with Australian-raised children of migrants Attila Abonyi and John Watkiss and the Australian-born players Max Tolson, Col Curran, Ray Baartz and Johnny Warren, while Harry Williams, a speedy winger from St George-Budapest, was the first Indigenous man to represent an Australian national soccer team.

In the final five matches – two against Iran and three against South Korea – Australia scored six goals and conceded four, but no goal was more spectacular than Jimmy Mackay's winner in the decisive game against South Korea. From 25 yards out, it flew off his right boot like a tracer bullet through the humid Hong Kong night, past the keeper's outstretched hands and into the top left hand corner of the net. '[A] superb shot,' noted the *Sydney Morning Herald*, 'and one worthy of providing a win after such an arduous campaign.'[20]

In the parliament, Dettre's boss Frank Stewart paid tribute to the Socceroos. 'I desire to offer congratulations to our Australian soccer team [...] I am sure Australia is proud of this splendid team which so clearly emphasised the multi-national character of our country.'[21]

★

The Socceroos coach, Rale Rasic, led the hearts-and-minds mission with an iron will and a charm offensive. In Gough Whitlam, he saw a rare Australian politician who had vision and class.

'What impressed me about him was not politics, but the intellect of the man,' Rasic would later recall. 'Gough was most eloquent and elegant. His speech manner always was emotional, it always had something to carry weight in every word that he said. Opening the door to the world – people became dreamers. Not convicts, dreamers.'

Andrew Dettre first met Rasic in the summer of 1969. He shared with him hotel rooms, socialist values and blistering arguments. He wrote honestly of Rasic's 'manipulation of the press' and 'massive ego', commenting that 'he is a difficult man to like incessantly' and that 'he sees himself as the saviour of Australian soccer'. Rasic, wrote Dettre, was 'the eternal good copy'.[22]

With his sharp suits, polished shoes and immaculately coiffured hair, to the public Rasic was a statesman, a man of purpose and clear vision who placed the national interest at the centre of his grand speeches. Away from the cameras, however, he was cunning, authoritative and serious, earning the respect and loyalty of his players and the ire of frustrated soccer officials.

Born in Mostar, Yugoslavia, Rasic arrived in Victoria in 1962 as a journeyman player disillusioned with European soccer. His mind for tactics and organisation was far more advanced than his playing ability. After serving a brief stint in the Yugoslav national army, Rasic returned to Australia in 1966 to coach JUST.

His ascent from JUST to the Socceroos via Melbourne Hungaria and St George-Budapest was meteoric. At each club he had demanded the highest standards of professionalism from players, staff and committee. Like Gough Whitlam, his style could be described as 'crash-or-crash-through'. From team meals to dress code to the choice of rooms in hotels, if there was a right way it was Rale's way.

His predecessor Joe Vlasits was nicknamed 'Uncle' by the players, but Rasic was a benevolent dictator.

'I respected Joe Vlasits,' Rasic once said. 'He wasn't old, but he was elderly to them. They called him "Uncle". I didn't want anybody to be called Uncle. I do business, I'm in charge, I must have some title.'

One of Rasic's first acts as coach of JUST was to order the committee out of the dressing room. When he was appointed Socceroos boss he demanded that all state selectors be eliminated to give him total control. In Iran, he almost caused an international incident when he told the media that he represented a 'superior race'. He embarrassed

ASF officials by picking 22 players instead of 18, and demanded that the fixtures be tailored to suit the Socceroos.

Just as Rasic had moved from Melbourne to Sydney in search of the top job, he gathered most of his players around him at the top Sydney clubs. In September, just before the Socceroos played the decisive qualification matches against South Korea, Rasic led Marconi to the NSW first division title. It was his third consecutive grand final victory, and *Soccer World* duly named him coach of the year.

Rasic was a confident man with his own colourful brand of team psychology. In the final game of St George-Budapest's tour of Asia in 1971, Attila Abonyi and Adrian Alston had insisted that Rasic start them in the forward line, bargaining that if they both failed to score in the first half, he could substitute them for the second.

Rasic agreed. Abonyi and Alston fulfilled their end of the deal, both netting a goal in a stunning 3–0 first half performance. Never one to take instructions – especially from his own players – Rasic substituted them anyway.

During a national team camp, he left two bottles of beer in Jimmy Mackay and Jimmy Rooney's room. Knowing that Rasic had banned alcohol, the pair came rushing down after one particularly hot training session to inform Rasic that someone had planted beer in their fridge. Appreciative of their hard work at training he ordered them to enjoy the beers and, for their unwavering loyalty to his doctrine, sent them six more.

Yet for all of Rasic's prodigious talent as a coach and player manager, he was a terrible politician. He refused to use the president Sir Arthur George's honorific title, even though he had been knighted in 1972, and as he grew close to Gough Whitlam, Sir Arthur quickly went from loyal backer to bitter enemy.

As Rasic later described it, Sir Arthur once introduced him to NSW Liberal premier Sir Robert Askin as 'the greatest coach and the biggest son of a bitch'. Rasic shook Sir Robert's hand and replied, 'Pleasure to meet another son of a bitch'. On a separate occasion, in front of several dignitaries, Rasic grabbed Sir Arthur by the collar and threw him out of the dressing room. Dettre would describe their relationship as 'like two king tigers at each other's throat; neither lets go, neither succumbs. It's a fight to the end.'[23]

In April 1974, as Uruguay arrived to play two World Cup warm-up matches against the Socceroos, Australia was in the peculiar situation of having two national anthems. An Australian Bureau of Statistics poll showed that 'Advance Australia Fair' was the most popular anthem, and so Gough Whitlam announced that it would replace 'God Save the Queen'. Yet the Returned Services League and NSW Premier Sir Robert Askin demanded that 'God Save the Queen' be played on Anzac Day.

'Faced with a boycott of its preferred national anthem at Anzac Day next Thursday,' read one editorial in the *Age*, 'the Federal Government compromised to suggest that six bars of the "Queen" be immediately followed by eight bars of "Australia Fair". This absurd hybrid is apparently to be played in Victoria, NSW and the Federal Territories; in other states the RSL organisers are still insisting that only "God Save the Queen" will be played at Anzac Day ceremonies.'[24]

It was one of the most emblematic episodes of the battle between the old 'British to the bootstraps' Australia and the new, outward-looking multicultural nation.

On 27 April, just two days after the Anzac Day anthem debacle, the Socceroos lined up against Uruguay for its last game on home soil before the World Cup. At the Sydney Sports Ground were the prime minister Gough Whitlam, the minister for tourism and recreation Frank Stewart, the deputy leader of the opposition Phil Lynch, and Sir Robert Askin. Whitlam's presence and opening speech brought the house down, and before the match the Socceroos lined up to sing 'Advance Australia Fair'. It was the first Australian sporting team to do so.

Ray Baartz scored the first goal, Peter Ollerton the second, and Australia won 2–0. But the match was a bittersweet affair. Baartz was karate chopped by one of the Uruguayan players, which forced him from the field, nearly leaving him paralysed and later caused his early retirement. Yet as the Socceroos scored two unanswered goals, men born in Europe cheered for Australia, their children banged empty soft drink cans against the corrugated iron sheets of the Paddington stand, and the crowd sang 'Waltzing Matilda'.

Days later, as Australia went to the ballot box for the second time in three years, Dettre told his readers in *Soccer World* that soccer 'has received more attention from the Whitlam Government in sixteen months than it did from their predecessors in 72 years'.[25] The Whitlam government personally invited Socceroos midfielder Johnny Warren to their election launch, and as the Socceroos prepared to leave for Germany, Rasic went to a huge Labor Party rally at the Sydney Opera House. Playwright David Williamson, historian Manning Clark and author Patrick White all gave speeches in support of Whitlam, and as one of the distinguished guests, Rasic told the crowd of the Whitlam government's enlightened approach to sport.

'After that Arthur George told me I shouldn't have done it,' Rasic told Dettre years later. 'From then on I was treated like a ballboy.'[26]

★

On the night of the 1974 World Cup draw, the qualified nations were divided into three pots. West Germany, Brazil, Uruguay and Italy were the top-seeded teams in pot one, while Argentina, Chile, Scotland, Holland, East Germany, Poland, Bulgaria, Yugoslavia and Spain were sorted into pot two.

Australia, in pot three, was classified as a rank outsider alongside Zaire, Haiti and Sweden. Created from these three pots were four groups consisting of four teams each. The draw commenced in relative silence until West Germany was drawn into Group One alongside Australia, Chile and, notoriously, East Germany.

Along with Zaire and Haiti, bookmakers listed Australia as 250-to-1 chance of winning the tournament. Their opponents and the international media treated the Socceroos with a mixture of disdain, mockery and downright confusion.

In Australia, however, the mood was rather different. The Socceroos briefly became Australia's favourite national team, cloaking themselves in green and gold, kangaroos and other symbols of Australiana. Mulga Bill's Bicycle Band, a seven-piece folk-country ensemble, was sent to perform at the opening ceremony with sponsorship from the newly created Australia Council of the Arts, while the Socceroos mascot dressed in a kitschy green-and-gold tracksuit with the words 'Advance Australia Fair' arched over the shoulder blades.

'At the opening ceremony there was a significant number of Australian supporters,' Sir Arthur George once recalled. 'Curiously, most of them who had adopted Australia as their life, as their country … When they played the Australian national anthem, I felt tears go down my face and I looked around and I was relieved to see the same was happening to every Australian there. That was a wonderful moment for me.'[27]

Australia had by far the most multicultural team at the World Cup, but on the home front, where the ABC broadcast the World Cup into Australian living rooms, the players were transformed from the weird mob of fifth-column wogs to working-class underdogs. 'Australia's World Cup players may come from many nations,' said Rale Rasic, 'but when we are together we are all Australians.'[28]

Peter Wilson, the captain, worked down in the coalmines. Jimmy Mackay was a roof tiler, Manfred Schaefer a milkman. John Watkiss was a scrap-metal dealer, Branko Buljevic a fitter and turner. Attila Abonyi worked as a painter after starting his career in the rag trade as a tailor.

'I lost four jobs,' Abonyi once remembered. 'In '67, when I first got into the Australian team, I was working in a little place called TD Noon in Melbourne. It was my first job after leaving school. You can imagine walking up to an Australian boss who knew nothing about soccer. I said, "Mr Noon, I've got to go to Sydney because we're in camp." Then I was off to Vietnam for six weeks. He said, "I'm really happy for you, but I can't have you travelling because I need you to work." But I had to leave – soccer to me was everything in life. A lot of players lost jobs.'

The Australians revelled in their outsider status. David Bateson, usually a quiet and reserved children's author from the Blue Mountains, began writing excited columns, letters and poems for *Soccer World*. In one jaunty poem, Bateson wrote about a group of outsiders – Joey,

Snowy, Garry, Larry, Micky McNab, Pincher Crabbe, Polly and Dolly – who played soccer on 'Garbo Street' before graduating to the local C-grade as 'mini Socceroos'. Bateson's team of fictional misfits caused an upset, winning the game 1–0. The last stanza read: '"A good big 'un beats a good little 'un," I've heard chatter, but a team of Jimmy Rooneys, well that's another matter.'[29]

The Socceroos lost the first game against East Germany 2–0, the second against West Germany 3–0 and drew 0–0 with Chile in the last match. An Australian player found the net just once, during the opening match against East Germany. After an impressive display in the first half, left-back Col Curran gave the Germans a lead after 56 minutes, turning the ball into his own goal. Joachim Streich's goal in the second half put the game to rest.

Next day, however, the front page of the *Sun-Herald*'s sports section read 'NOT DISGRACED', while the article inside was titled 'AUSTRALIA WIN CROWD SYMPATHY'.[30] Vignettes of the Socceroos' gallantry were matched by descriptions of how the team's 'fighting spirit' won the hearts of those in attendance.

The parochialism matched the genuine affection from the opposition. During the Socceroos' 3–0 loss to West Germany, the home fans began cheering for the Socceroos and booing their own team. Adrian Alston and Branko Buljevic were approached by German clubs, while interest was also shown in Jimmy Rooney and Peter Wilson. An English columnist for the *Guardian* commented that Australia was 'by far the best equipped' of the emergent nations and the Australian Soccer Federation received a telegram from the East German Sports Ministry inviting them back to play in 1975. *Der Spiegel*, one of Germany's largest-selling news magazines, wrote: 'The Australian soccer team is what the World Cup is all about. Unknown and grossly under-rated when they arrived, they were transcended by the World Cup and delighted countless millions with their surprisingly high standard, fighting spirit and sportsmanship before returning home firmly entrenched as a soccer nation that now matters.'[31]

The Socceroos arrived home to a heroes' welcome on Thursday, 27 June 1974. At Sydney Airport were a gaggle of family, friends, supporters, journalists, and the minister for tourism and recreation, Frank Stewart. As photographers snapped pictures of wives and children reunited with their fathers, the Socceroos team manager, John Barclay, predicted that a national league would be a 'distinct possibility' for 1976. 'There is no choice,' he said, 'we have to go professional.'[32]

'For a team of part-time players, they did remarkably well in their first appearance in the World Cup finals,' read one editorial in the *Australian*.

> They aroused tremendous interest back home; people who have never been to a soccer game in their lives sat up to watch the games televised early in the morning. Soccer's image in Australia has steadily changed from a migrant sport to a populist game, and the World Cup challenges both in Munich and the earlier games in Korea and Iran highlighted and hastened this trend. The growth of the game raises some interesting possibilities [...] it is quite possible that soccer could be Australia's national winter game in the next twenty years or so.[33]

At *Soccer World*, Andrew Dettre and Lou Gautier published articles and readers' letters in support of a national league, recommended that the Australian Soccer Federation send a delegate to the 1974 Congress of the Asian Football Confederation, lobbied for Rale Rasic to be re-appointed as national coach, and implored Australian coaches to adopt a new tactical approach.

St George-Budapest was granted permission to build a new soccer stadium on the banks of the Cooks River overlooking the runway from Sydney Airport. The Australian Schoolboys played for the first time against the England Schoolboys. The Australian Women's Soccer Association established its inaugural national championship, with five states taking part. Andrew Dettre and Johnny Warren published a book called *Soccer in Australia*. The Ministry for Sport and Recreation promised to redevelop a soccer complex in Newcastle, and approved a

$15,827 grant to fund two junior soccer championships. Johnny Warren and Ray Richards took over as player-coaches at St George-Budapest and Marconi, while Adrian Alston scored on his debut for English club Luton Town. And Ron Barassi, the coach of North Melbourne, said that Australian Rules was 'facing the biggest challenge from soccer in the history of our game'.[34]

On 29 September, a crowd of nearly 11,000 people witnessed St George-Budapest beat NSW premiers Hakoah in the 1974 grand final. After a seesawing hour of play, in which two goals were scored by Hakoah and one goal by St George-Budapest, Attila Abonyi brought the scores level. During the 30 minutes of extra time, St George-Budapest scored two more to win the match 4–2. The final goal, nominated by *Soccer World* as the goal of the season, arrived from the boot of the captain-coach.

'John Warren stole a ball at the halfway mark and with nobody running off the ball, burst through on his own,' reported Dettre. 'When he got to about fifteen metres, and being pushed towards the left, he sliced the ball with his right, curving it like a croissant, just inside the post – something a Rivelino or Tostao can perhaps imitate at their best.'[35]

Warren, 31, left the field immediately and was carried around the ground by his teammates after the final whistle. It was his final act as a professional footballer. In a farewell column titled 'Epitome of a Sportsman', the *Sydney Morning Herald* called him 'the All-Australian boy ... the son every mother hopes for ... the man every sportsman should live up to'.[36]

★

The forward march of soccer soon ground to an unexpected halt. Australia's official bid to affiliate with the Asian Football Confederation was rejected, and a planned tour of Asia was cancelled soon after. The federal government decided to curb the flow of migrants, making it much harder for clubs to recruit new players from abroad.

The total crowds for the season had dropped right around the country – in Sydney reaching their lowest ebb since 1958. Nobody could figure out why the crowds stayed away, especially in light of the Socceroos' performance at the World Cup, but the empty terraces were a clear sign that something was not right.

Rale Rasic, perhaps the most recognised man in Australian soccer, was ostracised by the Australian Soccer Federation. Unappreciated by the soccer bosses, he was appointed to a select study group by the Department of Tourism and Recreation in late September 1974. He, Andrew Dettre and six other experts travelled through Europe, researched the success of other national training centres, and wrote a feasibility study for the creation of an Australian institute of sport.

The Whitlam government had already begun to dismantle the symbols of the old Australia, attempted to re-calibrate the political attitude towards Indigenous people and immigrants, and commenced establishing new national institutions. Under Whitlam the British imperial honours were replaced with the Order of Australia. Whitlam turned the National Gallery of Australia from blueprint to bricks and mortar. His government set up the first multicultural and youth radio networks, created the Medibank Health Scheme, expanded funding into the development of Australian film and television, and fought for women to have access to refuges, the contraceptive pill, equal pay, single-mother pensions and no-fault divorce. It was Whitlam who passed the *Environment Protection (Impact of Proposals) Act 1974*, ratified the World Heritage Convention, established the Australian Heritage Commission and started a political discussion about land rights for Indigenous people.

Sport was just another part of this process of social and cultural renewal. As Frank Stewart once told the Australian Sports Council, in a speech penned by Dettre:

> There can be no more doubt that the influx of postwar migrants played a tremendously important and direct part in all this transformation and that today's Australian way of life, as we know it, is a mixture of the old and the new, not merely a continuation of the prewar customs.
>
> In the same vein, there has been a growing realisation for some

time that sport, physical recreation and many of their sideshoots may not be able to carry on forever on either sheer enthusiasm or on a shoestring hemmed together from donations and chook raffles.[37]

The soccer-loving European migrants had nation-building in their DNA. Despite a narrow and parochial sporting culture based around state-based competitions and federations, the migrants had created a national soccer federation, a national soccer newspaper, the Australia Cup and the most inclusive national team in the country. They had adopted Australia's first independent national anthem and ventured into uncharted territory in Asia to qualify for the world's most important tournament. More than any other sport, soccer had dragged Australia out of the 1950s.

On 5 April 1975, 25 clubmen from Sydney, Adelaide, Newcastle and Brisbane met at Soccer House, the home of St George-Budapest. The conveners of the meeting were St George-Budapest's Alex Pongrass and Hakoah's Frank Lowy. Both were Hungarian-speaking disciples of the soccer revolution of the 1950s, the next generation of migrant leaders who had carved out their own lucrative business careers.

Lowy was the head of Westfield Shopping Centres; Pongrass was the owner of Pongrass Brothers Pty Ltd, with a stake in many different industries around the country. Both men lost their fathers in Auschwitz. Pongrass arrived in Australia in 1950 by way of an Austrian refugee camp; Lowy via a stint fighting for the Haganah in occupied Palestine. They had arrived in Australia hungry and wide-eyed, eager for opportunities. Instinctively, they were men of action, not words.

Yet their dream for a national league was threatened by the intransigence of the Victorians. Led by Michael Weinstein of Melbourne Hakoah, the Victorian clubs objected to the high cost of the enterprise, the threat of irrelevancy for their state competition, and the lack of promotion and relegation. They called the national league a 'closed shop' and refused to allow Tony Kovac, the president of JUST, to attend the first meeting. Other potential problems included the number of teams in each city, the question of 'nationalistic club names' and the role of state and national federations.

Not realising the enormity of these issues, St George-Budapest called on the representatives to 'sustain this spirit of adventure', and after four hours a resolution drafted by Dettre, who took the minutes of the meeting, was signed by the representatives to 'start such a league in 1976, if possible'.[38]

Yet by the winter of 1975, the progress of the national league had stalled, the Socceroos were still without a full-time coach, and Attila Abonyi was ready to retire from the national team. When Manchester United toured Australia, however, United coach Tommy Docherty offered him a run in a match against a Queensland XI. Abonyi played the second half for his favourite boyhood club, and scored the final goal in a 3–0 win.

As he returned to St George-Budapest, the Australian Soccer Federation ended months of speculation and finally dumped Rale Rasic as Socceroos coach. Brian Green, a seriously under-qualified Englishman, was the replacement.

'What I find more depressing than the mere matter of personalities,' wrote Dettre, 'is that the ASF seems hell-bent on prodding Australia even further towards becoming a pale imitation of English soccer.' To illustrate the point, he headlined the story: 'ANGLOMANIA PREVAILS – RASIC DUMPED.'[39]

This began an unhappy period for Dettre. He was frustrated by soccer's internal politics and impatient for the creation of a national league to capitalise on the 1974 World Cup. In his day job, he was forced to defend the government's extravagant spending, particularly the activities of the Department of Tourism and Recreation, which had just sent the study group on a costly round-the-world trip.

By September, the *Report of the Australian Sports Institute Study Group*, known as the Coles Report, had been tabled in the parliament. The timing could not have been worse. The Whitlam government was beset by scandal, neutered by a worldwide oil crisis and paralysed by a hostile Senate.

Led by Malcolm Fraser, the leader of the Liberal Party, the opposition used their favourable numbers in the Senate to block the budget and effectively hold the Australian economy to ransom. Just as Rasic fell out with Sir Arthur George, his friend Whitlam was betrayed by the governor-general, Sir John Kerr. Just after midday on 11 November 1975 – following a backroom deal between Kerr and Fraser – Kerr told Whitlam that Fraser had the authority to form a new government.

Some said it was a 'constitutional crisis'; others called it a coup d'etat. As an angry mob formed at the foot of Parliament House, Whitlam delivered his immortal line: 'Well may we say "God Save the Queen", because nothing will save the Governor-General.'

Fraser won the election that December. The Dismissal had worked. The Department of Tourism and Recreation was disbanded, Dettre lost his job, and the plans for a national sports institute were discarded.

The collapse of the Whitlam government and the sharp recession in Australian soccer seemed to bring out the best in Dettre. His writing became more free, his sense of humour sharpened and his ideas grew more radical. No longer burdened by day jobs at the *Daily Telegraph* or the Department of Tourism and Recreation, he gave away the pseudonyms 'Paul Dean' and 'Mike Renwick', and for the first time in *Soccer World* began to write under his own name. He labelled the Fraser government 'sanctimonious' for its dismissive attitude to sport, accused the mainstream media of ignoring soccer, and embarked upon a military-style recruitment campaign to get people back to soccer grounds, printing front-page slogans such as 'MAKE SOCCER A HABIT', 'SOCCER: 2nd BEST HOBBY', and 'SOCCER NEEDS YOU!'

While the rest of the soccer community discussed the prospect of a national league, Dettre suggested that the NSW federation create an international league, with teams representing Poland, Holland, Hungary, Greece, Croatia and so on. 'Australia today is more of an ethnic country than ever before,' he reasoned, and predicted that soccer 'can only be saved by migrants'.[40]

The idea immediately set the news agenda and found traction among club officials and foreign companies. Among the ethnic press, the plan was supported by *La Fiamma*, *Il Globo*, *Hellenic Herald*, *Hungarian Life* and *Nova Doba*. Even the *Daily Mirror* and the *Australian* picked up the story. But Peter McCann, the president of the NSW federation, rejected the idea, telling reporters that he would 'not stand for blood on the terraces and riots in the stands'.

Dettre reproduced these comments in *Soccer World* with a cheeky editorial note: 'The trouble is our crowds are becoming so small that we haven't got enough even for a minor riot any more.'[41]

The joy of the World Cup had almost completely receded to memory. As the game's officials searched for a way out of the crisis, the Socceroos' new coach Brian Green was caught shoplifting at a record store. He fled the country to howls of laughter.

Rale Rasic and Johnny Warren applied to replace him, yet they were both overlooked for Jim Shoulder, another relatively unknown Englishman. He was just 29, younger than many of the senior Socceroos, and had almost no top-level coaching experience. Rasic threatened to leave soccer altogether and take up rugby league, Warren warned against the 'Anglomania' that had taken hold of the ASF, and Dettre, tired of the politics and the bickering, wrote: 'No other Australian sport, no matter how impoverished or poorly administrated, is quite capable of such masochistic performances. We must really despise ourselves some-where deep down in our psyche to keep handing top soccer jobs to either complete outsiders or to starry-eyed, unqualified newcomers.'[42]

Yet soccer should have been the envy of every other sport. The tours of Asia, the World Cup, the new women's championship and the recent support from the federal government should have provided a solid foundation on which to build. Instead the new vistas in Asia were slammed shut and the progressive political consensus disappeared. 'What happened to Gough Whitlam, who is a personal friend, was a disgrace,' Rasic would later recall. 'In a way that's what happened to me.'[43]

Soon after Malcolm Fraser disbanded the Department of Tourism and Recreation, Australia sent a team of athletes to the 1976 Montreal

Olympics. Instead of 'Advance Australia Fair', a racy, upbeat version of 'Waltzing Matilda' was played at the opening ceremony. When the Australian athletes returned home with no gold medals, just one silver and four bronze, the Fraser government unsuccessfully tried to quell the public outrage by suggesting that Australia's participation was more important than medals. Eventually, Fraser was forced to commission an inquiry into the matter.

For Andrew Dettre, who had been advising, studying and writing on this topic for five years, it was cruel vindication. Yet his work had already been forgotten, and the Coles Report – victim of Fraser's austerity measures – gathered dust in the parliamentary library. Furthermore, he no longer had the ear of government, and his criticisms of Fraser went no further than the readership of *Soccer World*. It was akin to shouting in the wind.

At least in soccer there was a faint glimmer of hope. The Victorian boycott of the national league had been broken by Mooroolbark United, a tiny club from the far eastern suburbs of Melbourne, and applications to join the league were soon dispatched by Fitzroy United Alexander, South Melbourne Hellas, Footscray JUST, Essendon, Sunshine City and George Cross-Courage. By the end of July 1976, the national league sub-committee had arranged the infrastructure of the competition, signed a range of sponsors, and announced Alex Pongrass as chairman and John Frank, another Hungarian, as manager. It had also selected 14 teams for its inaugural season.

The enormity of this commitment can't be underestimated. Australian Rules football did not yet have a national league. Rugby league didn't either, nor did rugby union. The National Soccer League was the first national sporting competition in Australian history, and perhaps the most diverse national competition in the world.

★

Nearing 30, Attila Abonyi had achieved more in his career than he could have ever imagined. Between 1967 and 1976 he had led

Melbourne Hungaria to its first state and national titles, won the NSW first division with St George-Budapest, played at a World Cup and in the battlefields of Vietnam, started a lifelong friendship with Johnny Warren, and scored a goal for Manchester United. Yet he was uncertain for the future.

'Something had to be done about the set-up of soccer in Australia, and the national league is a step forward,' he wrote for *Soccer Action*, a new specialist newspaper based in Melbourne.

> But I'm not quite sure it will be a goer. A lot of clubs will find it hard to cope from a financial viewpoint [...] and attendances at matches was much better and bigger ten years ago. I honestly believe the game has dropped back a bit since then.
>
> Australia is not a great sporting nation and this is where we are totally different to the European countries [...] We just have to look at what we've done in the Olympic Games in Montreal to realise our apathy [...]
>
> Interest in Australian soccer picked up when we qualified for the World Cup finals a few years back, but over all the sport has not progressed.[44]

For the first time in his senior career, Abonyi left the Hungarian clubs and signed for Sydney Croatia, an ambitious club in the NSW first division. He would never play in the NSL. This was the beginning of the end.

A GOLDEN OPPORTUNITY

1977–1979

Ethnicity was turned into multiculturalism. The idea as such had been conceived by the ethnics themselves [...] they had foolishly believed they could be partners in this exciting venture. As it turned out, an Anglo-Australian public placed a stranglehold on it and has steadfastly refused to let go.

Pino Bosi
Who Is Afraid of the Ethnic Wolf?, 1986[1]

Between Sydney and Melbourne, Australia's two largest cities, is Canberra – the national capital. Before the surveyors and town planners and construction workers took to it in 1913, it was a quiet panorama of meadows and farm country, bordered by undulating mountains, the Brindabella Ranges and the drought-prone Lake George. The dry, flat plains had few remarkable features and even fewer people.

The 'bush capital' was selected for its isolation, in the hope that it would transcend state rivalries and engender feelings of national unity and progress. Sir Robert Garran, an architect of Federation, once remarked that Canberra 'is undoubtedly an integrating force in a country that has a longer period of disunion behind it than of union, so that its citizens need an occasional reminder that they are more than

Queenslanders or Victorians – they are Australians. Canberra is more than a city, it is an idea; and as the city grows, the idea grows with it.'[2]

By 1977, Canberra was home to more than 200,000 people and many of the institutions of Australian society. It housed the Parliament of Australia, the national library, the national gallery, dozens of foreign embassies, the mint, the national war memorial and the national university. And in the outer suburb of Bruce, a national sports stadium was under construction.

Every inch of the city was meticulously planned and built for purpose – brutalist modern architecture, extravagantly wide streets, suburbs named after prime ministers. Canberra was, as Andrew Dettre once observed, 'the eternally spoilt child of a munificent federal government [...] where resplendent and *nouveau riche* buildings spring up like mushrooms after rain; where a maze of geographically perfect avenues and circles, suburbs and estates, empty hospitals and deserted lakesides keenly await the arrival of people, more people, real people, to make this a living city'.[3]

Those who did move to Canberra were the kind of people who wanted to shape Australia's future – politicians, middle-class professionals, policy wonks, public servants and academics – as well as a willing crop of migrant labourers who quietly built that future. The Australian National University, a sprawling campus on the banks of Lake Burley Griffin, was home to Jerzy Zubrzycki, the father of Australian sociology. He studied migrant settlement, community and social inclusion and became the most vocal advocate of multiculturalism.

On 23 March 1977, Zubrzycki chaired the inaugural meeting of the Australian Ethnic Affairs Council in Canberra. The nation's historic challenge, he told an audience of ethnic community leaders and the federal minister for immigration and ethnic affairs, 'is that of harnessing the plurality of cultural, social, ethnic and religious groups for the common good without losing any original values that are part of these groups' heritage'.[4]

The Liberal government sponsored a review that would offer practical guidelines to meet this challenge. Under the leadership of

Prime Minister Malcolm Fraser, multiculturalism became a bipartisan policy. It should have been of great consequence to soccer – here was a government-backed mission that was not only encouraging migrant institutions but also hoping to include them in the national decision-making process.

Yet multiculturalism was never clear in the minds of the general public. 'Like most other societies, Australia is composed of a majority population from a roughly homogeneous ethnic background and a number of minority populations,' wrote Zubrzycki in the council's first submission to the Fraser government.

> [T]he established institutions reflect and confirm the various interests, ways of life, values and world views of the majority. We use the term Anglo-Australian for this majority population and culture [...] We describe as 'ethnic' the people who form the minority populations of non-Anglo-Australian origin and their institutions; apart from the Aborigines, the overwhelming majority of ethnics in Australia are migrants or the children of migrants.[5]

And so the Anglo-Australians were never asked to think of themselves as just another group in the 'Family of the Nation'. Instead they saw themselves as representative of mainstream or 'real' Australia.

This was the structural flaw that allowed assimilation to continue as an idea, even if it would no longer be expressed in public policy. No matter what Al Grassby, Fraser or Zubrzycki said, the dominant Anglo-Australian population was no closer to inviting an Indigenous person into their home, barely more appreciative of the European migrant experience, and continued to see South Sydney Rabbitohs or Richmond Football Club as more authentically Australian than Pan Hellenic or Wilhelmina or Adelaide Croatia.

Yet it was these migrant soccer clubs that had pioneered the practice of multiculturalism before it became policy. In rugby and cricket and especially Australian Rules, the Anglo-Australians already had sporting teams that had been built in their own image. Although migrants did play and watch those games, they were rarely found in positions of power or authority. Rather, these sports added to the long list of institutions that Anglo-Australians were over-represented in, including the parliament, the justice system, the corporate boardrooms, the public service and the media.

The Anglo-Australians were not asked to do anything – they were not forced to learn any of the migrant communities' languages, were not asked to seriously come to terms with the ongoing dispossession and mistreatment of Indigenous people, and, for the most part, were not consulted about the rapid social and ideological transformation from 'assimilation' to 'multiculturalism'. They were expected simply to tolerate the lexical change and continue with business as usual.

This tension at the heart of the Australian identity became the nation's central topic of conversation and the foundational debate in Australian soccer.

'Migrants are perfectly entitled to form whatever association or union they want, be that a church choir, welfare agency, scout group or soccer team,' Dettre once wrote. 'The trouble lies elsewhere; Australians (born here) are perfectly entitled to ignore these. And they do.'[6]

★

Before there was an Ethnic Affairs Council, there was the Philips Soccer League (PSL), Australia's first national club competition and its truest multicultural institution. It began in 1977 thanks to the missionary zeal and cooperation of Brisbane Lions and Mooroolbark, both founded by Dutchmen; the Greeks of South Melbourne, Fitzroy United Alexander and Sydney Olympic; the Italians at Marconi, Brisbane City and Adelaide City; the Yugoslavs at Footscray JUST; the Anglos at Western Suburbs; the Jews at Eastern Suburbs Hakoah; and the Hungarians at St George. Only one club was created specifically to compete in the PSL – Canberra City.

Just as the city of Canberra was artificially constructed to assimilate the notion of one united Australia, so too was its soccer club. From the outset, the directors of Canberra City envisioned that the club would be a new way forward for Australian soccer, beyond the scope of migrant clubs and free from the tradition of ethnic rivalries. Its major benefactor was Brian Pollock, a local car salesman, and the board comprised men of different faiths and nationalities.

'The Australian public will support soccer if they see quality football, marketed professionally,' wrote David Dillon, the club's first president, in Canberra City's application to join the league. 'The public will be quick to see that the proposed members of the 1977 League merely represents ethnic groups, and the Australian public as a whole will not identify with an ethnic group. Hence the promotions manager will not be able to market his product adequately. The National League needs support from the migrant communities but not at the expense of losing the potential Australian market.'[7]

Canberra City's first promotions manager was Steve Doszpot, a polite and conservative firstborn son of Hungarian refugees. Doszpot had arrived with the great wave of Hungarians in 1957, fleeing cold Soviet tanks on hot Budapest streets, and found refuge at St George-Budapest. He had played in the reserve grade side and followed the first team week in, week out.

By March 1977, however, he was nearing 30 and working as an executive in the computer industry. Physically and emotionally he had moved on from the warm embrace of the ethnic club and was determined that Canberra City would be seen as a team for the entire region. He saw the new club, with its diverse population base and distinct regional identity, as representative of a multiculturalism in which ethnic groups played a role in the institutions but did not dictate their conversations or identity. This new club structure would serve two interrelated functions: first, the migrant supporters would no longer be referred to as Hungarians, Greeks, Scots or Italians but as Canberrans; and second, their invisibility would precipitate the involvement of the Anglo-Australian sporting public.

'The Hungarians didn't live in enclaves,' Doszpot once explained. 'We assimilated, not because we didn't want to be Hungarian, but my parents always taught me that this was our new home and we have to thank Australia for giving us refuge.'

Quietly, Canberra City became imbued with the best of St George-Budapest. The club's blue-and-gold emblem was designed by Doszpot in the same shape as the Hungarian coat of arms. At Doszpot's recommendation, Johnny Warren – St George-Budapest's favourite son – became Canberra City's first coach. His assistant was the Argentine Vic Fernandez, another St George-Budapest alumnus.

The Kunz family – headed by the patriarch Frank Kunz, a Hungarian-born scholar who wrote about migration and refugee flows – formed Canberra City's first supporters club. Frank's son Chris began writing regularly for *Soccer World*, and in late March 1977 predicted that Canberra had a 'golden opportunity to gain supremacy' over the other football codes to become a 'true soccer city'.[8]

On Saturday 2 April 1977, Canberra City hosted West Adelaide in the first national league match. At Manuka Oval, a small cricket ground not far from Parliament House, a little more than 1500 people saw the home side go down 3–1.

Across four states, 14 sides played their first PSL matches to a total crowd of 28,400 people, at a respectable average of 4050 per game. Canberra City versus West Adelaide was the clearest example of the two competing visions of Australian soccer, and two competing ideas about Australian multiculturalism.

West Adelaide – known to most simply as Hellas – was a club firmly rooted in the South Australian soccer community. The players wore the blue and white of Greece, the fans flew Greek flags at games and celebrated on Greek national days. It was a traditional club with traditional aims: serve the community, produce players and win titles.

By contrast, at Canberra City there was no social club, no junior sides, no history and no clear mandate from the local soccer clubs. At City's first training session, there were no soccer balls. The club owed more to concept than to reality. Canberra City, wrote Johnny Warren in the first of his weekly columns for the *Canberra Times*, 'had to be achieved from scratch'.[9]

The first national league goal was scored by West Adelaide striker John Kosmina. It was his fourth game in six days. On Sunday 27 March 1977, he had scored one goal for the Socceroos and set up another in a spellbinding performance against New Zealand in Sydney. Three days later he had played 90 minutes for the Socceroos against New Zealand in Auckland. He then farewelled Polonia, his local club in Adelaide, by scoring a last-minute goal in the South Australian Ampol Cup final. After scoring the first national league goal the next day, one reporter called it 'a unique double'.[10]

Kosmina had a frame like a greyhound's: thin, fast but with the requisite mongrel to fit in among much older, battle-hardened men. He was named after his father, Alex, a Polish immigrant, but he took the name John and learned just a few phrases of his father's language. In many ways he was the typical Australian larrikin, and his ruthless competitive attitude and supreme confidence quickly found admirers. Along with John Nyskohus, he was rated the brightest talent to emerge from South Australia.

The national league brought the states together on a weekly basis, in turn creating opportunities for players and clubs outside soccer's traditional strongholds in Sydney and Melbourne. After three rounds of competition, Kosmina had scored three goals, and both Adelaide sides – City and West – attracted large crowds to their games.

Yet the enormous distance between Adelaide, Brisbane, Melbourne, Sydney and Canberra soon became a problem. In Round 6, air-traffic controllers went on strike and grounded flights around the country, leaving politicians, holiday-makers and national league soccer players stranded. 'Although nobody was wearing gas masks,' reported Dettre, 'the Philips Soccer League office this week resembled a war office. [PSL] Manager John Frank and his staff were studying maps, train and bus schedules, negotiating with charter airlines and almost everything else except rent-a-kayak outfits.'[11]

In order to reconcile the round of matches, a bus was rented to take the Fitzroy players back to Canberra. Once the players decamped from the bus, Marconi players got on and were ferried back to Sydney.

Adelaide City, meanwhile, had to take a long, torturous bus trip back home after its match against Eastern Suburbs Hakoah. The rest of the matches were postponed until June and July.

The strikes inadvertently allowed for one of the most memorable matches of the season. The Round 6 match between St George and South Melbourne was postponed until 15 June, and in the intervening period St George lured Arsenal legend Charlie George, while South Melbourne signed the Newcastle and Arsenal star Malcolm 'Supermac' Macdonald.

The pair joined several other high-profile foreign players, including the Scottish pair John 'Dixie' Deans and Graeme Souness. Dettre, although a purist, was resigned to their necessity. 'The fans who abandoned soccer gradually over the last ten years have failed to return to the terraces,' he wrote. 'The PSL clubs must now realise that only very big-named overseas stars could appreciably alter this trend.'[12]

George and Macdonald fitted the bill perfectly. Both were long-haired and boyishly good-looking, with charm, talent and charisma. In his legendary memoir, *Fever Pitch*, Nick Hornby wrote that George was representative of 'a time when football was beginning to resemble pop music in both its presentation and its consumption'.[13] Macdonald, meanwhile, was described by sportswriter Patrick Mangan in his own memoirs as 'part footballer, part rock star, part mystic'.[14]

Although they played just a few games in Australia, they delivered exactly what the promoters had hoped for. In an end-to-end thriller that finished 3–2 to St George, Macdonald scored two for South Melbourne and George scored the winner for the visitors.

A 12-year-old Angelos Postecoglou and his father, Jim, were among the 15,000 people there at Middle Park. The lucky ones crammed into the creaky wooden stadium to find a seat; the rest stood on the concrete terraces to see the two great sides and their exciting guest players. '[F]or me it felt like I was at a ground in Europe and experiencing in person what I had seen on my TV,' Postecoglou would later remember.[15]

In the national capital, Canberra City was already lining up a guest player of its own. Its man was not a foreigner, however, but Socceroos hero Adrian 'Noddy' Alston. Following the World Cup in 1974, Alston had played for Luton Town in England, Cardiff City in Wales and the Tampa Bay Rowdies in the North American Soccer League. But when his former teammate and Canberra City coach Johnny Warren came calling, he responded: 'I'd love to help.'[16]

Alston joined a hastily assembled squad of relative no-names. Some, like Tony Henderson, Ron Tilsed, Jim Cant and Oscar Langone, were genuine imports brought to Australia specifically for the purpose of playing in the PSL. Others, such as English defender Mike Black, Croatian midfielder Ivan Grujicic and Fijian forward Keni Kawaleva, had come up from local and state league sides.

It was not a glamorous team, and each player worked a job to help finance his soccer career. *Soccer World* labelled them 'known fighters' for their never-say-die attitude, while Warren pointed out that they had fared respectably against richer teams with players who had been together for years. 'We're not a magic side,' Alston conceded, 'but they're a great bunch of lads.'[17]

In the United States, Alston had been introduced to the crowd on his debut by a spectacular helicopter drop. In Canberra the reception was considerably less extravagant, but still his presence took immediate effect. He spoke well to the press and travelled with Warren to Griffith, a regional town four hours west of Canberra, to conduct a coaching clinic. In his first match at Manuka Oval, he scored the third goal in a 4–0 win over Sydney Olympic. 'Obviously since appearing with Tampa Bay, "Noddy" has learned what the publicity game is about,' noted Chris Kunz for *Soccer World*. 'He handled his many engagements with effortless ease, and indeed an engaging charm.'[18]

Alston was just 28 years old, in the prime of his career, yet by August he was curiously absent from the Socceroos squad. His non-selection was a major embarrassment to the ASF, which required that he be selected for the Socceroos to extend his stay as a guest player at Canberra City.

Keeping him out of the Socceroos was John Kosmina. Since scoring the first goal of the season, everything had gone Kosmina's way. In July, during an 11-day fiesta of football that included the Socceroos, English first-division club Arsenal, Scottish giants Celtic and Yugoslav powerhouse Red Star Belgrade, he had scored the Socceroos' first goal in a famous 3–1 victory over Arsenal. Dettre reported that Kosmina was 'devastating, classes above the highly rated Arsenal stars'.[19] And in August, during a crucial World Cup qualifier against South Korea, he had scored two late goals in a 2–1 win.

For the next qualifying match against Kuwait, however, Alston was recalled to the squad. He started up front alongside Kosmina, and was soon joined by his old World Cup teammate Attila Abonyi. But the Socceroos lost 2–1, sending its campaign into total disarray. In the final four games, all played away from home, the Socceroos drew one, won one, lost two, and failed to qualify for the 1978 World Cup.

Alston never played again for the Socceroos. He had made 62 appearances for 17 goals. He soon returned to Florida. For Canberra City, he made ten appearances for three goals.

Abonyi also retired from the national team, while the Socceroos coach Jim Shoulder was sacked. Cries of 'Pommy mafia', which became in vogue after the dismissal of Rale Rasic, hit fever pitch. Shoulder's young assistant coach, Ron Smith, also a migrant from England, would have to deal with this charge for the next three decades as he moved into different coaching roles.

'The "Pommy mafia" was just a label,' he once recalled. 'Because in the mid-1970s Eric Worthington – who was of English heritage – was the director of coaching. He tried to set up a formalised coaching structure in every state. There was a notion at the time that he appointed everyone in the states, when in actual fact he didn't.'

The PSL season ended with an $8000 total loss, but overall the experiment had been a success. Eastern Suburbs Hakoah, one of the architects of the new league, won the inaugural premiership in an exciting final round. John Kosmina scored 12 national league goals, almost a third of West Adelaide's total, and was voted the under-21 player of the year by the Australian Soccer Press Association, receiving double the votes of his nearest rival.

For his achievements he was invited to join Alston at the Tampa Bay Rowdies. Instead he chose to make the big step up to Arsenal. The inaugural season of the PSL propelled him from the Antipodes to the centre of the world.

Canberra City finished in second-last place, but received widespread acclaim in the season postmortems. 'Within one year,' wrote Dettre, 'Australia's capital city, the long dormant public service haven and a backwater in major sports, has gained national prominence through soccer.'[20]

For Johnny Warren, Canberra's success was determined off the pitch. 'In its first nine months, City has achieved many positive things,' he wrote for the *Canberra Times*. 'It is reasonable to say that City's concept of a truly Canberra team not based on one nationality is a first in Australia and a good thing for our football.'[21]

Andrew Dettre had already arrived at a similar conclusion. As the season drew to a close, and the attendances in Sydney failed to rise, he suggested that the PSL 'be transformed into mass entertainment' through modern marketing, clever promotions and generous sponsorship.[22]

He was a man of big and often contradictory ideas, trying as always to resolve soccer's existential crisis. One year after he had suggested that an international league should be formed, with a view to making soccer more ethnic, he now took the view that the national league must rid itself of its ethnic image.

Having witnessed the splintering of Sydney's supporter base, as well as the growing, unrepresented South American and Lebanese communities, Dettre proposed that the five Sydney clubs be replaced by two superteams. His grand, almost utopian plan was to merge the administrative knowledge of St George, Sydney Olympic and Eastern Suburbs Hakoah to create a new club called 'Wentworth United'.

The big question to be resolved is this: are the Sydney clubs ready to face realities or do they prefer to sink into oblivion under their own name and banner?

I am convinced that there is no other way out of this crisis than a daring, intelligent and selfless move to bring Sydney's PSL soccer under two big umbrellas [...]

Sydney can and will support two PSL teams – but only if those two teams belong to much larger and broader groups than hitherto and through their neutral name, organisation and composition, also appeal to the average, uninvolved Australians.[23]

Once the scattered Sydney scene was resolved, Dettre believed that other superteams could be established in Hobart, Perth and New Zealand. It was perhaps the most prophetic article ever written in the history of Australian soccer, but at the time there was no institutional will to take it from dream to reality.

In the first round of 1978, Dettre's vision was validated in stunning fashion. In the capital, Canberra City drew a record 6000 people to the new national stadium; and in the Hunter Valley, more than 100 kilometres north of Sydney, Newcastle KB United drew more than 15,000 spectators to its first ever competitive match against Eastern Suburbs Hakoah.

Newcastle had taken the place of Mooroolbark, the little club from Melbourne that finished last in 1977. In 1976 it had been Mooroolbark that broke the Victorian boycott of the national competition, but now, without a trace of sentimentality, it was sent back to the Victorian state league. Fittingly, the range of commemorative dinner plates adorned with the logos of the founding PSL clubs had only a pair of question marks where Mooroolbark's logo should have been. Mooroolbark United would be the first national league club to be discarded, forgotten, and nearly erased from history. But it would not be the last.

Newcastle KB United represented a growing regional centre of 300,000 people, with an image that was desirable to both PSL officials and Dettre's 'uninvolved Australians'. The 'wogball' tag just wouldn't stick in a soccer community that had traditionally been patronised by hardworking British coalminers, and to get the parochial juices flowing, local players such as Lloyd Hardes, Neil Endacott, Joe Senkalski, John Sneddon and Col Curran were recruited.

Newcastle's best player, however, was a 27-year-old British import named Ken Boden. A painter by trade, he had sublime skills that moved one sportswriter to label him 'an intriguing artist' in the same breath as Vincent van Gogh and Rembrandt. Before he arrived in Newcastle, Boden had played at clubs so obscure they almost sounded fictional – Matlock FC, Bridlington Town, Scunthorpe United. Yet he hit the ground running. Although his debut match ended in a loss, the quiet Yorkshireman scored Newcastle KB United's first national league goal.

The PSL was injected with a near-lethal dose of British players. In 1977 there were 57 Englishmen, 59 Scots, three Northern Irishmen and one Welshman, forming 42 per cent of the total and 75 per cent of overseas-raised players. The days of the spellbinding European import were over. No player reflected this decline better than Ulysses Kokkinos, Australian soccer's first playboy.

Born to Greek parents in Turkey in 1949, Kokkinos arrived in Australia in 1966. He had bought a ticket to tour the migrant ship *Patris*, but as the other tourists filed on and off the boat, he hid underneath in the workers cabins. When the ship left for Australia, he was still on board, ready for a new adventure. A young migrant without family, friends or money, he knew that there was soccer in Melbourne – good-quality soccer, with big crowds – and lots of Greeks. He joined the South Melbourne Hellas Soccer Club.

Kokkinos was a genuine star, with the charisma to cross over from the ethnic communities of Victorian soccer to the mainstream. Yet his independent spirit was his greatest quality and his greatest flaw. Depending on how you saw it, he was either a charismatic free spirit or a self-obsessed philanderer. His hair was a large black afro, his shirts open at the chest and his mannerisms smooth and confident. His perfectly chiselled jaw was flecked with dark stubble, and his brooding gaze suggested mischief and adventure. The Greek men in Melbourne, many of them factory workers, wanted to be like him. Many women found him irresistible.

Kokkinos reciprocated the love and affection with interest. 'My ideal Saturday night before a game is to relax, have dinner with a nice girl and have sex,' he once told reporters. When rumours swirled that he was in charge of a massage parlour, he had responded: 'I wish the reports were true ... I would give up soccer forever.'[24]

By 1978, as the former West Adelaide striker John Kosmina trained with Arsenal, Kokkinos was vying for the spot Kosmina had vacated up front. He was no longer a great player, however, and to soccer he had added two more vices that he pursued with considerable enthusiasm: whisky and gambling.

By the fourth round of the season, he was hauled before the County Court of Victoria and sentenced to 18 months in prison. His crime: extortion. When Kokkinos moved to Adelaide, he had struck up an affair with a pretty young woman. To feed a lavish lifestyle, he threatened to tell her family and the media of their affair if she didn't provide him with money.

'The offence was a callous one,' said the judge. 'You told lies to the young lady involved and didn't have any real concern for her feelings. Your thoughts were on yourself and on the chance of obtaining some easy money ... apparently to be used for gambling.'[25]

His incarceration brought a final, tragic end to soccer's swinging sixties. Kokkinos would never again play top-flight soccer.

★

Eight days after Ulysses Kokkinos was sent to Pentridge Prison, Newcastle KB United travelled for the first time to Canberra to play the opening match of Round 5. 'Like Canberra City, Newcastle KB United is a completely new club, created solely for the purpose of maintaining a presence in the national competition,' noted *Canberra*

Soccer News. 'The wisdom of this method of entry into the League has received the early approval of the Australian public and the immense local support by way of crowds is evidence of this. In fact, this could well be the pattern for the league in the future.'[26]

Canberra Soccer News was the neatly arranged match program of Canberra City Soccer Club. It published team line-ups, news and tidbits about the goings-on of soccer in Canberra and carried columns by players, the promotions manager, Steve Doszpot, and regular fans.

While many of the ethnic clubs were built upon networks of Hungarian or Greek or Italian families, who shared a common language, history and culture, the Canberra City supporters came together in an ad hoc fashion, inspired only by their desire to watch high-quality soccer. In this context, *Canberra Soccer News* helped to create a sense of atmosphere and togetherness among the loose coalition of supporters.

'What we did was a tremendous exercise in showing people that soccer can attract the average Australian who hasn't seen a soccer match before,' Doszpot later explained. 'I had friends who were involved in rugby league, Aussie Rules and basketball all coming out to watch Canberra City because they didn't feel different there.'

Many onlookers were impressed by Canberra City's organised supporter group, which would dress in club colours, travel to interstate matches and chant enthusiastically for their team. Headed by the Kunz family, they congregated in a specific area of the stadium, handed out instructions to new supporters, and hung banners on the railings to mark their territory.

After one match in Sydney, Johnny Warren congratulated the supporters club for making the trip north. 'This,' he wrote, 'was the first time in my soccer days in Australia that I had heard a crowd support a team when it was behind.'[27]

The fans themselves claimed to be the first active supporter group in the country. 'Within months, the Canberra Cheer Squad became a legend in Australian soccer,' wrote its founder Frank Kunz, 'interstate soccer writers, coaches were writing about us with envy and the crowds began to grow.'[28]

Doszpot dubbed the cooperation of *Canberra Soccer News*, the match day cheer squad, the supporters club, the ground announcer and the ground manager 'The Home Game Machine'. The unity of the supporters was complemented by the professionalism of the committee. In 1978 Canberra City moved to the newly opened national stadium, established a clubhouse in town, and organised for Prime Minister Malcolm Fraser to become the club's number-one ticket-holder. Fraser was brought into the fold by Charles Perkins, the deputy secretary of the Department of Aboriginal Affairs and the newly appointed vice-president of Canberra City.

Perkins joined a board full of experience in Canberra's commercial, cultural and political life. President Doug Holman was the head of a real estate firm, Victor Falko worked at the National Library of Australia and Peter Windsor worked in the Department of Immigration. Bill Arnold was a local pharmacist, Doszpot the manager of Sanyo, and Theo Moulis ran the popular Bacchus Tavern.

When *Soccer Action* published a three-page spread on the 'wonder team', many of these men took out advertisements in the newspaper. After ten rounds, however, Canberra City was languishing at the bottom of the ladder, unable to register a single win in front of their home fans. And yet the crowds were booming – the Round 10 match against Marconi drew a club record of 7450 spectators.

Across the competition, the crowds seemed to have more to do with off-field promotion than results. The best club in the league, Eastern Suburbs Hakoah, could barely attract 3000 people to any of its games, even though it played at Wentworth Park, an historic soccer ground in the heart of Sydney's bustling metropolis. But Newcastle KB United, which, like Canberra City, had won just a single match in the first ten rounds, was regularly drawing more than 6000 spectators to its home games.

By Round 14, on the same day that just 3500 people watched a Newcastle rugby league side play against New Zealand, nearly 7000 spectators witnessed Newcastle KB United beat Western Suburbs at the International Sports Centre. In the final round, Newcastle again broke all records as more than 16,000 people turned out to watch English legend Bobby Charlton don the cinnamon, green and white Newcastle jersey against Marconi-Fairfield.

Both Canberra City and Newcastle KB United missed the finals series, although Ken Boden won the PSL Golden Boot award with 14 goals and Newcastle's aggregate home attendance was 110,707, a staggering increase of almost 700 per cent on Mooroolbark's from the season prior.

Max Talbot, the club president, put the success down to capturing the imagination of an entire city. 'We can only improve on an area basis,' he told *Soccer World*. 'One major area against another [...] Perhaps Sydney would do better with two teams, and so would Melbourne.'[29]

For as long as soccer had existed in Australia, it had been viewed as a threat to the other codes of football. Generations of soccer supporters had tried to present the game to the public in the best possible way, in the hope that they would see the light and become soccer converts. In this context, pooling the resources and the supporters of an entire city into one or two superteams was a new method of achieving old objectives.

First, it would take apart the tribalism of ethnic club soccer and put it back together again in a more attractive way for the dominant Anglo-Australian population. Second, the economies of scale in these united superteams would provide stiffer competition to the popular, state-based rugby league and Australian Rules competitions.

If Canberra City and Newcastle KB United could overcome the entrenched sporting interests in their respective cities, why shouldn't the broad-based model be replicated in Perth, Townsville, Wollongong, Adelaide, Melbourne and Sydney?

September 1978 laid bare the fractured nature of Australia's sporting loyalties. While the PSL hosted its first finals series, won by Eastern Suburbs Hakoah in front of more than 9000 people at the Sydney

Sports Ground, the other codes of football attracted much larger crowds for state-based grand finals.

Earlier that year, a labour historian named Ian Turner had tried to explain this peculiarly Australian phenomenon in his final Ron Barassi Snr Memorial Lecture. Turner called the imaginary diagonal border that separated the Australian Rules states in the south-west from the rugby league–obsessed states in the north-east 'the Barassi Line'. It ran directly through Canberra – Australia's budding 'soccer city'.

As Turner was an Australian Rules supporter, he did not dwell upon soccer. And yet, apart from cricket, soccer was the only sport that could claim true national status. In Queensland and NSW, the laws, traditions and culture of Australian Rules were mostly foreign. In the remaining states, you would have been hard pressed to find a rugby league ball. Rugby union, meanwhile, still existed essentially among Australia's landed gentry and elite private schools.

By contrast, the PSL was the only weekly national competition, with tentacles that stretched to six major cities. 'Soccer is now a national as well as international game here in Australia,' wrote Herman Huyer, the chairman of Philips Industries, in March 1979. 'If it is to realise its potential we all know it has, there must be a real competition on the field and real cooperation off the field.'[30]

However, soccer's two major problems – the tyranny of distance and the concentration of political power in Sydney and Melbourne – were inherited by the PSL. Canberra City and Newcastle KB United had shown the great potential of the regional areas, and that by forming new, non-ethnic superteams, soccer could find a market among the Anglo-Australians.

Yet the paralysis of the ASF inspired neglected regions and participants to go in their own direction. The Australian Women's Soccer Association pressed ahead with its own fledgling competitions in NSW, Queensland, the ACT and South Australia, while in Queensland a revolutionary new men's state league kicked off on the final day of March 1979.

The Queensland State League (QSL) featured Mareeba United and Townsville Kern United from the far north, Rockhampton-Frenchville from central Queensland, Across the Waves from Bundaberg, and Gold Coast City, Ipswich United and four Brisbane clubs from the south-east.

The teams were a potpourri of Queensland's population – Townsville was full of Englishmen, Mareeba was run by Yugoslavs and Italians, Southside Eagles were once Germania, Grange Thistle were Scots, and Across the Waves were an Italian side founded by cane-cutters who literally named their club after their journey to Australia.

In a state that covers nearly 2 million square kilometres – an area seven times larger than Britain – the QSL was a tremendous logistical achievement. When Mareeba United in the far north travelled nearly 2000 kilometres to meet Gold Coast City on the southern border, the trip was as far as any made in the PSL.

'Ambitious players now have somewhere to go,' said Alan Vessey, the secretary of the Queensland Soccer Federation, in an interview with *Soccer World*. 'Many squads have plenty of 18-year-olds who never previously had the chance to progress and drifted out of the game ... This is another Philips League in the making.'[31]

In Rockhampton, a beef-producing regional town roughly equidistant between Townsville and Brisbane, Michael Cockerill, a sandy-haired, square-jawed son of a newspaperman, was in his first year as a journalist for the *Rockhampton Morning Bulletin*. He was 18, fresh out of school and playing for the Yeppoon Eagles in the local competition. He would climb aboard the bus to travel with Rockhampton-Frenchville throughout the state. It was his first major assignment as a soccer journalist. His experience at the *Morning Bulletin* would influence his reportage for the next four decades, as he repeatedly encouraged the national league to support its regional centres.

'I came in with a passion to make writing about football my life,' Cockerill later recalled. 'I went from thinking I'd be writing the occasional story about the Rockhampton first division – and hopefully playing in it – to suddenly writing about a proper state league.

It was exciting, I grasped the significance of that pretty quickly and ear-bashed my sports editor about it. I was the guy who wanted to do everything, I wanted to change the world. We had a state league in Queensland that went up to Far North Queensland and down to the Gold Coast, we had a national competition, so in a geographic sense, I thought this sport was going somewhere.'

In Rockhampton the crowds hovered between 1000 and 2000 people, while Townsville Kern United's first game drew 2200 spectators – more people than had turned up to Brisbane Lions' PSL match held just five days earlier. Backed by Kern Brothers, a well-heeled local building firm, Townsville seemed the most likely to join the national league. Rudi Gutendorf, the Socceroos' newly appointed coach, told *Canberra Soccer News* that the PSL should expand to new centres. 'Rather than national sides from places with PSL teams already,' he said, 'I favour Wollongong, Geelong and even Townsville being in the league.'[32]

The ripple effects of the QSL also reached Newcastle, where a chirpy Yorkshireman named Stefan Kamasz was impressed by the scope of the new competition.

Kamasz was a 'ten-pound Pom' who had arrived in Australia after answering an advertisement from Newcastle-based Weston Workers Bears in an English newspaper. The club had sponsored him to move down under, and within two years his brothers and parents had followed him. By 1979, he had retired from soccer, was training to be an accountant and was the treasurer of Maitland Magpies. He was an unfailingly pleasant young man, a keen learner and had a passion for the game that kept him awake at night.

'I wanted to emulate what had been happening in Queensland,' Kamasz later recalled. 'Our league was basically Newcastle and the coalfields. We set about creating a proper state league for Northern NSW. We had to get rid of some of the clubs and bring in Tweed Heads, Coffs Harbour, Armidale and Tamworth – because Queensland had brought in Rockhampton and Townsville.'

Although they were not under the umbrella of the PSL, the growth of the Australian Women's Soccer Association, the rise of the QSL and the budding new league in Northern NSW had proven beyond all doubt that soccer was now a truly national game. You could drop a pin almost anywhere on the map of Australia and, if it were inhabited by people, there would be a soccer team.

Marginal though it may have been, soccer was capable of galvanising every possible ethnic, regional, metropolitan, gender and political group from Perth to Sydney, Darwin to Adelaide, Cairns to Hobart. This presented an historic opportunity.

★

The architecture of Australia's multicultural society had been fortified by 1979. The Galbally Report, the outcome of a government-sponsored inquiry into services for migrants, noted that 20 per cent of Australians had been born overseas, more than 100 different languages were spoken across the country, and around 60 different ethnic newspapers were in circulation. It decreed that Australia was 'at a critical stage of development of a cohesive, united multicultural nation' and that the most 'significant and appropriate bodies to be involved in the preservation and fostering of cultures are the ethnic organisations themselves'.[33]

The authors of the report also noted that there was some ongoing tension and inequalities between the Anglo-Australians and the migrant groups. 'We are convinced,' they wrote, 'that provided that ethnic identity is not stressed at the expense of society at large, but is interwoven into the fabric of our nationhood by the process of multicultural interaction, then the community as a whole will benefit substantially and its democratic nature will be reinforced.'[34]

At the time of its publication, the most successful clubs in the Philips Soccer League were West Adelaide, Marconi, Fitzroy United Alexander, Adelaide City and Eastern Suburbs Hakoah, which had been rebranded as 'Sydney City'. Each of these clubs had ethnic foundations – Greek, Italian, Jewish – and each had a squad made up of players of various backgrounds. They were following the recommendations of the Galbally Report to the letter: they were the ethnic organisations that would foster the preservation of culture; they had each adopted district names so as not to stress their ethnic identity at the expense of society at large; and, by mixing with other teams in the PSL, they were actively engaged in the process of multicultural interaction more than any other facet of society.

If multiculturalism meant 'migrants getting in on the act', as the Ethnic Affairs Council once decreed, then it was the ethnic soccer clubs that should have been seen as the ambassadors.

Yet the broader public had long detested the ethnic soccer clubs, and now the soccer community was losing faith in them too. Despite having sacrificed its foundational 'Budapest' title and opened a beautiful new soccer stadium in the district, St George was in severe crisis. Andrew Dettre started to joke with his son, Steve, that the club, which was famous for its *langos* – an artery-clogging, deep-fried Hungarian flatbread – was killing off its own supporter base. 'The most stunning blow to the Saints,' he wrote, 'must have been their failure to attract "Australians" to their matches.'[35]

Instead it was Canberra City and Newcastle KB United – the two 'non-ethnic' clubs – that were seen as the future of Australian soccer. The tension between these two club models would define the next three decades of national league soccer. This was Australian soccer's great national question.

There was also a looming question about the involvement of women. Founded in 1974, the Australian Women's Soccer Association (AWSA) had accumulated more than 200 teams, nearly 5000 registered players, adopted its own badge, its own constitution, and formed its own national team with players drawn from around the country. In the absence of partnership or support from the Australian Soccer Federation, AWSA affiliated with women's associations in NSW, South Australia, Western Australia and Queensland.

In Canberra, the first ever women's competition was underway. Heather Reid, the daughter of Scottish labourers who had worked on the Snowy Mountains Scheme, became the first secretary of the Australian National University Women's Soccer Club.

'The women at the ANU club were proud feminists,' Reid once explained. 'We were on the back of International Women's Year in 1975, the Whitlam Labor government saying women's rights are human rights, and the rise of feminism in a broader context – any woman could do anything. In soccer the biggest challenge that we had was dealing with the gender politics. It's so entrenched in males that for the women to come in and find a space was going to be difficult.'

Canberra City – which was eager to establish strong foundations and take soccer to new fans – threw its support behind the women and created its own team to play it in the local competition. The club also formed a fruitful relationship with Newcastle KB United. It recruited ex-Newcastle boss Max Talbot to work as its secretary-manager, the supporter groups built a terrific rapport, the promotions managers liaised regularly, and together the two clubs had established a new cup tournament.

'The idea of playing annually for a trophy between two clubs with virtually no ethnic affiliations – compared to the other PSL clubs – came from City coach Johnny Warren,' explained a reporter for the *Canberra Times*. 'It was later expanded by the club board and culminated in the prime minister, Mr Fraser, giving permission to call it the Prime Ministers Cup.'[36]

At one Canberra City match, an Indigenous man performed a boomerang-throwing demonstration as pre-game entertainment. Charles Perkins had assumed the role of president of Canberra City, becoming the first Indigenous person to lead a top-flight sporting club in Australia. And Harry Williams, the former St George-Budapest and Socceroos star, had also joined the club. Like Perkins, he divided his time between soccer and the Department of Aboriginal Affairs.

Other well-known Indigenous people such as John Moriarty and local journalist John Janke were engaged to promote the club, and within a few years the Canberra Nomads – perhaps Australia's first Indigenous soccer club – would be formed in the local Canberra competition. It included Perkins, Janke, Moriarty and Steve Doszpot, one of the few white players in the team.

'This is the thing about soccer – we were in a place where our passions and our lives weren't governed by politics,' remembered Doszpot, who became the vice-president of Canberra City under Perkins. 'Charlie was put through so much hell in politics. But when we were at the soccer, Charlie was totally immersed. I think it kept him motivated in his political life. He could just be himself.'

Canberra City entered reserve teams in the local competitions, sponsored a local woman to enter the Miss Australia contest and reorganised the recruitment policy to focus on the development of junior players. The club took part in the Canberra Day Parade, and invited the prime minister and the governor-general and handicapped children as guests of honour to its games.

It was the biggest, the best and the most progressive sporting club in Canberra. Yet it continued to struggle to get results. Both Canberra City and Newcastle KB United finished the 1979 season outside the top four. Theirs was an off-field contribution – the pioneering examples of how a new type of soccer club could be formed.

It would take another quarter of a century for the one-town-team model to be applied across all the clubs in the competition. But in the Canberra City clubhouse, behind the main bar, a blue-and-gold club scarf was wrapped around a green, brown and white scarf of Newcastle KB United. 'The official reason given is that this is the knot of eternal friendship,' read a supporters' column in *Canberra Soccer News*. 'The symbolic uniting of the first two city-based non-ethnic clubs in the PSL.'[37]

WE TOOK THEIR NAME AND THEIR GAME

1980–1982

The Eagles will scoop on the Rams
With Gunners on alert,
The Demons will bewitch the Hawks,
As Arrows hit the dirt.
Gladiators will go marching on
While Strikers seek a strip,
The Stingers make a stingy bite
The Slickers lick a tribe.
Giants will hunt for tame Lions,
Olympians, salute!
The Raiders have captured the Bears
And Warriors the loot.
The game will now be persilwhite
And dinky-di, to boot, [...]
We've got the problems licked at last
But one snag still remains;
Who will remember what the hell
Were his club's maiden names?

Andrew Dettre
Soccer World, 1981[1]

On the evening of 29 October 1979, as the Socceroos' captain, Tony Henderson, emerged from the players' race of the Sydney Showground, he was amazed to see spectators spilling out of the stadium and onto the grass. What should have been an oval became a tight rectangle as nearly 60,000 people crammed into a 40,000-seat stadium.

It was the biggest crowd Henderson had ever played in front of, and opposite him in the tunnel was his idol, Franz Beckenbauer. Upon seeing the regal German, the crowd went berserk. Without missing a beat, Beckenbauer turned to Henderson and quipped: 'Well, you're very popular here.'

The Socceroos were up against the New York Cosmos, the largest club in the North American Soccer League (NASL). The Cosmos were in Australia thanks to Johnny Warren, who had finished his coaching duties at Canberra City and moved north to work as the promotions manager for Sydney City, the club formerly known as Hakoah. In his regular column for the *Sunday Telegraph*, Warren wrote about the potential for such a tour to kickstart Australian soccer, and a promotional group called International Artists quickly agreed to fund the operation.

Between 1975 and 1979, the New York Cosmos signed Pele, by then the greatest player in the world, and attracted huge crowds to its games. The NASL created new clubs out of nothing and pushed soccer into the mainstream of American social and cultural life. Unburdened by tradition, the Americans called clubs 'franchises', relocated them around the country according to the tides of popular support, and when they found a rule they didn't like they just changed it.

Star players had followed Pele like moths to the flame – George Best went to LA Aztecs in 1976, and when he left to join the Tampa Bay Rowdies in 1978, the Aztecs replaced him with Dutch icon Johan Cruyff. When Pele moved on, the Cosmos signed Beckenbauer, the king of German football.

Soccer in the USA and Australia shared the same demographic opportunity, and suffered the same xenophobia and the same shortage of mainstream attention. But, in 1977, the New York Cosmos were attracting crowds of more than 30,000 people, a figure greater than the average weekly attendance for all 14 PSL clubs put together. By 1978, the PSL marketing manager, John Frank, and Western Suburbs' Mike Laing were dispatched to the United States on fact-finding missions.

For most Australians, however, the Cosmos tour of 1979 was the first opportunity to see the results of American soccer's rapid transformation.

Unsurprisingly the New York Cosmos, not the Socceroos, were the selling point of the tour. On advertisements heralding 'once in a lifetime soccer', not a single Socceroos player was listed alongside the Cosmos superstars. And at a pre-match dinner held at the APIA club in Sydney, the visitors had been given prime seating in front of the press, while the Socceroos were seated at the back. 'There's nothing worse than feeling like you're making up the numbers,' Henderson later recalled. 'We were determined to give them a go.'

A journeyman footballer from Newcastle, England, Tony Henderson played a few seasons in South Africa before arriving in Australia in 1977 to play for Canberra City. A colossus in defence, Henderson was the classic English centre-back who led with a tough brand of soccer and a no-nonsense attitude. He was accomplished with both feet, good in the air and popular among his peers.

By 1979 he had moved to Sydney to join Marconi and had made his debut for Australia, a natural successor to the outgoing captain of the 1974 side, Peter Wilson. The match against the Cosmos was just his fourth appearance for the Socceroos, yet he was given the captain's armband and the job of marking the notoriously difficult Italian striker Giorgio Chinaglia. Not that this worried Henderson, a towering bruiser bred on the mud-heaps of northern England. 'I could be pretty,' he once said, 'but I generally wasn't. Especially not against players like Chinaglia.'

After 77 minutes Chinaglia scored what appeared to be the equalising goal. Moments before full-time, however, Jimmy Rooney delivered a dangerous corner, which was nodded home by Henderson. The 2–1 win for Australia was a perfect ending to a revelatory tour.

The popularity of the New York Cosmos tapped into something much bigger occurring in Australian society. Americanisation had reached its peak in the 1960s, and became all-pervasive in the 1970s. Australians tuned in to American television shows such as *Happy Days* and *The Brady Bunch*, watched Hollywood films, sang along to songs by the Village People and Bruce Springsteen, and danced to disco music.

Many Australians lived in 'California bungalows', kept their food fresh in American-designed refrigerators and started eating at McDonald's, which opened its first store in Sydney in 1971. Kerry Packer's revolutionary World Series Cricket tournament was influenced by baseball, Australia's first National Basketball League tipped off in August 1979, and American innovations such as cheerleaders and mascots began to feature throughout the football codes.

Among the soccer community, discussion was raging about the possibility of forming a superteam in Sydney to replicate the New York Cosmos. Sydney City president Frank Lowy said that he 'completely favoured the scheme', while Peter Sheean, one of the men behind the plan to redevelop Cumberland Oval into Parramatta Stadium, said that he wanted to run a Cosmos-style soccer side out of the Parramatta Leagues Club.[2] And at *Soccer World*, Andrew Dettre was captivated by the NASL.

At the end of 1979, Dettre travelled to the United States, where he traded ideas with American soccer administrators and journalists. In New York he met with a fellow Hungarian, Otto Radich, who told him that dropping ethnic club names and replacing them with glitzy monikers like Chicago Sting, Houston Hurricanes and San Jose Earthquakes had led to greater acceptance from middle America.

At the Rockefeller Center in Midtown Manhattan, Dettre had an epiphany: the PSL should copy the NASL and play in summer to escape the clutches of the rival winter sports. Upon his return to Australia, Dettre wrote a four-part series titled 'Soccer Made in the USA'. He commented favourably on American innovations such as celebrity players, the one-town-team concept, summer soccer, corporate involvement and franchised clubs.

'Is it possible to imitate or emulate the success of soccer in America?' he wrote. 'I am sure it is. But we are on completely the wrong track. We had the chance when we created the Philips League – but blew it. Instead of creating an entirely new structure on new foundations, we thought it would be enough to throw out the "ballast" (unfashionable clubs) and continue in the same vein. The effects of this mistake are still felt, especially in Sydney and Melbourne.'[3]

Not for the first time, his dispatches reverberated through the corridors of power. In July 1980, the ASF's hired marketing hand, Rik Booth, announced that the PSL 'will be remodelled over the next four to five years on the North American Soccer League'.[4] Booth's suggestions included new broadcast deals, summer soccer, an indoor soccer competition and, perhaps most importantly, a plan to attract big business to support the game.

'Clubs, we hope, will change their names, all club emblems will be redesigned,' Booth promised. '[W]e will de-ethnicise it in every way.'[5]

★

Of all the American innovations, Andrew Dettre was most convinced by summer soccer. He had been lobbying for its introduction since his trip to America and, by the end of July 1980, he thought the battle had finally been won.

It was winter, in the middle of the PSL's fourth season, and the signs were not good. Clubs such as Canberra City and Newcastle KB United, once heralded as the future of the league, were struggling to get supporters along to games. Crowds had also slumped for both the Adelaide clubs, South Melbourne, APIA Leichhardt and Brisbane City.

In *Soccer World*, Dettre printed simple questionnaires for readers to fill in and send back for submission to the ASF. To his delight, 67 per cent of readers felt it was a good idea to shift the season to summer, while less than 4 per cent rejected the idea out of hand. Most readers felt that Friday-night matches would be ideal, would create a better television product and would attract new fans to the game.[6]

By September, an ASF Marketing report had arrived at a similar conclusion. The PSL Council of Clubs agreed that the competition should switch to the warmer months between October and May, and Frank Lowy, the chairman of the PSL, came out to publicly support the idea.

Buoyed by the response, Dettre derided those who opposed summer soccer as 'stubborn traditionalists raised in the winter slush of Europe', and implored his fellow journalists – many of whom were resistant to the plan – to see soccer as just one part of a 'rapidly changing society'.[7]

'When Dad was promoting summer soccer, I was at AAP,' recalled Steve Dettre. 'I still remember the tension in the press boxes when we'd turn up. It wasn't just the concept of summer soccer, a lot of these guys had a very cosy existence. They covered football in the winter, and then they covered cricket or horseracing or something else in the summer.'

Dettre stuck to his vision. Fail to try summer soccer in 1981, he warned, and the game would suffer 'yet another decade of stagnation'.[8]

It was a deeply frustrating time to be involved in soccer. The 'ethnic issue' remained unresolved and the rules relating to promotion and relegation between state and national leagues were hazy at best. Many of the clubs were bleeding money and support, and although everybody had their own ideas about how to take soccer to the Promised Land, no one had the power or authority to follow them through. To make matters worse, the state federations, particularly in Sydney and Melbourne, saw the PSL as an enemy rather than as complementary to their own state-based competitions.

'Familiarity, they say, breeds contempt,' Dettre explained in an article. 'And in our soccer, everything is familiar. Everybody knows everybody else; the actions, utterings, views and mistakes of one and all are remembered, colored, exaggerated and, like the parables of the New Testament, passed from father to son, with an extra hue added here and there. This sad tribal compound in which soccer exists accommodates genuine zealots, verified madmen, innocent idealists, mercenary opportunists, egomaniacs, loud-mouth dilettantes, pro and anti-ethnics, a few conmen and a fairly large number of amazed bystanders.'[9]

As chairman of the national league, Frank Lowy began advocating for complete autonomy from the ASF. He wanted the league to run as a separate entity to the governing body, leaving the PSL clubs free to determine their own destinies.

Sir Arthur George refused. His focus was on ending the resistance of the mainstream media. At a press conference in Sydney he lamented that although roughly 37 per cent of the Australian population was not of Anglo background, the broadcasting tastes of the television networks remained resolutely white. Decrying the 'isolationist Australian "ocker"', George said that 'the support and exposure given by the established electronic media to soccer bears no relationship to the huge growth in the numbers of participants'.[10]

Salvation soon arrived in the form of 'multicultural television'. After several reviews into the lack of diversity in Australian broadcasting, the Fraser Liberal government established the Independent and Multicultural Broadcasting Corporation, which came to be known as the Special Broadcasting Service (SBS). Designed to act as a link between the ethnic communities and the Anglo-Australians, its foreign-language films were subtitled for the English speakers and its first slogan was 'Bringing the World Back Home'. The intent was to break down stereotypes and contribute to the development of a cohesive multicultural society. To this end, soccer became SBS's number-one sport.

It was a marriage of great convenience. In 1979, back when SBS began as a short program on the ABC known as 'Ethnic TV', Andrew Dettre had introduced the station to viewers in his soft Hungarian lilt. 'Hello, and welcome to the very first sports show on Ethnic TV,' he had said. 'For the first item on our program let's turn to the most popular sport in the world – soccer, football, *fussball*, *calcio*, call it what you like.'

He was a better writer than he was a presenter. His eyes were down-cast, his demeanour wooden, and although his elocution was perfect, his voice was abrupt rather than friendly and inviting. By the time SBS became its own independent network, with its own dedicated channel, the face of its sports coverage was Les Murray, a 32-year-old journalist who was working at the *Sun* newspaper.

Born Laszlo Urge in Hungary, Murray arrived in Australia in 1957 in much the same fashion as Dettre – daring escape, long passage across continents and time zones, followed by a stint in a migrant hostel and social acceptance at St George-Budapest. He had a freshly shaven, boyish face to match wavy hair and smart suits. He was a crooner in a rock 'n' roll band and a slave to pretty football played in the spirit of Alfredo Di Stefano's Real Madrid or Ferenc Puskas' Hungary.

Like Dettre, he saw his own culture as rich and romantic, nothing at all like this mongrel outpost at the end of the earth. At school, Murray had despaired at the local children's lack of soccer knowledge, dismissed Australia's own football game as 'eggball' and refused to consider it as a worthwhile pursuit. He inherited this superiority complex from his father and viewed Australia's indifference to soccer not as the failing of migrants but as a sign of a flaw in the nation's character. He took it as his responsibility to provide the remedy.

First and foremost, Murray was a child of the soccer boom of the 1960s. He first felt like an Australian in the summer of 1969, when he sat among fellow migrants watching the national team play Israel in a World Cup qualifier. He was a passionate St George-Budapest supporter – his family twice donated a full set of kits – and an intel-lectual disciple of *Soccer World*. He grew up reading Dettre and Lou Gautier and fostered dreams of following in their footsteps.

In 1971 Dettre had published one of Murray's very first articles, and when Murray moved to England in 1975 to resolve an identity crisis – was he European or Australian? – Dettre elevated him to European editor of *Soccer World*. Although Dettre and Murray were never close mates, there was a mutual respect akin to the relationship of a master and an apprentice.

'Andrew and Lou [Gautier] were one of us, and I was one of them,' Murray once explained, 'both ethnics, both passionately loving football and understanding it – loving it the way it should be played. The journos who wrote in the daily papers were either imported from Britain, like David Jack or Tom Anderson, or junior cadet types who didn't get the rugby league gigs. They weren't that good. Andrew and Lou were real thinkers of the game. Andrew always struck me – although he had a fantastic sense of humour and was very funny – as a bit of an intellectual snob. He had this belief that his intellect was higher than anyone else's. In many cases, it was. When SBS started, Andrew had visions of either himself, or his son Steve, becoming football presenters. His son did audition, and appeared a few times. Then I came along and I got the job there, commentating and then presenting.'

Yet for all of his continental bohemia and derisive attitude towards English soccer, Murray was also heavily influenced by the famous British commentators Kenneth Wolstenholme, Hugh Johns, Brian Moore and Martin Tyler. In London he had sought out his favourite soccer writer, Eric Batty, and travelled with him on long road trips to the continent. This British education also became part of his identity as a journalist and a broadcaster. So much so, in fact, that in Murray's early years as a commentator, Dettre would review his performance by noting: 'He would be even better if he didn't insist on imitating the Brian Moores and Hugh Johns of TV fame [...] throwing in an occasional "wee Jimmy" which, without a genuine Scottish accent, sounds hilariously funny and uproariously inappropriate.'[11]

Les Murray's first major assignment for SBS was to call the 1980 PSL grand final between Heidelberg United and Sydney City. It was a brilliant, innovative day for soccer. SBS broadcast the match live to the eastern states and more than 11,000 supporters piled into Canberra's national stadium to be entertained by cheer squads, sky divers, marching bands and an address by Prime Minister Malcolm Fraser. The referee, Don Campbell, theatrically gave Fraser a red card, which he received with good humour, while two Heidelberg fans offered him a swig from their hip flasks.

The man to watch was Gary Cole, the 24-year-old workmanlike Heidelberg striker with blond hair, the face of a racehorse and thighs to match. He once described himself as having 'limited technical ability', yet all throughout 1980 he had attacked the opposition goal like a one-man blitzkrieg.

In Round 2 he scored the fastest hat-trick in Australian national league history, netting three times in the first 11 minutes against West Adelaide. Soon after, he bagged two hat-tricks in consecutive matches, and by Round 16 he became the first player to reach 50 national league goals. He also scored in an international match for the Socceroos against England, the country of his birth, and by season's end his record-breaking tally stood at 21 goals, 17 of which were scored in the first 12 matches. 'He had trouble trapping the ball, quite frankly,' remembered Murray, 'but he scored a lot of goals.'

And so he did in the grand final. The first arrived just after the half-hour mark, when Cole latched onto a deep pass and slid the ball beneath the goalkeeper. Ten minutes later, he converted a penalty-kick to make it 2–0, and on 77 minutes he scored the third and decisive goal with a tidy right-foot finish.

As the crowd filtered out of the stadium and the Heidelberg players celebrated their victory, Murray and his co-commentator, Johnny Warren, sat back and exhaled, having completed the call without fault. It was their first match as a commentary pair. Their exchanges were breezy and comfortable – Les calmly describing the play in his exacting Hungarian twang, Johnny chipping in with expert analysis in his distinctive Australian drawl.

'Murray and Warren played it like old pros once the match started,' reviewed the *Sydney Morning Herald*. 'Many other sports commentators would do well to follow their example.'[12]

The partnership of 'Les and Johnny' was an authoritative mix of passion and professionalism, and it would come to define soccer in Australia. Johnny was the ex-player with boundless energy and a voracious intellect, while Les became known for his impeccable pronunciation of foreign-sounding names.

Under their editorial guidance, it would not take long for SBS to earn the nickname 'Soccer Bloody Soccer'. The PSL nestled snugly between telecasts of soccer matches from Italy or Brazil, foreign-language news bulletins, Swedish love stories, and programs hosted by presenters with names such as Basia Bonkowski, Vlado Lusic and George Donikian.

Yet some people also queried why soccer, a sport trying to shed its image as the 'ethnic game', would partner with the multicultural broadcaster. The *Daily Telegraph*, for example, greeted SBS with a cartoon of a man sitting in front of a soccer game on television, next to his wife and a pile of foreign-language dictionaries, trampling on a newspaper that said 'Ethnic TV' and screeching: 'QUICK! QUICK! GREEK PHRASE FOR BLOODY GREAT MUG GALAH REFEREE.'[13]

Three months after the PSL grand final, on Australia Day 1981, Prime Minister Fraser again visited the national stadium in Canberra. This time he was there to launch the Australian Institute of Sport (AIS), a luxurious training centre where young athletes could receive scholarships and expert coaching in their chosen sports. Australia's sporting decline would end, Fraser told the crowd, but there was no mention of the Whitlam government, the Department of Tourism and Recreation, the pioneering study tour in 1974, the Coles Report, or Andrew Dettre. It was not the first time his work and ideas had been repurposed and credited to someone else, nor would it be the last.

The AIS was established to meet the demands of a nation still angry about the medal-less Montreal Olympics in 1976, and so its primary focus was on the development of athletes. This was the opposite to Dettre's vision: he had recommended that the AIS develop top-level coaches, which he believed would provide a long-term benefit for a wider group of athletes.

Still, soccer was one of the major beneficiaries of the AIS program. Its first coach was Jim Shoulder, the former Socceroos boss, and the first intake of young players included Mauritian-born midfielder Jean-Paul de Marigny and the Argentine-born playmaker Oscar Crino. Over the course of the next three decades the institute would produce dozens of players for the national league and for the various Australian national teams. Together, SBS and the AIS were the Fraser government's two great gifts to soccer.

★

SBS shared many similar characteristics and the same internal tensions as soccer's ethnic clubs. Both were places of comfort and opportunity for the ethnic communities, yet both also had the wider remit of familiarising Anglo-Australians with the migrant groups and their various cultures. SBS, like the PSL, was supposed to be the bridge and not the ghetto.

There existed an internal dialogue in soccer between those who felt that ethnic club names were part of this education process, and those who felt that the names militated against the aim. Of all the issues that plagued Australian soccer in the postwar period, few debates encouraged such tribal passion as this one.

When the PSL was established, Club Marconi argued that its name – taken from the Italian engineer Guglielmo Marconi, inventor of wireless transmission – was not ethnic. Pan Hellenic took the name Sydney Olympic, which it believed had 'associations with Greece and a pleasant ring with the Australian population in general'.[14] The Hakoah Club felt that it was a religious not an ethnic group and thus became Eastern Suburbs Hakoah.

APIA Leichhardt had long taken the view that APIA – an acronym for *Associazione Polisportiva Italo-Australiana* – was just as Australian as it was Italian. And the South Melbourne supporters chanted *Hellas*, Adelaide City sang for *Juventus* and Heidelberg United cheered for *Mega Alexandros*: Alexander the Great.

Had you wandered onto a soccer ground in 1981 and asked ten people their view, you would likely have received 11 different answers. David Jack, journalist from the *Sun* newspaper, wanted them anglicised.

Laurie Schwab, a German-born journalist at the *Age* and editor of *Soccer Action*, used the ethnic names even when the authorities threatened to revoke his press credentials. The Queensland Soccer Federation had simply banned them all in the early 1970s.

Johnny Warren had a bet each way, supporting the right of the clubs to label themselves as they wished while orchestrating a campaign to have Hakoah rebranded as Sydney City. Even the great English midfielder Bobby Charlton weighed into the debate, arguing in 1970 that 'Australian soccer will be poorer the day the clubs shed the exotic names'.[15]

The policy of outlawing ethnic names also swung uncomfortably close to Australia's racial discrimination laws. Al Grassby, the godfather of Australian multiculturalism, once advised that rejecting ethnic names was akin to rejecting their culture. 'It is a very serious subject,' he said, 'and one with which the ASF should approach very cautiously because of its far-reaching effects, not only those involved in soccer.'[16]

Les Murray knew this only too well. When he started working as a commentator for Channel 10 in 1977, he had been ordered to find a more pronounceable name than Laszlo Urge. Murray, he felt, worked as a Hungarian name also – 'Mura' taken from the River Mura that snakes through Hungary, and 'y' being Hungarian for 'of that place'. The name stuck and he soon became Les Murray by deed poll. He was one of thousands of ethnic Australians to anglicise their name.

The attitude towards the ethnic club names had more to do with power than principle. The leaders of clubs and federations, often rich, well-connected businessmen, were more inclined to the name changes. The rank and file, often factory workers, shopkeepers and labourers, mostly opposed them. Frank Lowy, for example, would argue for years with the membership of the Hakoah Club about the name Sydney City, and Sir Arthur George changed his tune as he moved further up the hierarchy of soccer administration.

'Those people harping on about the effects of nationalistic names suffer from a massive dose of inferiority complex,' he had said in 1965, while he was representing the Pan Hellenic club. 'Why should clubs change their names? One out of four people under 21 now in Australia was born elsewhere.'[17]

Yet by 1978, after he had assumed the presidency of the ASF, he became one of the great advocates for de-ethnicisation, arguing that 'soccer is not being regarded as an Australian sport, due to the names adopted by so many clubs at present'.[18]

Nobody was as haunted by the issue as Andrew Dettre. In principle he was for retaining the ethnic names, believing they were the glue that held soccer clubs and communities together.

However, the intensity with which the Croatian community took to soccer tested his patience, and after a particularly fierce riot between Sydney Croatia and Yugal in 1970 (Yugal being an acronym for 'Yugoslav Australian League'), Dettre warned that ethnic names were a 'threat to the game' and served 'no practical purpose except perhaps to fan the embers of chauvinistic sentiments among groups of minorities'. He had also recommended that clubs be forced to change their colours and their names to 'East United, South Wanderers [...] BUT NOTHING EVEN IMPLYING foreign countries, cities, crests, flags, etc.'.[19]

Yet by 1976, he had adopted a completely different view, arguing for a full re-ethnicisation of soccer clubs in Sydney, not only in presentation but also in participation. And then in 1980, after witnessing firsthand the success of the North American Soccer League, he was stuck somewhere in the middle.

He could see the logic of de-ethnicisation without ever reconciling with the principle. At the beginning of the 1981 season, as teams half-heartedly adopted gimmicky nicknames such as Slickers, Warriors, Giants, Demons, Gladiators, Arrows, Olympians, Strikers, Raiders, Gunners, Wolves, Hawks, Leopards, Rams and Eagles, Dettre lamented: 'Ever since I became involved in Australian soccer, I have been watching with decreasing interest and diminishing passion the perennial argument about club names.'[20]

Throughout the 1981 season, ASF Marketing worked on a report aimed at resolving the issue once and for all. Its findings were released at a major press conference at the Boulevard Hotel in Sydney, on 12 August 1981, in front of an audience of weary pressmen and wary club executives.

On page one was a speculative look into a fantastical future in which the 'Parramatta Eels' would beat the 'Gold Coast Surfers' in the national league grand final of 1990, racing identity John Singleton's son Patrick would score four hat-tricks, Kerry Packer would own a national league 'franchise', and the inclusion of the 'Gosford Boatmen' and 'Townsville Sharks' would bring the total number of national league franchises to 20. Mixed boys and girls teams would play in schools, there would be a national indoor soccer league, Australia would lose the semifinal of a Women's World Cup held in a new, 30,000-seat indoor stadium in Newcastle, and FIFA would allow the use of a revolutionary green-and-gold soccer ball with 'wind channels cut into the surface' and a 'built in transistorised microphone' which would allow television viewers to 'hear the thud and whistle of the ball as it is kicked around the field'.[21]

By now there was a realisation that football competitions could not survive on tradition alone. The proliferation of television sets in Australian homes, and the introduction of colour television in 1975, had led to an increased sophistication of sports broadcasting, which in turn brought a rolling snowball of commercial sponsors, expansionist ideas, and demands for higher wages and better conditions for players.

In Australian Rules football there was a growing desire to expand the Victorian competition to Adelaide, Hobart, Perth and the virgin territories of Sydney and Brisbane; while in rugby league the introduction of the State of Origin series between Queensland and NSW proved immensely popular, and plans were hatched to expand the Sydney competition to Illawarra and Canberra.

Soccer's crisis, however, was driven by changing demographics as much as it was by commercialisation. Four seasons of the PSL had proven that the great majority of Anglo-Australians refused to be involved with the ethnic clubs. Thus, in a competition that relied heavily on the patronage of Greek, Jewish, Italian, Hungarian, Macedonian and

Dutch communities, continued inwards migration from those countries was a necessary precondition for growth.

Yet by 1981 Australia's migration program had pivoted to Asians – as many Indonesians arrived as did Italians, while Filipino arrivals outnumbered Greeks by nearly two to one. Almost as many immigrants arrived from the Subcontinent as did people from the republics of Yugoslavia.[22]

Moreover, the children of soccer's leading ethnic communities were better educated than their parents, spoke English with much greater proficiency and were more inclined to other interests. The ASF Marketing report, in a section titled 'The Facts of Life: The Players and Spectators of Today', noted that an older generation of supporters had 'not assimilated properly into the Australian community' and represented a 'dying market'.[23]

'Today children aspire to be like Flash Gordon or Superman,' the report read.

> They emulate their heroes in play by building imaginary space ships and fighting inter-galactic battles with laser guns. Teenagers paint their faces in black and white and stick their tongues out to emulate their pop heroes, the Kiss [...] [and] drink Big M or Moove milk because the commercials say it makes them sexy and part of the 'in crowd'.[24]

Echoing a point that Dettre had made in late 1977, the authors concluded that soccer 'cannot develop on the premise of sport for sport's sake', instead it 'must provide entertainment'.[25]

To this end, the authors recommended the introduction of summer soccer, an increase in Australian-born players, the franchising of clubs, the re-zoning of the league into two separate conferences, and an end to promotion and relegation. And in between pages ten and 11, attached in a glossy foldout, were 16 snazzy new logos. Each one featured bright colours, garish designs and a green, gold and white soccer ball with a kangaroo.

Canberra Arrows were given an archer dressed like Robin Hood, Marconi-Datsun Leopards a big angry cat, Sydney Olympians a naked man throwing a discus. South Melbourne Gunners' logo featured two Greek men in traditional garb, holding a flaming torch and firing a cannon, while most controversially of all, the proposed logo for Sydney Slickers featured a wealthy-looking man in a pinstripe suit, a monocle and a bowler hat. Predictably, many of the Hakoah members objected to it on the grounds that it would encourage anti-Semitic tropes of the 'rich Jew'.

'We <u>do not</u> seek to <u>de-ethnicise</u> an individual club,' promised the report. 'We do seek to Australianise the whole image of the league.'[26]

In the appendices to the report, ASF Marketing included letters from English and American soccer officials, medical articles from FIFA, and a report from the ASF doctor, Brian Corrigan. Each seemed to support the introduction of summer soccer.

Yet it was summer soccer that became the most controversial of all the recommendations. Significant opponents included the Marconi-Datsun Leopards president Tony Labbozzetta, Sydney Olympians president John Constantine, NSW federation president Karl Rodney, as well as *Australian Soccer Weekly* – a new rival to *Soccer World* in Sydney. Edited by David Jack from the *Sun* newspaper, *Australian Soccer Weekly* gathered as much negative information on the concept as possible and published it relentlessly. 'If any country in the world does NOT need summer soccer,' decided Jack, 'that country is Australia.'[27]

By Saturday 5 September 1981, however, the PSL clubs voted 11 to five in favour of switching the season in October 1982.

A week after the vote, Sydney Slickers wrapped up the PSL title with a record four-point margin. In five years of the PSL, it had won the league three times and never finished lower than third place. Its style of soccer was outgoing and aggressive, the team was backed by the prosperous Hakoah social club, and Johnny Warren was the public relations officer. With Ken Boden and John Kosmina up front, Steve O'Connor and Kevin Mullen at the back, little Joe

Watson and Ian Souness and Murray Barnes pulling the strings in midfield, and youngsters John Spanos, Jim Patikas and Grant Lee pushing their way into the senior team, the Slickers should have been the model club.

Yet at the final game of the season, which the Slickers won 5–3 against Adelaide Giants, barely 2000 people showed up. Many of the supporters had given up on a team that had, by giving up its traditional name, given up on them.

'Over more recent years the Hakoah-sponsored team has been known as Hakoah Eastern Suburbs, Eastern Suburbs Hakoah, Sydney City or Sydney Slickers,' reported the *Jewish Times*. 'The latest nametag, Sydney City, has failed to "bring in the crowds" from the Sydney City area and only the handful of hardened and loyal Hakoah fans support the team.'[28]

Dettre had grown frustrated and tired, sick of the politics, sick of the constant squabbles and, most of all, sick of the fact that soccer was still considered a third-rate sport. The game had become so predictable that he had foreseen the brouhaha over ethnic names in a fictional story that he wrote for *Soccer World* in 1979. The story was of an old man reciting to his grandson the history of Australian soccer. The old man explained that the migrants had set up enterprising clubs, but nobody came along to watch them play. He recalled how the ethnic presidents searched frantically for an answer until somebody told them 'in good old plain Australian' that 'the game wouldn't sell because it had a strong ethnic image'.

The old man then described how the ethnic soccer clubs, players, officials and journalists had to change their names from 'Hakkabi' to 'Meatpie United', and 'Papazzetta' to 'Parkchester', while the ethnic supporters needed to be fingerprinted, tested for garlic and subjected to a language test before every game. 'All club officials who couldn't trace their ancestry back to the Eureka Stockade,' remembered the old man, 'were asked to hand over the clubs to fair dinkum locals.'

Dettre gave this fictional story the title 'A Sad Thing Happened on the Way Out …' and concluded: 'The grey-haired old man paused for a moment, leaning forward in his rocking chair. "Well, grandson, that's what did happen, gospel truth, cross me heart. You can still hear a few whinges here and there that we took their name and their game."'[29]

Like many people, Dettre had come to the view that soccer had won no new fans by adopting Americanised nicknames, and had probably turned many more away by ridding itself of its traditional titles. His frustration and flight into fiction showed that what he wanted, most of all, was for a re-creation of the soccer boom of the 1960s.

Yet the commercial demands of the national league had pushed the game further away than ever from that romantic golden age. The names were unrecognisable, the players a new breed of Australian boys and journeymen Britons, and the rationale of the game had transformed from a community-oriented halfway-house for migrants to a profit-seeking enterprise with a national focus.

But even then the business of the game was not adequately managed and the structure of the organisation was a mess. Rik Booth and ASF Marketing were ostracised, and their findings were soon forgotten. Traditional crests would replace the logos, and the nicknames would be dropped entirely.

Yet despite the report's far-out predictions, it was the first piece of research to thoroughly analyse all aspects of the game not for the benefit of the present but for the demands of the future. It was the first time that the soccer community was forced to recognise that top-flight sport was going to be an industry and no longer a pastime.

In the rush to set up the national league, the clubs should have been required to make an enormous step up. The increased professionalism and its associated costs should have been reflected in the promotions, the administration, the grounds, the quality of the play – everything. But few of the existing clubs had the capacity to herald the new era that Australian soccer so desperately sought. Burning questions about their identity were far from resolved. For the most part, the PSL was dominated by over-extended state league sides. Confidence fell to an all-time low.

By the end of 1981, the league's naming rights sponsor, Philips Industries, withdrew its financial support and the clubs passed a motion of no-confidence in Sir Arthur George. His major opponent was Frank Lowy. Lowy was critical of the way the game was being promoted and of the lack of coordination between the various federations and the national league. He had fought unsuccessfully for greater autonomy for the PSL from the ASF and, when he failed to get his way, he resigned from the national league executive and returned to Sydney Slickers. 'The strength of Australian soccer,' he predicted, 'depends on the strength of the clubs.'[30]

Even Sir Arthur predicted that the national league would wither and die. It was, as Dettre wrote, 'like the Pope forecasting the demise of the Vatican'.[31]

★

On the final weekend of February 1982, as the North American Soccer League was in recess, Tony Henderson flew to Florida with a view to joining the Fort Lauderdale Strikers. The Strikers were one of the richest NASL clubs, attracting star players such as Dutch goalkeeper Jan van Beveren and Peruvian striker Teofilo Cubillas.

Yet cracks had already started to appear in the league's foundations. The California Surf, Atlanta Chiefs, Dallas Tornado, Calgary Boomers and Washington Tornado were all pronounced dead before the season even got underway, while the rest of the teams were in heavy debt and the league had lost its major broadcast partner.

As the NASL plummeted into freefall, all theories were canvassed as to the cause of its demise. Some said the league expanded too quickly, from 18 teams to 24 in 1978, placing franchises in areas with no love or understanding of the nuances of the game. Others proposed that soccer was too dull and low scoring for Americans. Most agreed that the New York Cosmos had created an illusion of success and raced too far ahead of the pack. No other franchise could keep up with their freewheeling and dealing.

In the end, Henderson failed to agree to terms with Fort Lauderdale

Strikers and returned to Marconi, which had dropped its 'Leopards' nickname. He went back to work for Datsun, Marconi's major sponsor, and he took over from Johnny Warren as presenter of the SBS program *Captain Socceroo*, a television show designed to popularise soccer among children. The American experiment, both for Henderson and for the PSL, was well and truly over.

'It appeared to me that Fort Lauderdale looked very professional on face value, and that's all,' Henderson told reporters. 'In other words, no back-up to the image they projected.'[32]

THEY'RE OUR FUCKING WOGS

1983–1985

If you had seen Mr Lukic outside the Olympic Park Stadium on a wintry Saturday afternoon, calmly waiting for the tram to Flinders Street Station, you would have felt sure that he was a peaceable old man [...]

But if you had glimpsed him a little earlier, before the soccer match was over, you would have received a different impression. You would have seen him then, surrounded by other fervid supporters, yelling Boot-cher! Boot-cher! *at the referee who, cruelly and deliberately, had overlooked a foul against a member of Mr Lukic's team, Sava [...]*

Jure Lukic was Croatian.

David Martin
Who Says A Must Say B, 1981[1]

From Germany to Greece, England to France, Spain, the Soviet Union and Yugoslavia, soccer competitions have always been determined by the team that finishes with the most points at the end of the season.

The Australian sporting culture, however, is rather different. Rugby league, cricket and Australian Rules football decide the winner through an end-of-season grand final. The debate in Australian soccer, as always, was between those who wanted to hold on to tradition and those who wanted to adopt the Australian way.

The first five seasons of the National Soccer League were concluded with an uneasy compromise – the top clubs would play a finals series, but the winner of the grand final was not considered the overall champion. That accolade would belong to the team that finished with the most competition points. In other words, when Sydney City won the 1978 and 1979 grand finals, and finished top of the table in 1977, 1980 and 1981, only the latter three counted as national league titles.

In 1982, Sydney City looked to prove its dominance by finishing at the top of the table as well as winning the grand final. By the end of the regular season it had scored more goals than any other, conceded the fewest, lost just five matches and finished a record nine points clear of its nearest challenger. It then qualified for the grand final against St George, an old, neighbourly rival with many similar traits.

Together Sydney City and St George had established the national league and led the way in dropping their original ethnic names. Both teams were stocked full of Australian-born juniors and British journeymen, and both had watched their mostly Hungarian support base decline rapidly since the 1960s.

'The big derby I remember growing up was between St George-Budapest and Hakoah,' Les Murray once said. 'They were very fierce battles with a lot of Hungarian supporters on both sides. The St George fans were mostly non-Jewish Hungarians and they resented the fact the other Hungarians didn't support their club.'[2]

If 1982 was a season of expectation for Sydney City, for St George it was the season of revival. While Sydney City became the most successful club in Australia, St George had gone into freefall for the first five seasons of the national league. It finished sixth in 1977, seventh in 1978 and 11th in 1979. In 1980, after finishing in last place, St George was relegated to the NSW first division. The committee promptly sacked the coach, and for the fourth time in 11 years hired Frank Arok to mastermind a recovery.

Ferenc 'Frank' Arok was born to Hungarian parents in Novi Sad, a Yugoslavian town not far from the Yugoslav-Hungarian border, in 1932. On the other side of the border was Szeged, Andrew Dettre's hometown.

Dettre and Arok shared an instinct about soccer, born out of their similar cultural and historical circumstances. Both Hungarian speakers and journalists by trade, the pair had become pen-pals in 1962, and at the 1966 World Cup in England Arok strode over to Dettre in the press box of Wembley, slapped him on the back, and introduced himself.

In many ways, Arok was *Soccer World*'s greatest gift to Australia – Dettre conducted the courtship and negotiated for him to join St George-Budapest in 1969, while Dettre's colleague Lou Gautier was the one who handed Arok the contract in Mexico.

In 1972, during Arok's second stint with St George-Budapest, the club won an historic treble – the Ampol Cup, the Federation Cup and the NSW first division. In 1981, during his fourth stint, Arok brought with him Dezider Marton, a 32-year-old semi-retired striker. Marton, from Yugoslavia, could not speak a word of English and had confused Australia with Austria when signing his contract, but managed to score a record 42 league goals in a single season to earn St George promotion back to the national league.

For this unprecedented achievement, Arok literally painted Marton's boots gold, and auctioned them off to raise money for the club. Arok's devotion to St George, Dettre wrote in 1982, was 'the strictest form of soccer monogamy you can wish to see'.[3]

Due to St George's parlous financial position, Arok was not able to build an impressive squad for 1982. Very few of his players had big-game experience, and even he admitted that most of them were replaceable. As such, St George went into the 1982 PSL grand final as rank outsiders. Sydney City, as one reporter noted, 'have proved all along that they are a superior team. They have had the measure of St George in their three previous clashes, and it is hard to imagine Saints turning the tables at this late stage of the season.'[4]

To attract new supporters, the game was taken to Penrith Park, a suburban ground at the foot of the Blue Mountains, an hour west of Sydney. In front of a healthy crowd, on a bright sunny day, Marton scored three goals. The match finished 3–1 to St George, described by the local newspaper as 'a fairytale comeback into the Philips Soccer League'.[5]

Yet in *Soccer World*'s season review, Andrew Dettre lamented a year of torpor. To him, the handling of the national team was 'bordering on disgrace', the crowds had 'slumped' and the administration was 'inept'. On the international scene, Dettre believed that player wages had 'spiralled' and that the North American Soccer League was 'about to collapse'. He worried that many of the most famous European and South American clubs were struggling to survive, and decried the lack of organisation and tactical innovation at the 1982 World Cup.[6]

The ray of hope was St George. Dez Marton, wrote Dettre, 'is perhaps the most accomplished and deadliest striker to come to Australia since the halcyon days of the great Austrians, Baumgartner and Co., and certainly many measurable degrees above the dozens of pedestrian British imports'.[7]

This would be the final edition of *Soccer World*. By the end of 1982, after 25 years of unparalleled authority in the soccer community, *Soccer World* ceased publication. *Australian Soccer Weekly* had cannibalised many of its readers, writers and advertisers, and Dettre's son Steve had moved on to work for AAP.

The 1982 FIFA World Cup in Spain was their swan song as a father–son duo. Indeed the newspaper was, by the end, very much a family operation. Andrew's wife, Colleen, would stay up late at night, packing each edition into a parcel to send out individually to subscribers. Her work, Dettre would repeat for years, 'was the real heroic story'.

By the time *Soccer World* closed down, it was debt-free, and not a single subscriber had been left out of pocket. Yet the sense of doom and gloom was palpable. For a newspaper that had reported all the intricacies, the politics, the personality clashes and the very idea of a national league, the great leap forward never arrived. Without Philips Industries as a major sponsor, the NSL plunged into a deep financial crisis. And summer soccer – Dettre's biggest idea, which he promoted tirelessly through *Soccer World* – was postponed indefinitely.

The recession had ripple effects across the country. The Northern NSW State League had been restructured and rebranded, losing much of its regional appeal, while the Queensland Soccer Federation decided to break up the once-revolutionary Queensland State League. The cost of flying teams from Mareeba to the Gold Coast had proven to be too great.

Michael Cockerill, who had moved south from the *Rockhampton Morning Bulletin* to Sydney's *Manly Daily*, reported that the areas north of Brisbane were in open revolt against the decision. Fittingly, Townsville Kern United won the premiership in the final season of the QSL as well as the Ampol Cup – the first Queensland club to achieve such a feat. It drew bigger crowds than many national league sides, better local sponsorship and plenty of interest in the local *Townsville Bulletin* newspaper.

Yet with no more state league soccer and no invitation to the national league, the club had nowhere to go. Townsville Kern United folded.

There was precious little money in the sport, barely any sustainable streams of revenue and a crushing lack of interest from the great majority of Australian sports fans. Some, like the editor of *Australian Soccer Weekly* and many of the heads of the state federations, wanted to kill the national league entirely and return to state league soccer. The logic was simple: if the crowds would not turn up, why continue funding the enterprise? Wouldn't it be better for soccer to simply live within its means?

The biggest crowds of 1983 came to see England, in June, during a brief tour of Australia. For the three games Frank Arok was appointed caretaker coach of the Socceroos. He selected four St George players in his squad, and introduced Charlie Yankos and Phil O'Connor to the national team set-up.

The Socceroos drew the first match 0–0, lost the second match 1–0, and held England to a 1–1 draw in the final match. The improbable results pushed Arok into the realm of celebrity. Goalkeeper Terry Greedy, defender Yankos and striker O'Connor were rated as the best players in the Socceroos side. O'Connor, who was born in England, instigated many of the Australian attacks and terrorised the England defenders. It was his best ever game for the Socceroos.

Yet the result had little effect on the domestic leagues, and the crowds vanished as soon as England departed. Desperate to bring back the supporters, Arok promised to reimburse them if St George's matches didn't provide adequate entertainment.

Still hardly anyone showed up. It didn't matter that St George was near the top of the ladder, or that the conclusion to the 1983 season was one of the closest and most exciting in the NSL's short history. No one was interested. O'Connor predicted that the national league would be regionalised to save money and that soccer would not become a professional sport within his lifetime.

There was no finals series in 1983. The NSL executive decided that competition points would determine the champion team, and so the season came down to an exciting final round. St George and Preston were equal at the top on 52 points, while Sydney City was second on 51 points.

It was Dez Marton, Arok's most reliable player, who made the difference. In the final game of the season against Brisbane City, he scored two late goals and set up two more. The game finished 4–0, and as Preston lost its final match, St George finished top on 55 points. It would stand forever as one of the greatest comeback stories in the history of Australian sport: relegated in 1980, NSW premiers in 1981, NSL grand final winners in 1982 and national champions in 1983.

'The teams I had with St George in the past were stacked with international players and were expected to do well,' said Arok after the final whistle. 'This year, because of a tight budget, we had a bare ten field players and two goalkeepers. Only one player missed a training session all season, and that really sums it up.'[8]

Arok was awarded coach of the year, and for a third season running

Marton was St George's top goal-scorer. The national league coaches agreed that Wollongong striker Phil O'Connor was the most valuable player of the season and the press gallery voted him player of the year.

But O'Connor's gloomy prediction soon came to pass. After seven seasons of a single, unified national league, the NSL expanded to 24 teams and split across two regional conferences, in the desperate hope that crowds would be driven up and that costs would be driven down by the reduction in travel.

The decision very nearly brought an end to the NSL. The Victorian, South Australian, Queensland and NSW federations each protested against the decision, and advocated a reversion to Super State Leagues with a national playoff at the end of the season.

Stefan Kamasz, who had moved from the Northern NSW Federation to the NSL executive in 1982, was now faced with an incredible situation. The president of the QSF, Ian Brusasco, was openly advising Brisbane Lions and Brisbane City to return to the local competition, while a board member of the South Australian Federation accused the NSL of bias in favour of Sydney and Melbourne. And in NSW, the federation demanded reimbursement, claiming the expanded NSL competition would leave them tens of thousands of dollars out of pocket.

The NSL survived, but chaos ensued. The ASF Marketing report had suggested regionalisation in 1981, but back then it called it 'zoning' and recommended that the NSL spread to new centres such as Perth, Hobart, Gosford, Townsville, Tamworth, the Gold Coast, Bathurst, Albury/Wodonga and even Mount Isa.

Instead, by late 1983, the NSL executive decided to spread its franchise thickly across the metropolitan centres in NSW and Victoria, and, as a concession to the regional cities, classified Newcastle, Wollongong and Canberra as 'development areas' that could not be relegated from the competition. It was decided that the 'Australian' or 'Northern' conference would house the teams from NSW, while the 'National' or 'Southern' conference would accommodate the rest, strangely including Brisbane, which was the northern-most team in the competition.

Instead of creating new, superteams in strategic areas and regions, as Dettre had recommended back in 1977, the NSL extended a welcome to ambitious state league sides. By far the greatest beneficiaries of this decision were Melbourne Croatia and Sydney Croatia.

★

In 1984, Mark Anthony Viduka and Marko Ante Rudan were playing for the junior sides of Melbourne Croatia and Sydney Croatia respectively. Both were eight years old, born to Croatian parents in Australian suburbs, and crazy about soccer. Their fathers worked hard during the week, taught their children to respect their elders, and took them to watch the Melbourne Croatia and Sydney Croatia senior teams on the weekend.

'Every single week used to revolve around me going to the game, home and away,' Viduka once recalled. 'Me and my dad, we were part of this whole thing. I've got four sisters and they used to come to every game. We watched Melbourne Croatia play and hoped to God. When I look at a player who is not Croatian, and I think of him playing for my club, I probably loved him more than I did the Croatian players. I grew up with people – not just Croats – different nationalities. We were a football family. We were Europeans. It was natural for us to play football, because that was what our parents showed us first – that was their game, a European game. Aussie kids who were born here with an Australian background, usually they went to play cricket or footy or something else.'

The Croatians were the most enthusiastic, the most nationalistic and the most difficult supporters in Australia. There were Croatian churches, social clubs and restaurants, but nothing galvanised the community quite like soccer. Wherever there was a community of Croats there was a soccer club, and wherever there was a Croatian soccer club, there was a frustrated official who wished to curb its patriotic tendencies. The soccer club was a place for networks of Croatian families to coalesce, for their children to play together and learn the language, and – if fate was on their side – to meet a wife or a husband.

Croatian clubs had grown in the steel city of Whyalla in South Australia, on the docks at Port Hedland in Western Australia, in the tobacco fields in Far North Queensland and among the orchards of Glenorchy in Tasmania. The most influential clubs were in Sydney and Melbourne, centred around the biggest population clusters.

Invariably these clubs were called Croatia, took to the field in red shirts, white shorts and blue socks, and were considered pseudo-national teams at a time when Croatia itself was subsumed by the 'brotherhood and unity' of communist Yugoslavia. For Croatians, sport was politics.

'We see not only a leather ball,' wrote one supporter to *Spremnost Hrvatski Vjesnik*, the Croatian newspaper in Sydney, 'we see red, white and blue, and that will always sustain us and draw us together.'[9]

For the first seven seasons of the national league, both Melbourne and Sydney Croatia had been refused entry due to their insistence on keeping their nationalistic name. In this context, admitting Melbourne Croatia and Sydney Croatia into the revamped NSL for the 1984 season – along with Blacktown, Penrith City, Brunswick Juventus, Melita Eagles, Green Gully and Sunshine George Cross – was a huge risk. Some feared that by allowing the Croatian clubs into the league, the debate around names and logos and ethnic nationalism would be inflamed, locking the game irretrievably into an ethnic ghetto. Others felt the Croatians deserved a chance.

'Of course we are basically an ethnic club,' said the Sydney Croatia president, Tony Topic. 'Of course so are most of the others. And what's wrong with that? Ninety per cent of soccer spectators are ethnic too. It's high time we stopped pretending. If we do get 4000 or 5000 fans at our matches, I'm not going to run around asking them whether it's the game or patriotism that has brought them out. I only wish every club had support like we do, soccer would be miles further ahead down the road.'[10]

When Stefan Kamasz was dispatched to the Croatian club in Punchbowl to explain why Sydney Croatia's home ground needed to be upgraded to meet the competition standards, he and the club president were met by more than 500 members.

'[Tony] had to calm them down, because they were in a frenzy,' Kamasz once remembered. 'People were getting up making passionate speeches: "We will not move from Edensor Park! You say it is full of mud? We live in the mud, we will die in the mud!"'

As Kamasz rose to speak, chants of 'CRO-A-ZIA! CRO-A-ZIA! CRO-A-ZIA!' reverberated around the auditorium. As he left, a large bodyguard tracked his every move, and when he returned home, police were called in to monitor his family after he received death threats.

After seven seasons of trying to downplay the league's ethnic heritage, the conference system now allowed space for four Balkan clubs, three Maltese sides, as well as the numerous Greek and Italian clubs. Yet there was no team north of Brisbane, only two sides from Adelaide and not a single representative from Perth. Such was the reliance on the ethnic communities that in Melbourne, Soccer Action printed foreign-language columns for the Italian, Yugoslav and Greek communities.

This turn back to ethnic soccer, which encouraged the great tribes, the various languages, the multiple identities and the dual loyalties, drove many Anglo-Australian supporters away from the game while also enfranchising many children of migrants.

Remo Nogarotto, a 23-year-old accountancy student from Fairfield in Sydney, was one of the latter. Elected to the board at Marconi in 1983, he joined a group of men with names such as Mariani, Fontana, D'Amore, Labbozzetta and Cavagnino. He wore large glasses beneath an extravagant mane of black hair. He was tall, urbane, smart and extremely ambitious.

'It was politics at the base level,' he later explained. 'The vehicle of football gave this community – generically called the ethnic community – empowerment in a country in which there were very few vehicles of empowerment. While I played rugby league, soccer was always an important part of my life. If someone would have come along at the time and said, "Remo, we want you to be on the board of your beloved St George Dragons in rugby league", would I have jumped at that? Probably yes. But how many rugby league clubs at the time had a wog on the board? That channel was not open for someone like me. There's no doubt that the Marconi club gave you a vehicle that you were completely comfortable with, in a sport that you loved, within a community that was your own, and within a very formalised structure that was the national competition. For a young buck like me, in the early 1980s, it offered everything that a young, ambitious, enthusiastic person wanted to do in the world of sport.'

The same was true for many soccer players. Like all migrant parents, the Viduka and Rudan families had come to Australia for a better life. It didn't make them any less attached to their homeland, but it did sharpen their focus on the future. The parents wanted their children to be upstanding citizens, to integrate with the new society, but also to remember where they were from. Melbourne Croatia and Sydney Croatia's inclusion in the NSL gave the Viduka and Rudan children a clear pathway to achieve each of these aims.

'My father put me into Sydney Croatia to integrate with the Croatians,' Rudan once explained. 'Not to become a footballer – that was never his plan – I had to learn the language, because it was only Croatian at our dinner table.'

★

On the final day of March 1984, in front of less than 2000 people at the International Sports Centre, the Newcastle KB United players were warned that the Round 5 match could well be their last. They won 3–0. Yet when the club was pronounced dead three days later, it was met with a rather muted local reaction. The club simply folded, and the responsibility to run the team was handed to Adamstown Rosebud – an historic but seriously under-capitalised local team from the Northern NSW first division. For the soccer community, which in 1979 saw Newcastle KB United as the future of the Australian game, it was a grim return to reality.

'What it pinpoints,' noted the *Newcastle Herald*, 'is the difference in attitudes between the European supporter and Australians. One regards football as a religion, the other sees it as a hobby. Newcastle United's experiment did not work because it failed to convert the greater percentage of its followers, the Australian supporter, to the soccer religion.'[11]

There were other reasons too, of course. The local television network had stopped broadcasting its matches, the relationship with the local federation could certainly have been better, while the NSL provided little financial assistance to keep the club afloat. And the decision to cut the NSL into two conferences had clearly removed the glamour from the competition.

One supporter, Howard Bridgman, believed it was 'a lesson to other sports in national competition'.[12] And therein lay the tragedy of Newcastle KB United: it was the first club from Newcastle to participate in a national sporting competition on a weekly basis, yet it would be remembered as a footnote, not as a pioneer.

Its collapse would also begin the most tumultuous season in the history of Australian soccer.

Two weeks later, on an average Sunday afternoon in front of an average crowd at Middle Park, the South Melbourne Hellas' young defender Alan Davidson collapsed suddenly and hit the turf with a dull, sickening thud. With the ball at the other end of the field, few people around the ground initially noticed 'Davo' turning blue and struggling to breathe.

Bill Siavalas did. The Hellas supporter vaulted the fence and applied mouth-to-mouth resuscitation. Davidson, born to a Japanese mother and an Australian father, was one of Hellas' brightest young stars. As he was carted from the field, a young Angelos Postecoglou – 'Angie', as he was called by those in attendance – came off the bench to make his first senior appearance for Hellas. Postecoglou took his place at left-back, and the match finished 0–0.

Davidson only just survived. 'I helped him as much as I could,' Siavalas told reporters after the match. 'I was disgusted by the attitude of one of the Sydney City players who kept yelling that we should drag Davidson off the ground and get on with the game.'[13]

Many blamed John Kosmina. Although Davidson could remember being struck by someone, he conceded that he couldn't remember who did it. One reporter wrote that the South Melbourne Hellas fans stormed the Sydney City bus after the game, and that Kosmina had to be escorted separately to the airport in a police van. This was hugely distressing for Kosmina, and he issued a writ against the newspaper for incriminating him in Davidson's injury. Only Johnny Warren came to his defence, pointing to video evidence that showed Davidson collapsing at least 40 metres away from Kosmina.

'I didn't see the incident,' remembered Kosmina's teammate Steve O'Connor. 'Kossie said he didn't do it. He made a bit of money out of that, he sued a couple of Melbourne newspapers. But knowing Kossie, I wouldn't put it past him. When he was playing for West Adelaide he caught me in the mouth with an elbow, and I was trying to get him back. Those days were a lot more physical. It would be brutal – there were elbows a-go-go. You went up for a header and you had to protect yourself. It was tough, certainly.'

Kosmina was 27, the captain of the Socceroos, and in the prime of his career. At the time of Davidson's injury, he was scoring a goal a game, and Sydney City was unbeaten in its opening six matches. When City finally played its Round 6 match against Newcastle Rosebud United, which had been postponed after the collapse of Newcastle KB United, Kosmina scored a hat-trick in a whopping 8–1 victory.

Four days later, in Round 11, Melbourne Croatia and Footscray JUST met for the first time in NSL history, rekindling an explosive Croatian–Yugoslav rivalry that stretched back to the mid-1960s.

The match finished 0–0, but at half-time tyres burned in the car park and four supporters were in handcuffs. The police claimed that their operation had gone to plan, but when JUST officials unlocked the gates the next day they found all electricity to the ground had been cut, the canteen had been firebombed and the windows to the press box smashed in. Worse, the pitch had been burned with a large U – signalling 'Ustase', a Croatian revolutionary movement that had collaborated with Fascist Italy and the Nazis during World War II.[14]

As general manager of the competition, Stefan Kamasz flew to Melbourne to survey the damage. 'I've got a stupid sense of humour,' he would later recall. 'When I went to inspect the ground, I went with Tony Kovac from Footscray JUST. Les Shorrock took a photograph of the president pointing to all the damage that had been done: broken windows, everything. And when Les had finished taking the photo, I said to Tony, "Mate ... at least you could have smiled in the photo".'

In Sydney there was chaos of a different kind. By Round 12, Sydney Croatia had already sacked two coaches and was onto its third. Attila Abonyi was fired after eight matches, while Mick Jones was relieved of his duties after just three. Bruno Vidaic took over for three matches, and then in Round 15 passed the baton to Englishman Harry Noon. It was under Noon's short reign as coach that Sydney Croatia almost caused an international incident by signing Vedran Rozic from Hajduk Split in Yugoslavia.

Born on the Adriatic coast of Croatia in 1954, Rozic was a classy footballer, composed on the field, quiet off it, and one of the most popular players in the country. But when it was announced that he would leave Yugoslavia for Sydney Croatia, his character was immediately brought into question. He was accused by the Yugoslav media of betraying 'brotherhood and unity' in the chase for money. One journalist from Belgrade decried the fact that Sydney Croatia had pictures of Ante Pavelic, the Ustase leader, on the clubhouse walls, alongside 'the dirtiest anti-Yugoslav defamations'.[15]

To many Yugoslavs, joining Sydney Croatia was akin to joining the infidels. To the Croats in Australia, it was a point of pride and defiance. The board members of Sydney Croatia greeted Rozic at the airport and a photo of him signing his contract on the hood of a Holden Kingswood was taken. It was the classic Croatian-Australian welcome.

'I came to Australia to play football and I do not want to enter any political games and machinations,' Rozic promised. 'Right upon arrival I went to the Yugoslav embassy with the board members of "Croatia" [...] I said that everything that is being claimed in relation to my connection with the anti-Yugoslav emigre community is not true. If I had felt, even only by a gesture or word, or if during my playing there will be some incidents that insult my country and our brotherhood and unity, I swear that I will leave Australia right away and return.'[16]

Rozic's signing brought even more chaos to the league. In Round 17 he made his debut, helping Sydney Croatia to a 2–1 win over Brisbane Lions, but by Round 22 he was sidelined after the Yugoslav Federation telexed their Australian counterparts to inform them that clearance had not been granted by Hajduk Split.

'It is a farcical situation,' said the ASF secretary. 'We are backing up [Sydney] Croatia's right to use the player, as all the usual procedures were followed before he was registered. The foul-up occurred at the Yugoslav end.'[17]

To resolve the issue, Sydney Croatia simply fired Noon after Round 23 and hired Rozic to take over. He became the club's fifth coach for the season – an NSL record. Noon left complaining of politics, but Rozic, who knew little English but knew his football, guided the club away from the relegation zone and into sixth place in the Northern Conference.

In 1984, during the National Soccer League's most multicultural season, the economic historian Geoffrey Blainey published a book titled *All for Australia*. He argued that multiculturalism was corroding a sense of national kinship, cataloguing a range of niche and unusual grievances which included, but were not limited to, phlegm-covered footpaths, 'ethnics' driving expensive cars and parking them in inconvenient places, and Asians drying noodles where laundry was supposed to hang.[18]

With Australia no longer moored to the White Australia policy, Asians arrived at a rate not seen since the gold rush in the 1850s. The new migrants came from China, Vietnam, Hong Kong, Malaysia and the Philippines. The xenophobic backlash that followed narrowed in on Asians, but had roots in the broad tropes that stretched back decades. Australia's immigration program had always been fairly evenly spread, and its discontents were generally academic rather than vigilante. Up until the 1980s, however, immigration had always been coupled with economic growth. Yet as the economy spiralled into recession, many Australians clung to old notions of assimilation with growing alarm. They feared the erosion of a recognisable Australian identity and worried that multiculturalism would gradually splinter the nation along tribal lines. Above all, Australia feared concentrations of new migrants in ethnic ghettos.

Refuge from these tectonic demographic shifts had always been available in cricket, Australian Rules football and rugby league. Here were the last vestiges of the old, white Australia, either ignoring migrants and their children altogether or assimilating them into pre-existing suburban clubs, federations and traditions. Migrants were afforded no opportunity to create new clubs or federations in those sports. They had to fit in. If these sports were the myth of multiculturalism, soccer was the mess. '[T]o many people of Anglo-Saxon descent,' concluded one reporter, 'soccer remains Wogball. A sport without heroes.'[19]

Soccer was a Scot captaining a Croatian club, an Argentine playing for a Greek club, or a Macedonian turning out for a district side. To the rest of Australia, sport was a group of happy Anglos beating the English in cricket, or Queensland versus NSW in rugby league: state against state, mate against mate. Sport was Australian Rules football, with rival fans sitting side by side, good-naturedly ribbing each other over the result while gaily singing show tunes. Above all, sport was a sacred space where Australians could imagine a clear, collective national identity, uninterrupted by the dubious theatre of one ethnic group hurling projectiles and indecipherable abuse at another.

And so soccer, the most genuinely multicultural sport, was abandoned by sponsors, by administrators and, above all, by the supporters. 'Soccer in its present state,' wrote Les Murray, 'is no commercial proposition and where commercial sponsors won't help it, governments should. That is unless a sports version of a Professor Blainey discovers first that the emergence of a foreign game creates disharmony in Australian society.'[20]

The resurgence of the stridently ethnic soccer clubs and the collapse of the non-ethnic one-town-team seemed to go hand in hand. Newcastle Rosebud, Wollongong City and Canberra City all finished the 1984 season at the bottom of the competition ladder, with crowds plummeting to an all-time low. The lowest crowd in national league history was recorded when Wollongong hosted Canberra at Dapto Showgrounds: just 150 hardy souls showed up, and even that crowd figure was suggested to be an exaggeration.

As the league steadily contracted, the much-vaunted local derbies didn't bring in the expected crowds, attention or revenue. One match between APIA Leichhardt and Wollongong City attracted less than 700 spectators. Yet despite Wollongong finishing last in the Northern Conference, with terrible crowds and even worse performances, Melita Eagles, a club representing Sydney's Maltese community, was relegated to the NSW first division. Wollongong only survived thanks to its classification as a 'development area'. It was deemed too important to fail. Melita, on the other hand, was expendable.

At the end of the season, a finals series was contested by ten sides: Sydney City, Sydney Olympic, Marconi-Fairfield, APIA Leichhardt, Blacktown, South Melbourne, Heidelberg United, Melbourne Croatia, Brisbane Lions and Brunswick Juventus.

The star of the series was Oscar Crino, a 22-year-old playmaker born in Argentina and raised in the south-east of Melbourne. He was tall, handsome, with black hair and rare poise; a throwback to an earlier era where skill and artistry reigned. Soccer fans spoke about him in the same reverential, epochal way they had about Leopold Baumgartner. Les Murray would remember him as 'the finest midfielder Australia has ever had [...] indispensable to the national team, the classic playmaker, the jewel on which all his team-mates gazed with both pride and envy'.[21]

Crino arrived in Australia at the age of ten. His father, a Sicilian by birth, immediately adopted an Australian identity. Young Oscar was told to work hard, learn English and fit in with the new society. Soccer, however, was non-negotiable. At primary school, when one of the teachers encouraged him to choose the best possible secondary school, he replied: 'It doesn't matter where I go to school, I'm gonna be a soccer player.'

In 1981, Crino was part of the first intake at the Australian Institute of Sport, and by the age of 19 he had made his senior international debut before he played in the national league. Incredibly, he achieved all of this while hiding an acute case of compartment syndrome in his calves, which made it almost impossible for him to run for extended periods.

Early in his career some coaches and fans thought him lazy, so he decided to drop back to sweeper and focus on his passing to make up for his lack of pace and mobility. In constant, silent agony and frustrated at having to play out of position at half pace, he was on the verge of early retirement. Then he met a brilliant surgeon named David Young, underwent an operation, and burst back onto the scene with a renewed enthusiasm for the game.

In essence, Crino was a product of the street-against-street, house-versus-house games of Buenos Aires. He was a classical virtuoso who attracted the rough attention of defenders, but he learned to give as good as he got. As a kid missing the atmosphere of home, he would race to Middle Park to watch South Melbourne Hellas play. Although it was nothing on the white-hot intensity of La Bombonera in Buenos Aires, for him it was the closest he could get to a real soccer atmosphere.

Yet despite Hellas' passionate supporter base, the club was the biggest under-achiever in the NSL. Crino went there with a mission to change that. In 1983, his first season at Hellas, he helped it to fourth place and won the under-21 player of the season award. By 1984 he, alongside Ange Postecoglou and Alan Davidson, formed one part of Hellas' dynamic youth triumvirate.

All three lined up for South Melbourne Hellas in the 1984 Southern Conference final against Heidelberg United. The winner would progress to the NSL grand final against the winner of the Northern Conference.

Hellas were 2–1 down at half-time before Crino changed the game. First, he drew a foul from Heidelberg defender Charlie Yankos, for which the referee gave Yankos a red card. This gave Hellas a one-man advantage with more than 40 minutes to play. Soon after, from almost the same spot as he had been fouled, Crino lashed a right-foot drive into the back of the net. Scores level at 2–2, the Hellas fans temporarily invaded the pitch to congratulate him.

In the 80th minute, John Yzendoorn's powerful header put Hellas ahead, and four minutes later Crino completed the comeback with a silky, one-touch finish. 4–2. This time, the pitch invasion was absolute pandemonium.

In the grand final, a Greek derby between South Melbourne Hellas and Sydney Olympic played over two games, Crino scored the first goal of the second game, and the match finished 4–2 on aggregate to Hellas. It was the club's first NSL title, capping off a terrific season that also included victories in the National Youth League and the Hellenic Cup.

Alan Davidson, by now fully recovered from his collapse in Round 7, jetted off to join Nottingham Forest in the English first division. Ange Postecoglou cemented his place in the first team. And Oscar Crino turned his attention to qualifying for the 1986 World Cup.

★

'Few players who have donned the green and gold for Australia had as much pure skill as Oscar Crino,' once remembered the economic historian Roy Hay. 'Statistics will never accurately reflect Crino's contribution to the game, for it was how he glided through matches in total control of the ball [...] which drew the fans.'[22]

Hay, a bespectacled, bookish Scotsman, arrived in Australia in 1977 to write study guides for the newly opened Deakin University in Geelong. After helping establish the Deakin University Soccer Club in 1978, it took until mid-1985 for Hay to move from the Sunday leagues to a wider, more authoritative role in the local game.

On 29 May 1985, just prior to the European Cup final between Liverpool and Juventus, 39 fans were killed as a wall inside Heysel

Stadium collapsed. Incredibly, despite the fact that bodies lay in the car park, the match went ahead.

The reverberations were felt all over the world. Playing for Liverpool was the Australian star Craig Johnston, and in Sydney, Les Murray and Johnny Warren were presenting the game live on SBS. Told to buy time by his producers due to the delayed kick-off, instinctively Murray defended soccer and warned against those Australians who would try to exploit the tragedy to bash the game. 'Editorialising at such a time was probably insensitive,' he later conceded. 'I now regret doing it.'[23]

Insensitive they may have been, but Murray's words were prophetic. In Geelong, an industrial city south-west of Melbourne, the local newspaper splashed a provocative headline about the threat of 'soccer violence'. Hay fired off a letter to the editor. 'Sir,' he implored, 'in all the justified horror and outrage following the European Cup final, much nonsense is being spoken and written about the relationships between soccer and violence.'[24] He went on to detail the law-and-order questions facing soccer authorities not just in Britain but around the world, as well as the under-reported incidents of violence at Australian Rules football games.

It was typical Roy Hay: endlessly committed to fact rather than opinion, impeccably researched and, on the whole, a far more sober assessment of the situation than the *Geelong Advertiser* had provided. In fact, he had been quietly researching the relationship between sport and violence for years and, miraculously, his letter to the *Advertiser* found a willing audience.

In response, the editor tasked him with covering the Geelong and Western Victoria soccer competitions. A new career was born. Hay threw himself into covering the game, and by doing so was introduced to the coalface of multicultural Australia. Geelong was a microcosm of Australian soccer – Croats, Macedonians, Hungarians, Italians and Greeks.

Hay's fellow Scots were the most clannish of the lot, yet mergers were not uncommon, and there was a gallows humour among the nationalities, who all played second fiddle to Australian Rules. When the Macedonians joined forces with the Scots, for example, Hay witnessed one Scotsman turn up to a game and remark: 'What are all these fucking wogs doing here?' Another man tapped him on the shoulder. 'Shut up, Johnny,' he said, 'they're our fucking wogs.'

A stickler for detail but never a stylist, Hay's exacting match reports provided all that you needed to know in the clearest possible manner. He committed to writing short, sharp sentences, with a word or two thrown in to expand the readers' vocabulary.

'I would have terrible battles with the subs on the *Advertiser* when I tried to introduce words of more than two syllables in the soccer column,' he once explained. 'Why? We had all these little migrant kids whose parents probably didn't speak English at home. They were as bright as a button – I knew they were going to succeed, but if all they read was the soccer column to see what I'd written about them, at least they would be reading! I wanted to make sure these kids were getting some recognition that what they were doing was as good as this [Australian Rules] footy stuff, and I also wanted to make sure that each column stretched them a little bit.'

Hay's involvement in soccer gave him a terrific subject of academic enquiry. For the next three decades, his career as an historian would be invariably tied to the game as he studied the role of identity, citizenship and ethnicity in Australian society.

Six weeks after the Heysel disaster, a riot broke out at a match between Sydney City and Sydney Olympic at Pratten Park. Soccer's latest disgrace unfolded almost as a commemoration of the 20th anniversary of the infamous Anzac Day riot of 1965, complete with a wild pitch invasion and a targeted assault on the referee.

The incident began when Marshall Soper, the Sydney Olympic striker, was sent from the field after an altercation with Sydney City defender Gerry Gomez. As Soper made his way into the dressing sheds, Sydney Olympic midfielder Peter Raskopoulos waved to the frustrated home crowd, inviting a section of Sydney Olympic fans to invade the field. The supporters grabbed corner flags and medical boxes and charged at the referee. A crazed fan brandishing a flagpole chased Sydney City coach Eddie Thomson into the dressing room, and the referee was enveloped by a mob and punched and kicked to the ground. As a crowd of 30 opposition supporters chased Sydney City goalkeeper Tony Pezzano, his mother collapsed in the stands. After the game, Pezzano told reporters that he was going to give up soccer forever.

'Quite often the media would beat things up,' once recalled the NSL official Stefan Kamasz. 'There was a fascination with the soccer violence in England, and when things happened here it would get blown out of all proportion. You could normally argue it was bias – but you couldn't on this occasion, the riot was way over the top. I'd never seen anything like it.'

The Pratten Park riot of 1985 was splashed across the media and the fallout continued for more than a week. And, like the Anzac Day riot, it was blamed on ethnic politics when in fact it had more to do with a heated on-field rivalry. 'The Pratten Park riot,' once explained Sydney City defender Steve O'Connor, 'was really out of Olympic's frustration that they couldn't beat us.'

NSW Premier Neville Wran set the tone of the debate by labelling the event 'anti-Australian'.[25] Columnists immediately and gratuitously compared the riot to the Heysel disaster, some called the spectators 'animals', while the *Sun* newspaper questioned whether soccer's 'ethnic links' helped to 'increase rivalry and tension' and relayed calls for any migrants involved to be deported.[26]

None were as steamed up as the letter-writers, however. A Toongabbie resident wrote to the *Sun*, suggesting soccer fans attend a rugby match to learn good manners, while a Bondi man blamed 'a multi-cultured country' for the disturbance. To one man from Canberra, the solution was simple: 'It's high time we declared Australia a soccer-free zone.'[27]

In *Soccer Action*, Andrew Dettre tried to make sense of the cacophony of outrage. He acknowledged that 'the rubbish dump known as Pratten

Park' had woefully inadequate facilities to deal with large crowds, and that violence was an affliction plaguing soccer all over the world. 'At long last, soccer again has gained public attention,' he lamented. 'True, it needed the prodding of an ugly riot, the mindless savagery of a few dozen or perhaps hundred lunatics – but we've made it.'[28]

Just one month after the Pratten Park riot, Roy Hay travelled with the Victorian Country Region under-13 squad on a tour of Europe. After the major sponsor pulled out, Hay had taken on the role of fundraising organiser and moved heaven and earth to raise the $66,630 needed for the tour, which included his young son, Ross. He had door-knocked and raffled everything that he could get his hands on: colour televisions, table lamps, bottles of wine, even an electric tin opener.

When the target was reached, a story in the *Geelong Advertiser* was headlined 'Lamington Lads Are Bound for Europe's Best Pitches' in recognition of the successful lamington drives.[29] The trip was a great success, with the children playing games in Germany, Holland, Wales, Scotland and England. The star was Kris Trajanovski, who would later graduate to play in the NSL and for Australia.

Back home, the Socceroos were preparing for their World Cup qualification campaign against New Zealand, Israel and Taiwan. For the first time since 1974, St George played a major role in the campaign. St George Stadium became the Socceroos' unofficial home base, while goalkeeping coach Ron Tilsed, physiotherapist Charlie Jurisic, and players Terry Greedy and David Ratcliffe divided their time between St George and the Socceroos. Frank Arok, who had masterminded the greatest underdog comeback with St George, was tasked with doing the same with the Socceroos.

On 11 September 1985, Arok arranged for the Socceroos to play a testimonial game for Dez Marton at St George Stadium. At 37, the 'old man' of the NSL had led his club back from the brink to a national title, scored 40 goals in 95 NSL matches, and inspired a generation of young Australians. Marton picked many St George players, including Robbie Slater, the O'Shea brothers and Pedro Ricoy. The Socceroos won 2–0, with goals to David Mitchell and Tom McCulloch. Marton had a short run on the field, but uncharacteristically failed to score a goal.

'For a supporter who was always searching for that special brand of soccer, Dez was the favourite,' read a farewell article in the St George *Soccer House Journal*. 'His "magic touch", that "Marton magic", was instrumental in the success of the club over the past four years.'[30]

That's the kind of club St George was – generous, welcoming, always keen to honour its heroes. Many players were given part-time work by the board members and fans to supplement their soccer income. Both Marton and Phil O'Connor – who played with St George between 1977 and 1979 – had worked at Atlas Printery in Alexandria, which was owned by a Hungarian supporter.

Yet while Marton retired of his own accord, O'Connor was taken too soon. In the early hours of 23 September 1985, O'Connor veered off a dangerous stretch of Appin Road, crashed into a tree, and died instantly. He was just 32 years old. In total, he made 222 appearances in the NSL and scored 88 goals. During his career he had played for Luton Town in England, St George, Wollongong and Blacktown City in Australia, as well as a few games for the Socceroos. Sadly, both of his earlier predictions – that soccer would not become a professional sport in his lifetime, and that the league would need to be regionalised into two conferences – came true.

On the other side of the world, Roy Hay's father-in-law also passed away. With the Victorian Country Region under-13 touring party already in Britain, Hay followed his wife, Frances, to Scotland for the funeral. It dawned upon him that his return ticket to Australia was for 19 November, just one day before the Socceroos were due to play Scotland in the first leg of a crucial World Cup qualifier in Glasgow. The profundity of the occasion demanded immediate action. The return flight was re-arranged.

For the first time, Hay faced his own national question: did he owe loyalty to the country of his birth or his new homeland? In the first leg at Hampden Park, Hay introduced his son, Ross, to Joe Watson and Kenny Murphy, two of the Scottish-born Socceroos, and promised them: 'At least you'll have one supporter in attendance, it just won't be me.' Scotland won the match 2–0 in front of a raucous crowd of 60,000 people. Hay flew back to Australia a happy man.

Before the second leg in December, Hay remained committed enough to the Scottish cause to send a dossier of information about the Australian squad to Scotland manager Alex Ferguson. What many might have seen as a treasonous act to the Australians was met with sincere gratitude from Ferguson. 'Dear Mr. Hay,' he responded, 'Many thanks for the information you sent me recently on Australia, I appreciated the thought and every bit helps. I have received many letters and tapes from brother Scots and their help and kindness will all go towards Scotland's World Cup hopes.'[31]

Hay did indeed consider himself a 'brother Scot'. A passionate Ayr United supporter and the grandson of James 'Dun' Hay, the first Protestant captain of Glasgow Celtic, his mannerisms and outlook would remain resolutely Scottish. Letters would be signed off with the phrase 'Yours aye, J. Roy Hay'.

Yet on the night of 4 December 1985, as he watched the Socceroos relentlessly charge at the Scots, something changed.

The Socceroos entered the second leg of the World Cup qualifier as rank outsiders. The team had been labelled 'mad dogs' by both the Australian and Scottish press after Frank Arok said that he wanted his players to 'fight like mad dogs' earlier in the qualification campaign. He had delivered the quote to Steve Dettre, who reproduced it for the newswire service AAP. It had spread like wildfire, picked up by national and international press. The Israeli media were outraged, mistaking his comments as a derogatory reference to their team and to Jews. An international incident was only narrowly avoided.

'Frank had an incredible ability to motivate players, to talk about other things rather than put pressure on the players,' once remembered Dez Marton. 'Maybe he wasn't a great coach, but he was a great motivator.'

Arok's qualities as a tactician, man-manager and spokesperson for Australian soccer all revolved around psychology. He knew how to outfox an opponent even before a ball was kicked, and how to use the media to tap into the Australian psyche. Like Rale Rasic before him, however, Arok's vision butted up against the totalitarian rule of Sir Arthur George and the general incompetence of the Australian Soccer Federation.

For the qualification matches against Scotland, Arok's captain was Kosmina, and he relied again on the strength and leadership of Steve O'Connor (unrelated to Phil O'Connor) and Yankos in the backline, the skills of Crino through the middle and the speed of Davidson on the wing, while the quartet of Watson, Mitchell, Murphy and Dunn were all hoping to put one over the country of their birth.

The most famous Australian player, however, was Craig Johnston. Johnston had been on the Socceroos' radar since 1977, but in 1984, when Arok met him at the Newcastle Rugby Club and put it to him that he should play for Australia, the young striker was hesitant. Back in England he had a wife, a child on the way, a mortgage and a first-team place to hold down in a very competitive Liverpool squad.

'Despite my rampant nationalism, I knew that a move into the Socceroo ranks from the English first division would be a retrograde step,' he would later write in his autobiography, *Walk Alone*. 'I wanted to play for Australia, but not at the risk of what I had achieved.'[32]

Yet as Arok continued to work on Johnston, the ASF publicly concluded that he was ineligible due to his previous appearances for the England under-21 side. Despite a written letter from Ted Croker, the general-secretary of the England FA, and assurances from FIFA that he was free to represent Australia, Johnston never played for the Socceroos.

For the most part, Australians laid the blame squarely with Johnston, remembering his unfortunate throwaway line: 'Playing soccer for Australia is like surfing for England.' Of course, with the standard of professionalism shown by the ASF administration in handling his case, he wasn't far wrong. The *Bulletin* called it 'one of the strangest sagas in the suspect history of Australian sports administration'.[33]

The federation's second mishap, however, was far more costly. Needing to win by three goals in the second leg, Arok wanted to play on a bumpy pitch in extreme mid-afternoon heat in Darwin. It was straight out of the Arok playbook – win the psychological battle, play to your strengths, never give the opponent an inch. 'Why be nice guys?' reasoned Arok. 'I've never been a nice guy. Why should I change all of a sudden?'[34]

Yet he was out-politicked by the ASF, which sought instead to capitalise financially on the large Scottish community and the sudden interest in soccer. The federation booked Olympic Park in Melbourne, cut the grass perfectly for the visitors and scheduled the game in the cool temperature of the evening. Alex Ferguson even said that 'you could play snooker' on the pitch and that the weather was like being 'in paradise'.[35]

Even so, the Socceroos threw everything at their opposition. By half-time, Australia was clearly the better side, yet could not find the back of the net and the match finished 0–0. Yankos, a colossus at the back, was named man of the match; Jimmy Patikas was a constant menace; and Murphy and Mitchell fought bravely for Australia, showing no sign of contested loyalty. The press fell back to that familiar trope from 1974 – Australia as valiant underdog, as gallant losers. The *Sun* said the Australians 'bowed out [...] with heads held high'.[36] The *Australian* labelled the Socceroos 'Australia the brave'.[37] The *Age* praised the team for 'fighting like tigers', while the *Sydney Morning Herald* called it 'a night to remember' and 'one of the finest performances ever produced by an Australian team'.[38]

Yet it was Scotland, not Australia, that went to the 1986 World Cup. While Johnston sat high up in the commentary box, Arok was left to wonder what might have been. And for Roy Hay, who had started the match in support of Scotland, it was the final consummation. By full-time he realised that he had fallen in love with the Socceroos. 'After seeing that game,' he would later recall, 'my allegiances, like those of many present, were to Australia.'[39]

THE FINAL WINTER

1986–1989

Above all, I am worried about the misguided and misinformed man who goes to the Hakoah Club to say Kaddish to a sports team. It demonstrates his ignorance of Kaddish, which causes him to prostitute his prayer [...]

Because the Kaddish is said for martyrs, who gave their lives so that Judaism survives, so that the Kaddish represents their sacred memory as well as the Jewish struggle against tyranny and oppression;

Because, for those Jews that have drifted so far from Judaism that they keep nothing else, the Kaddish is a road back, a lifeline to parents, to synagogue, to Jewish heritage.

For those who say Kaddish for a ball club; to what is such a Kaddish a lifeline? [...] An idolatry?

Rabbi Dr Nisson E Schulman
Jewish Times, 1987[1]

In the first week of February 1986, Dragoslav Sekularac arrived at Footscray JUST accompanied by three players hand-picked from the Yugoslav first division. They were Vlada Stosic, a baby-faced Serbian striker; defender Vojislav Vukcevic, who had played in Sweden and for the New York Cosmos; and Zoran Nikitovic, a tousled-haired goal-keeper from the Montenegrin town of Krusevac.

Sekularac, or 'Seki' as he was known by his players, was on a mission. 'We must try to play entertaining soccer to draw the crowds,' he announced. 'That is just as important as winning, otherwise, in the long run, no one will want to watch the sport anymore.'[2]

Joining Footscray JUST was a risk. The facilities were prehistoric and the team had finished last in the Southern Conference the season prior. And Sekularac had a name and a reputation to protect. In the 1950s and 1960s he was the idol of Yugoslav football. Cedo Cirkovic, a former Footscray JUST player and coach, once claimed that in Yugoslavia he was 'more popular than Tito'.[3]

It was Sekularac's charisma and popularity that enticed Nikitovic, 28 years old at the time, to join him in Melbourne. At first Nikitovic was hesitant – he had a comfortable enough existence in Yugoslavia, a contract offer from top Austrian side Rapid Vienna, and on his one previous trip to Australia with Partizan Belgrade in 1978 he had left in despair after watching Yugoslavs and Croats battle it out on the terraces of Australian stadiums. But Sekularac wouldn't take no for an answer. The wily coach asked him to try it for four months and, if he didn't like it, he was free to move on to Vienna. Nikitovic relented.

Zoran Nikitovic was the quintessential Yugoslav. An Orthodox Serb from Montenegro, he identified with the multiculturalism of socialist Yugoslavia and made friends with Croats, Slovenes, Serbs, Montenegrins and Macedonians. His wife was Croatian. So was his *kum* (best man). 'In Yugoslavia, nobody ever ever ask me who I am,' he once remembered. 'But then coming here, if you're Yugoslav, they hate you ...'

He arrived in Australia with a decent resume: several seasons in the Yugoslav first division, numerous appearances for the Yugoslav national youth teams and one extra special match for Partizan Belgrade in the Yugoslav Cup final of 1979. If Sekularac wanted entertaining soccer, Nikitovic was the perfect goalkeeper. With wild, friendly eyes and an unvarnished sense of adventure, he was an unorthodox player, confident enough with his feet to take penalties and willing to come off his line and play as a makeshift sweeper. Within weeks of his arrival, he was involved in a match described as 'one of the most remarkable games we've seen at Middle Park – or anywhere else for that matter'.[4]

It was a pre-season cup match against Sunshine George Cross, an NSL club run by Melbourne's Maltese community. Footscray JUST scored first after 40 minutes, and looked to have gone two ahead on the hour mark after the ball ricocheted off the crossbar and down over the goal line. Yet the referee called play on, and the agitation of the JUST supporters only increased when George Cross equalised 20 minutes later. The Yugoslav fans unleashed a torrent of abuse at the referee, rattled the fences and muttered darkly to one another – this referee was either incompetent or corrupt.

But the vaudeville was not yet complete. In the final ten minutes the referee sent off a player from either side, and awarded a penalty to Sunshine George Cross in the final minutes of extra time. Nikitovic saved the penalty, but to his surprise the referee found an infraction and ordered it to be taken again. Relieved, George Cross striker Don Maclaren had another go. Again Nikitovic palmed it away, and again the referee insisted he had moved too early.

This was too much for the JUST supporters. One man hurdled the fence and rained blows on the referee, knocking him to the ground. As the unruly fan wheeled away from police, Maclaren had his spot-kick saved by Nikitovic for a third time. Rattled from the punch, the referee let the save stand, and the match went to a penalty shootout. Both sides converted the first round of five penalties, but on George Cross' ninth attempt Nikitovic saved his fourth penalty of the evening, leaving his teammate to finish his penalty and win the game. 'Nikitovic Saves Four Penalties,' read the headline in Soccer Action. 'Fan Punches Referee.'[5]

Rival players and coaches were soon marvelling at Sekularac's side. They called his work 'magic', while one opponent said that Footscray JUST were the 'only NSL side I'd pay to watch'.[6] In that 1986 season, JUST rocketed up the ladder to finish second in the Southern Conference, and were knocked out in the playoff series by the eventual champions, Adelaide City.

Nikitovic settled quickly. He fell in love with the club, opened his own business in Fitzroy and dined frequently at Tony Kovac's Vineyard restaurant in St Kilda, which he felt was like being in Yugoslavia. Life was good.

All around him, however, soccer was in a state of ruination. Although the conference system had created the most inclusive conditions ever seen in the NSL, it had also brought it to the brink of financial collapse. A total of 26 clubs, including tiny sides such as Inter Monaro, Green Gully and Canterbury-Marrickville, had featured in the space of just three seasons. Crowds were steadily contracting, and confidence in the NSL had all but evaporated.

★

In the first week of April, just days after the first round of the 1987 season, Frank Lowy called NSL executives to a meeting at his Westfield offices in Sydney's CBD. Lowy, a founding father of the NSL, had fought long, bitter battles with Sir Arthur George, resigned from the NSL executive in 1982, and witnessed the game go backwards. Against all protests, he announced that Sydney City would withdraw from the league.

Ignoring a rescue package put together by several leading club figures and supporters, Lowy described the club's terminal position as 'cold, hard facts'. No matter how well Sydney City played, it could not attract a 'worthwhile level of attendances', and worse, the budget to participate in the NSL would require the Hakoah Club to run at a loss. He argued that soccer only served a minority of the Hakoah Club membership and thus 'it does not mean that everything must be sacrificed for the dubious honour of sponsoring a professional sporting team'.[7]

This was a classic problem, rooted in the DNA of Australian club soccer – to what extent were these soccer clubs or ethnic social clubs with a soccer team attached to them? When the going got tough, to whom did the administrators owe loyalty? The general ethnic community that patronised it, or the soccer fans that came to the games on a Sunday?

That debate was carried out in the Hakoah Club and in the pages of the *Jewish Times*. Bill Kadison, generally a supporter of Lowy and a man who had been involved in Hakoah since the 1950s, reminded the membership that soccer was the 'sole basis' for the social club's existence.[8] More annoyed was Peter Scott, a young journalist from Rose Bay who contributed regularly to *Soccer Action*. Sensationally, he accused Lowy of running a 'one man dictatorship', and accused the board of being highly incestuous and of having a 'misguided ghetto mentality' towards the name Hakoah.[9] Scott was also convinced that Lowy had a personal vendetta against Sir Arthur George and that the *Jewish Times* was ignoring the team.[10]

A group of members cheekily took out a space in the *Jewish Times* to publish an obituary. 'We sadly mourn the untimely loss of our beloved SYDNEY CITY S.FC. (48 Years) (HAKOAH),' it read. 'Taken from us suddenly, following a short, misdiagnosed illness.'[11] Another supporter wrote an open letter to Lowy, announcing that his decision 'deserves the utmost contempt of every Jew in Australia, whether a soccer supporter or not'.[12]

Meanwhile, Rabbi Dr Nisson E Schulman from the Central Synagogue in Sydney implored Jews to forget soccer and worry instead about the perils of AIDS, apathy, assimilation, homosexuality and intermarriage. In particular, Schulman took umbrage at a soccer supporter who had pledged to 'say Kaddish' for Sydney City. 'Because the Kaddish was used as a prayer for the forefathers of our people, whose memory is demeaned by perverting it,' the rabbi protested.[13]

The trauma of Sydney City's exit was not confined to its supporters; this was a repudiation of the national league as a concept, and a sobering assessment of the state of Australian soccer in its entirety. Incredibly, by the time Frank Lowy and his board pulled the pin, Sydney City was by far the best side in the country. Since the establishment of the national league in 1977, City had never finished outside the top five and had amassed a record four national league premierships and one NSL Cup title.

Sydney City's squad consistently featured the who's who of Australian soccer, from Agenor Muniz to Gerry Gomez, John Kosmina to David

Mitchell, Frank Farina, Ken Boden, Steve O'Connor, Murray Barnes and Eddie Thomson. And the administrative talent was without peer, from Walter Sternberg leading the NSW soccer revolution in 1956 to Dr Henry Seamonds forming the Australian Soccer Federation in 1962 and Frank Lowy kick-starting the national league in 1975.

In an ultimate irony, when the NSL ditched the conference system in 1986 and cut the competition from 24 clubs to 14, the league bosses rated City as the best equipped for the season ahead.

'We didn't know it was going to come to an end, although there were signs,' Steve O'Connor once remembered. 'They sold Frank Farina and other players off to Marconi, Kossie went to [Sydney] Olympic, so we knew there was something going on. We were disappointed because although we had lost players, we still had a strong team. We felt that we could be challenging at the end of the season.'

In every other country, the rewards for such on-field excellence would have included new supporters, generous sponsorship, financial bonuses and a permanent space in the national imagination. Films are made, hagiographical accounts are produced and coffee-table books printed. The club becomes an intrinsic part of the city's cultural pulse. Sydney City was often referred to as 'the Liverpool of Australia', but in the nation's biggest city it was, to put it generously, a marginal presence.

The club's success was met with declining attendances, recurring identity crises, financial instability and complete disinterest from the general public. The million-dollar premises, where the club members danced, broke bread, played cards, exercised, gambled, got married and attended bar mitzvahs, were the envy of the soccer community, but even the social club had lost faith in the team.

Sydney City was the first NSL club to surrender to reality. Just as Andrew Dettre had opined back in 1977, there were too many top-flight soccer clubs in Sydney, and for the most part the rationale for their existence was almost completely incompatible with the modern era of sport. It is worthwhile remembering that the first Hakoah team back in 1939 was a restless group of young Jewish men, fresh off the refugee boats from Europe and playing recreational soccer at Rushcutters Bay in Sydney's eastern suburbs. That was the purest expression of an ethnic soccer club – look after your own first and use sport as a means for fitness, health, networking and cultural replenishment.

The Hakoah of 1987, with its utterly meaningless 'Sydney City' moniker, dwindling attendances and entirely non-Jewish squad, simply had no reason to exist. No longer a true Jewish club, it certainly wasn't a club for all of Sydney. It was a very good bunch of players with an excellent coach cut adrift from everything that made it whole: geography, supporters, culture.

Lowy had tried nearly everything to transition the ethnic club to a club for the entire city. But the city never cared for it, and the move made absolutely no difference to Hakoah's popularity. 'At the height of the club's soccer successes,' wrote Lowy in 1987, 'spectators did not come to watch the team, whether it played under the name of Hakoah, Hakoah Eastern Suburbs or Sydney City.'[14]

The soccer club was still patronised almost exclusively by ageing migrants – Dettre would later describe a Sydney City match as 'a few old Jewish men with varicose veins half-asleep in the sun' – while Johnny Warren remembered Lowy telling him: 'John, our biggest problem is that our support is literally dying out. We have more supporters in Rookwood Cemetery than we do at the games.'[15]

Indeed, the closest Sydney City ever got to truly 'branching out' was in the early 1980s when a gang of skinheads started coming to games, complete with the hooligan regalia of Doc Martens, stovepipe jeans and polo shirts. Although these young men weren't Nazis, seeing skinheads supporting a Jewish soccer team made for the most unusual sight in Australian sport.

On 3 April 1987, ten years and one day to the date since the club's first national league game, Sydney City officially pulled out of the NSL. The club had won 155 of its 273 matches, lost just 52, and scored 527 goals. It was the end of Hakoah's investment in soccer, and the beginning of Lowy's long hiatus from the game.

Since the establishment of the NSL, 1987 was the first season in which every single participating club was supported by an ethnic community. The conference system had been discarded, but the league was still 'national' in name only.

Of the 13 remaining clubs, only Adelaide City came from outside the metropolitan centres of Sydney and Melbourne. Gone were the one-town-teams in Canberra, Newcastle and Wollongong. Brisbane was not represented at all, and Perth and North Queensland might as well have been in different countries. Blacktown and Penrith retreated to the NSW first division, with the latter becoming 'Uruguayan Penrith'.

As Andrew Dettre observed in his weekly dispatch for *Soccer Action*, 12 of the NSL clubs were supported by communities originating from the Mediterranean – Croats, Greeks, Yugoslavs, Italians, Macedonians and Maltese. Central Europe, once a cradle for Australia's soccer clubs, was represented in the NSL only by the Hungarians at St George, while in the lower divisions the clubs belonging to Austrians, Jews, Dutch, Czechs, Germans, Poles and Hungarians were fading into oblivion. Slavia Melbourne was dead, Prague long buried. Not long after Sydney City pulled out of the NSL, Melbourne Hungaria – the 1967 champions of Australia – collapsed.

Below the NSL, newer migrant groups had already established their own ethnic clubs. In the NSW state competition, for instance, the South Americans could be found at clubs such as Argentinian Lidcombe, Colo Colo, Haberfield Peru, Santiago Wanderers, Chile Sports and Trasandinos, while the Arabs played for sides called Crescent Star, Green Island and Lebanon. There was even a club called simply 'Assyrian' that represented a group of stateless people from the Middle East.

Meanwhile, Footscray JUST scouted Minh Tri Vo, a newly arrived refugee and former Vietnamese international, from a local ethnic World Cup tournament. And in Melbourne's indoor-soccer competition, eight families from East Timor formed an enterprising little side called the Buffalo Mets.

Yet these new migrants did not seem to push soccer with the same zeal and enthusiasm as their forebears. The Vietnamese, most of whom had arrived as refugees following the Vietnam War, may well have had good soccer players, but their priority was work and education. Moreover, the social and economic conditions had changed since the 1950s, making it much more difficult to establish new clubs, competitions and breakaway federations.

The fate of Australia's ethnic soccer clubs could be pegged to the natural evolution of Australia's migration program. As the postwar migrants died out or assimilated, most of the clubs began to wither and collapse. The seeds of decline were planted in their modus operandi.

'It was the end of large-scale migration, and the change in character of residual migration that meant that the numbers were not there to support the clubs,' Roy Hay once explained. 'Plus they had worked at converting their existing children into Australians. A success story in cultural and social terms that left soccer behind. Sad from a soccer perspective, but hugely important for Australia.'

For Andrew Dettre, soccer's interminable crisis became too much to bear. His weekly column for *Soccer Action* became increasingly cynical, maudlin and occasionally downright bitter. He predicted that the 'true-blue, dinky-di, non-ethnic Australians of this great land will embrace soccer when they swap their Fourex for Chianti, their meat pie for empanada and their lamb chops for raznici'.[16]

By now he was all written out. Over the course of nearly three decades he had reported on soccer during a time of great social, political and demographic upheaval, and yet he could not find an adequate answer to his great national question. It did not matter whether the government policy was 'assimilation', 'integration' or 'multiculturalism' – in the minds of most Australians soccer remained a foreign sport. For someone who had written about soccer as if Australia depended on it, this was deeply dispiriting. And for an immigrant who had pegged his own acceptance in Australia to the acceptance of soccer, it was unsettlingly personal.

His work had taken him to Europe and all over the Americas. Along with his colleague Lou Gautier, he travelled to all parts of Asia, championing integration with the region well before it was in vogue with politicians and Australia's intellectual elite. He was there at the birth of the ethnic clubs, at the coalface for the revolutions of the late 1950s, the boom times of the 1960s and the dizzying high of the 1974 World Cup.

He had watched his beloved St George-Budapest go from the migrant camp in Bathurst to the heights of Asia and become champions of Australia, all the while providing numerous Socceroos and building a plush social club and a boutique stadium it could call its own. He was responsible for bringing Frank Arok, possibly Australia's favourite national coach, to these shores.

Soccer provided him the experience and the authority to move into government, and he had come within touching distance of setting up a national sports institute, only to watch the Fraser government take credit for its eventual establishment in 1981. Nobody ever thanked him for the work he had put in to create the model for the Australian Institute of Sport. 'That was my idea,' he would repeat for decades. Nobody listened.

He had taken on everyone, from star players to club officials, from media outlets to the SCG Trust, from federation heavyweights to prime ministers. He had devoted countless hours to making his beloved newspaper, *Soccer World*, rise from a little pamphlet to the most respected soccer paper in the country, before it died in sudden and painful circumstances. He had authored several books, including *Soccer the Australian Way*, which became a veritable bible for many youngsters. He had been there at the beginning of SBS, only to see Les Murray get the job of soccer presenter ahead of his son. He had switched from pro-ethnic names to anti-ethnic, and then back to the pro-ethnic camp again. He had suggested that the national league revert to a one-town-team structure, franchise the clubs to invite private capital into the game, and switch to the summer months. Mostly, his suggestions fell on deaf ears, and when he was heard, almost nothing was done to carry out the vision.

So when the *Age* newspaper ceased publishing *Soccer Action* in 1987, Dettre decided it was time for him to write about other things. Soccer's finest journalist quietly departed the game, almost broken by the pain of unfulfilled promise.

'It's with almost unspeakable sadness that I begin to write this valedictory to a fine newspaper solely devoted to the affairs of soccer,' he wrote, in what would be his final column.

> For some time I have been fearing for the future of soccer in this country at the current semi-professional level.
>
> Recent signals appear to make my fears well founded.
>
> Two weeks ago Australia's most successful soccer outfit ever, Sydney City, decided to withdraw, for financial reasons, from the NSL; now it's a fine newspaper that packs it in for similar reasons.
>
> Oh, I know, soccer won't disappear; nothing does in nature. Things merely change place or shape.
>
> The same is happening with soccer, which will shrink even further to serve a narrow ethnic market at NSL level, with the appropriate publications in the supporting role.
>
> One small consolation is that we all know the date of death: today.
>
> This is something I didn't know about *Soccer World* when I ceased to publish it as a weekly in 1981 and then as a monthly in 1982, thus missing our own obituaries [...]
>
> As for myself, I think I will switch now to becoming a mere observer of the passing parade.
>
> Soccer, as I said, will survive. But for me it won't be the same.[17]

Soccer would never be the same without Andrew Dettre. Nobody would ever have such soaring ideas, such a gift for language, and such a surety of purpose. He was Australian soccer's greatest intellectual.

Soccer Action collapsed before his final article went to print. Cruelly, Dettre was not even granted the 'one small consolation' of farewelling his readers and publicly reflecting on his time in soccer. Twice he was denied the opportunity, as he put it, to write his own obituary.

What remained, however, was his national question. In December 1987, in response to a call by Stefan Kamasz to get 'the Australian people more involved' in soccer, Dettre wrote a letter to the *Sydney Morning Herald*. Repeating an argument that he had been making for more than 25 years, he wrote: 'All those involved are Australians – born here or migrants of various backgrounds.' What had changed, however, was the tone. His youthful optimism was gone. Soccer, he predicted, 'is simply not Australia's national sport and never will be'.[18]

★

With darkness engulfing domestic soccer, the national team was a glimmer of hope to administrators, a rope-ladder out of a gloomy underworld to players, and for the supporters it was a fan for a dying flame.

Frank Arok was entering his fifth year as Socceroos boss, and by 1988 the squad had found stability, adding the youthful energy of Alex Tobin, Robbie Slater and Frank Farina to the strong core retained from the failed 1986 World Cup qualification campaign. Safe passage to the 1988 Olympic Games in Korea had arrived in March, with victories over Taiwan, Israel and New Zealand.

The Socceroos' qualification for the Olympic Games dovetailed conveniently with Australia's bicentennial celebrations. As part of the year-long carnival, several large-scale events were held to boost a sense of national pride and belonging. The largest event was the World Expo '88 in Brisbane, while air, car and railway shows entertained crowds in NSW and Victoria.

On the first day of the new year, Channel 9 broadcast *Australia Live*, a nation-wide television extravaganza. The Australian Bicentennial Authority was granted a slush fund to help generate a sense of national pride throughout the population. Among many other things, it partially funded James Jupp's monograph, *The Australian People: An Encyclopaedia of the Nation, Its People and Their Origins*. The book was launched by Prime Minister Bob Hawke, who praised it as a testament to the nation's multiculturalism. In its pages the book paid tribute to soccer people including Andrew Dettre, Branko Filipi, Marin Alagich, Frank Kunz and Jim Bayutti.

Multiculturalism was a constant theme of the bicentenary, yet there remained a great incoherence in the national narrative. After 200 years of European settlement, nobody quite knew what it meant to be an Australian.

Two years prior, the film *Crocodile Dundee* had portrayed Australia through a brazen blond-haired bushman. Although people could imagine an Australian type in the rugged larrikin, Dundee was unrepresentative of Australia's changing demographics; in fact, Australia boasted one of the most urbanised populations on the planet. In 1987, a top-rating Australian play titled *Wogs Out of Work* led to a new genre of ethnic comedy, but its primary power was in cleverly subverting the existing stereotypes, not in recasting the face of the nation.

Rather than coming from a groundswell of authentic, deeply ingrained nationalism, the bicentennial celebrations were shoe-horned into Australian households and public spaces by an army of pen–pushers, event planners, government bureaucrats and advertising companies. For a nation uneasy with itself, lacking a clear set of national myths and symbols to draw upon, sport filled the gaping void. In a pamphlet produced by *Sport '88*, the authors wrote that sport was 'Australia's national religion'.[19]

In total, the Australian Bicentennial Authority funded 76 sporting events and endorsed another 456. There were bicentennial events in women's cricket, rugby league and rugby union, Australian Rules football and golf.

For once, soccer was high on the list of priorities. The Bicentennial Gold Cup was contested by the Socceroos, Saudi Arabia, Argentina and Brazil. *Australian Soccer Weekly* proudly labelled itself a 'Bicentennial 1988 Publication', while in the *Sydney Morning Herald*, Michael Cockerill wrote that the tournament 'may provide just the catalyst the game needs to make some real inroads on the hearts and minds of a mass audience'.[20]

Yet several issues plagued the tournament. The Socceroos almost boycotted after being offered measly match fees, while a confluence of factors including bad weather, exorbitant ticket prices and the ABC live telecast worked against getting people through the turnstiles. And the Argentines were furious at being forced to train at a park with rugby goalposts at Rushcutters Bay.

All the negativity was quickly forgotten, however, after Australia's shock victory over the reigning world champions. With the Socceroos' resident Argentine, Oscar Crino, bed-ridden by a stomach bug, Footscray JUST midfielder Vlado Bozinovski made his international debut. In front of nearly 20,000 people, Australia won 4–1, with two goals to Charlie Yankos, one to Paul Wade and one to Bozinovski.

Yankos' first would remain etched in the memory of every Socceroos fan. Just before half-time, from some 40 yards out, Yankos blasted a free-kick into the top right-hand corner of the goal. It was a classic captain's intervention, putting Australia a goal ahead for the second half. After the match, Arok called it 'a beautiful goal', and predicted 'he'll never score one like that again in his life'.[21]

Having faced more than a decade of international disappointments and a rapidly declining national league, Australian soccer supporters straightened their backs a little. 'Australia won the Bicentennial Gold Cup soccer series yesterday everywhere except on the field,' noted one reporter after the Socceroos lost the final game to Brazil. 'Everyone from coach Frank Arok to captain Charlie Yankos to the fans who poured in from the suburbs could not stop talking after the game about Australian soccer's bright future.'[22]

Just four days later, however, Sydney Olympic hosted Melbourne Croatia at the Sydney Football Stadium, and only 1200 people turned up. 'Those who had hoped the euphoria of the Gold Cup would spread to the National League,' lamented Michael Cockerill, 'were soon brought back to reality.'[23]

The problem, as always, was one of identification. As they had done several times before, the Socceroos presented to middle Australia a completely neutral image. The team momentarily transcended ethnicity, becoming illustrative of a soft and fuzzy multiculturalism. But when the attention turned back to the NSL, fans were left with teams run by Croats, Greeks or Italians.

The 1988 NSL grand final between Sydney Croatia and Marconi, for instance, included a melting pot of players. It was like a United Colors of Benetton ad, perhaps the most raw and authentic expression of Australia's multicultural society, but it didn't matter – in the minds of the average sports fan, the names 'Marconi' and 'Croatia', and the Italian and Croat men who ran the clubs, were seen as proof of soccer's ethnic separatism.

The NSL presented a society radically different from the one Prime Minister Hawke had promised with his 'Living Together' bicentenary slogan. It was messy and unpredictable, the tensions often impossible to navigate, and completely incongruous to those who wanted to see Australians as one tribe. It was a living, breathing example of community self-determination in a country that clung quietly to an old, insidious notion that immigrants and Indigenous people should assimilate. As usual, soccer had the worst-attended grand final of any football code that season.

Against this bleak backdrop, the Socceroos departed for Korea with the nation's Olympic contingent in September 1988. The team lost against Brazil, but shocked the world by beating both Nigeria and Yugoslavia. For Frank Arok, a Yugoslav by birth, the latter was extra special – a final high point in a national team career that would conclude at the end of the year. The goal-scorers were John Kosmina and Frank Farina. Kosmina, 32, was the master, probably the best striker of the NSL's first decade; Farina, his apprentice, was the great hope for the future. Yet by year's end, he too would leave the NSL to embark on a career in Europe.

This marked a new credibility crisis for the NSL – while rugby league and Australian Rules could boast the best players in the world by virtue of their insularity, soccer could no longer hold on to even the best Australian players. The talent drain had begun.

During the Bicentennial Gold Cup, Sir Arthur George stepped down as president of the Australian Soccer Federation. It marked the end of a long, often-tyrannical reign that lasted almost two decades. Stefan Kamasz went to his farewell function, but for the first time in years he was there on unofficial business, having resigned from the NSL executive three months earlier.

Kamasz was fed up with soccer politics, crestfallen at the national league's lack of progress and deeply frustrated by the lack of vision within the organisation. In late 1987, he had presented a discussion paper to his fellow administrators, suggesting, among other things, the introduction of summer soccer, the employment of promotions and development officers at each club, minimum standards for grounds, an end to promotion and relegation, and stricter controls over club licences. None of his suggestions found an audience. Before his departure, Kamasz had pleaded with Frank Lowy for months to return to the game. Much to Kamasz's dismay, however, Lowy formally refused his overtures.

If you think of the development of Australian sport in the 1980s as a tectonic shift, the other sports rode the changes to higher ground while soccer fell into a deep crevasse. Rugby league had established its hugely popular State of Origin series between Queensland and NSW, and the showpiece competition had become national by the inclusion of five new teams based on the one-town-team concept – Canberra Raiders, Illawarra Steelers, Newcastle Knights, Gold Coast Giants and Brisbane Broncos.

In 1987, Australian Rules football had introduced the West Coast Eagles from Western Australia and the Brisbane Bears from Queensland, while the Sydney Swans – which had relocated from South Melbourne in 1982 – had been sold to Dr Geoffrey Edelsten in mid-1985. It was an historic moment in Australian sport, ushering in an era where private interest would reign over the membership-based, community-owned model.

'I walked away when Frank said he wasn't going to come back into the game,' remembered Kamasz. 'The day Frank's letter arrived on my desk, within a matter of minutes I rang [NSL executives] Sam Papasavas and Tony Labbozzetta and said, "I'm resigning". One of the reasons I got out was because we couldn't convince the NSL to go to summer soccer. It made complete sense to me – it opened up the availability of stadiums that we couldn't use in winter. I'd rather sit on a grassy hill on a balmy summer's evening than in the middle of winter. This, in my view, should have happened in 1980–81.'

By 1988, soccer officials and fans were still arguing over summer soccer's implementation. *On the Ball*, a popular SBS panel show, had invited Kamasz and Eddie Thomson to discuss its relative merits, while *Australian Soccer Weekly* continued to run many negative articles and letters on summer soccer. One woman, describing herself only as 'Soccer Widow of the Present Divorcee of the Future', wrote to the newspaper to accuse soccer officials of plotting to destroy the family unit.[24]

Eventually it was decreed that the first NSL summer soccer season would proceed in 1989–90. The 1989 season would be the final winter. As if to prove a point, it was beset by terrible weather. Many matches needed to be postponed; many more went ahead in atrocious conditions. In the third weekend of May, a match between Heidelberg and Blacktown City highlighted everything wrong with soccer in the 1980s. Rain bucketed down, a general gloom fell over the dimly lit stadium, and the pitch was in a severe state of disrepair. Pockmarked grass on the fringes merged into a dark slush in the middle.

The players, socks stained black from the mud, slid around hopelessly and hoofed the ball in the air. Early the second half, a Blacktown defender slid horribly into the back of a Heidelberg midfielder, leaving him screaming in pain and writhing in the mud. As the ball trickled towards the sideline and the Blacktown defender hastily ran away from the scene of his crime, an enraged Heidelberg player booted the ball into the face of an opponent, who also hit the turf. It was like a scene from a black comedy sketch, but for the 192 hardy souls huddled underneath umbrellas on the terraces, summer soccer couldn't come fast enough.

★

Zoran Nikitovic never played summer soccer. His NSL career ended on 17 July 1989, after an emotional, winner-takes-all battle between Melbourne Croatia and Footscray JUST.

The rivalry between the two sides – the former backed by Croatians, the latter by Yugoslavs – was based in part on their shared location in the western suburbs of Melbourne. Footscray JUST played at Schintler Reserve, a decrepit old soccer ground that sat in between Footscray Road and the banks of the Maribyrnong River, not far from the Croatian social club.

Nobody hated Schintler Reserve more than the Croats. On the scoreboard and on JUST's shirts, the state-owned JAT Yugoslav Airlines sponsor was seen as proof that JUST were another branch of the Yugoslav propaganda machine. Many of the visiting Croatia fans, so as to avoid giving the Yugoslav club their hard-earned cash, would perch themselves up on the railway line behind the goals, hurl abuse and piff projectiles at those inside the fence.

To the naive Australian, the conflict between Yugoslavs and Croats made no sense. They spoke a common language, the food and drink was indistinguishable and their migrant experience was essentially the same. They lived in the same suburbs and worked similar jobs. But the politics of the homeland kept them apart, and in soccer the Melbourne Croatia–Footscray JUST derby became a battle between two competing visions for the Balkans.

Just one month prior to the decisive match between Melbourne Croatia and Footscray JUST, the Croat nationalist Franjo Tudjman formed the *Hrvatska Demokratska Zajednica* (Croatian Democratic Union), which would lead Croatia to independence within a year. Many of his supporters were nationalistic emigres in Australia. In the Republic of Serbia, meanwhile, Slobodan Milosevic stoked ethnic divisions in Kosovo, encouraged Serbian nationalism and put in place many free-market reforms. With Tudjman and Milosevic in power, the socialist, multicultural nature of Yugoslavia was finished.

Two of the hallmarks of Yugoslavia's death – a loss of identity and privatisation – were both visited upon Footscray JUST between 1987 and 1989.

To Nikitovic, the beginning of the end came when Footscray JUST was sold to a consortium of people that included his *kum*, Alf Bulic, and his teammate Oscar Crino. After a short stint in Cyprus, Crino had joined JUST in mid-1987 and soon became an investor. To an outsider, the decision seemed insane – why would a young, enterprising Australian player of Argentine heritage put his own money into a dying Yugoslav soccer club? The way Crino later explained it, the privatisation of the Sydney Swans in 1985 had given him an idea: by bringing in new money, he hoped that JUST could be transitioned into a club for the entire city.

To privatise and de-ethnicise a Yugoslav soccer club was a great risk, but Crino and his cohort gambled that Melbournians would embrace the changes and gradually create an identity stronger than the ethnicity of the existing supporters.

'A lot of migrants come here with a postcode in their heads,' Crino would recall. 'A lot of them are transfixed in that and stay like that, and they actually don't progress. I said that to a lot of people in those days: that is the biggest downfall that we've got here. By identifying yourself as a political entity you're no longer a sporting entity.'

Just as Hakoah's transition to Sydney City did little to increase their support base, Footscray JUST gained nothing by switching its name to 'Melbourne City'. People still felt it was a Yugoslav club and, in a competition where Croats and Macedonians had their own soccer teams but not their own independent nations back home, it was a recipe for disaster.

The festering hatred for Footscray JUST was born out of a geopolitical situation thousands of kilometres from Australia, and Nikitovic, who as a goalkeeper stood closest to the supporters, copped it with extreme prejudice. 'So many people call me gypsy,' he later recalled. 'To one guy, I said: "Why did you call me a gypsy? Do I look like gypsy? You know who I am, my name is Nikitovic Zoran!"'

For his teammate Drago Deankovic it was even worse. Deankovic had actually started his Australian career for Melbourne Croatia in 1984, but after three successful seasons he became one of the few

Croatia players to transfer to Footscray JUST. The committee was furious and the fans were ropable. Melbourne Croatia secretary Frank Burin accused Deankovic of misleading his club, using a trip back to Yugoslavia as a diversionary tactic to allow him to return to JUST. To the Croats, who hated Yugoslavia with every fibre of their existence, Deankovic's move was high treason. Not long after, his house was firebombed.

In the six seasons that Melbourne Croatia and Footscray JUST were both in the NSL, the two sides had met 11 times, against a backdrop of fistfights, rock-throwing, general abuse, firebombs, arson attacks and some very good football. JUST was the dominant side, winning five matches to Croatia's three, with three games ending in a draw. To the NSL officials' eternal relief, the two sides had never met in a final. This game, then, was the battle royale.

The Middle Park crowd of 5000 favoured Melbourne Croatia. With everything to play for, there was little time for showmanship or pretty moves. The match was conducted in a state of emergency, with tackles flying in thick and fast and midfielders searching frantically for space to exploit. By the end of the first half, the scores were locked at 0–0. In the second half, Croatia simply ran over the top of their opponents, with goals to Zeljko Adzic and Joe Caleta.

The go-ahead goal was scored by Adzic. The young, blond-haired Croatian had arrived in Melbourne only a few months prior, after stints with Dinamo Zagreb and Canadian side Hamilton Croatia. He was a natural goal-poacher, scoring with his head, his right foot, his left foot, inside and outside the box, tap-ins and thunderbolt drives. In his first 13 games he scored ten goals. None, however, was more important than his glancing header in this all-important game.

As Adzic celebrated, right arm raised towards the sky, Nikitovic stood hands on hips in a state of shock. Moments later, his thoughts were interrupted as Croatia fans rained flares down into his goal-mouth, engulfing him in acrid red smoke and chants of 'CRO-A-ZIA! CRO-A-ZIA!' You could not have scripted a more poignant end to his

NSL career, and indeed to Footscray JUST. The loss meant the club was relegated from the NSL for the first time in its history, accelerating a dramatic fall from grace matched only by Sydney City's collapse two seasons earlier.

At season's end, Nikitovic sold his house in Melbourne and moved back to Yugoslavia. He tried to return to his old life, but the Yugoslavia of his youth was disintegrating.

In the months to come, Nikitovic would return to Melbourne, fight for unpaid wages from Footscray JUST, and try to get on with life. His teammate Oscar Crino, meanwhile, would be left to smooth the pillow of a dying club.

The demise of JUST, Australia's most prominent Yugoslav soccer club, occurred in tandem with the decline of Yugal in Sydney. The identity that had sustained both clubs for four decades had been subverted by the nationalism that had taken root in the republics of Yugoslavia. Families frayed. Friends drifted apart. Towns and cities were divided along ethnic lines. And for the next decade and a half, the Balkan communities in Australia would internalise all the stress, the angst and the pain, and let it out on the soccer field.

The expensive clubrooms and facilities that Crino and his partners had built at Schintler Reserve were rendered virtually worthless. Without a presence in the NSL, there were no fans, no identity and no future. Crino would soon depart the club, and quietly drift out of the game as one of soccer's saddest stories. The conditions of Australian soccer could never properly support and nurture his talent. Neither of his dreams – to take Australia to the World Cup and to make domestic soccer a big deal – had come to fruition.

'That cost me a lot of money,' Crino would later comment of his investment in Footscray JUST. 'Financially it set me back probably 15 years. I had to start all over again, and all for the game. We were really dreaming that we were going to reshape the league. When you're young, you think you can do things …'

PART II

THE UNINVOLVED AUSTRALIANS

'[...] only if those [...] teams belong to much larger and broader groups than hitherto and through their neutral name, organisation and composition, also appeal to the average, uninvolved Australians.'

Andrew Dettre, 1977

FOR THE HOMELAND

1990–1995

our eyes transfixed
on the game
clear cut loyalties back then
we barracked
for the Greek team
near hysteria at every goal
and the odd brawl
providing laughter
and heated debates
momentary diversions
from the backbreaking toil
of the coming week.

Konstandina Dounis
Soccer at Middle Park, 2009[1]

On the eve of summer soccer's very first season, in the nervous spring of 1989, Michael Cockerill decided to investigate the cause of the game's decline. Although just 28 years of age, more than any other journalist he had seen soccer's potential in far-flung corners of Australasia. He had reported on the rise and fall of the Queensland State League for the

Rockhampton Morning Bulletin; witnessed New Zealand qualify for the 1982 World Cup while working for a Christchurch newspaper; and, in 1983, divided his time between Sydney's *Manly Daily*, Melbourne's *Soccer Action* and the *Australian Soccer Weekly*.

He had also briefly tried his hand working as a journalist in London, but soon realised that with his Australian passport he would never be taken seriously as a soccer writer. So he had returned to Australia to land a job at the *Sydney Morning Herald* – a role that would define his career for more than three decades. Through his travels he had learned to write, and developed an authoritative voice and a toughness that appealed to newspaper editors. Skin in the game, as he called it.

Cockerill's greatest commitment was to statism. In a searching, six-part series for the *Herald* in October 1989, he suggested that the teams in Sydney and Melbourne be rationalised, and that the steel cities of Wollongong and Newcastle be strengthened. With rare intricacy and detail he canvassed expansion opportunities in Perth, Brisbane, Adelaide, Canberra, the Gold Coast, Townsville and Tasmania. 'One of the major bugbears of the national league in recent years is that it has become less and less national,' he concluded. 'For the national league to regain some of its lustre, every mainland state must be represented.'[2]

The National Soccer League entered the 1990s with 14 teams. Just two – West Adelaide and Adelaide City – came from outside Victoria and NSW. Canberra City, Newcastle Rosebud, Brisbane Lions and Brisbane City had all been relegated to their respective state leagues, and Wollongong City was the only club to represent a regional centre. Otherwise the clubs came from the Italian, Greek, Croatian, Hungarian, Macedonian and Maltese communities of Sydney and Melbourne.

It was more international than it was national. And it was a far cry from the recommendations in the 1981 ASF Marketing Report, which had predicted that, by 1990, 20 franchises would stretch from Western Australia to Wollongong, Tasmania to Townsville. Indeed, by 1990, there was another review creating headlines in the soccer community. Graham Bradley, an academic from the University of NSW, had been commissioned by the Australian Soccer Federation to whip around the states, interview the various stakeholders, associations and clubs, and report back on the 'structure and functioning' of the national competition and the governing body. His recommendations, known as the Bradley Report, delivered a holistic rebuke of the way in which soccer had been operating. He found that the ASF did not represent all of the game's constituent parts, leaving soccer riven by fragmentation and sectional interests.

Perhaps the greatest failure of the ASF was in its neglect of women's soccer. By 1990 the Australian Women's Soccer Association was entering a new phase of growth. It had a successful national side, conducted regular interstate tournaments and was competing with the ASF for grants from the Australian Sports Commission. It had also appointed a full-time marketing director, Heather Reid, who began publishing the very first women's soccer magazine.

'I called it *The Far Post* because I felt like I was in an outpost,' she once recalled. 'We contributed to the Bradley Report, and I think the concern was whether we could trust the ASF. If we handed everything over, could we trust [them] to manage the business of women's soccer? Would they give the women the same priority that the AWSA was giving it? We'd had a range of delegations from the ASF telling us they would take care of the ship, and one promise after another just fell over.'

The Bradley Report recommended that the ASF become involved in women's soccer, but most of the points were a rehash of the recommendations in the 1981 ASF Marketing Report, particularly with regard to ethnicity, to promotion and relegation, and to the structure, composition and geographic spread of clubs in the NSL.

'In the long term,' Bradley noted, 'the ASF needs to create the image that soccer is Australian not ethnic.' To this end, he recommended that SBS – which he labelled 'the ethnic television station' – be replaced by the ABC as the broadcast partner, and that the clubs 'include a district name in their overall club name'.[3]

Bradley recommended that the seven NSL sides from Sydney be reduced to four; that Hobart, Perth, Newcastle and Brisbane be included in the competition; and that promotion and relegation be decided on factors other than the competition ladder, in a manner that would cause the least possible instability in the league. He came up with a complex points system in which the clubs from Sydney and Melbourne would face relegation more often than those in the other areas.

Never a soccer person, Bradley formulated his recommendations in the interests of best business practice, without deference to sentiment or tradition. He asked soccer officials to see supporters as akin to 'shareholders in a company', and while the purists saw his fiddling with club identities and promotion and relegation as tantamount to heresy, Bradley simply pressed ahead with what he felt would enhance organisational stability and growth. 'The game,' reasoned one reporter in response to Bradley's recommendations, 'is gradually being taken over by the Australian-born – on the field and off it.'[4]

One of this new breed was Andrew Howe, an obsessive, awkward-looking young man with a beaky nose, chestnut-brown hair and sharp eyes. Howe discovered soccer not long after his 19th birthday, on the second Sunday of May 1988. For reasons nobody can quite remember, he, his brother Rod and a couple of their mates hopped on a train and left the Sutherland Shire for Lambert Park in Sydney's inner west.

After vaulting the fence to avoid paying the entry fee, Howe and his friends settled in to watch APIA Leichhardt lose 2–0 to Marconi. For Howe, the crowd that crammed into APIA's creaking old grandstand was the main attraction. In his excitement, he had rushed onto the field after the final whistle, performed an impromptu breakdance move on the halfway line, and then scampered away to the delight of his mates. He was hooked.

When soccer officials spoke about broadening the base of support for the NSL clubs, Howe was the kind of person they had in mind. He came from the largest and the most un-integrative ethnic group in Australian society – the Anglos. Here was a group that played soccer on the weekends, watched English soccer on television, but had long excluded themselves from Australia's national league. The Anglos had not created their own successful NSL clubs, and for the most part refused to support those from different ethnic groups.

At face value, Howe seemed like the quintessential Anglo. He was young, well educated, from a rugby league family in the whitest suburb of Sydney. His childhood had been spent at Cronulla Sharks matches among the Harrises, the Watsons, the Fitzgibbons and the Millers of middle Australia. Yet when he departed for his fantasy world of the NSL, he was surrounded by the Yankoses, the Gomezes, the Nastevskis and the Milosevices. His father, who had never been to a soccer match, once warned him: 'You know they take knives to the soccer, don't you?'

Undeterred, Howe entered Australian soccer in the same spirit as the Pevensie children entered Narnia in *The Lion, the Witch and the Wardrobe*. Soccer, like Narnia, was stuck in what seemed like an eternal winter. Lambert Park was Howe's wardrobe, and the ethnic club was his Mr Tumnus. It was a new world, a secret society, and a place that he could believe in.

'Basically every week for the past five years I'd been to a rugby league game,' he once explained. 'There was the occasional Sharks chant, but there wasn't the buzz that I was getting from this packed inner-city ground, in a completely different sport that was far more tense. The ethnic element was a real eye-opener for me – I wanted to learn more about these ethnic communities, and why they were following these soccer teams. I wanted to know more about the clubs in terms of the history, the narratives, but also the stats. I've always been a stats person. I was just trying to catch up – the NSL had its yearbook, but that wasn't enough for me. It was just my way of being involved.'

Once Howe had been exposed to Sydney Croatia, Preston Makedonia and South Melbourne Hellas, the Cronulla Sharks suddenly seemed anodyne. He started watching SBS television. He bought the foreign-language newspapers that covered the games, particularly the Italian *La Fiamma*, the Yugoslav *Novosti* and the Greek *Neos Kosmos*. His parents thought he had lost the plot as he sat up late at night, listening to radio broadcasts from matches in Italy or Greece, not understanding a word of the commentary but revelling in the romance and the grandeur of a world game.

In 1989, he had joined the Croatian society at Macquarie University, and with a group of mates established a team called Miranda Croatia in the Southern Sydney Churches competition. He had never played the game before and none of his friends had any family ties to Croatia, yet in the style of the Croatian teams of the NSL they wore blue socks, white shorts and red shirts with a homemade *sahovnica* badge and chanted '*CRO-A-ZIA! CRO-A-ZIA!*' from the sidelines.

Miranda Croatia lost nearly every game, some by double figures, but it mattered little. During the week Howe would modify the draw to ethnicise the Southern Sydney Churches competition so that in his imagination, at least, St Philips was 'Filipino', St Giles became 'Macedonian', Fairfield LDS was 'Latvian' and Mortdale Baptist was 'Turkish'. It wasn't that he was a converted Croat nationalist, however. When he wasn't watching Sydney Croatia he would listen to Yugoslavia's most famous pop star, Lepa Brena, and even went to the Yugoslav club in Canberra to see one of her shows. He fell in love with soccer in its entirety, without allegiance to any particular team. Whether he was among the Croats at Sydney United, the Greeks at Sydney Olympic or the Italians at APIA Leichhardt, he felt comfortable and inspired.

He was one of those rare Anglo-Australians who voluntarily left their own enclave and became fully involved in the multicultural society around them. By being a soccer fan, Howe realised that he was witness to epochal, continent-rattling history. This sort of stuff didn't happen in rugby league.

Within a few months of his first NSL game, Howe had started to build his own database of national league statistics, cross-referencing every result since 1977 from at least two different newspaper match reports. It was a labour of love, an unexplainable passion and a peculiar way for a young man to pass his weekends. Although Andrew Dettre had stopped writing regular soccer columns, Howe began to understand the weight of his work through reading old, bound copies of *Soccer World* and *Soccer Action*. He chuckled at soccer's insane politics, marvelled at the all-conquering Hakoah club, and wondered what had become of the pioneering Newcastle KB United.

What linked Dettre and Howe was their eye for the eternal. Through writing and archiving, they sought to record soccer's past for the sake of its future. What made them different was how they negotiated this information. While Dettre had worn his heart on his sleeve, Howe was much more guarded. If Dettre had been the passionate reformer, Howe was the silent watcher.

The fact that Andrew Howe had ventured into soccer as a supporter and not as a participant made him an extremely rare commodity. As the Bradley Report had noted, soccer had developed a huge participant base, yet it had borne almost no fruit for the NSL. Soccer's inability to convert participants to spectators was, as many people recognised, the game's greatest unresolved problem.

In Victoria, South Australia and Western Australia, boys and girls would play soccer with their mates in the morning, talk about Australian Rules footy at lunch, and watch an AFL game with their parents in the evening. The same relation between soccer and rugby league existed in Queensland and NSW. The vast majority of weekend soccer players had no interest whatsoever in the NSL. As Graham Bradley had bluntly concluded, the NSL made soccer appear to be 'a game for ethnics'.[5]

This fact became the central theme of enquiry for a new fanzine called *Inside Soccer*. It was the hastily stapled-together organ of a collection of juvenile soccer hooligans, an incredibly vulgar and occasionally brilliant trash catalogue that combined lacerating wit with outrageous slurs and far-right provocations.

It was first published in June 1990, with a cover story that had suggested that four prominent soccer officials had entered into an orgy with a transsexual, a goat, a sheep, two hens and a python. That set the tone for the rest of the fanzine's short existence. *Inside Soccer* would break the 'news' of the Iraqi dictator Saddam Hussein's desire to coach Heidelberg United, make endless jokes about Bulgarians and gypsies, stoke as much hatred as possible between the Macedonian and Greek clubs, and mock up a regular column for Pat Brodnik, a Wollongong City player who had refused to play on Sundays due to his Seventh-day Adventist faith. Each 'Religious Round-Up with Reverend Pat Brodnik' would conclude with the advice 'Until next month … REPENT SINNERS REPENT!' Each edition was mailed to the offices of the ASF, with the aim of offending as widely and liberally as possible. Soon the fanzine attracted police surveillance.

Although Howe secretly enjoyed the gallows humour of *Inside Soccer*, as a budding young demographer it was obvious to him that the NSL needed to expand beyond its traditional boundaries. It was also clear that the competition was only serving a fraction of its potential support base. And yet on a personal level, it was this ethnic identity that had him hooked in the first place. If it weren't for soccer's ethnic clubs, he would have remained a rugby league fan.

This paradox set him on his own journey to resolve soccer's great national question. First, he needed to equip himself with the game's history. In the first decade of the competition, all of which he had missed out on, Howe noted that no single non-ethnic or district side had won a title, and if you put aside Sydney City's four titles and St George's victory in 1983, the remaining five titles were shared by the Greek and Italian clubs. Demographically, this made sense: the Greeks and the Italians had consistently been the largest non-British ethnic groups since the postwar migrant boom.

Howe's greatest intrigue, however, was the rise of the Croats. By 1990, the Croats and the Slovenes had left the Yugoslav Congress, and Croatia had elected Franjo Tudjman's ultra-nationalist Croatian Democratic Union to govern the republic. Just eight weeks later, the Croatian club Hajduk Split travelled to Australia to play a series of matches.

Fittingly, the one in Sydney was Howe's very first Socceroos match. Hajduk had become a potent symbol of the emergent Croatian state, and as the players ran onto the field at Parramatta Stadium they literally tore the logo, which featured the socialist red star of Yugoslavia, off their shirts. The mostly Croatian crowd went wild.

Australia won 1–0, but as Paul Trimboli's wonder-strike sailed into the net, all eyes were drawn to a gaggle of Australian Croats behind the goal, dancing joyously beneath a mass of Croatian flags among the thick red smoke of a flare. The Croatian ascendancy had begun.

As Sydney Croatia and Melbourne Croatia rode this wave of nationalism, St George, once the best club in Australian soccer, was sent back to the state league. Using the Bradley Report as justification, the ASF axed St George from the NSL towards the end of the 1990–91 season. Les Murray, who had grown up with the club, said that he was 'sickened' by the decision:

> Bradley, in his suggested criteria for NSL membership, spoke of making the game more attractive to 'Australians'.
>
> Yet St George, which shed its ethnic name 25 years ago, was rejected. Several of the accepted clubs appear only interested in the migrant communities they represent.
>
> Bradley spoke of financial viability, yet Heidelberg and West Adelaide who, we are told, allegedly owe plenty, were accepted, and St George, which is liquid, was rejected.
>
> Bradley spoke of facilities. St George, which owns its highly acclaimed stadium on which countless internationals have already been played – close to the centre of the city – was rejected. Some of the accepted clubs have not a patch of dirt they even rent much less own, while others play on just that: a patch of dirt.[6]

Almost exactly 16 years since that fateful day in 1975 when the St George-Budapest social club had hosted the first meeting of the national league, its final NSL game was played on Sunday 7 April 1991. Thanks in part to two goals scored by a young striker named Andrew Harper, St George beat Sydney Croatia 3–0 to finish its final season in tenth place.

It was dumped not because of its on-field results, however, but due to a political decision by the ASF. Although few realised it at the time, the mercenary logic that underpinned St George's exclusion would herald the beginning of a cinematic, decade-and-a-half-long collapse, as soccer's sacred stadiums, great clubs and distinct culture would all be brought down by the rapacious commercial desire of a hungry, half-finished sport.

★

The first club that Andrew Howe became intimately involved with was Canberra Croatia, an ambitious side from the NSW first division. Like its sister clubs in Sydney and Melbourne, Canberra Croatia turned out in red, white and blue and its supporters chanted '*CRO-A-ZIA! CRO-A-ZIA!*' from the terraces. Howe had moved to Canberra to take a job with the Australian Bureau of Statistics, and at Canberra Croatia he joined a promotions committee aiming to take the club all the way to the National Soccer League.

On the morning of Sunday 3 March 1991, Howe hopped in his Nissan Pulsar and drove to Melbourne for the 1991 NSL grand final between South Melbourne Hellas and Melbourne Croatia. After 15 seasons, it was the first grand final to be contested by two clubs outside Sydney. Howe wandered around the ground, snapping pictures as the Hellas and Croatia players stood in line for the Australian national anthem. The first few bars went by without a hitch. Then, with the intensity of a wildfire, a chant of '*HELLAS! HELLAS!*' swirled around the terraces. To the horror of the soccer officials, the crowd then burst into a spine-tingling rendition of the Greek national anthem, completely drowning out the strains of 'Advance Australia Fair'.

Howe didn't mind. He just chuckled, shook his head and continued taking photos.

On the bench sat the South Melbourne Hellas coach, Ferenc Puskas, in his day one of the greatest attackers ever to lace up a football boot. Puskas had arrived at Hellas in 1989, after a playing career that inspired millions around the world, and a coaching career that took him from Europe to South America and the Middle East.

The Hungarians, who were steadily declining as a soccer nation, built an identity around Puskas. Andrew Dettre loved him. Les Murray credited him for all that was good and holy in soccer. And here he was, coaching the biggest club in Australia. In Puskas' first season in charge, Hellas rocketed up the ladder from eighth to second place, and attendances at Middle Park soared.

'His techniques were derived from his era as a player,' once recalled the South Melbourne striker Kimon Taliadoros. 'He was a great showman with the crowd in an understated way. There'd be 10,000 people at the game and he'd make them feel like it was their own private show. He would get up and gesticulate or raise his eyes in a way that brought them into the game. He understood and played for the crowd.'

Puskas was an extravagant man with a large, round gut, slicked hair, dark sunglasses, polo shirts, sweat jackets and slacks. He looked more like a mafia don at a Sunday barbecue than a football coach. Legend has it that at one post-match dinner at Club Marconi, he ate a bowl of pasta that was supposed to feed the entire team.

But his touch never left him. At training sessions he would waddle around, flick the ball casually from one foot to the other, and send it with terrifying accuracy past stunned goalkeepers. He placed his faith in individuals rather than tactics, arranging the players in a 4–3–3 formation and encouraging the fullbacks to overlap on the wings and the wingers to press high up the park.

Players, fans and neutral spectators loved this attacking style. 'I'd often pick him up from his house and drive him to the ground,' once recalled Ange Postecoglou, who became Puskas' chauffeur and translator, as well as club captain. 'I spent a lot of time chatting about football with him. I loved it. He was so much more open than the previous coaches, who were so regimented and structured.'

The final started well enough for Melbourne Croatia, with young midfielder Andrew Marth scoring a dramatic opening goal from some

35 metres out. Yet as Croatian flags fluttered proudly in the stands, the chant of 'CRO-A-ZIA! CRO-A-ZIA!' grew louder, and the South Melbourne Hellas fans began to leave the ground before full-time, Paul Trimboli collected possession and, in one swift motion, threaded a perfect pass across the field to Joe Palatsides. The tall number ten buried the ball in the back of the net with just moments left to play. 1–1.

As darkness began to engulf the ground, Melbourne Croatia missed three penalties in the shootout to lose 5–4. In the gloom Postecoglou and Puskas held the trophy aloft, while the Croats left Olympic Park in devastation. It was, many agreed, the most exciting NSL grand final yet. It would leave a huge impression on Mark Viduka, a 15-year-old Melbourne Croatia ballboy who had held aloft the run-through banner before kick-off. 'We snatched defeat from the claws of victory,' he later recalled.

The winter of 1992 brought Mark Viduka and Marko Rudan together for the very first time. They were both 16 and had spent most of their lives at the Croatian soccer clubs of Melbourne and Sydney, and had both been awarded scholarships to the Australian Institute of Sport in Canberra.

'What nationality are you?' Viduka asked Rudan. 'Croatian,' came the response.

They became inseparable. They would talk about Hajduk Split, their favourite club in Croatia, and compare passports to decide which was the more Croatian. It was decided that the name 'Marko Ante' Rudan trumped the anglicised 'Mark Anthony' Viduka.

But on the wall above his bed at the AIS, Viduka hung a picture of the Croatian president, Franjo Tudjman, and in his wallet he kept a picture of Zvonimir Boban, the Croatian soccer-star-turned-independence-hero. Together Viduka and Rudan would belt out Croatian songs after games, and teach their AIS teammates the words to sing along.

'At school we were called a lot of names, the biggest one being a "wog",' Rudan once remembered. 'After a certain amount of time, you get used to that term and [it] becomes part of who you are. You then look for allies, other wogs, because you know you're more comfortable in that environment. Not to say that there weren't any Anglos in the team – there were – but we made sure it was their job to fit in with us. If they did that, they were accepted.'

Rudan and Viduka were part of perhaps the best generation to pass through the AIS – a group that included Craig Moore, John Aloisi, Robbie Middleby, Robbie Enes, Josip Skoko and John Angelovski. They came from all over the country, and from many different cultural backgrounds. Clint Bolton, a shy, fair-haired goalkeeper from Bundaberg in Queensland, was introduced to a world that would leave him changed forever.

'I didn't know about multiculturalism that much,' he later recalled. 'I thought a wog was an Italian specifically, I didn't realise it covered a whole European area. It was only when I went to the AIS at 16, when I was just thrown in the mix with all these guys from different cultures. I started eating *maznik* and *zelnik* from the Macedonian parents, Rudan was a big figure, and Viduka started teaching me Croatian songs, particularly "*Veceras je nasa festa*". They were so patriotic. You know Viduka had these bedsheets that were white, and he'd paint them red so they were like the Croatian flag.'

In charge of this diverse and enthusiastic young group was the ex-Socceroos assistant coach Ron Smith, who had taken over from Jim Shoulder as head coach of the AIS in 1986. Smith was as passionate about player development as he was about the progress of Australian coaches. He appointed Gary Cole, the ex–Heidelberg United striker, and Steve O'Connor, the ex–Sydney City defender, as his assistants.

By 1992, the AIS soccer program had been in operation for more than a decade, and under Smith it had grown into a sophisticated finishing school. He was employed not by the ASF but by the AIS, giving him the freedom to experiment with training loads, strength and conditioning programs, international tours, sports science and testing to determine a player's best position according to their physical profile.

The influence of Smith – in a quarantined, professional environment where the players could learn good on- and off-field behaviours, without fear of making mistakes – had a seismic impact on a generation of Australians. He gave Rudan, for example, a new name and a new position. Under Smith's guidance, 'Marko' the midfielder became 'Mark' the centre-back.

The AIS soccer program, in combination with the opportunity granted to these young men in the NSL and the demands of summer soccer, began to produce players who could mix it with the best in the world. After more than four decades of inhaling soccer players from all corners of the globe, Australia began gradually to exhale, becoming an exporter rather than an importer of talent.

It began with the 1992 Barcelona Olympics, in which the Olyroos – a select squad of elite under-23 players – finished fourth behind Spain, Poland and Ghana. Most were Australian-born, some were graduates of the AIS, many were the children of ethnic soccer clubs, each had enormous potential. 'The Olyroos in Barcelona,' Michael Cockerill once said, 'was the best Australian team I've ever seen.'

Yet at the start of the tournament, only three players were based overseas. By the end of 1992, however, Ned Zelic, Dominic Longo, John Filan, Milan Blagojevic, Shaun Murphy, Tony Vidmar, John Aloisi and Paul Agostino would sign for clubs in Belgium, Germany, England and Switzerland. And Frank Farina had become the first Australian player to play in Italy's Serie A after a record-breaking $3 million transfer from Club Brugge to Bari.

This was a source of enormous pride to Australian soccer fans and a statement of the game's global potential, yet the departure of so many talented players served to further damage the credibility of the NSL as a commercial product. The water-cooler conversations of rugby league, AFL and cricket supporters revolved around the best clubs, the best players and the best competitions. Soccer fans, meanwhile, had to feebly explain the enormity of Zlatko Arambasic playing for KV Mechelen.

★

With his impeccably Greek name and classic Mediterranean features, Kimon Taliadoros seemed to most a chip off the old block, the quintessential 'wog boy' of Australian soccer. Yet his entry into the game was far from pre-ordained.

He was a child migrant from South Africa, arriving in Australia with parents who were totally uninterested in soccer. Where his teammates were the sons of the working class, Taliadoros' parents were businesspeople. He was sent to Camberwell Grammar School, where he played cricket with the sons of Melbourne's aspirational class and learned to speak with an elocution that would have impressed the Queen. He was a highly urbane and adaptable young lad with a thoughtful sensitivity not usually afforded to strikers. His best mate was his girlfriend, he drove an open-topped Mini Moke around the eastern suburbs of Melbourne, and when he wasn't scoring goals for South Melbourne Hellas he studied to be an accountant.

The soccer community expected great things of Taliadoros. His was a frame strong and athletic, perfect for a striker, and his enthusiasm for scoring goals was limitless. He had run riot during season 1991–92, scoring a league-leading 15 goals, more than a quarter of South Melbourne Hellas' total output. The supporters loved him for his intensity and for his exuberant goal celebrations. Here was a player who had developed from a skinny kid to a ruthless competitor under their watchful gaze. Here was an ambassador for the club, a leader who could take Hellas into the 1990s – with a Greek surname to boot. This, the supporters felt, was one of their own.

Yet in the winter of 1992, as Ferenc Puskas departed South Melbourne, Taliadoros made a career-defining move north to Marconi. Soccer was just a part-time undertaking, but he had a family business opportunity in Sydney, and Remo Nogarotto, the soccer director at Marconi, had made him an attractive offer. Nogarotto was one of the more forward-thinking club officials and, with the weight of Marconi's reputation and finances, he had signed quality players from all over the country. When he organised a sit-down with Taliadoros, however, he was surprised to find him accompanied by a bookish young lawyer named Brendan Schwab.

Despite Taliadoros being off contract, George Vasilopoulos, the South Melbourne Hellas president, prevailed upon the Marconi directors to suggest that the transfer would murky the otherwise friendly relations between the two clubs. Pressure was placed on Nogarotto to call off the deal, while Taliadoros was accused by Hellas of going behind the club's back and of using 'business interests' as a ruse to sign with Marconi.

Taliadoros was just 25 years old, but with Schwab at his side he refused to be cowed by the contract negotiations. He knew his rights. With Nogarotto pulling the strings, Marconi paid the transfer fee and the matter was quickly resolved.

'What remained,' remembered Taliadoros, 'were the core issues. One, I was one person who happened to have a good friend who was capable of helping me. Two, I was a reasonably high-profile player and I had some influence, and there was some demand for me at Marconi, so they were prepared to go on the journey. I was very privileged not to suffer at the hands of the system. It occurred to me that players wouldn't be as fortunate as me and their careers would be affected.'

The deal would raise awareness about the rights of the individual against the might of the clubs, put the entire transfer and compensation system under the microscope, and hasten the advance of professionalism in the NSL. It would change soccer in Australia forever.

Nogarotto had a Bachelor of Economics, Taliadoros an accountancy degree; Schwab was a trainee industrial lawyer. It was not the usual round table.

'I'd spent eight years negotiating contracts with players, and Brendan Schwab was the first third-party, other than a wife or girlfriend, in the room negotiating,' Nogarotto later recalled. 'The first time ever. That was my sense things were changing. I think you can probably trace the seeds of the footballer representative movement to around that time.'

For as long as there had been organised, competitive soccer in Australia, there had been players screwed out of their contracts or left out of pocket by penny-pinching clubs. Before 1992, there had been several failed attempts by the players to organise collectively. As early as 1959, a goalkeeper named Ron Brown wrote a letter to *Soccer World* encouraging the players to unionise.

More than three decades on, the issues remained the same, but the partnership of Kimon Taliadoros and Brendan Schwab was the crucial variable.

Schwab first met Taliadoros at high school and the pair had quickly developed a bond. They opened the batting in the school First XI, kicked a soccer ball at lunchtime, talked Australian Rules footy during breaks, and played subbuteo for laughs. As opening batsmen in cricket, Schwab would always face the first ball of the innings, while Taliadoros would score the most runs. In school soccer, goalkeeper Schwab would belt the ball long from the back for Taliadoros to do the business up front. They formed an intuitive team.

Brendan Schwab was the eager son of Alan Schwab, a hugely respected AFL official. Alan Schwab was unlike the Australian Rules men of his generation: he had travelled widely, modelled Richmond Football Club on Matt Busby's Manchester United, and looked to America for inspiration. Throughout the 1980s, as he helped reform the Victorian Football League into the national Australian Football League, he would bring home high-level reviews and reports for his sons to rake through. Brendan was fascinated by his work.

'My father was a successful cricketer, he played for Transvaal in South Africa,' Kimon Taliadoros once explained. 'And of course Brendan's father was an outstanding sports executive, so the perspective we brought to football, because we hadn't been brought up in the football culture, was completely objective through the lens of professionalism and industrial relations. That perspective helped us to question the status quo.'

At the time of Taliadoros' transfer to Marconi, Schwab was an articled clerk not yet admitted to practise law. He was 25, worked at Holding Redlich, a well-regarded Labor law firm, and was looking to establish himself in sports administration. He was an intense young man, with an appearance that suggested maturity beyond his years.

He wore round spectacles, was of average height and build, and had pale skin and thinning brown hair. He was driven almost to distraction by his sense of injustice, possessing a prodigious work ethic and a cunning, strategic mind.

The Schwabs were people of policy detail and reform, not polemic and revolution, and by virtue of his father's role in footy Brendan felt at home in the society as it existed around him. Never a radical, he could see the capacity for individuals to make change through existing institutions. He joined the Labor Party while at university, and when his father learned of his ambition to start a players association, he handed him a copy of Marvin Miller's *A Whole Different Ball Game: The Sport and Business of Baseball.*

More than anything else, this book taught Brendan valuable lessons in how players unions could lead the reform of sporting organisations. Still, sensing some creative tension between their politics, Remo Nogarotto gave him the nickname 'Trotsky'.

What Nogarotto perhaps failed to realise, however, was that soccer players needed a Trotsky, someone with the requisite vision, intelligence, loyalty and commitment to the cause.

'I had a chat one day with a club president who said, "We've lost three on the trot, if these players expect to get their money, they might be waiting a while. Until I get a good performance I'm not going to pay them,"' remembered *Sydney Morning Herald* journalist Michael Cockerill. 'I thought, that's not really how it should work – this is wrong. And there were legion stories about players not getting paid, and a real obvious need for them to be represented. But it was more than that – there was also an incredible desire for the game to get better, not just at the narrow industrial level but the whole level.'

And so the battlelines were drawn: clubs and federation on one side, Schwab and his cadre of players on the other. Bosses and workers. On 27 April 1993, Schwab convened a special players meeting in the law courts at Chifley Square in Sydney's CBD. Thirty players joined the meeting, many in person, some via teleconference. Greg Brown, a colossal English striker at West Adelaide, was elected president, while

John Kosmina became his deputy. 'For too long,' Kosmina wrote in 1989, 'the system has been geared towards the financial interests of the clubs rather than the future of the players.'[7]

By September 1993, Braham Dabscheck, an industrial relations academic from the University of NSW, had become a close adviser. Since the early 1970s, Dabscheck had written numerous papers on the difficulty of forming players associations, but when he met Schwab, he wrote himself a little note that read: 'I have reason to be optimistic.'

The players also merged with the newly created professional sports branch of the Media, Entertainment and Arts Alliance, allowing it the funds to appoint Taliadoros as the chief executive. The union was concerned primarily with a transfer system that had allowed clubs to place huge fees on the heads of players, even after they had reached the end of their contract.

In no other industry did this make sense. If a baker or a labourer or a bank manager moved from one workplace to another, the new employer was not required to compensate the old one. The transfer and compensation system, as it was called, was deeply unpopular among the players. One poll found that 88 per cent wanted to see it abolished, while 94 per cent supported free agency to move to their club of choice.

The first effects of collective bargaining were evident in October 1993, as the Socceroos went down in a World Cup qualifier to Argentina. The players, who once received as little as $250 per game, earned $5000 thanks in part to the intervention of the players union. The biggest battles still lay ahead, however, not only to reform soccer's employment contract but also to solidify the union's longevity as an organisation. That month, investigative journalist Robert Galvin wrote an article for *Inside Sport* outlining the previous player movements that had been thwarted or simply collapsed.

'The lucky few will escape overseas,' he concluded. 'The rest will stay here, condemned, to soccer's great shame, to a life of sporting slavery.'[8]

★

As the players agitated for professional domestic career paths, the clubs instinctively pushed back, but they soon began to realise the magnitude of their obligations in this new, commercially oriented world. The Australian Unity Soccer Players Association reported that 70 per cent of the NSL players had signed up to the union, arousing fear among many club officials of increased wage demands and spiralling costs. Aware of the need to enliven the national league, the Australian Soccer Federation ploughed money into marketing and advertising. The 1994–95 season was launched by pop star Peter Andre, with the slogan 'Let's Get It On', while penalty shootouts were made mandatory for every match that ended in a draw. All eyes were firmly focused on the future.

On the first weekend of the new season, Peter Filopoulos, the South Melbourne Hellas general manager, made the familiar trip down to Middle Park. As young men filed into the ground in colourful baggy T-shirts and shorts, Albert Park Lake sparkled in the sun and the city skyline shimmered in the distance. Filopoulos' father, George, arm linked with his wife Joanna, wore sunglasses with his usual Sunday finery of shirt and slacks. The blue and white of South Melbourne was complemented by the familiar sound of Lefteri's trumpet and the sweet smell of souvlaki. It was a time to say goodbye.

Sunday 23 October 1994 was the opening round of the 19th season of the NSL and the final game at Middle Park, soccer's first cradle in Australia.

Middle Park, or Oval 18 as it was once known, sat on an old landfill site in between the Albert Park Lake and the St Kilda railway line. As many as 18,000 supporters could cram inside, and for the big games they sometimes did. Built on land that was once shared with cyclists, the ground traced the shape of a velodrome, and a tin-shed grandstand with wooden seats faced north-west towards the lake. Spectators were free to wander around the ground to select the best vantage point, but from the bleachers you could see all the way back to the city. When it was full, as it was for the final match, between South Melbourne and Heidelberg United, it was a fortress. Kimon Taliadoros once described playing at Middle Park as 'like riding a wave of emotion'.

South Melbourne needed to beat Heidelberg that day, not only for the competition points but to honour the memory of Middle Park. On the bench was coach Frank Arok and his young assistant Ange Postecoglou; on the field was an all-star cast that included Kevin Muscat, Paul Trimboli, Con Boutsianis, Mehmet Durakovic and Paul Wade.

South Melbourne went ahead after just three minutes through a Boutsianis goal, but when he left the field with an injury half an hour later, Peter Tsolakis pulled a goal back for Heidelberg. He was an ex-South Melbourne player and as he wheeled away in celebration he reminded the home fans of that fact. 'It was a Greek derby,' Francis Awaritefe later recalled, 'but although there was an intense rivalry between the clubs there wasn't any nastiness.'

Born in London to Nigerian parents, Awaritefe was one of the many soccer players who became Australians at Middle Park. Having arrived in Australia in 1988, he had gone for a trial at Middle Park because it was the closest national league ground to his home in Elwood. It was not a successful experience. Told to try his luck in the state league, in 1989 he went to Melbourne Croatia, and by 1992, he scored 14 goals to finish just one behind Taliadoros.

South Melbourne, who lost Taliadoros to Marconi during that off-season, bought Awaritefe in the winter of 1992. He was soon recognised by the soccer community as a lethal striker and as a sex symbol. With midnight-black dreadlocks and a long, slender frame, Awaritefe was slick on the pitch and effortlessly cool off it. He wore the latest threads, listened to good music and talked with a sophisticated accent. He smiled a lot, and the media loved him for it.

When the *Soccer Australia* magazine profiled him, they asked an astrologist to give an 'unbiased angle' on his character. 'Francis exerts a childlike, restless energy' was the assessment, 'fiery, impulsive and impatient, but when channelled, it transforms into power and propelling speed.'[9]

After half-time, Awaritefe put the home side 2–1 ahead with a tremendous goal from an acute angle. As the momentum shifted, Ivan

Kelic scored two goals for South Melbourne to complete a famous second-half comeback.

The game finished 4–1 to South Melbourne, and Middle Park was given the farewell it deserved. 'You had a sense that something historic had happened,' remembered Awaritefe. 'Middle Park just had a magic and a history that the others didn't. It was a privilege to be able to play the last game at that ground. I remember people running on, hugging and thanking us – it was a big deal that we didn't lose that last game.'

After the final whistle, Peter Filopoulos walked slowly around the pitch. Old men were crying. Several supporters had ripped wooden panels off the grandstand and were digging up patches of turf to take home as a souvenir. This was it.

In Filopoulos' head, he knew it was the right move – the old place was crumbling, and he was convinced that the new arrangement would to lead to South Melbourne Hellas' renaissance. But his heart was heavy. Middle Park had been a place of devotion for generations of Greek families in Melbourne, including his own. He had been introduced to Middle Park by his uncle Jim, and as a kid he ran around the ground with friends as South Melbourne transitioned from state league to national league. As a teenager he stood on the terraces and marvelled at Oscar Crino; as a young adult he worked out of the crammed offices underneath the grandstand.

Middle Park was what made South Melbourne a proper soccer club. The stadium, the car park, the social club and the junior fields were all organised on one self-contained piece of land. 'It was a place where you met a girl, a place you made friends, a place you played soccer,' Filopoulos once explained. 'Everything at the core of a young man's life.'

The demolition of Middle Park was brought about by Jeff Kennett, the then Victorian premier who partnered with Ron Walker from the Australian Grand Prix Corporation to bring the car race to Melbourne. Middle Park was in the way.

If history is written by the victors, perhaps it was fitting for the old soccer ground to be bulldozed to make way for another sporting event. From the early days, soccer people fought for Middle Park in the face of local opposition. As Australian Rules football bullied the other soccer clubs, mostly backed by immigrants, into marginal areas of outer Melbourne, Middle Park remained soccer's refuge in the heart of the city. If Albert Park is 'the lungs of Melbourne', then Middle Park provided the crucial oxygen for the world game. When the last light was turned out at Middle Park, and the supporters filed out of the ground for the final time, something died. The Victorian soccer tribe had lost their most sacred meeting place.

Middle Park was destroyed as a result of an uneasy coalition between the state government and the South Melbourne board. South traded their home for a $3.8 million reimbursement package and a new stadium at Lakeside Oval, which was still in the Albert Park precinct. Jeff Kennett became an enthusiastic supporter of South Melbourne and the number-one ticket holder. The place where Middle Park once stood became the pit lane for the Formula 1 Grand Prix.

With St George consigned to the NSW first division, the game's two spiritual homes – St George Stadium and Middle Park – would never again host a national league match. Their abandonment would pave the way for the abandonment of all the old ways, as soccer hurtled headlong into a future of new stadiums, new clubs, new people and new traditions.

'That final day just forced you to think about all those times, and the fact you weren't going to be able to show people the grandstand and the dressing rooms and the history,' Postecoglou once remembered. 'It was the end of an era.'

Directly across town, on the wrong side of the Maribyrnong River, Mark Viduka ran onto a well-placed pass and, as the opposition coach screamed at the referee for offside, calmly slotted the ball into the back of the net. The match finished 1–0 to Melbourne Knights. A week later, Viduka scored a double against Wollongong, and within four matches his tally was four goals. By Round 7, as Knights recorded its seventh straight win, setting a new record for the best start to a national league season, Viduka was motoring along at a goal a game.

On the railings of soccer grounds around Melbourne, a long white banner began to appear. In between two Croatian coats of arms were the words '… AND ON THE 7th DAY, GOD CREATED VIDUKA'.

By 1994 the AIS had taken in new students, and the class of 1992–93 had been cast out into the world of top-flight soccer. Craig Moore and John Aloisi had gone overseas. Clint Bolton had almost signed with Marconi, but decided instead to join the Brisbane Strikers. There was never any question about where Mark Viduka or Mark Rudan would end up. They had returned to Melbourne Croatia and Sydney Croatia, which after a decree from the Australian Soccer Federation had dropped the name Croatia for 'Knights' and 'United'.

Of all the AIS graduates, Viduka was the quickest to adapt to men's soccer. He had made his NSL debut in 1993, and had scored his first senior goal in just his second match. After each goal he would run to the sidelines, right arm raised, left hand tugging at his shirt to kiss the club badge.

This immediately drew the ire of those who wanted to see the worst in his community. 'Is it necessary for him to give the fascist salute and kiss the Croatian flag on his shirt every time he scores a goal?' complained one letter writer in 1994. 'If he loves Croatia so much, he should return to the land of his parents.'[10]

When asked on national television why he performed the celebration, Viduka just smiled, shrugged his shoulders and replied: 'Because the oldies like it.'

With his devotion to his club and respect for the elders of his community, Viduka represented all that was good and right about Australian soccer. He stood at over six feet tall, with shy eyes, a small grin and a floppy haircut. He possessed unshakable balance, a combination of poise and power not seen before or since. By 1994, Melbourne Knights games had become the Mark Viduka variety hour, his opponents reduced to props in a one-man theatrical performance.

But he was as lazy off the field as he was luxurious on it. He didn't train particularly hard, and he would not go to the gym unless ordered to. He ate fast food, and spoke his mind. When asked by one reporter what he did away from soccer, he said he liked to sleep. When pressed on post-career plans, he said he wanted to 'live it up'. He had swagger. Even the way he wore his jersey, with the front always slightly untucked, gave him an air of casual assurance.

Not everyone saw these qualities straight away. If his surname were Fitzpatrick instead of Viduka, if his club were Collingwood instead of Melbourne Knights, if his sport were Australian Rules instead of soccer, he would have been the delight of an entire nation. Instead, outsiders and soccer's assimilationists queried his loyalty to Australia. Others wondered if he had the temperament to match his talent.

Viduka buried these concerns in an avalanche of goals. In 1993–94, his debut season, he had scored 17 goals in 21 appearances, winning the Golden Boot, the under-21 player of the year, and the senior player of the year. This was an historic personal achievement, but he longed for a championship – not just for himself but for his club, which had lost three grand finals in four seasons. Seven goals in seven unbeaten games was a good way to start.

By Round 20, everything appeared perfect at Melbourne Knights. The club sat on top of the ladder on 61 points, 11 clear of second-placed Adelaide City. Coach Mirko Bazic's investment in youth was reaping a fruitful harvest, and he had the side playing consistent and clinical soccer. Viduka was top of the goal-scoring charts. And with Middle Park demolished, the Croatian Sports Centre – later known as Knights Stadium – had become the best soccer-specific venue in Victoria. The supporters could not be happier.

Then their captain, Joe Biskic, a 35-year-old club legend and an idol of Viduka's, dropped a bombshell. Selangor, a cashed-up club from Malaysia, had made him an incredible offer that would secure his future. After 278 NSL games for Knights, having anchored the midfield for more than a decade, 'Biska' played his final game against

Heidelberg United. Melbourne Knights won 6–2. The goalscorers for Knights were Steve Horvat, Oliver Pondeljak, Vinko Buljubasic, David Cervinski and, of course, Mark Viduka. It signalled the arrival of a new generation.

Yet for the final two rounds and the two major semifinals, Melbourne Knights were forced to continue without Viduka, who was on leave with the Australian under-20 team in Qatar for the World Youth Championships. There he wrapped a red, white and blue captain's armband around his green and gold sleeve and, along-side former AIS teammates Mark Rudan, Clint Bolton and Josip Skoko, qualified for the knockout stages of the tournament.

With Viduka on national team duty in Qatar, Knights lost the two-legged playoff to Adelaide City, forcing it into a preliminary final against South Melbourne at Olympic Park. 'We are one team with Viduka,' admitted coach Mirko Bazic, 'and another team without him.'[11]

It was the third time in three seasons that South Melbourne and Melbourne Knights had met in a finals match. South Melbourne had the clear psychological advantage, having won two, including the grand final in 1991. But in 1991 Viduka was a ballboy. In 1995 he was a lethal striker looking to make up for lost time.

After just 13 minutes, in pouring rain, Knights midfielder Danny Tiatto careered along the wet turf and clumsily upended a South Melbourne midfielder. The referee flashed a red card in Tiatto's face and ordered him from the field. It should have been advantage to South Melbourne, but Kresimir Marusic – the nimble midfielder brought over from Croatia to replace Biskic – had other ideas. He created two opportunities for Viduka, who finished both to put Knights 2–1 ahead at half-time. On 53 minutes, Viduka scored again – his second hat-trick of the season, and the winning goal. 'I really only had three chances and I took them all,' he said simply after the match. 'That's what I'm paid to do.'[12]

With the South Melbourne hoodoo put to rest, attention turned to the grand final against Adelaide City. Twice in the previous three seasons City had beaten Melbourne Knights to win the NSL trophy. And although Viduka hadn't agreed to any contract offers, the Knights fans knew it would be his last game for the club. When asked in the pre-game build up where he was headed, Viduka was evasive. 'I think I'd be able to fit in most parts of Europe,' he mused. 'I'm not too fond of England, I just think it's a bit too quick for me, and I'm sort of a lazy player. I don't really like running that much. Anywhere in Europe – Germany, France, you know, wherever I can get a good contract.'[13]

Just as he did in the 1991 grand final, Andrew Marth, the Melbourne Knights captain, scored the opening goal. This time Knights did not let the lead slip. With just minutes remaining before half-time, Viduka picked up possession on the left, drew the attention of three defenders, and slid a neat pass to Marusic. With the Adelaide defence out of shape, Marusic crossed for Joe Spiteri to secure a famous 2–0 victory for Melbourne Knights.

For the second season running, Viduka won the Golden Boot, the under-21 player of the year and the senior player of the year. He had been the first player to win the clean sweep of awards, and the only person ever to win it in consecutive seasons.

Australian soccer would never again see a man like him. Not only for his goal-scoring prowess and his records, but because of what he represented. Since the age of six, he had only ever appeared for Melbourne Knights – the club that he was born to play for. He would never play for another Australian club. In an increasingly mercenary age, he was truly the last of the Mohicans.

When the team arrived back in Melbourne, a throng of jubilant supporters mobbed the players at the airport. Croatian flags were thrust in front of television cameras, and a reporter noted that the fans had 'failed to adapt to the name change' as chants drowned out the terminal. At the centre of it all was a sweaty, wide-eyed Viduka, grinning from ear to ear. Like a rock star entering a mosh pit, he chanted 'CRO-A-ZIA, CRO-A-ZIA, CRO-A-ZIA!'

★

'Melbourne Croatia was very, very welcoming,' recalled Francis Awaritefe, who played with the club between 1989 and 1992. 'The people were unbelievable. They're conservative people, mostly, however they're very community-oriented and they care about the collective. The football club is a big part of their community – to play for the football club was a big deal.'

Five weeks after the 1995 grand final, the newly elected Croatian president, Franjo Tudjman, flew into Australia on diplomatic business. Thousands of Serbs marched in protest in Sydney, Melbourne and Perth. Amid cries of 'Tudjman: Fascist!', the Croatian president stood at Sydney Airport and encouraged Australian Croats to return to the homeland. 'There is more than half of Croatia's population living overseas because of the previous government,' recognised Tudjman, 'but in the past five years we have established a government that guarantees our future. Come with your skills, know-how and your money, but more importantly, just come.'[14]

To understand the intensity of feeling among Australia's Serb and Croat communities, one needed only to look to the fate of Yakka Banovic's indoor soccer centre in Geelong. The former Socceroos goalkeeper had established the business in 1993 to rave reviews. The centre thrived, attracting all of Geelong's multicultural community, including Banovic's fellow Croats. Fatefully, however, when Banovic asked the *Geelong Advertiser* to run an advertorial, the newspaper used the term 'Yugoslav'. The Croats were furious, a boycott was arranged, and the centre collapsed within a year.

In this context, Tudjman's visit was a delicate matter for the Labor government. Recognising that it was impossible to please both the Serb and Croat communities, Prime Minister Paul Keating decided on the path of least resistance. He welcomed Tudjman to Canberra with a flourish befitting Croatia's first diplomatic visit, pointing to the tremendous contribution of Croats to the Australian economy, from the gold rush of the 1850s to the builders, farmers and fishermen of the 20th century. Acknowledging that Croats 'helped build modern Australia', Keating said: 'Along the way, Croatian-Australians have introduced their love of soccer through players such as this year's player of the year, Mark Viduka.'[15]

A republican by instinct and conviction, Keating waxed lyrical about the privileges and responsibilities of Croatia's hard-won independence. He told Tudjman that Croats had helped develop Australia's sense of self. 'They have done this, as they must, with their loyalty to Australia first,' he promised.[16]

Next day, Tudjman continued to Melbourne. In a rousing 40-minute speech at the sports precinct in the heart of the city, he was cheered on wildly by 8000 loyal Croats. A writer and historian, he traded in propaganda, myth and legend.

To the Croats in Australia, with their frustrated, long-distance nationalism, Tudjman embellished the Croatia that had incubated in their imagination. After thanking them for the years of support from afar, Tudjman promised to 'liberate' all the remaining parts of 'real Croatia'. One reporter noted that 'he saluted the crowd like a prize fighter, clasping his hands over his head and gesturing to all parts of the stadium'.[17]

Diplomatic mission complete, Tudjman sought an audience with Mark Viduka not once but twice. First, they ate at Vlado's, a dimly lit steakhouse run by a kindly Zagreb-born restaurateur. It was the perfect setting – small, plain-white tables, Croatian music, and antiques and photos from the old country. Then, before he flew back to Croatia, Tudjman entertained Viduka in his private jet. The president had strong ties to Dinamo Zagreb, one of Croatia's top clubs. Indeed it was under Tudjman's watch that the name 'Dinamo', which he associated with the communists, was replaced by 'Croatia'.

Here was an unprecedented scene in Australian sport: Viduka, the young prince of Australia's Croatian community, being courted by a president they idolised. For an ethnic group that had explicitly used soccer for political and nationalistic ends, this was glorious affirmation.

Tudjman was impatient, asking the young striker to come to Croatia immediately. Although Viduka had also attracted interest from clubs all over Europe, including Real Madrid, and a $1 million offer from Japan, within a week he was on a plane to Croatia. In his diary, Viduka wrote that he arrived at Zagreb Airport in the afternoon.

'Many reporters are there to greet me and all are curious about why I have chosen Croatia to further my soccer career,' he noted. 'My main reasons are that I am of Croatian origin, I want to learn the language properly and I want a club where I will actually get to play every week rather than sit on the bench or be in the reserves. Other clubs offered more money, but I know that I will be more comfortable over here.'[18]

Viduka joined three other Australians of Croat parentage. At Hajduk Split were Paul Bilokapic from Sydney Croatia; Steve Horvat, alumnus of North Geelong Croatia; and Josip Skoko, from Mount Gambier Croatia in South Australia. All except Bilokapic, who returned to Sydney after his trial, would become well-known players in the Croatian first division.

Viduka noted 'an atmosphere of fear as well as one of patriotism' and during Operation Storm, the last major battle of the Homeland War, he learned that his father's village had been liberated from Serb occupation.[19] This happy news was clouded by worry for the wellbeing of his cousins, who all fought in the Croatian army. And in his first big derby against Hajduk Split, he scored the winning goal. It made him immensely popular. In one match, the crowd chanted for him to take a penalty instead of the usual penalty-taker, Josko Jelicic. As Jelicic threw his shirt to the ground in disgust, Viduka scored to complete his first hat-trick for Croatia Zagreb.

Still, his idealised version of Croatia began to crumble. When he travelled with his father to their ancestral village, he found razed houses and his grandfather's grave rendered unrecognisable by vandals. He could see the skeletons. As homesickness crept in, he longed for his mum's cooking and the relaxed atmosphere of Melbourne Knights. Back home he could go to nightclubs, muck around, talk to girls and enjoy being young. In Zagreb, when he went to restaurants and bars he was enveloped in his own celebrity. His sense of identity started to shift. He wasn't a Croat born in Australia; he was an Australian of Croatian heritage. A small distinction, perhaps, but an important one.

By October, as autumn leaves covered Zagreb's handsome streets, Viduka celebrated his 20th birthday with a bowl of Weet-Bix and a phone call from his sisters. 'Every morning a thick fog covers the city,' he wrote in his diary. 'It usually starts to snow in December but by then I will be back in Melbourne for my mid-season break – and I can't wait.'[20]

A GENEROSITY OF SPIRIT

1996–1998

It's about attitudes and vision. It's about removing forever counter-productive rivalries and power bases. It's about acknowledging the ethnic community's indisputable contribution to Australian soccer, without alienating the growing non-ethnic throng of soccer players and supporters. It's about the future, not the past.

George Negus
Sydney Morning Herald, 1996[1]

Soccer entered 1996 beset by rumour and recrimination, and in the shadow of a national scandal. For more than 12 months, a coalition of player representatives, journalists, federal senators and a crime-fighting Supreme Court judge, the Honourable Donald Stewart, had aired allegations of corruption at the heart of the Australian Soccer Federation.

Stewart had recommended, among other things, that Socceroos coaches Eddie Thomson and Les Scheinflug be sacked, that the activities of former Socceroos bosses Frank Arok and Rale Rasic be further investigated for criminal conduct, and that club officials Tony Labbozzetta, Berti Mariani and Alfio Bulic never again hold any position of power within the game. When the first Stewart Report was published, one reporter called it 'the worst week in the history of Australian soccer'.[2]

There were concerns, relayed through public and private channels, that coaches and officials had pocketed bribes for the selection of
players, and appropriated transfer fees from overseas clubs for personal
gain. Perhaps the highest-profile cases were Paul Okon's 1991 transfer
to Club Brugge, which brought Labbozzetta's integrity into question,
and Thomson's role in the transfer of Ned Zelic to Borussia Dortmund.
As the courts had no power to subpoena or protect witnesses, however,
the allegations never shifted from opinion to judicial findings, and one
by one the individuals had been cleared of wrongdoing.

'There was a moment in the hearings at Parliament House,' recalled
Sydney Morning Herald journalist Michael Cockerill, 'where I was
looking out of the window seeing the Olyroos training in the Domain,
of which half a dozen of those players were listed in the [Stewart]
Report. There they are, literally outside the window training, instead
of being in there substantiating anything. Why weren't they inside
giving evidence? They had a bit to say off the record, but they never
fronted up to their day in court.'

Still, the scandal helped to entrench a view that the union had been
prosecuting for years: that the game was riddled with corruption, and
that the players had been unfairly treated by their clubs. And it was the
players, through their union, who were the biggest beneficiaries of the
sorry episode.

The Senate inquiry supported Stewart's recommendation that
players be granted better conditions, and that the domestic transfer fee
'be abolished entirely'. This recommendation was soon complemented
by a demand from the Industrial Relations Commission that transfer
and compensation fees should be phased out 'by the end of 1996'.[3] And
then, thousands of kilometres away in the European Court of Justice,
the Bosman Ruling decreed that players were free to move at the end
of their contracts, and that restrictions on foreign players in European
leagues be eased.

Cumulatively, the results of the Stewart Report, the decision of the
Industrial Relations Commission and the Bosman Ruling shifted the
balance of power from clubs to players, led to the rise of player agents,

and sent European talent scouts to the uncharted territories of Africa, Australasia and the Americas. The Industrial Relations Commission decision, in particular, would force the governing body and the clubs to meet with the union and negotiate soccer's first ever collective bargaining agreement. The players union, which had rebranded as the Australian Soccer Players Association, was content with the progress it had made.

'We wanted to give every player the opportunity to achieve the most they could,' Kimon Taliadoros once explained. 'Those that were talented – there's a market out there and it's not in Australia. So it's in the players' interests, and their own financial interests, to pursue it if they want. But in addition to that, we were obsessed and committed to providing local, domestic career paths.'

The acute demands brought forward by the players and the pressures of an increasingly globalised football economy gave rise to fears for the future of the National Soccer League. More than ever before, soccer had become a business. Players began to see themselves as workers, clubs as commercial enterprises, and officials as bosses. The clubs and federations could no longer survive on passion alone – they needed new streams of revenue, high-level officials and corporate support.

Yet the administration of soccer had neither the function nor the reputational strength to meet these challenges. The Stewart Report and the subsequent Senate inquiry had torn through the game like a tornado, leaving in their wake a splattered picture of corrupt men presiding over a small kingdom of broken homes and incompetent institutions.

Many found it impossible to recover from the intense scrutiny. Eddie Thomson resigned as Socceroos coach and took a job in Japan. Kimon Taliadoros, who for more than a year had worked closely with the reporters and given evidence at the hearings, became public enemy number one at many of the clubs, while Michael Cockerill was ostracised for years by the soccer fraternity for his investigative reporting.

One journalist wrote that soccer was 'split more ways than a kid's birthday cake'.[4] Senator John Coulter called soccer 'mafia-like', while

Senator Michael Baume had been even more blunt. 'The game is in need of an enema,' he said. 'It won't like it but it will make it feel a lot better.'[5]

David Hill, the Australian Soccer Federation's swashbuckling new chairman, had been handed the rectal syringe and a group of totally uncooperative men. Elected on 1 April 1995 – April Fools' Day – his first nine months in office had brought the biggest sea-change to the organisation since its inception in 1962.

He changed the federation's name to Soccer Australia, signed a lucrative contract with pay television network Optus, brought television journalist George Negus onto the board, appointed basketball administrator David Woolley as the chief executive and repatriated Stefan Kamasz to run the NSL. And he cut Heidelberg United, Brunswick Juventus and Melita Eagles from the competition, replacing them with Newcastle Breakers and Canberra Cosmos, which brought the total number of clubs in the NSL to 12.

Born in England in 1946 to a destitute, determined mother and an absent father, Hill was sent to Australia as a child migrant. He quickly adjusted his vocabulary as he learned that football meant rugby league or Australian Rules, not soccer, and he matched his support for Manchester United with a new allegiance to North Sydney Bears, a rugby league team that he played for and presided over between 1989 and 1992. He had previously been in charge of the NSW State Rail Authority and the ABC, and his career detailed the life of a reform-minded, head-kicking, union-busting public servant.

He was a precise republican, a white-marble nugget with thinning grey hair swept off his forehead, beady eyes and round shoulders that seemed to start at his jawline. He spoke with a soft English lilt, claimed to be a Labor man without faction, but, as one NSL player put it, he was 'further right than Genghis Khan'. Those within soccer saw him as a meddling outsider. Hill, on the other hand, saw himself as representative of a silent majority. 'What was lacking in soccer,' he once explained, 'was a generosity of spirit. There was such entrenched interests.'

Together Hill and Negus formed an enterprising team. They were both known throughout Australia's intellectual class and well versed in the language of the Anglo old-boy networks. Both were self-styled cosmopolitans, and their greatest wish was to localise the world game – to hear it hold court at the water coolers of corporate boardrooms, on the shop floors and in the schoolyards. They sought a mandate for reform from regular supporters just as much as they did from club officials.

This was perhaps best illustrated in the winter of 1995, when they hosted the first and last soccer summit in Melbourne. It was packaged as a forum for new ideas and a renewed spirit of cooperation, with the editors of *Studs Up*, a newly formed fanzine from Melbourne, invited to give a presentation.

From the inaugural issue in December 1994, *Studs Up* had set out to kick heads and take names. It gave Hill reserved support, prioritised articles written by regular fans, and published history columns, feature interviews and a bulletin board for other supporters to advertise their own fanzines. The lively 'Did That REALLY Happen?' section provided supporters an entertaining wrap-up of life following the always-outlandish NSL.

'Soccer is funny,' once explained Matthew Hall, a freelance journalist and occasional contributor to *Studs Up*. 'It's hilarious – the characters you have in the game are ridiculous, the things that occur off the pitch are comedic. This was a time when there was so much material for someone just to poke fun at all the self-righteous posturing that was going on.'

Studs Up was the brainchild of Kevin Christopher, a scruffy, democratic editor who smoked too much, wore crumpled clothes and loved heavy metal. He worked odd jobs to make ends meet, and ploughed his money and time into the fanzine. There was never a lot of cash, however, and for its entire existence *Studs Up* was printed in black and white, on 18 sheets of A4 paper folded in half, stapled together, and mailed out to subscribers, members of the soccer media, and the heads of state and national federations. Apart from being stocked by Santo

Caruso's Elizabeth Street bookstore, Melbourne Sports Books, it relied mostly on word of mouth for sales.

Christopher's house in Oakleigh, the heart of Greek Melbourne, had quickly become a drop-in centre for soccer supporters. He was a long-distance West Ham fan and a casual South Melbourne supporter, and many of his friends were Greek, including his assistant editor, Harry Georgiadis.

When Georgiadis met Christopher, he was roped into playing soccer for his Sunday amateur team and came to see the game in a different light. 'A real bugbear of Kevin's was that the ethnic component of the clubs held the game back a bit,' Georgiadis once recalled. 'We needed a competition that was for all Australians, and could take the game into the mainstream. Being the son of migrants, I had my club; I had South Melbourne. I never thought of it until I met Kevin. He was like, hang on, why can't this game be bigger than it is? Why can't this game be mainstream?'

Many people, particularly David Hill, agreed, and it was at the soccer summit that he first prosecuted the case. Both Hill and Negus spoke about 'Australianising' the game, while Damien Stenmark, an adman, called for the national league to start anew with one, privately capitalised team from each city.

The famous actor and Sydney Olympic member Lex Marinos implored the existing ethnic clubs to broaden their base of support, while Wanda Jamrozik, a journalist from the *Australian* newspaper, made the controversial suggestion of a media ban on ethnic accents.[6]

Jamrozik's intervention was representative of a fast-growing number of first- and second-generation Australians who had lost patience with soccer's attachment to ethnicity. Not long after the summit, she likened the ethnic clubs to 'secret societies', accusing them of being 'inward looking', 'paranoid' and 'dependent on a whole range of cues and codes, some of them not so subtle, to exclude outsiders'.[7]

This assimilationist tendency was soon supported by prevailing political winds. In March 1996, as Melbourne Knights defended its NSL title with a grand final win over Marconi, the Liberal Party returned to power after more than a decade in opposition.

The small, reanimated political corpse of John Howard came to office promising that he was the 'average Australian bloke'. His campaign ad – 'For all of us/Not just for one/For all of us/Not just for some' – was a sharp rebuke of the identity politics of the 1990s. He pined openly for the 1950s and told Australians to be 'comfortable and relaxed'. He had long opposed multiculturalism on the grounds that it had eaten away at a 'common Australian culture' and that it had forced Australians 'to pretend that we are a federation of cultures and that we've got a bit from every part of the world'.[8] And when Pauline Hanson, the flagrantly obnoxious leader of the racist One Nation party, called for a return to assimilation, Howard's response was to acknowledge that her views 'were an accurate reflection of what people feel'.[9]

Like David Hill, Howard had played soccer as a child, and like so many Anglo-Australians they had both drifted away from the game and developed a passion for rugby league and cricket. Neither appreciated the presence of ethnic teams. They, like tens of thousands of the uninvolved Australians, saw the NSL as anathema to the Australian sporting tradition.

Right or wrong, this perception had cost the game supporters, administrators, corporate dollars and many talented players. Before he became a star batsman in the Australian cricket team, Steve Waugh had excelled as a soccer player at Sydney Croatia. But he believed cricket was the national sport, and in his autobiography he would complain that 'being Anglo-Saxon was a major hindrance' in soccer because he could not speak Greek or Italian 'or whatever language was the basis for their conversations'.[10]

So while Waugh became a national hero in cricket, Australian soccer continued to debate its three central issues – ethnicity, commercialism and professionalism. The tension between an aggressive players union, a powerful lobby of traditional clubs and a forthright, reformist chairman brought the three major conversations together at terrifying speed.

By the middle of 1996, as the NSL prepared for its 21st season, the founding fathers were either dead or departed, and just five of the original 14 clubs – Marconi, South Melbourne, Adelaide City, Sydney Olympic and West Adelaide – remained.

Yet the view that the ethnic clubs would gradually evolve and find wider support, which had been the dominant school of thought for more than two decades, had come to sound fanciful. Meanwhile, the one-town-teams in Canberra, Wollongong, Brisbane and Newcastle struggled along, full of potential but short of both money and interest.

From the moment the league began, soccer authorities had allowed these competing club models to exist side by side. During the 1996–97 season, however, something would snap. Distrust between the game's great tribes and the soccer assimilationists would reach fever pitch. A revolutionary new team would arise in Perth, another would rise and fall in Melbourne, and there would be calls for the end to the ethnic clubs and for breakaway leagues.

Even before the season kicked off, the editors of the *Greek Herald* accused Hill of saddling all evil on the backs of immigrants, 'as Hitler did to the Jews', and called on him to resign.[11] So began the most politically unhinged season in the history of the NSL. It was a final showdown – the season in which the Australian soccer community decided that it wanted a national league, not a league of nations.

★

By objective calculation, soccer was the most popular football code in Australia. During 1995 and 1996, the Australian Bureau of Statistics had collected participation data of all sport and recreation activities, concluding that Australian Rules football had 146,400 players, rugby league 83,000 and rugby union just 69,600.

Soccer, meanwhile, had 162,700 total players, and if you were to include indoor soccer the number would rise to nearly 200,000 participants. Significantly, between the ages of five and 14, soccer had nearly double the number of participants than that of Australian Rules football, and triple that of rugby league.[12] Soccer was also vastly more popular among women, and had a wider geographic spread across the country.

The signs of this dominance were everywhere. Every evening through the winter months, parks and council grounds would be packed with children and parents at soccer training, and the word 'soccer mum' had become part of the Australian lexicon. The rise of the English Premier League, broadcast on SBS on Monday nights, gave Australians unprecedented access to one of the richest sporting competitions in the world. The Australian Women's Soccer Association, despite more than two decades of separate and unequal development, was ready to launch the first ever national women's league of any football code. And the internet gave supporters new ways of engaging with overseas leagues and with each other.

One of the first Australian soccer websites was *OzSoccer.net*, set up by two fans named Thomas Esamie and Greg Baxter, which functioned primarily as an emailing list between supporters from around the country. Many of the contributors were *Studs Up* subscribers, and the website and fanzine soon developed a symbiotic relationship. *Studs Up* dedicated a page to 'Internet News', *OzSoccer* advertised *Studs Up* on its homepage, and when Andrew Howe started a supporters' tipping competition for *OzSoccer* he published the results in the fanzine. Their partnership allowed supporters to have frank, honest and unmediated discussions about the issues facing the domestic game, and helped foster valuable friendships that would last a lifetime.

These were fabulous conditions for the NSL to capitalise upon. The challenge for David Hill was to capture the new wave of enthusiasm, convert soccer's demographic opportunity into supporters at the gate, and assimilate each of the game's constituent parts into a coherent and marketable whole. With the Socceroos aiming to qualify for the FIFA World Cup in 1998, Hill had little more than a year to drastically revitalise the NSL.

In 20 seasons, the competition had existed on the verge of total collapse, forever struggling for attention, always desperate for new money, and perennially sidetracked by intractable questions over image and identity. Privately, Hill wished he could simply wipe the slate clean and place brand new clubs in strategic areas with anglicised names and non-denominational logos. In the knowledge that this was a utopian dream, he decided instead to introduce a few new clubs and, as George Negus often put it, 'Australianise' the existing ethnic teams.

On the eve of the new season, in mid-August 1996, Soccer Australia circulated a letter to the NSL clubs ordering them to 'remove all symbols of European nationalism from club logos, playing strips, club flags, stadium names and letterheads'.[13]

Of particular concern was the Italian tricolour and the Croatian *sahovnica* on the crests of Adelaide City, Melbourne Knights, Sydney United and Marconi. Even the letter 'H' on the grandstand at Bob Jane Stadium, which formed one part of the South Melbourne Hellas acronym, was deemed too ethnic. When the clubs protested against the order, Hill simply threatened them with expulsion.

'As part of the broadening of the appeal of soccer, we're about to launch a new plan to sell national soccer gear throughout Australia,' he reasoned in an article for the *Daily Telegraph*. 'It is [...] important that we market gear which has maximum appeal to the broadest mainstream of Australian society.'[14]

Hill was correct in the diagnosis but wrong in the prescription. In the two decades leading to 1996, it had been proven that the ethnic clubs were incapable of attracting a wide cross-section of supporters. Yet history had also shown that cosmetic changes did nothing to reverse that trend – Hakoah had not drawn bigger crowds as 'Sydney Slickers', Footscray JUST were no more popular under the name 'Melbourne City', and, if anything, de-ethnicisation had turned the traditional supporters away from the game.

Unsurprisingly, the issue split the soccer community in two. Supporters screamed about racial discrimination, while club officials spoke of protests to the Human Rights Commission. It was front-page news for several weeks in the *Australian and British Soccer Weekly*, and the cause of much debate in *Studs Up*. In the *Sydney Morning Herald* and the *Daily Telegraph*, the editors dedicated double-page spreads to the issue, inviting submissions from a variety of different viewpoints. 'By failing to adopt a truly Aussie image,' wrote one reporter, 'soccer shot itself in the foot.'[15]

Perhaps the most strident critic of David Hill and George Negus was Johnny Warren. At his farm in Gold Creek, he nicknamed his two pet goats 'David' and 'George', and in a column for the *Sydney Morning Herald* he denounced Soccer Australia's policy as 'racist and discrimina-tory', and 'a microcosm of the whole nation's problem'.[16] In response, Negus called Warren 'spiteful and personally jaundiced'.

The logos and letterheads became landmines in a bitter, territorial war for the game's spiritual heartland. Warren lobbed the heavy artil-lery, defending the ethnic clubs as '*real* soccer people', while Negus played the divide-and-rule game of a colonial diplomat, promising that the ethnic community had a role in the game's future even if 'they don't own it!'.[17]

Soccer had been through this imbroglio at least twice a decade since World War II, tried countless combinations of nicknames and logos and, ultimately, achieved no consensus on the matter. The only NSL club that remained essentially as it had been in the 1950s was Marconi. For almost 30 years it had defied all the orders, kept its name, its colours and its badge and, by doing so, the name Marconi had become synonymous with soccer in the western suburbs of Sydney.

Of all the logos in the NSL, few were as handsome or as heavily imbued with symbolism as Marconi's. Designed in 1958 by the artist Guido Zuliani, it combined a light-blue globe with a red, green and white boomerang in the foreground and a tall electricity tower in the background. Together, the composite parts elegantly represented the club's Italian heritage and its Australian future. And, as the members often said, the club was named after an Italian inventor who once switched on the lights at Sydney's Town Hall from a distance of 22,000 kilometres. It was, therefore, no more Italian than it was Australian.

For a decade, Club Marconi had been ruled by Tony Labbozzetta, the charmingly cunning son of Calabrian migrants. He had gone to school over the road from the club, joined as a member in 1969, and had grown into a figure so large that he frequently referred to himself in the third person.

With Labbozzetta in charge, Marconi won several trophies, expanded its membership base, improved its financial position and widened its sphere of influence. Yet it also attracted investigation from the Liquor Administration Board of NSW and the Honourable Donald Stewart. Labbozzetta also put many members offside, and fell out spectacularly with Remo Nogarotto, his once-loyal director of soccer.

Comfortable in his power base and mostly resistant to change, Labbozzetta was the antithesis of everything that David Hill wanted for soccer, and when Hill threw him off the board of Soccer Australia in early 1996 they became mortal enemies. Labbozzetta enlisted all the forces of the Fairfield district to make Hill's life hell.

On the issue of Marconi's logo, three local Labor members – Janice Crosio, Joe Tripodi and Morris Iemma – leaped to the club's defence. And when Hill and Stefan Kamasz went to Club Marconi to try and sort through a resolution they were bombarded by a gathering of school children waving Italian national flags.

In Adelaide, Mike Rann, the leader of the South Australian Labor Party, released a statement saying that 'wearing a logo with the Italian colours is totally consistent with Australian multiculturalism'.[18] In Sydney, both NSW Labor premier Bob Carr and the Liberal opposition supported Marconi's case. Iemma, the Labor member for Hurstville, even called for a breakaway league comprising the ethnic clubs and, as he so stridently put it, 'previous victims of earlier attempts at ethnic purging'. He also narrowed his attack specifically on Perth Glory and Brisbane Strikers – both one-town-teams – labelling them 'pale imitations of American sporting franchises'.[19]

Soccer fought this civil war to resolve an internal dilemma, but in the lively contest of ideas it approached questions of national significance. Why, after a generation or two of life in Australia, should people of Greek or Italian or Croatian heritage need a soccer club to call their own? Were these institutions of multicultural Australia still relevant to the nation? And if they were, was it still necessary for them to be so strongly identified with their ethnic community?

In the letters pages of the *Australian and British Soccer Weekly* and *Studs Up*, an interesting debate began to emerge. Enraged by the governing body's belligerent rhetoric, a group of soccer fans argued that because migrants had built the national league it would be nothing without the contribution of clubs such as Marconi, Melbourne Knights and Adelaide City.

Another ever-growing group, however, called for the league to be completely de-ethnicised and restructured along geographic lines. Armed with soccer's massive participation statistics, they reasoned that there was a huge mass of people waiting to watch the game, so long as it was packaged in the right way. 'Times are changing,' read one such letter, 'and Australian football no longer needs ethnic clubs to survive.'[20]

The spectators at Victoria Park for Collingwood Warriors' first ever NSL game witnessed the terrible collision of these competing arguments. On a warm Sunday afternoon in October 1996, in front of a crowd of around 15,000 people, the Collingwood Warriors beat Melbourne Knights 3–0. Captain Kimon Taliadoros, playing for his fourth club in four seasons, scored two goals in an inspired second-half performance.

But there was no match program, the AFL stadium was totally unsuited to soccer and, most importantly, people realised that Collingwood, the historic Australian Rules football side, had done little more than provide a Trojan Horse for Heidelberg United to get back into the competition. Perhaps the saddest metaphor for the charade was the club jersey, which interrupted Collingwood's famous black and white vertical stripes with lashings of Heidelberg yellow.

Over the next two home games, the attendances went into freefall, dropping by more than 75 per cent. 'That first Collingwood game at

Victoria Park, I think it was one of the biggest NSL crowds in history, but there were no Collingwood scarves,' remembered David Hill. 'And the chant was *Mega Alexandros* – Alexander the Great. People said, "This isn't Australia – this is fucking Greece."'

Collingwood Warriors, the Frankenstein merger of the Collingwood AFL club and Heidelberg United, suffered from a lethal combination of poor planning, a lack of faith between the AFL people and the soccer people, and, most of all, terrible timing. As the debate over club names and logos continued into the summer, and the antipathy between the pro- and anti-ethnic crowds grew increasingly heated and personal, the club sat uncomfortably between the traditional NSL club model and Hill's vanilla vision for the future. It was nicknamed 'Collingberg' by *Studs Up*, and disliked by nearly everyone.

Nearly every decision seemed to be met with suspicion and claims of cultural bias. When Hill appointed the famous English manager Terry Venables to take over the Socceroos in November, Johnny Warren complained that it ran counter to Hill's aim to 'Australianise' the game. Rumours swirled that Zoran Matic, the coach of Collingwood Warriors, had been overlooked for the Socceroos job because of his thick Serbian accent.[21] And the wild arguments narrowed with acerbic focus on Joe Simunic, a young Melbourne Knights centre-back, who announced in December that he would rather play for Croatia than for Australia.

Letter-writers labelled Simunic ungrateful to the country that provided him a childhood 'uninterrupted by wars or racial hatred', while reporters accused him of taking 'foreign money'.[22] And the *Sydney Morning Herald* turned him into an avatar for the de-ethnicisation debate, wondering if Simunic would have played for Australia had he 'not played for a club with Croatian emblems on its jersey and which continues to identify with Croatia'.[23]

It was in this context that three Italo-Australian businessmen emerged to try and move the NSL beyond the ethnic communities. Lou Sticca, a former Brunswick Juventus committee member, announced the creation of Carlton Soccer Club for the 1997–98 season. Remo Nogarotto, the former soccer director of Marconi, began working on a new, privately owned franchise to be based out of the northern suburbs of Sydney from the 1998–99 season. And Nick Tana, a former director of the Perth Italia club, drove the success of Perth Glory, the newest, hottest team in the NSL.

In Round 12, as the season reached its halfway point and Collingwood Warriors' crowd bottomed out at just 3000 people, Perth Glory drew nearly 15,000 spectators to a match against the Melbourne Knights. Glory went two goals up before half-time, lost the lead early in the second half, but won the game 3–2 thanks to a last-minute wonder-goal to Scott Miller.

Like Collingwood Warriors, Perth Glory was participating in its first season of the NSL. Unlike Collingwood, however, it was a completely new side, without affiliation to any pre-existing club. The players wore garish purple and orange jerseys, took the name 'Glory' from an advertising agency, and was privately owned by Tana, a man who made his money from fast food franchises and spent big on advertising and promotions.

Before the very first game at Perth Oval, a handsome black singer crooned 'I Am Australian' while cute children walked onto the field, which was covered with a giant Australian flag. The opening verses to the club song, which was belted out after the national anthem, called for revolution:

> We're in the dawning of a new age
> With the birth of our new code
> Yes we're basking in the Glory
> With our colours they're so bold.
> Our game's a great tradition
> Let the future now unfold
> When the Perth Glory marches on.

That it took 20 seasons for the national league to reach Perth was reflective of soccer's hopeless administration. As early as 1978 there had been attempts to bring the NSL to Western Australia; indeed Tana had tried for years to get Perth Italia into the competition without success. The biggest change had arrived in 1994 when Perth Kangaroos, a brand new franchise established by the state association, won the Singapore Premier League but almost collapsed under the cost of the undertaking.

'Conceptually, what the Kangaroos were all about was good,' Tana later recalled. 'It was just targeted at the wrong league.'

He had taken over, removed the hierarchy, changed the name and colours, and sold the vision to Soccer Australia. David Hill quickly became an enthusiastic supporter. Many of the Perth Kangaroos staff, including coach Gary Marocchi, had been carried over to the Glory. And despite Perth Glory winning just half of its first 12 NSL matches, it managed to draw a large average crowd of nearly 10,000 spectators to the first six home games. 'The inclusion of Perth proved they have been admitted years too late,' concluded an editorial in *Studs Up*, 'while the jury is still out on Collingberg.'[24]

In the most isolated city in the world, the sun shone down brightly on Perth Glory, nourishing the roots and allowing it to grow rapidly in a fertile microclimate. Even David Hill had reservations about the non-traditional name and colours, but as the club flourished like the purple morning glory flowers in summer bloom, he hastened in his conviction that soccer needed to be totally rebuilt.

In a city with the highest population of British migrants per capita in Australia, Hill and many other soccer fans marvelled at the English atmosphere at Perth Oval. But Tana believed the success of Perth Glory had foundation in its structure. As a wholly private entity, the board was not answerable to its supporters, a social club, or to any one ethnic group. This was an epochal shift in the administration of Australian soccer.

Yet it was never enough for Perth to simply join soccer's federation of cultures. 'My biggest concern,' Tana said after the rollicking win over Melbourne Knights, 'is that if the other clubs don't adopt the same attitude – if they don't move with the times – then the public here will quickly become disillusioned. The truth is that Perth can only succeed if the league succeeds.'[25]

★

The Australian Soccer Players Association was the centrifugal force driving the growth of top-flight soccer. Led by Kimon Taliadoros and Brendan Schwab, and with a committee that included Socceroos and Adelaide City captain Alex Tobin, Marconi striker Francis Awaritefe and South Melbourne striker Warren Spink, the union was fighting battles on several fronts.

Together Awaritefe and Schwab had drafted soccer's first ever Equal Opportunity Code after Awaritefe had been on the receiving end of racist abuse, while the union represented West Adelaide player Cyrille Ndongo-Keller in a landmark unfair-dismissal case. But the union's crowning achievement, and one with the most far-reaching consequences, was the first ever NSL collective bargaining agreement, which came into effect during the 1996–97 season. As Taliadoros would later explain, it shifted the NSL 'from a cottage industry to a legitimate industry'.

'The agreement contained two particular provisions which enhanced the economic rights of players,' once wrote Braham Dabscheck, an industrial relations academic who acted as an adviser to ASPA.

> First, players who did not receive an offer of employment from their current club 30 days prior to the expiration of their contract, on 'terms and conditions no less favourable than their previous contract', automatically became free agents. Second, players aged 26, or who had played six seasons with the same club, automatically became free agents.[26]

For the first three years of ASPA's existence it had run essentially as a coordinated industrial campaign, with an intense focus on the domestic issues facing the NSL. In January 1997, however, as the Socceroos prepared for a four-nations friendly tournament, the union was called to represent the players in a pay dispute with Soccer Australia. The disagreement stemmed from the Socceroos games that had been played between September and November in 1996. Tobin had complained to Schwab that the players had not received fees or prize-money for the matches, which included two successful Oceania Cup games.

In the ensuing negotiations, Schwab and David Woolley, the chief executive of Soccer Australia, began to talk about a collective agreement for the national team to complement the one already in place in the NSL. Yet by 14 January, the players and Soccer Australia management were still no closer to a resolution. The Socceroos decided to boycott training on 16 January, and voted 21–1 to hold industrial action for the upcoming game against Norway.

'I filed the paperwork to the Industrial Relations Commission which threatened a work stoppage,' recalled Schwab. 'Hill hated this stuff, and hated us. He had a view that he was trying to reform the game, make it popular, and we were a small-minded union fighting over crumbs. That was his very simplistic view of what we were trying to do. When we filed the document to negotiate the enterprise agreement, David Woolley rang me. He said, "Brendan, the chairman would like to speak to you." And Hill took the phone and said, "I've got your document. I fucking dare you to, you pissant."'

After some compromise, the Socceroos ended up beating Norway 1–0 in Sydney, but the relationship between the union and Hill had been stretched to breaking point. The players refused to meet with Hill after the Norway match, and so in retaliation Hill decided to cancel the scheduled meeting with Schwab.

The cold war between the union and Soccer Australia continued into March, as the Socceroos prepared to play a friendly match against Hungary in Budapest. Hill offered those in Budapest – mostly overseas-based players – a $154 daily allowance and a $750 per game match fee, with bonuses of $250 for a draw and $500 for a win. The players were promised $1000 for each qualifying match for the upcoming Confederations Cup, $5000 for tournament selection and an extra $5000 if they progressed past the group stage.

It was the best package ever tabled to an Australian national team, but with neither the players union nor any NSL players present for the negotiations Schwab claimed that Hill was trying to 'drive a wedge' between the overseas and the domestic Socceroos.[27] 'I don't give a stuff about the union,' Hill told the *Sydney Morning Herald*. 'I won't be discussing anything with them.'[28]

On the domestic front, Hill already had his hands full with a crisis that threatened to derail the NSL. In February, the Collingwood Football Club had officially pulled out of the Collingwood Warriors venture, causing the forfeiture of its Round 17 match and placing its future in grave doubt. Things had become so bad that in one match reserve goalkeeper Dean Anastasiadis was forced to participate as an outfield player due to a lack of available substitutes. By the end of March, Soccer Australia had seen enough. Collingwood Warriors would play its final five matches and then be wound up forever.

The dramatic failure of Collingwood Warriors was terrible for the image of the NSL, damaging to Hill's reform program, and catastrophic for Lou Sticca's Carlton Soccer Club, which was due to enter the competition under a similar arrangement with the Carlton AFL club.

Those hardest hit by the collapse, however, were Warriors coach Zoran Matic and his players. Having uprooted his family from Sydney to join the new team, Taliadoros was one of the worst affected. His two-year contract, which included a promise to pay for his Bachelor of Business degree at Melbourne Business School, was rendered virtually worthless. He and his wife were forced to move in with her parents. Eventually, they would move north so Taliadoros could rejoin Sydney Olympic. Collingwood Warriors, wrote one journalist, 'will be remembered as one of the great follies of Australian sport'.[29]

★

There were few prouder times to be a Croatian-Australian than in the 1990s. The war of independence had been won, Mark Viduka and Josip Skoko were stars of Croatia's two biggest clubs, and Croatia was preparing for its first World Cup. Between 1991 and 1995, Croatian-backed sides had won four NSL premierships and had participated in four of the five grand finals. And in season 1996–97, Sydney United lost just four times in 26 matches, and scored at a rate of 2.58 goals per game, setting a new record by finishing on 56 points – nine points clear of second place.

That challenger was Brisbane Strikers. Geographically and philosophically the two clubs were from different worlds. Sydney United lived and died by its Croatian community, and was staffed with players called Kalac, Plesa, Zdrilic, Kupresak and Milicic. Brisbane Strikers was backed by the Queensland Soccer Federation and staffed with players called Gwynne, Hunter, Cranney, Brown and Bolton. Sydney United was coached by Branko Culina, a bespectacled product of the Australian Croatian community; Brisbane Strikers was coached by its centre-forward, Frank Farina, the former Socceroos star who had returned home to boost the profile of soccer in Queensland.

The rivalry between the two sides flickered to life in the autumn of 1996, was consecrated that summer, and given national prominence in the autumn of 1997. It was born of two competing visions of the NSL, and enhanced by competitive, seesawing games. Thanks to the unusual NSL draw, in Round 13 and Round 14 they had met twice in the space of just nine days. In Brisbane, the Strikers won 3–0. In Sydney, United won 4–0. In 12 months, they had played each other six times, with three wins apiece.

Yet as the two sides entered the finals series, their off-field differences, not the on-field rivalry, would take on profound importance.

Life under the administration of David Hill had not been easy for Sydney United. With the explanation, 'It's pretty hard to market Croatian nationalism to non-Croatians,' Hill had ordered the club to change its logo, encouraged it to appoint former Liberal Party leader John Hewson to the board, and pushed for its games to be moved from Edensor Park to Parramatta Stadium.

'You would go to Edensor Park,' Hill once remembered, 'and on match day you'd walk past the King Tomislav Club with tables selling Croatian scarves, merchandise, videos, everything. And on top of the turnstiles there was a big sign that said, "Croatia Sydney". You honestly felt – Christ, have I got my passport? You go in and all the ground announcements were in Serbo-Croat. Nobody went there unless they had a Croatian family connection.'

Brisbane Strikers, on the other hand, was free to do as it pleased. It decided to move from Perry Park, which had a capacity of around 4000, to Suncorp Stadium, which could hold ten times that figure. Its board comprised Ian Brusasco, an alderman of the Brisbane City Council and a longtime head of the Queensland Soccer Federation; Clem Jones, the longest-serving mayor of Brisbane; and Frank Speare, a prominent local business identity.

Of all the states, Queensland was the most unified, the most decentralised and the least troubled by soccer's national question. Its divide was geographic, both for the state as a whole and for the north–south factions on either side of the Brisbane River. When the QSF became the first state to ban ethnic names back in the early 1970s, it received relatively little opposition from the clubs. In this context, the Brisbane Strikers were, in the words of its marketing manager Bonita Mersiades, 'a pan-Brisbane team'.

As the propaganda arm of the most parochial state in Australia, the *Courier-Mail* immediately jumped on board the Brisbane Strikers bandwagon. It was a rugby league newspaper in a rugby league town, but on the strength of the Strikers' performance it offered soccer front pages, back pages, features and comment.

Significantly, it also ran opinion pieces by Jeff Wells, a shock-jock journalist who once suggested that 'the national league is no place for ethnic fiefdoms'.[30] In the preliminary final between South Melbourne and Sydney United, Wells was given the ammunition to take this argument to its zenith. After a tense, hard-fought 1–0 win by Sydney United at Parramatta Stadium, sections of supporters from both sides had let off a barrage of flares, abused police and invaded the field.

'South Melbourne fans taunted their rivals with Serbian flags,' reported the *Sydney Morning Herald*, 'while the Sydney United supporters responded by waving Macedonian symbols.'[31]

Soccer Australia talked seriously and openly about expelling both Sydney United and South Melbourne from the competition, with Hill decreeing that the riots 'were on racist and European nationalist grounds'.[32] In the *Courier-Mail*, under the headline 'Soccer Sinking into an Ethnic Quagmire', Wells decided that the ethnic teams needed to be abandoned altogether, or at the very least diluted by enforced mergers.[33]

In this febrile political environment, the grand final between Sydney United and Brisbane Strikers loomed as a battleground for the future of soccer in Australia. Tickets to the game sold fast, as thousands of curious Queenslanders turned their attention for the first time to the NSL. David Hill predicted that Brisbane would overtake Sydney and Melbourne as the soccer capital in Australia, while an editorial in the *Courier-Mail* praised the Strikers as 'a new breed of Australian soccer club that has thrown off the shackles of ethnic-based football'.[34]

It was, as the Sydney United president Ivan Simic observed, 'like the wogs against Brisbane'.[35]

The case against clubs such as Sydney United was as old as the national league itself, underpinned by commercial logic and furnished by the aggressive identity politics of the era. By 1997 the Australian soccer community had completely lost faith in its ethnic institutions. They were castigated as being 'monocultural' and blamed for everything, from the game's poor image to the violence on the terraces – even for the collapse of Collingwood Warriors.

By contrast, the structure of the Brisbane Strikers was seen to encourage supporters and players from all different backgrounds to assimilate into a clear, unified Queensland identity. Glen Gwynne represented the tropical far north and Kasey Wehrman the remote north-west. Jeromy Harris came from Rockhampton, Clint Bolton from Bundaberg, Chay Hews from Toowoomba, Graham Ross from Townsville, Nick Meredith from the Sunshine Coast. And Alan Hunter, Wayne Knipe, and the Cranney brothers Troy and Sean were the Brisbane boys.

'The extent to which the Strikers fitted into the Hill agenda was accidental,' remembered Bonita Mersiades, 'but there was a view around that for the game to grow it needed clubs that represented regions.'

At the beginning of the season, bookmakers had listed the Brisbane Strikers as 66–1 to win the title, and despite the team finishing second on the ladder, not a single Strikers player had been selected for the Socceroos. Yet everything, save for the form guide and the pundits, seemed to favour the Strikers. On the day before the game it rained, but on grand final day the sun came out. As the mascots parachuted into the stadium, Sydney United's stumbled and fell, while the Brisbane Strikers mascot landed flush on his feet.

By kick-off, Suncorp Stadium had to be locked for fears of over-crowding. Chay Hews had the first shot on goal within the opening minute, and Glen Gwynne expertly tracked United's danger man Kresimir Marusic, restricting his creative influence and cutting off supply to the forwards. Clint Bolton was a colossus in goals, rising high to comfortably catch the first Sydney United cross.

Just after half-time, Farina scored the opening goal with a left-foot stab that had just enough power and precision to trickle into the net. It was his 101st national league goal, and by far his most important. And when Rod Brown scored to make it 2–0, his tally rose to 131 NSL goals.

By the time the Brisbane Strikers' assistant coach, Peter Tokesi, replaced Farina, there were just ten minutes left to play. Farina walked off to a standing ovation and a large banner that read, 'Thanks Frank'. The official crowd figure was 40,446, a new national league record. On the other side of town, the Brisbane Broncos hosted the North Queensland Cowboys in rugby league's Queensland derby. Less than 15,000 people turned up.

It was a stunning outcome, perhaps even more spellbinding than the Strikers' victory itself, and as the players did their lap of honour Tokesi stood in the middle of the field and gazed up at a full stadium. For a man who had chosen to play soccer instead of rugby league at age 14, this felt like vindication. Tears formed in the big man's eyes.

'Suncorp Stadium is hallowed turf for rugby league players,' he once remembered, 'and here we were, having to shut the gates for soccer. I thought of the struggles. It wasn't just that game – it was the struggle for soccer in Brisbane.'

As the party moved to the streets, Andrew Howe logged the match stats into his database from his Adelaide home and happily faxed SBS to notify them of the attendance record. For many observers, however, a different record was of greater consequence. For the first time in 21 seasons, a club without roots in an ethnic community had won the national league. Although nobody could have predicted the enormous changes that would follow in the coming decade, this grand final marked the beginning of the end of ethnic club soccer, and the rise of the one-town-team.

The dominance of the Croatian clubs was over, and for Sydney United the grand final loss was something of a tragedy: no team had ever been so dominant, and few teams had ever featured such an array of locally produced talent. Had the season been decided by the traditional first-past-the-post system rather than a grand final, Sydney United would surely have been remembered as the greatest NSL side, and as the perfect, eternal image of the Croatian community's commitment to the game.

But Australian soccer has never been kind to tradition. Season 1996–97 would instead be remembered for the success of Brisbane Strikers and the introduction of Perth Glory – those 'pale imitations of American franchises' that Labor politician Morris Iemma had decried just a few months earlier.

With fans and officials thrilled by the enormous crowd that had materialised in Brisbane, the story unfolded to further marginalise Sydney United. Everything about the day – the record crowd, the safe and comfortable atmosphere, and, of course, the result – seemed to justify the claims that had been made by Soccer Australia and its supporters for more than a year.

The *Courier-Mail* claimed it as the 'Greatest Day in the History of Australian Soccer', the *Australian* decreed 'A Win for Multi-ethnic Harmony', while *Studs Up* announced that 'the future of Australian football has arrived – and it's popular, successful and multi-ethnic'.[36]

Even the *Sydney Morning Herald* proclaimed: 'The event demonstrated the potential pull of soccer, if it is perceived as a game that is part of Australian culture.' The editorial continued:

> The future of soccer in Australia is the supporters of the Brisbane Strikers yelling out, as they did on Sunday, 'Strikers! Strikers!' This support reflects the fact that Brisbane soccer gave up ethnic-based clubs two decades ago. The future is not Sydney United supporters with their 'Croatia, Croatia' chanting. Critics have labelled the program of breaking the ethnic nexus with the clubs as a racist initiative. In fact, it is an initiative towards proper multiculturalism.[37]

Only in Australia could you have had such a farcical situation: for finishing at the top of the competition ladder, and in the process developing some of the nation's best young talent, Sydney United were now being told that they were bad for the sport.

Indeed the notion that there was a 'proper' way to do multiculturalism, both in soccer and in the rest of society, had become a central point of debate. Pauline Hanson, the federal member for Oxley in Queensland, called for the abolition of multiculturalism, and for 12 months Prime Minister John Howard had unrelentingly scorned the 'political correctness' of cultural elites and their 'black armband' view of history.

The idea that Australia could exist, as Howard had once put it, 'as a federation of cultures', was withering under toxic attack. Multiculturalism had come to be seen as a dividing force, not as a unifier. For the NSL, Australia's truest multicultural institution, the conditions were terminal.

Just one week after the Brisbane Strikers victory, a riot broke out at Belmore Oval in Sydney. In what would become known as 'The Battle of Belmore', police were attacked and fans could be seen brandishing national flags and banners. It was the first rugby league riot since 1928, and in the aftermath the blame narrowed on Canterbury Bulldogs' decision to hold a so-called 'multicultural day'.

'As the history of soccer in Australia has shown, racial prejudices are a travesty of multiculturalism,' concluded one editorial in the *Sydney Morning Herald.* 'True multiculturalism is based on tolerance and an acceptance of Australian sensibilities.'[38]

★

In the space of four weeks, from 11 June to 6 July, Australia played six World Cup qualifying matches. The Socceroos won all six, scored 31 goals, conceded just two and tested 25 players in the process. Coach Terry Venables experimented with several different line-ups and combinations, yet in nearly every match Craig Foster started in the centre of the midfield. Along with captain Alex Tobin, he was also one of the few regular starters to be based in the NSL.

Foster was a hyperactive young man with soot-black hair, dark eyes hidden beneath a heavy brow, and sharp cheekbones framed by a permanent five o'clock shadow. On the field he wore the expression of the Grinch, barking at teammates to pass him the ball or find space around him. His life was soccer, and soccer was serious business. One journalist called him 'the new-age grafter'.[39]

From Goonellabah, a small town on the far north coast of NSW, Foster was never beholden to any one club or ethnic group. His greatest loyalty was to the players union, and to the Socceroos. He entered the Australian national team in a state of breathless excitement, enlivened by the opportunity and humbled by the company. He treated every game as his last and requested his teammates to autograph jerseys, goalkeeping gloves, polo tops and any other piece of equipment not nailed down.

He was the Socceroos' Charlie Bucket, that unlikely character in the children's book *Charlie and the Chocolate Factory.* The Socceroos shirt was the Golden Ticket, his most sought-after prize that kept him awake at night; while Venables played the part of Willy Wonka, recognising qualities in him that few others saw or bothered to cultivate.

'Venables had an incredibly positive impact on the players, particularly Foster,' recalled Brendan Schwab. 'I think he revolutionised Fozz's attitude to the game. Craig was really motivated by that, and he real-ised he had been exposed to a completely different level of coaching. Fozz was a bit of a lad; he was a very exuberant sort of personality and had a bit of a larrikin streak in him. Venables was the one who really brought him out.'

By August, Foster had signed a contract with Portsmouth, Venables' club in the English first division, joining a committee of Australians including John Aloisi, Zeljko Kalac, Robbie Enes and Hamilton Thorp. With the Stewart Report and the Senate inquiry not long in the memory, many felt that Venables had a clear conflict of interest. After all, one of the central recommendations by the Honourable Donald Stewart was for national team coaches to stay out of player transfers. David Hill promptly dismissed the claims; Venables was his handpicked appointment.

Venables was a born showman, a colourful cockney who, in between his considerable on-field achievements, found time to write pop songs, an autobiography, a futuristic soccer novel and another book, titled *The Greatest Game in the World*. He worked as a media pundit and incorporated his own name.

At the time of his appointment to the Socceroos, he was the chairman of Portsmouth Football Club, as well as the owner of a nightclub in London's West End, and had had two books published about him. Hill paid him $400,000 for an 18-month gig, which he worked at part-time. He was by far the most expensive Socceroos coach in history, but Hill promised that it would be great business. The usually uninterested Australian press put him on the front and back pages: here was a coach they knew from the television, with a name they could pronounce, and from the mother country.

Most importantly, the players loved him. Venables filled them with confidence and clear, valuable instruction. He probed the defenders' intelligence, rotated the minds and bodies of the midfielders, and said 'there's nothing up there for you' when the strikers hit shots over the crossbar.

'I'll never forget his first session – it was straight out of the Barcelona log book,' Foster recalled. 'I later asked him, I said, "The system of play you gave to the Socceroos, you didn't get that in England. Where did you get it?" He said, "I got it at Barca." We'd be playing in a certain way, he'd have the cones out for the zones we should move into. This was all new, but I got it immediately, which is why he must have picked me. He immediately recognised that I could play the system. It was brilliant.'

By November 1997, 31 of the 32 World Cup spots had been decided. Europe had 15 spots, South America and Africa five each, Central America and Asia three. Oceania was only granted half a spot, meaning that Australia needed to defeat the fourth-placed Asian side to qualify.

In 1996, David Hill had tried to shift Australia out of the Oceania Football Confederation and into the Asian Football Confederation, but got rolled 170 votes to one at the FIFA Congress. And so Australia qualified through Oceania and then faced Iran, the fourth-placed Asian side, in a winner-takes-all clash played over two legs in Tehran and Melbourne.

On 22 November, 129,000 intensely partisan Iranian men welcomed the Socceroos into the Azadi Stadium. In the cool mountain air of Tehran, they waved little Iranian flags, paid deference to the looming, intimidating portraits of Ayatollahs Khamenei and Khomeini, and whistled loudly throughout the Australian national anthem. Like a patriotic soldier preparing for war, Craig Foster slung his hand theatrically over his heart and defiantly belted out his best rendition.

The whistling continued whenever an Australian went near the ball. 'It was very difficult to play in,' Foster later explained. 'It was like being Marcel Marceau – communication is a big part of my game as an organising midfielder. In that game I was screaming at guys two metres away and they couldn't hear shit. It was the loudest noise I'd experienced. The one player who stood up was Harry. Nothing affected him.'

Harry Kewell, a 19-year-old cherub-faced upstart playing just his second match for the Socceroos, scored the first goal of the game. As

Australia clung on for a 1–1 draw, match reporters singled out Mark Bosnich for his sequence of stunning saves in the second half, and Terry Venables said he was 'delighted' with the result. Exhilarated by the intense nationalism of the Iranians, David Hill frantically called Stefan Kamasz at his home in Sydney. Kamasz, who had spent the past two years trying to remove national symbols from soccer stadiums, now woke to an executive order: 'Get me 50,000 Australian flags'.

Needing only a scoreless draw to progress to the World Cup, expectation was at an all-time high. The expected crowd rose from 70,000 to 90,000 in the space of a week. At their peak, tickets sold at a rate of 1000 per hour. The *Australian* commissioned Mark Bosnich to write a column, the *Age* published a diary entry from Harry Kewell, while Michael Cockerill from the *Sydney Morning Herald* was working feverishly on a book to be published in time for the World Cup. Kamasz ordered posters of Bosnich to be hung all over the city, from telegraph poles to trams and on freeway overpasses, with a caption that read 'Aussie Rules Soccer'.

For the first time in history, the Australian soccer team was booked to play at the Melbourne Cricket Ground. The 'G is Australia's largest and most holy sporting stadium, reserved for cricket and Australian Rules. The press had a field day when they learned that Melbourne-born Mark Viduka had never entered it, while Bosnich admitted that he had always dreamed of playing at the MCG 'dressed in whites, shirt sleeves rolled up, face covered in zinc, cricket ball in hand and thundering it down for Australia in a Test match against England'.[40] When Peter Desira, a Melbourne reporter who spent his working life at the cold, half-built outposts of soccer, asked his colleague Ron Reed for directions, Reed retorted: 'A Melbourne sportswriter asking where the MCG press box is – that's a disgraceful question.'[41]

On the afternoon of Saturday 29 November 1997, at the Cricketers Arms Hotel on Punt Road, the *Studs Up* fanzine organised its largest-ever meet up. Nearly 100 readers congregated at the back of the pub from mid-afternoon, dressed in an array of Socceroos jerseys, some of them meeting one another in person for the first time.

Andrew Howe and Kevin Christopher drank and smoked together and tried to keep a lid on their excitement. They knew that success would catapult soccer, their little secret society, into the bright lights of the Australian mainstream. Every soccer fan knew that World Cup qualification would either make or break David Hill's reform program. Failure was too scary to even contemplate.

The mood at the Cricketers Arms was expectant and euphoric. Within a few hours the pub had been drunk dry. Two hours before kick-off, David Hill went for a stroll around the stadium. He walked slowly, letting his eyes take in the cavalcade of human emotion, pausing occasionally to reflect on the turbulent two years that had just passed. He looked out to a kaleidoscope of colours, foreign jerseys and the badges of overseas clubs, noting happily that every supporter wore a piece of green and gold. 'It was the most beautiful experience of Australia at its best,' he later remembered.

In what was perhaps the most telling image of the Hill era, Stefan Kamasz rushed around like a man possessed, handing out Australian flags to everyone who passed. Finding entire cartons of flags abandoned at the turnstiles, he picked them up, thrust bulk boxes into the hands of supporters and told them to spread them to all parts of the ground.

A motorcade of the 1974 Socceroos rolled slowly around the perimeter, and as a green-and-gold inflatable ball bounced happily around the crowd, the band played 'Waltzing Matilda'. Craig Foster again slapped his hand over his heart and, this time, more than 80,000 people sang the national anthem with him.

Between 1977 and 1993, the Socceroos had failed in five consecutive attempts to qualify for the World Cup. But this was a golden generation on the field against Iran. The starting XI had an average age of just 26, with a wealth of international experience at club level. Only the captain, Alex Tobin, was playing in the NSL, and in a significant change from previous generations of migrant and journeymen Socceroos, every starting player was either Australian-born or Australian-raised.

Under Venables' reign the Socceroos hadn't lost a single match, and the team started the second leg against Iran with supreme confidence. Within six minutes, Aurelio Vidmar had already missed three very good opportunities to score. Stan Lazaridis tore up and down the left wing, Harry Kewell danced down the right, Zelic shimmied through the middle and Foster ran himself into a lather. 'In a boxing match you'd stop the fight, Australia is so dominant,' noted match commentator Johnny Warren.

On the half-hour mark, Kewell hoofed a wayward, looping cross from the far right side of the field to the far left. It landed softly at the feet of Vidmar, who, with his back to goal, shaped to go right and then broke left, bamboozling his marker completely. He swung a sharp cross in the direction of Viduka, who dived forward, missed the ball by a fraction, and landed heavily on his stomach. The onrushing Tobin was also just out of reach.

But lurking at the far post, just six yards out from goal, was Kewell. He tapped the ball into the back of the net, finishing the move that he had started, and swaggered away in celebration. As millions of Australians watched him run to the crowd, the television cameras cut to a young woman in a Croatia jersey, hopping up and down on the spot and waving an Australian flag.

By the half-time break, Australia were so dominant that Bosnich – who was barely troubled in the first 45 minutes – remained on the field to keep warm with the Socceroos trainer. On television, former Socceroo Alan Davidson told SBS presenter Les Murray that Australia was 'a bit unlucky' not to be 5–0 in front. There was a confidence in the Socceroos' step.

Three minutes after the restart, Kewell instigated a cascading move that drifted from right to left, finding Lazaridis free on the wing. Lazaridis' deep cross was bumped back across goal to Foster, who looped a header over the keeper and onto the crossbar. Vidmar was on hand to slam the ball home. As the crowd exploded into a deafening roar, Venables nodded excitedly on the bench. He was just 40 minutes away from coaching in his first World Cup.

Then everything changed.

A crazed, peroxide-blond man named Peter Hore, a serial pest who had made his name disrupting high-profile events, invaded the field and broke through the netting on the Iranian goal. As the match was delayed, a wave of trepidation fell over the stadium. In the VIP area, David Hill turned to fellow board member Basil Scarsella, who was fidgeting with nerves. 'Calm down, Basil,' Hill ordered. 'You can pack your bags for Paris!'

But he had spoken too soon. The final 20 minutes unfolded as operatic tragedy: in the 71st minute, a goalmouth scramble drew Bosnich off his line, and in the ensuing mess the ball was swept home by Karim Bagheri. 2–1. Just four minutes later, the Iranian striker Khodadad Azizi sprung the offside trap and side-footed past Bosnich to make it 2–2.

Panic took hold among the players, and a familiar sick feeling rose in the throats of Socceroos supporters. Long, hopeful passes were sent in the direction of the Iranian goal. With minutes left on the clock, Viduka had a glancing header fly wide and high over the crossbar. Then Graham Arnold, a late substitution, had a diving header saved. As the referee blew his whistle for full-time, Australian soccer's moment of truth mutated into a dark night of the soul.

With scores locked at 3–3 over the two matches, the Socceroos had not lost, but they had not won either. Iran qualified due to the fact they had scored two goals away from home to the Socceroos' one. Amid the wreckage of the MCG, an SBS sideline reporter dragged Craig Foster in front of the television cameras. The colour had drained completely from his face. Withered by defeat, he shook his head repeatedly at the injustice. But as he stumbled over his words and stammered out a postmortem, the statesman emerged from the sadness.

'We win as a team and we lose as a team,' he promised. 'We'll stick together, and, I dunno, we'll pick up the pieces tomorrow.'

In living rooms across the country, Socceroos fans watched SBS commentator Johnny Warren break down live on air. 'You just feel for them,' he wavered. 'They are representative of so many people who make soccer their life.'

The dressing room was a morgue. Alex Tobin sat slumped, eyes glazed over, catatonic at the result. Others howled in pain and were physically ill. With Tobin inconsolable, David Hill took his place at the post-match press conference alongside Terry Venables.

In the gallery, Michael Cockerill's mind wandered briefly to his book manuscript. *Australian Soccer's Long Road to the Top*, despite the misleading title, would be one of the best books on Australian soccer, a thorough and entertaining examination of both the Hill era and the growth of the Socceroos. But without the ecstasy of World Cup qualification, it wouldn't sell. As Cockerill would later admit, 'it lacked the punchline'.

That night Stefan Kamasz locked himself in his hotel bathroom and bawled his eyes out. The tears were shared by the players on the field, the supporters in the stands, the officials in corporate boxes, and in the homes of thousands of Australians. Across the front page of the *Sunday Age*, a special World Cup edition led with the words, 'The dream is dead'.[42]

Andrew Howe took an early flight home to Adelaide. His sandshoes were ruined by flares, his heart shattered into a million pieces and his plans for France 1998 dashed. In the taxi home from the airport, the driver shared in his misery. 'He was so down that he lost a couple of hundred dollars in wages just because he couldn't face the outside world,' Howe recalled.

The *Studs Up* crew, who had stood together on the terraces at the MCG – at first loud and exuberant among the burning red flares, by the end silent and still in the indignity of defeat – were perhaps the hardest hit by the loss. The *OzSoccer* email list was transformed into a message board of grief, while Kevin Christopher decided to name issue 28 of *Studs Up* 'The Black Issue'. It was published with a heavy, matt-black cover instead of the usual glossy white, with no words or pictures.

'The decision had been made within five minutes of the final whistle,' read the editorial. 'You know which one. *That* final whistle at the MCG. *Studs Up* 28 would be encased in black as a permanent reminder of *that* game. For a few hours we even toyed with the idea of winding up *Studs Up*. But with a good night's sleep and a healthy dose of vitamin B came the realisation that Australian soccer needs *Studs Up* more than ever before.'[43]

★

The tears returned in early December in a cold terminal of London's Heathrow Airport. Removed by thousands of kilometres from the scene of disaster, the overseas Socceroos met for a flight to the Confederations Cup in Saudi Arabia. They had recovered from the shock but were still mourning the lost opportunity: words were scarce and emotions ran high.

Craig Foster, joining the overseas Socceroos by virtue of a mid-year move to Portsmouth, sat with Stan Lazaridis and together they faced their heartbreak. They cried at the pain of the two late Iranian goals, and for each other, and for the future of their troubled sport. Foster called it 'the grief flight'.

The Socceroos had qualified for the Confederations Cup in November 1996, just before Terry Venables took over as coach, by defeating Tahiti 5–0 in Canberra. Had they managed to hold on to that two-goal lead against Iran, the Confederations Cup would have been the final tune-up before France 1998. Instead, Australia played for pride against an illustrious group of nations readying themselves for the World Cup.

The players had been led to believe that there was big prize money for the Confederations Cup, and expected to receive a fair share. David Hill, however, refused to increase their share of the largesse. A relationship that had been disintegrating for months finally collapsed.

As the opening match against Mexico loomed, Foster went to Venables to explain the players' discontent. He told him that Socceroos squads had suffered pay disputes as far back as the 1974 World Cup, and that brinkmanship was always used as a weapon by the governing body. Although successive generations of players had lobbied ferociously, they never had the benefit of an organised union backing them up. This time, Foster told Venables, things would be different.

It was high noon for the Australian Soccer Players Association. Brendan Schwab and Kimon Taliadoros had succeeded year-by-year in their bid to overturn the transfer and compensation system in the courts, establish free agency, enshrine a standard national league contract and draft soccer's first Equal Opportunity Code. Although the domestic situation was of greatest importance to the union, the Socceroos were always crucial to its strategy. The national team was the headline grabber, and contained the players that the public felt an affinity with.

Alex Tobin, the Socceroos captain, was also the president of ASPA. 'Alex was an outstanding leader, but he was very quiet,' Schwab once remembered. 'He led the players association the way he played. He'd be there when he had to be: clear the ball, pass it out, he never looked like he was sprinting. That was the way he handled disputes.'

Foster, on the other hand, was much more adversarial. 'I was probably the most militant guy,' he later explained. 'I've never been shy about my own opinion. If I feel strongly about an issue I don't give a shit who I'm talking to.'

Robbie Slater, who had been in the Socceroos for a decade, through good times and bad, didn't appreciate Foster's attitude. He had paid his own airfare to play for the national team and refused to put a price on the green-and-gold shirt. When a vote was called to boycott training, he, Ned Zelic and Steve Horvat were the only three players to vote in the negative.

In his biography, *The Hard Way*, Slater would criticise the leadership of Tobin and say that he was ostracised for disagreeing with 'the party line'.[44] 'Foster [...] was such a dominant personality that many players followed his line,' Slater wrote. 'When we had a vote to strike, there was a call for a show of hands and there were only three dissenters. The whole thing didn't feel right, so I called for a secret ballot. From memory, about eight players were against taking such extreme action.'[45]

Although the training boycott went ahead, the Socceroos performed brilliantly in the matches, defeating Mexico and Uruguay to reach the final, which they lost 6–0 to Brazil. By the end of the tournament Foster, Zelic and Mark Bosnich were named in a list of 33 FIFA All Stars. It would be Foster's final major tournament, and Slater's last match for the Socceroos.

Hill resigned as chairman of Soccer Australia not long after. His was a thankless task, and he departed to a cartoon in the *Australian* that depicted him with knives lodged in his back. His star recruit, Terry Venables, also left the Socceroos after a depressing 7–0 loss to Croatia in June 1998. Farcically, the 19-year-old winger Ante Seric was picked by both the Socceroos and Croatia, and in what felt like a final blow to Soccer Australia's reform agenda, Seric chose to play for Croatia.

As soccer once again plunged into deep disarray, it was again the Australian Soccer Players Association that emerged the strongest.

'I wasn't heavily involved in that [Confederations Cup] dispute,' remembered Kimon Taliadoros, 'but there were enough leading people in among the Socceroos to drive it – Foster, Tobin, Lazaridis – really strong personalities. The most significant thing about that was that our greatest stars, the players who'd left our shores to pursue careers overseas, came back and validated everything. That was almost like a shot of adrenalin into the players association and across the bows of Soccer Australia. It was tremendous.'

In the years to come, the players union would take a commanding role not only in protecting players' rights but also in reshaping the domestic competition. Its membership base would grow and reformers such as Taliadoros, Foster, Tobin, Greg Brown and Francis Awaritefe would each be inducted as life members.

When the first ever Socceroos collective bargaining agreement was signed, adding a contractual framework to the long-standing culture of collectivism, every Socceroo would be paid the same – regardless of whether they played abroad or in the national league. Money would also begin to flow back from the national team to the players union.

'We did that in 1997,' Foster once explained. 'To me it was the principle. Every man in that group gave to the NSL players through the players union. A percentage goes to them to look after the domestic players. The discussion in the room was we have to give back there. That created the connection between the local league and the Socceroos, which can never be broken.'

THE SONS OF IMMIGRANTS

1999–2002

Sadly now the ethnic clubs [...] are dying [...] and what will replace them will be commercially bent franchises, units of the big soccer corporation only concerned with a business agenda: profile, positioning and profit, caring not a hoot about the culture, language, race or political ideology of their following [...]

The clubs they will replace will die, some faster than others. Their mementos will be the plaques in their honour in community halls.

Some will live on as State league or amateur clubs, playing in stadiums built with unselfish passion for a more extravagant future, with a handful of ageing fans, out of sentimental duty, watching them.

The saddest part will be that the new clubs, soccer's new era, will make hay from the foundations these clubs made.

And soon nobody will remember them.

Les Murray
Australian and British Soccer Weekly, 1999[1]

The *Studs Up* fanzine celebrated its fourth birthday in January 1999. Although the readership might still have been small, it was the only fanzine that brought soccer supporters together from across the country. By any standards, the four years had been an incredible feat of endurance. Few other media outlets, whether amateur or professional, were able to capture the mood and tenor of the time. As advertised, *Studs Up* was the voice of the people.

On 20 January 1999, *Studs Up* editor Kevin Christopher received a letter from Chris Kunz, who at the beginning of the NSL had been a young foundation member of the Canberra City Soccer Club. Citing the dwindling support for the ethnic clubs, Kunz called for the competition to be restructured along geographic lines and boosted by private investment and clever marketing. Using the success of Perth Glory as an example, he reasoned that only this formula could give soccer the potential to attract the broadest base of support. 'There is,' he wrote, 'inevitably a drift in the second-generation migrant away from the culture and traditions of the parent.'[2]

Lou Sticca, the general manager of the Carlton Soccer Club, was a living embodiment of this demographic drift. His boyhood club was Brunswick Juventus, one of the biggest migrant clubs of the 1950s and 1960s, but although it had won the national league in 1985 it grew smaller and became less relevant as its supporters passed away or assimilated.

As the NSL rapidly contracted through the 1980s, Sticca had watched on as his beloved mentors put their hands in their own pockets to refinance the club. He had seen families neglected for the sake of the club and the game. He had seen the Brunswick Juventus kitman mortgage his house so the players got paid on time. And he had seen a committee drowning in their deep love and passion for soccer, but without the requisite talents to take it to higher ground.

It was a similar story for Remo Nogarotto in Sydney, only it was Marconi instead of Brunswick Juventus in which he had lost faith. Out of their shared realisation came Carlton Soccer Club and Northern Spirit. Sticca and Nogarotto built their new clubs in almost total opposition to the old order. They were privately backed, appealed to a broad base of support rather than one section of the community, and frantically disassociated themselves from any ethnic links, whether real or imagined.

Carlton played out of a cricket ground shared with the Carlton AFL side and wore the navy blue and white of its parent club. Northern Spirit played at North Sydney Oval, a cricket ground that was also home to the North Sydney Bears rugby league side, and got its name from an ad agency and its money from the English club side Crystal Palace.

'I was a Judas, wasn't I?' once remembered Nogarotto. 'I had spent eight years with Marconi – rose to become chairman of the football club, won a premiership with them, seen to be the next president of the licensed club – and then I jumped ship and created this other thing. We were in every sense of the word *persona non grata*. The only friends we had around the table were Perth Glory and Carlton, because we sang off the same hymn sheet. My generation had a very different view of how the game should evolve. That's probably why people like Lou Sticca, Nick Tana and I had an alignment. We were a different generation to Tony Labbozzetta, Bob D'Ottavi, George Vasilopoulos and Tony Kovac – we were the sons of immigrants.'

Sticca and Nogarotto's realisation was shared by many players and a growing number of supporters. The ethnic clubs that they had grown up with were not necessary to shield them from the discomforts of migration or from social isolation; Australia was the only home they had known. They spoke English as well as anybody. They played cricket, rugby league and Australian Rules with the best of them. They moved with ease from the building site to the corporate boardroom to the halls of political power. Their communities were more diverse than ever, and Asians had become the new national punching bag.

In an environment where 'wogs versus Aussies' was more a schoolyard game than a serious social divide, what use was an ethnic soccer club?

Although both Carlton and Northern Spirit were inspired by Perth Glory's swashbuckling example, their experiment represented something far more combustible. While Glory started with a clean slate, Carlton and Northern Spirit were playing divide and rule in the country's two most congested and politically volatile cities. They competed with the established clubs not only for players and competition points but also for the corporate dollar, for media attention and for hearts and minds.

The aim was to break down soccer's tribal networks and reconfigure them into neutral, commercial-friendly and privately owned franchises. They had found institutional support from Soccer Australia, but in the traditional soccer networks their plans were met with resistance, doubt and personal animosity. Les Murray, for instance, warned that Northern Spirit was 'being run on purely corporate lines with a business agenda, rather than a social agenda'.[3]

More than anything else, Carlton and Northern Spirit wanted space. Geographically, culturally and philosophically, the clubs needed a *tabula rasa* to conduct their experiments in a controlled environment. Yet the NSL could only provide an anarchic world, largely free of commercial regulation, institutional discipline and strategic direction.

In response to this chaos, Lou Sticca called Carlton 'the club for all of Melbourne', while Remo Nogarotto, having scoured the west, east and southern suburbs for space, decided to build his Sydney franchise for the propertied class in the northern suburbs. His goal, as he would later admit, was to build a 'rainbow coalition football team ... in a part of Sydney that was overwhelmingly rugby-dominated, and with a strong Anglo-Saxon skew'.

While Sticca signed bona fide stars to drive the Carlton brand, ensuring that they dressed well and were clean-shaven, Nogarotto brought former Socceroos Robbie Slater and Graham Arnold home to become the captain and the player-coach respectively. He signed Phil Moss, a former *Manly Daily* journalist who claimed that he had been rejected by Sydney Olympic because he 'wasn't the right nationality'.[4] He splashed Harry Kewell's face all over the club advertisements, even though Kewell was playing in England for Leeds United. Kewell had grown up in the western suburbs of Sydney, not the north, and he had progressed through the ranks at Marconi. But there was a method in the madness.

'They knew what they were doing,' David Hill later explained. 'They got the Arnolds and the Slaters – the Anglos. They didn't want this thing to be seen as wogball.'

Sticca and Nogarotto were building more than soccer clubs; they were constructing empires of the mind. Yet they were fake empires, and almost all the commentary on Carlton and Northern Spirit furnished the myth. At a traditional club like South Melbourne or Marconi, supporters could vote for the board of directors and have a post-match meal in the social club. By contrast, Carlton was wholly dependent on Australian Rules, a sport that had maintained a visceral hatred of soccer for decades, while Northern Spirit was a shell soccer team, 70 per cent owned by Mark Goldberg, an Englishman who lived in London.

Along with Perth Glory, Carlton and Northern Spirit hoovered up the talent that had been nurtured and developed by the established clubs. Andrew Marth, David Cervinski and Lubomir Lapsansky, all Melbourne Knights boys, had moved to Carlton. Mark Rudan, Eddie Bosnar, Robbie Slater, Graham Arnold and Paul Bilokapic, each an alumnus of Sydney United, had gone to Northern Spirit. Kresimir Marusic, who had played for both Melbourne Knights and Sydney United, ended up playing for Carlton as well as Northern Spirit. By the time Carlton signed John Markovski, Australian soccer's most extravagantly proportioned and outrageously skilful midfielder, he had already played for six NSL sides.

This was the dawn of a new era in which the individual, backed by an aggressive players union, became more important than the clubs. Many of these individuals crossed over to the new world with a heavy heart – they weren't just turning their back on any old sporting club, they were leaving behind the most important community institution in their life.

For Mark Rudan, leaving Sydney United for Northern Spirit transformed soccer from an emotional pursuit into a professional tran- saction. He and Bilokapic arrived at Spirit as great mates, just as their fathers had been before them. So when Rudan and Bilokapic showed up to the Croatian club in Spirit colours, they were met with jeers and cries of 'Judas'. It hurt both men and their fathers, of course, but they were powerless to change this new world order.

'Economics had as much to do with the demise of the NSL as anything else,' remembered Nogarotto. 'Economics in terms of collapsing balance sheets, inability to fund the cost of running a football club, revenue shrinking, supporter bases shrinking – and then, out of the woodwork, comes clubs like Carlton, Perth Glory and Northern Spirit who say to the players "We want you to be full-time professionals". Rudan and Bilokapic did not leave their clubs because they fell out of love with them. They had to leave for economic reasons: better salary, better conditions, better standing in the sporting community. We offered them all that.'

The commercial demands of the new era created a sharp distinction between the privately owned and the community-run clubs, the rich and the poor, the new and the old. The players union, rebadged as Professional Footballers Australia, introduced a minimum wage in the collective bargaining agreement of 1999, which sent several of the smaller clubs to the brink of financial collapse.

The new, privately owned clubs waved big promises and even bigger chequebooks, and for soccer's traditional base it was change or die. In many cases the traditional ethnic clubs simply didn't have the means to match the wages on offer, while the players, cognisant of their unstable vocation, wanted contract security and better remuneration.

As attendances at the ethnic clubs dwindled, some supporters also started to question the sustainability of the enterprise. The crowds had grown only marginally since the 1950s and 1960s, when Sydney Olympic was Pan Hellenic, Adelaide City was Juventus, and Melbourne Knights was Croatia. This didn't feel like progress.

By January 1999, Sydney United was broke, and the club was placed in the hands of administrators. By March, West Adelaide owner Con Makris told the *Advertiser* that he was wasting his time putting money into the club. 'If it was good for business I would say goodbye right now,' he lamented. 'Business? What business? We are doing it because the club has been there for 60 or 70 years. The Greek and Italian communities started it when they came here 60 years ago. We are raising money because it is a cultural thing. Nobody will make money out of soccer in Australia.'[5]

It would prove to be West Adelaide's final season in the NSL. It would be the tenth foundation club to leave the NSL forever.

Sitting uncomfortably between the decline of the ethnic club and the rise of the professional franchise was South Melbourne. The introduction of Carlton, coupled with the changing demographics of the city, brought forward an internal debate over the future of the club. In the 1997–98 NSL season, South had finished first, Carlton second. In the grand final, held in front of 16,000 people at Olympic Park, South Melbourne had beaten Carlton 2–1 in an epic encounter. It was the club's third national league title.

Yet there was a realisation at South Melbourne that the future belonged not to the best soccer team, but to the team with the best public profile. Urged on by a younger group of fans that wanted to see generational change on the board, general manager Peter Filopoulos tried to reposition the club to appeal to a wider audience.

'We understood that we needed to broaden our support base,' Filopoulos once explained. 'We knew that non-Greeks were coming to our games, and we were really conscious of how they felt, so we tried to build a broad entertainment package. We had jumping castles and kids at our games, dancing ... Wherever we could we tried to make it as entertaining as possible to attract a mainstream audience. We had an attractive football team, but we knew it had to be about more than just the football.'

Of all the ethnic clubs in the NSL, it was South Melbourne that had the most potential to meet the challenges of the new millennium. Its headquarters were in the Albert Park precinct, just a short tram ride from Melbourne's CBD, and the move from Middle Park to Bob Jane Stadium had led to a mini renaissance. The new social club and administrative facilities had been built into a comfortable grandstand, and there was enough space in the stadium to fit 15,000 people. The romance of Middle Park had been replaced by the professionalism of Bob Jane Stadium.

By April 1999, as the season drew to a close, South Melbourne had missed out on the premiership by just one point. For a second time in three seasons, Sydney United finished at the top of the ladder. In the finals series, however, South Melbourne twice beat Sydney United to claim back-to-back titles.

It was one of the greatest NSL sides: Michael Petkovic in goals, Fausto De Amicis at the back, Goran Lozanovski and Steve Panopoulos in the midfield, Paul Trimboli and Vaughan Coveny up front. And of course the coach, Ange Postecoglou, the club's favourite son, who had experienced South Melbourne at every level – from a supporter in the 1970s to a player in the 1980s and now as the coach in the 1990s. It was, as Filopoulos later recalled, 'our proudest moment'.

The only impediment to South Melbourne's wider acceptance in Victoria, it seemed, was its continued identification as a 'Greek club'. For an older generation, that Greek heritage was of immense pride and importance, yet for the younger generations it held progressively less relevance to their daily lives.

'I think there was a push from a younger generation to continue to grow the sport, whereas a lot of the older generation were happy with the status quo,' once remembered Harry Georgiadis, the assistant editor of Studs Up. 'They were probably quite happy with their power bases. My uncles and cousins were all South Melbourne supporters. A lot of my mates were Greek, so we gravitated to South Melbourne, but by the time Studs Up came along, we had sort of grown out of it.'

★

In June 1999, as the 23rd season of the National Soccer League ended and the new millennium approached, the first history of the competition was published. The Un-official Beginners Guide to the History of the Australian National Soccer League was a humble 32-page booklet with pictures of old NSL match programs on the front cover and a smorgasbord of fanzines on the back. There were no promotional blurbs, but on the first page there was a short foreword from SBS commentator Paul Williams. 'Fans of soccer in Australia are starved of information about the local scene due to mainstream media's lack of foresight,' he wrote. 'No wonder then that it has taken a group of FANS to produce such a bible for the rest of us to enjoy.'[6]

The Un-official Beginners Guide was the crowning achievement of Kevin Christopher and the *Studs Up* crew. It was not a glamorous publication – in the introduction, Christopher even warned that 'there is certain to be a typo or two' – but it had heart.

With the help of Andrew Howe's statistics, Christopher compiled each NSL season in chronological order, from 1977 to 1998–99. At the back of the book was a section for the NSL Cup, which ran from 1977 until 1997, and a list of the best players, coaches, referees and goalkeepers. It directed readers to head to the *OzSoccer* website for more information and, like *Studs Up*, it would be sold at Melbourne Sports Books and by word of mouth.

One of *Studs Up*'s subscribers, Bonita Mersiades, was the communications manager of Soccer NSW. She helped organise for Christopher to be flown from Melbourne to Sydney to sell his book at the Soccer Expo at Sydney Olympic Park. The Expo, which was designed to coincide with the Socceroos' games against Manchester United and a World Stars XI in June, proved to be a flop. There was little cooperation between the federations, the NSL clubs and the Socceroos. 'Unfortunately, most international visitors would have left the Expo in a state of bewilderment,' reported *Studs Up*.[7]

The Soccer Expo was held at Stadium Australia, a huge new facility that had been built for the 2000 Sydney Olympic Games. Everybody had their eyes on the Olympics. In late 1999, the national women's team, the Matildas, posed naked for a calendar to raise sponsorship money for the tournament. Not everybody was happy about it, but the calendar sold in the thousands and created headlines around the world.

'I didn't like it, and most of the board didn't like it, but the players wanted to do it,' remembered Heather Reid, a long-time member of the Australian Women's Soccer Association. 'That put the Matildas on the map. There was no marketing strategy in place. The girls were saying: we're not men, we're real women playing football. The whole issue of sexuality was thrown out the window. Everybody knows who the Matildas are because of that calendar.'

The fact that it was necessary for the Matildas to use their bodies to raise money pointed to a deeper problem in the administration of Australian soccer. Soccer Australia and AWSA were still operating as separate entities, and both were effectively broke. And so was *Studs Up*. For nearly five years Christopher had put his heart and soul into the production of his fanzine, to the point that it almost became a full-time job. It never made him or Harry Georgiadis any money.

Season 1999–2000, however, was the first of a new century, one that many supporters and officials thought would herald a new beginning for soccer in Australia. Christopher had published *The Un-official Beginners Guide* in the spirit of progress. He hoped the book would mark the history of the national league, catch the prevailing winds of change, and be a part of the great leap forward.

On the first Sunday of May, Perth Glory won its final game to finish the season on 64 points. Its nearest challenger, Wollongong Wolves, lost theirs and finished second on 60 points. It was Glory's first premiership in four seasons of existence.

Four weeks passed, and Perth Glory and Wollongong Wolves kept winning until both qualified for the grand final. It was the first time in national league history that both sides were unaligned to an ethnic group, and the crowd of 43,242 broke the record set in Brisbane three years earlier.

It took just 20 minutes for Bobby Despotovski to score the first goal. As he ran to celebrate in front of the Perth supporters, he pointed to the crowd first, and then to the name on the back of his jersey. The name 'Bobby Despotovski' would become synonymous with Australian soccer.

Born in Perth in 1971, Slobodan 'Bobby' Despotovski had been raised in Pancevo, a town not far from the capital, Belgrade, in the former Yugoslavia. The Despotovski family were ethnic Serbs, and before the war, Bobby had played for Dinamo Pancevo in the second division, and worked as a cobbler in a factory that sponsored the team. The money had been good, the work easy, and the quality of soccer excellent – perhaps the best second division in all of Europe.

Yet by the time Despotovski joined the Yugoslav army to complete his compulsory year of service, the tempest of nationalism had ripped through the country, breaking apart families, beliefs, towns and the Yugoslav football league, which was replaced by national competitions throughout the republics.

'I went in the army and everyone was treated the same: Croatians, Slovenians, Bosnians, Serbs, everybody,' Despotovski recalled. 'All of sudden, three months into the army service, the army had to release Slovenians, and the border with Croatia closed. The banking system was collapsing, and they could not send money to their children. Obviously our banking system was working, so we give money to the Croatians to get out, buy themselves a ticket and go home. Which is a natural thing to do for kids. Everything escalates very, very quickly. I don't know where they ended up. Did they reach their homes? Did they go back into the army over there to fight against somebody else? We didn't know any of that.'

Self-harm had been the only way out for the remaining Yugoslavs. Despotovski had cut three deep wounds into his arm, causing the psychiatrist to declare him crazy and grant him his freedom. As war and inflation destroyed the economy and the soccer, Despotovski moved back to Perth in November 1992.

After wandering through the local competition, as well as a couple of Victorian NSL and state league clubs, he had signed for Perth Glory in the club's inaugural season in 1996–97. The 1999–2000 season was his first premiership victory, and the first time he played in a national league grand final. Perhaps no surprise, then, that he scored the first goal. He had led a life in search of small openings to big opportunities.

Despotovski's opening strike was the first of three goals for Perth Glory. With a seemingly unassailable 3–0 half-time lead, the mood was celebratory. The crowd heaved with expectation in the mid-afternoon sun, the lurid purple and orange shimmering like a vision of the future. On and off the field the Glory had become the league's standard bearers. Visitors to Perth would marvel at the gulf between west and east: every television channel – not just SBS – took an interest in Glory, the newspapers treated the club as the pride of the city and the airwaves hummed with the sound of soccer. The club paid its players as professionals and spent huge amounts of money on marketing and promotions.

Yet perhaps there was too much focus on the cosmetic. Confident with a three-goal lead, Bernd Stange, the Glory's magnetic German coach and one-man publicity machine, spent the half-time interval talking to reporters. After the restart, Wollongong coach Nick Theodorakopoulos reshuffled his line-up, and within 25 minutes Matt Horsley and Scott Chipperfield – two men born and raised on the South Coast of NSW – scored a goal each to make it 3–2. As the referee checked his watch, an equaliser to Paul Reid from Wollongong sent the game into extra time. Wolves eventually won 7–6 in a dramatic penalty shootout, and it was soccer, not rugby league, that brought Wollongong its first ever national league title.

The snatch-and-grab victory earned the players a ticker-tape parade down the main street of Wollongong, and left behind a stunned Perth Glory. 'Heartbreak' was the headline in the *West Australian* the next day. Out of the depths of despair, however, grew a renewed sense of purpose. The Adelaide City striker Damian Mori could sense a competitive desire that was equal to his own. He agreed to join Perth Glory for the 2000–01 season.

Nicknamed 'Frogger' for his wide, bulging eyes, Mori was a no-nonsense, rock-solid ball of muscle who always appeared to be in a state of ready alert. His father, Joe, a Slovene who migrated to Australia from Yugoslavia in the 1950s, was also a soccer player.

Mori wasn't particularly creative or skilful, but he had a ruthless streak that drove him to become Australia's greatest goal-scorer. He started his national league career as a fullback, and in the early days the soccer writers called him a 'utility player', but by the time he moved to Adelaide City in 1993 he had made the striker's position his own.

At Adelaide City he won his first NSL title in 1994 and began working for Best Bricks and Pavers, a company owned by City president Bob D'Ottavi and coach Zoran Matic. The relationship between these three men was illustrative of a rapidly dying soccer culture, a loveable but unstable semi-professional environment where the trust in personal relationships was more important than the cold bureaucracy of the contract. On and off the field Matic got the best out of Mori, helping him build his house and integrating him into his rigid system of play, while D'Ottavi took him under his wing.

'I was very close with Bob, they used to call him my second dad,' Mori once said. 'He looked after me like a son and treated my family very well.'

Mori was the youngest player to reach 100 national league goals. During the 1995–96 season, he had set the record for the most goals in a single season and achieved the fastest goal in history, belting the ball straight from the kick-off into the back of the net after just 3.7 seconds. It created headlines around the world, and attracted the attention of *The Guinness Book of World Records*.

Soon after, he left for Germany on loan to the first division club Borussia Monchengladbach. It was a steep but rewarding learning curve, but he couldn't hold down a spot in the first team. By 1997 he was back playing in the NSL.

The new millennium heralded the most decisive change in his career. In the winter of 2000, with 299 national league matches and 148 goals behind him, Mori packed his bags and moved west from Adelaide to Perth. Unable to resist the temptation of higher wages at Perth Glory, he left behind a seven-year love affair with Adelaide City and his job at Best Bricks and Pavers.

It hurt D'Ottavi, of course, but he didn't hold a grudge. He realised that Perth Glory had offered Mori something that few other clubs could: full-time professionalism.

★

By the year 2000, there were more privatised entities in the National Soccer League than community-owned clubs. This, above all else, was the legacy of Professional Footballers Australia and Perth Glory. The players union was the most stable and cohesive institution within the game, the most powerful collective voice, and the most impatient for change. The PFA had consistently demanded higher standards of professionalism, while Perth Glory had proven that these expectations could only be met under a privatised, corporate model.

In this enterprising new world, the ethnic clubs hung on like grim death. Most became wholly owned or privately funded by fraternal, sympathetic businessmen. Bob D'Ottavi plunged his own cash into propping up Adelaide City; three Greek-Australians formed the 'Friends of Sydney Olympic'; and Eastern Pride – the club formerly known as Morwell Falcons – leaned on Don Di Fabrizio for survival.

'Nobody wanted to get rid of the [ethnic clubs],' Brendan Schwab once explained, 'but they were going to collapse! Not only were they monocultural, they were also mono-generational. Young people had not taken over. Once we introduced the demands of profession-alism – and this is why there's probably some resentment towards us – these clubs went from being community owned to owned by a wealthy benefactor from that community.'

Privatisation wasn't simply a matter for the soccer clubs. In Australian Rules football, privately owned clubs had been formed with varying degrees of success in Sydney, Brisbane and Perth. In rugby league the first ever privately owned club, the Brisbane Broncos, became a powerhouse, winning four premierships in its first decade. And after the dirty Super League war broke out between Rupert Murdoch and Kerry Packer, two of Australia's richest businessmen, the rugby league clubs began to merge and restructure their operations to fit a hyper commercial new age.

Private interests frayed the traditions of all football codes, and even though it was the economics, not the identity, that was killing soccer's ethnic clubs, the game's national question remained at the centre of the conversation. 'There was only one way I could see soccer progressing in this country, and that was to break away from the little-ethnic-club model,' once recalled Lou Sticca. 'I did that with Carlton. The problem is that it's like having a glass of dirty water, and you put a little bit of clean water into it and it becomes polluted.'

Sticca's and Remo Nogarotto's experiments had lost both popular support and momentum. The Carlton Football Club pulled its funding from the soccer team after three-and-a-half seasons, and the team was forced to move to Olympic Park, and then to Epping Stadium in an unfortunate corner of Melbourne's northern suburbs. By December, the club was bankrupt, indebted to Soccer Australia and the Australian Tax Office. The NSL would have to limp through the remaining 22 rounds without it.

Northern Spirit, meanwhile, had lurched from one crisis to another after its owner, Crystal Palace chairman Mark Goldberg, declared bankruptcy just a few months into its first season. Northern Spirit players Robbie Slater, Ian Crook and Graham Arnold had thrown good money after bad in an attempt to recapitalise the club, but they too had lost a small fortune.

Nogarotto fought a long battle with the players union over his treatment of the senior players, who had informed the union of Spirit's breach of the award wage. The case ended up in the Federal Court. Things got very messy very quickly and, as the club was sold from Crystal Palace to Scottish club Glasgow Rangers, Nogarotto departed.

The Northern Spirit colours switched from white, red and yellow to the blue of Glasgow Rangers, and the Rangers crest was stamped on the sleeve. Just as Carlton's potential fanbase stayed away due to its association with one AFL club, many of Spirit's Catholic and Glasgow Celtic supporters shied away from a franchise that they now saw as a new arm of the Protestant Glasgow Rangers. It would never recover.

The failure of Carlton Soccer Club and the ongoing crises throughout the NSL prompted Professional Footballers Australia to reassess its role in the game. The fact that the NSL was actually forcing teams to have byes due to the withdrawal of Carlton was deeply embarrassing – more reminiscent of an under-12s carnival than a national, professional competition.

Led by Brendan Schwab, the PFA decided that it had to focus not only on the tit-for-tat industrial matters, but on the reform of the game as a whole.

'We had a meeting with Soccer Australia that I'll never forget,' Craig Foster once recalled. 'We were talking about creating equity and building the brand in an Anzac Day match, for instance, or a New Year's Eve match, perhaps. We started putting it to them, and we said, "Why don't you get the NSL draw, and let's look for windows where we can do this." The individual concerned said, "Oh, okay, I'll go get it." We had tea and coffee in there, we must have been 20 minutes waiting. The Soccer Australia officials came back in, with two sheets of foolscap paper, with a draw handwritten in pen. I remember looking at Schwabby and going, "Mate, this is over." Not long after, we had a meeting in Melbourne, and started strategising about how to close these guys down.'

In late December 2000, as the league reeled from Carlton's dramatic exit, the PFA registered the name 'Australian Premier League' and, with the financial help of Perth Glory owner Nick Tana, plunged $700,000 into research for a new national competition.

'Many are asking why the PFA is involving itself so heavily in driving policy – an area which, in an ideal world, would belong to the sport's administration,' reported Michael Cockerill.

> The answer is that rank-and-file players have tired of the endless chaos within their profession. Over the past five years, ten clubs have either gone into administration or fallen out of the competition. The players, with their livelihoods at stake, have lost confidence that Soccer Australia is able, or even willing, to help.[8]

The 'endless chaos' of the decade had taken its toll on Kimon Taliadoros. Nearing 33 years of age, he had seen it all: disputes with clubs and the federation, the collapse of Collingwood Warriors, the media spotlight during the Stewart Report, the intense scrutiny of the Senate inquiry, and the triumph of collective bargaining agreements. By 2001, the man once described as 'the revolutionary chief in the guerrilla warfare of industrial relations' was playing with Parramatta Power, a newly formed franchise that was funded by the Parramatta Eels rugby league side.[9] It was his fifth club in ten years.

On 9 February 2001, in front of just a few thousand spectators at Brisbane's Ballymore Oval, he collapsed to the turf with a nasty hamstring strain. In pain, he hobbled off the field for treatment. He would never return.

'That was it,' he later recalled. 'The only reason I joined Parramatta Power was because the coach asked me to come along and be part of the squad – he needed someone senior to help with the culture and the competitiveness. I was happy to do it, but I ended up playing more than I thought I would. They were full-time, and I would train 50 per cent of the time. The fitness and standard of the players were increasing relative to someone like me that was at the tail end of their career. There was nothing ceremonial about it – it was just exit stage left.'

At the very end, as full-time professionalism expanded throughout the clubs, he simply could not keep up with the standards that he had done so much to help create. Generations of Australian soccer players would go on to benefit from the sacrifices and the work that he had put in to build a professional and functional players union, yet he did not retire with a testimonial match, nor was he farewelled with glowing newspaper reports or tributes in the news bulletins. He just hung up his boots, and returned to his day job.

In total, Taliadoros played 244 NSL games in 15 seasons, won two championships, an NSL Cup, one NSL Golden Boot award, and scored 82 goals. For the Socceroos he scored two goals in nine games. Years later, when a reporter asked him to recount his playing career, he would chuckle and lament that it became 'a sideshow'.

Yet although few recognised it at the time, he was perhaps the most influential Australian soccer player of his generation. In 2001, clubs employed more than half of the players on a full-time basis, a far cry from when the PFA began back in 1993. Throughout his own career, however, Taliadoros never signed a full-time contract. He never benefited personally from the conditions that he had fought to enshrine.

Intent on revolutionising the national league, the biggest battles for the PFA were still to come. The NSL product, such as it was, carried the fetid stench of death. The PFA reported that 100 per cent of its membership under the age of 22 wanted to leave the NSL and pursue a career overseas. And in April 2001, four rounds before the end of the 25th season of the NSL, Eastern Pride collapsed.

The club formerly known as Morwell Falcons played its final game against Canberra Cosmos in front of less than 2000 spectators in Canberra. The senior players, who hadn't received wages for six weeks, went on strike on the Friday night before the game, and after Soccer Australia refused a postponement request from the PFA, Eastern Pride's youth team were forced to play instead. The teenagers lost 7–1.

★

By the turn of the century, the National Soccer League had become the secret society of Australia's most popular pastime. Soccer reigned in the participation statistics, in the schoolyard, at work lunches, on the streets and in the parks. The World Cup was a consistent ratings bonanza for SBS. Millions of Australians rose at ungodly hours of the morning to watch the tournament, even though the Socceroos hadn't qualified since 1974. By some measure, soccer was the most democratic, the most representative, the most educative and the most accessible Australian sport.

But no national sporting competition was ever so broken as the NSL was in 2001. Tony Labbozzetta – who just a few years earlier had been instructed to never again hold a position of authority in the game – was the president of Soccer Australia. The competition and its governing body reigned like an ageing dictator, disliked by almost everybody while remaining virtually immune from positive, lasting change. It maintained its power through the patronage of small cliques, a tangled web of loyalties and the cynical apathy of the masses.

In the first 25 seasons of the NSL, more than 40 clubs had come and gone. This was how the NSL began to die a spiritual death. Nobody liked the NSL; they liked their club, and for as long as the NSL supported their clubs' ambitions they were prepared to put up with it. But once Preston Makedonia or Canberra City or Brunswick Juventus or APIA Leichhardt or West Adelaide or Brisbane City went back to the state league, their fans lost interest and took up other weekend activities. It was a long, painful and losing battle of attrition.

By the end of April 2001, the lower reaches of the competition ladder painted a picture of cataclysmic failure. Carlton and Eastern Pride were left broken down at the bottom, behind Newcastle Breakers, Northern Spirit, Brisbane Strikers and Canberra Cosmos. The decline of each club represented a new kind of failure, whether it be cross-code cooperation, regional centres, foreign ownership or strategically placed one-town-teams.

On 3 May 2001, just days before the finals series began, Brendan Schwab, the chief executive of the players union, sent an angry letter to Stefan Kamasz, the general manager of the NSL. 'The NSL's problems do not merely lie with the poor management [...] of many of our clubs,' he wrote. 'They lie with the repeated failure of Soccer Australia over a long period of time to make decisions of the requisite quality to create the environment conducive to the growth and development of our clubs and the competition as a whole.'[10]

Every experiment to take soccer out of the ghetto, save for Perth Glory, had failed. Yet for the first time in its history, even Glory began to lose money. It didn't immediately affect the crowds, which hovered around the 15,000 mark, nor did it affect the quality of the team, which finished in third place.

This on-field success was maintained largely thanks to the brilliance of Damian Mori and Bobby Despotovski, who had become the deadliest strike partnership in national league history. They would play golf together every Friday and discuss tactics for the weekend match. In 2000–01, their first season together, over 26 rounds Mori scored 18 goals while Despotovski netted 17.

On 6 May 2001, Perth Glory travelled east for an elimination semi-final against Melbourne Knights. This was the most feared away trip in Australian soccer. Knights Stadium, located in a grim, industrial scrapyard in the western suburbs of Melbourne, provided almost every discomfort imaginable. The national colours and flag of Croatia were omnipresent, and the sponsors' boards were filled with fraternal butcher shops, construction companies and travel agencies. Chants of 'CRO-A-ZIA, CRO-A-ZIA, CRO-A-ZIA' rose from dirty terraces, caught the wind, and faded over the vacant wasteland that backed onto the ground. Angry wire fences separated players from spectators. Perth Glory owner Nick Tana called it 'the cold hole of hell'.[11]

For Despotovski, of Serbian background, Knights Stadium was never a welcoming atmosphere. This particular game, however, turned feral. It began with a Perth Glory defender being sent off, turned ugly as flares were let off on the terraces, and then became dangerous as a rocket flare was launched onto the pitch, narrowly missing the players.

After the referee blew full-time on a 0–0 draw, a group of wild Melbourne Knights supporters assaulted the Glory players on their way out of the ground. Despotovski was the focus of both the riot and its aftermath, as television replays clearly showed him gesturing to the crowd with a three-fingered salute.

'This very same salute was cited in the application to the International Court of Justice against Serbian war crimes during the Balkan conflict,' said a spokesperson from the Australian Muslim Public Affairs Committee following the match. 'The application provided evidence that Serbs were amputating Muslims' fingers so as to resemble this same salute.'[12]

Equally unhappy was the president of Melbourne Knights, Harry Mrksa, who claimed it was akin to entering a synagogue with 'a Heil Hitler greeting'.[13]

As Despotovski protested his innocence, the Serbian community came to his defence, with one community leader telling the Australian that the sign was a religious gesture that 'pre-dates the Battle of Kosovo in the 13th century'.[14] Not for the first time, the soccer community was dragged though a tragicomic crash course in Balkan history and politics.

Perth Glory furiously defended Despotovski. The club had been formed to transcend this kind of nonsense, and at one press conference after the match the song 'I Am Australian' was belted out, as if to drive a wedge between them and the Melbourne Knights. But Glory's star striker was no cleanskin. Only a few months prior, Ransford Banini, a Ghanian defender who played for Melbourne Knights, claimed that Despotovski had called him a 'black monkey'. The Human Rights and Equal Opportunity Commission had been called in to mediate.

From mass pitch invasions and assaults on referees to firebombed houses, weaponised fights, racist abuse and fascist iconography, the NSL had experienced almost every possible social disgrace. It was a garbage fire of personal, political, factional and sectarian jealousies and rivalries. The rest of the population watched on like strangers in their own country, uninterested in the cause but furiously indignant at the effect. One reporter for the *Sydney Morning Herald* concluded: 'Not what Al Grassby had in mind when he championed multiculturalism and purple suits in the 1970s.'[15]

The tragedy of all this was that soccer's ethnic clubs – which had been in the vanguard of the movement towards multiculturalism – had now become its own worst folk devil. Many people felt that the structure of the NSL clubs was keeping the ethnic communities in silos, rather than integrating them into broader society. The ethnic club was now seen as the failure, not the success, of multicultural Australia.

A few days after the incident, Melbourne Knights travelled west and beat Perth Glory in the second leg of the semifinal. The club was fined $30,000 for its part in the Despotovski drama, and even one of the Knights directors admitted that they deserved to be expelled from the league.

In the end, Melbourne Knights was eliminated before the grand final, and Wollongong Wolves went on to win its second consecutive NSL title. Despotovski returned to Perth as a hate figure of the Croatian community and a hero to the Serbs. Soccer Australia fined him $2000 and death threats arrived at his home. He lived, as he once joked, 'like Al Capone'. He never played at Knights Stadium again.

The reason he gave that three-fingered salute, he later admitted, was because of a provocative anti-Serb banner he saw in the home end. A decade after leaving the Yugoslav army, he still could not escape the Balkan War.

'I was taking a corner,' he remembered. 'What angered me was the banners on that particular day. They say how many Serbs they killed in Krajina. That's why I did what I did it. That banner is completely wrong. They celebrating how many Serbian kids and women and people died. Are you kidding me? We live in the best country in the world, and you doing that?'

★

In November 2001, four years after the tragedy against Iran, the Socceroos were back at the Melbourne Cricket Ground for a World Cup qualifier. Its opponents were Uruguay and the reward for qualification was even greater than in 1998: if the Socceroos could fend off the Uruguayans, it would be part of a World Cup that would be broadcast into Australian homes on prime-time television. In anticipation of this ratings bonanza, Channel 9 bought the rights to the tournament.

But the Socceroos collapsed in a style that had become all too familiar. It won the first leg in Melbourne 1–0, courtesy of a penalty to Kevin Muscat, before being bullied out of Montevideo in a 3–0 loss. The tears on the face of Tony Vidmar, a softly spoken 31-year-old Australian defender, were reminiscent of Johnny Warren's four years earlier. The Socceroos had become a byword for failure.

There was no 'Black Issue' of *Studs Up* to follow this latest defeat. The fanzine had been wound up, and boxes of *The Un-official Beginners Guide to the History of the Australian National Soccer League* were left unsold. In the last issue of *Studs Up*, a notice was printed on the back cover. 'We could really use some volunteers at *Studs Up* just to make sure the issues get out on time,' it read.[16] On the front cover was an incredible photo of Ransford Banini removing a flare from the pitch at Knights Stadium.

'The 2001 World Cup qualifier was probably the endpoint,' recalled Harry Georgiadis. 'The subscriptions hadn't increased to the level we wanted, and just the drudgery of putting out a new publication every month weighed on us.'

The World Cup was beamed back to Australia, and another generation of Australian children was forced to pick another country to support. The only Australians at the tournament were Joe Simunic and Ante Seric, who played for Croatia, and Christian Vieri, who played for Italy. Channel 9 screened just 16 of the 64 games – those it thought would rate well. SBS picked up the remaining 48 games, and Craig Foster joined Johnny Warren and Les Murray on an expert panel, settling into a new role that would come to define his career.

Newspapers sent only a few staff members to cover the tournament. The disinterest from Australia's blinkered media establishment belied the enthusiasm of the general public. 'I guess we knew the World Cup would be big but I don't think we knew it would be this big,' lamented one newspaper editor. 'It's been unpredictable, there've been upsets and it's obviously been a particularly exciting tournament. But we couldn't have foreseen all that.'[17]

SBS foresaw it. Since 1990, the multicultural broadcaster had made sure that Australia was connected to the World Cup, beaming all the matches back to Australia even if the Socceroos were never there. Foreign television crews would marvel at this commitment, but for SBS the reason was simple. The World Cup was Australia's tournament, the only sporting event that could energise both the ethnic communities and the uninvolved Australians. Only at SBS was there a recognition and a deep respect for Australian soccer's dual identities. SBS knew that there was a passionate Australian audience in the obscurity of South Korea versus Poland, or Saudi Arabia versus Cameroon.

The rest of Australia expected the ethnic communities to forget about life in the old country, to watch rugby league or Australian Rules or cricket, to give up on soccer and, most of all, to assimilate.

Six days after the 2002 World Cup final, Bobby Despotovski made his international debut for Australia. In the opening match of the Oceania Nations Cup, he joined Damian Mori in attack for the last half-hour against Vanuatu. By full-time, both Mori and Despotovski had scored to make it 2–0.

For generations, the best strikers in Australia had carried their form from the national league to the Socceroos. On the face of it Mori and Despotovski, both 31, were no different. The combination of these two men had strengthened during the 2001–02 season, with Mori winning the Golden Boot and Despotovski finishing third. Yet neither of them should have been playing for the Socceroos that day. The circumstances that brought them together in green and gold had more to do with institutional politics than individual prowess.

By 2002, Soccer Australia was imperilled by a deep financial crisis. It had been forced to go cap in hand to the overseas-based Socceroos, asking them to play for nothing at the Oceania Nations Cup and pay for their own flights back to Auckland. Only Scott Chipperfield agreed. The incompetence of the governing body began to dictate team selections, but tragically the overseas-based Socceroos copped some of the blame. 'There is no green-and-gold item of apparel that generates less passion than an Australian soccer shirt,' decided one sportswriter, blaming the legacy of an 'ethnically based' game.[18]

In the second match against New Caledonia, Despotovski netted four goals in an 11–0 win. An 8–0 victory over Fiji and a 2–1 triumph over Tahiti put the Socceroos into the final against New Zealand. Success would ensure qualification for the 2003 Confederations Cup and, more importantly, a $3 million payday for Soccer Australia.

With scores locked at 0–0 after 73 minutes, Despotovski was again brought off the bench to join Mori up front. Yet it was Ryan Nelsen, a New Zealand defender, who scored the only goal of the game.

Many people believed that Soccer Australia had got what it deserved. It had forced an underprepared, third-rate squad into battle, and when they failed, the federation was plunged into an even more parlous financial state. 'If any one day was symbolic of the death of Soccer

Australia, it was that game,' recalled Andrew Howe. 'I remember seeing the result and thinking, *Fucking hell, does it get any worse than this?*'

In Melbourne, Kevin Christopher tried to use humour to see through the gloom, joking with friends that he might not get to see the Socceroos play at a World Cup in his lifetime. Just days before the new season, the joke became a grim reality. He had cancer, and his body had grown gaunt and pale. On Sunday 4 August 2002, he passed away.

'I used to worry about him not eating enough,' remembered Bonita Mersiades, who had become a regular correspondent and friend to Christopher. 'He was a well-spoken Australian guy. He could talk – he wasn't a person that was magnetic, but if you start talking with him you'd want to listen. He told me that he had played soccer as a young-ster, and he just loved it. It was interesting – I almost got the feeling sometimes that he was envious of the wogs who'd grown up with the wog teams. He was a great guy. I loved him.'

Christopher left behind a young son and a family and a game of unfulfilled promise. He had formed a network of friends in this hopeful sport, and created for them a hive of opportunity. Assembling copy, writing articles, printing and mailing each edition to his readers: this, however small, was Christopher's contribution to soccer. Many fanzines were influenced by *Studs Up*, including *The Farr Post* from Brisbane, *Glory Daze* and *The Fat* from Perth, *My Blue Heaven* from the supporters at Carlton and *Wolf's Lair* from Wollongong. None, however, could ever replicate or match Christopher's beloved *Studs Up*. He was, as Roy Hay once remembered, 'an original'.

Not everybody had agreed with *Studs Up*'s editorial line, and some were unhappy with the bare-chested approach to reporting. Still, no other publication since the days of *Soccer World* and *Soccer Action* had been able to so accurately capture the spirit of the age. Christopher created something original, a lively, niche space for others to enjoy.

He was buried at Springvale Cemetery in the outer suburbs of Melbourne, while in Adelaide Andrew Howe lovingly archived the full collection of *Studs Up* in his garage and saved many of the unsold copies of *The Un-official Beginners Guide to the History of the Australian National Soccer League*. There they would remain as a painful metaphor for the final years of Australia's first national league; a competition that began in the throes of hope and reform, and ended in the acute stress of its own commercial naivety.

'Kevin was disappointed,' Harry Georgiadis would later remember. 'I think he took it to heart – he felt there was a real market for that kind of publication, and for football in general. We're all football fans, but Kevin really felt that the game had a future.'

DEATH TO THE NSL

2003–2004

Almighty God

It is your wish that all of us, whatever family or ethnic background, live together in peace and harmony.

In this new soccer club, Adelaide United, we see a sign of a unity that will enable great things to be achieved.

Let these players enjoy our wholehearted support. They are ready for the contest. Keep them safe from injury and harm.

Instil in them respect for each other and for the great game of soccer; and reward them for their hard work and perseverance.

By God's authority I commit Adelaide United, its players, managers and on ground staff to the care of Almighty God and the maternal protection of the Blessed Virgin Mary, Mother of God.

And so in God's name I bless you – the Father, the Son and the Holy Spirit – Amen.

Father John Fleming
Blessing of Adelaide United FC, 2003[1]

On the third weekend of September 2002, Australia's oldest national sporting competition kicked off in a state of severe distress. For its 26 seasons, the National Soccer League had mounting debts, an uninterested broadcast partner and no major sponsor. Player wages had been cut by dying, debt-ridden clubs, and more than 100 Australian players had deserted the league to play abroad. None of the six matches in the opening round drew a crowd of more than 7000 people, with the average attendance only marginally higher than that of the very first round back in 1977.

NSL commissioner Remo Nogarotto tried to put on a brave face, but he knew the league was effectively finished. The game, as he would later recall, 'was kept alive courtesy of the charity of its creditors, some sponsorship and, most importantly, government funding'.

Nogarotto had taken over running the NSL in 2001, after his part in orchestrating a bloodless coup that removed Tony Labbozzetta from the chairmanship of Soccer Australia. Labbozzetta had survived two government inquiries, an attempt by David Hill to throw him out of soccer and severe unpopularity among the game's rank-and-file. At one NSL grand final, he was booed off the podium in his hometown.

His downfall had been almost Shakespearean. Here was the master of the numbers betrayed by those he thought were his allies; soccer's most cunning general ambushed by a pincer move that had been organised in the shadow of the backroom. All sides of soccer's political spectrum lined up to celebrate Labbozzetta's removal, including the ex–Soccer Australia boss David Hill and the former Victorian premier Jeff Kennett. 'I never thought I'd see the day when Liberal and Labor would work so closely together,' said Labbozzetta as Ian Knop was named as his replacement.[2]

One of the silent plotters in this coup was Steve Doszpot, the president of Soccer Canberra and the former promotions manager of Canberra City. Knop and Doszpot were Liberal Party loyalists and had been close since their days at CanTrade, a Canberra-based company that had been pushing for increased trade with the Asian region throughout the 1990s.

By 2002, Australia's main export market was Japan, the main source of its imports was East Asia, and more than one million Australians claimed Asian ancestry. China and India had become the world's fastest-growing economies, and the FIFA World Cup was superbly hosted by Korea and Japan and watched by tens of millions of people across 200 countries.

During the final, Prime Minister John Howard was high in the sky, travelling from Sydney to Frankfurt for a meeting with the German chancellor, Gerhard Schroder. By the time he landed, news had filtered through that Germany had lost to Brazil. Before the trade talks commenced, Howard passed on his commiserations to his host. Soccer's greatest asset, Howard would later explain, is that 'it has a far greater reach than any other sport'.[3]

The geopolitical machinations of the 2002 World Cup were impossible to ignore. Howard saw two of Australia's most important trading partners host the biggest sporting event on earth, and he had wondered, along with millions of Australians, why the Socceroos weren't there. The question was obvious: why was the government funding a sport with so much potential for so little return?

In July 2002, as Soccer Australia's finances plummeted, Ian Knop had requested a $3 million bailout from the federal government. Howard and his sports minister, Rod Kemp, agreed, and used the opportunity to commission a root-and-branch inquiry into the management of the game. The inquiry, which became known as the Crawford Report, would sweep away the political fiefdoms, birth a new governing body, bring Frank Lowy back from his self-imposed exile and lead to the creation of a new national league. It would change soccer in Australia forever.

With Ian Knop in charge of Soccer Australia and the federal government engaged in the reform process, Steve Doszpot felt the game was on the precipice of true and lasting change – the kind of change for which he had been waiting for more than two decades.

But the process was slow. During Knop's short reign, Soccer Australia imposed a registration levy on all participants to help service the administration's debts, there was the Oceania Nations Cup debacle in New Zealand, and Channel 7 tried to wriggle out of the broadcast deal. Later it would be revealed that Channel 7 had deliberately buried soccer in the service of AFL. In one email, a Channel 7 director even lamented that the AFL had not given it enough credit after it had 'secured the soccer rights and suffocated the sport'.[4]

Getting the federal government involved may well have been Knop's crowning achievement, but the short-term picture was bleaker than ever. Moreover, many of Knop's fellow board members were furious at his appeal to the Howard government. In late October 2002, after repeated calls for his resignation, Knop fell on his sword.

The contenders to replace him included Paul Afkos, a former part-owner of Perth Glory who had fallen out with Nick Tana; Dominic Galati, the head of International Entertainment Corporation, who had just reached an out-of-court settlement with Soccer Australia over a marketing rights deal; and Remo Nogarotto. On the first weekend of December, Nogarotto was unanimously elected, becoming the fourth chairman of Soccer Australia in just four years. He emerged from the extraordinary general meeting preaching unity and progress.

But in the nation's capital Doszpot boycotted the election, labelled it illegitimate, and resigned from the presidency of Soccer Canberra. He placed all his remaining faith in the federal government inquiry. 'We needed an arbitrator that could break the nexus that existed between those who didn't want any change, and those that wanted change,' he later recalled.

As the factional warlords of Soccer Australia continued their political knife-fights, the players union prepared for revolution. In December 2002, Professional Footballers Australia finally published their research for a new national competition.

Titled *Australian Premier League: For the Fans*, it was a 15-page manifesto for the future. The PFA called for a brand new, ten-team competition based around what they called the '5 Pillars' strategy: quality, atmosphere, community, local brands and visibility. Each Australian Premier League club would operate at a budget of around $3 million and borrow from the example set by Perth Glory, which the PFA labelled 'a living model of the "5 Pillars" strategy'. Players would be paid as full-time professionals and fans would be crammed into throbbing boutique stadiums.

This document was the product of 18 months of market research, $700,000 of investment, and the undying faith of a players union that had done more than any other organisation to revamp Australian soccer. The PFA was in a fever of reform, boasting an impressive track record of achievements and an executive that included Alex Tobin, Craig Foster, Andy Harper and Francis Awaritefe. 'Soccer,' read the report, 'is the final frontier of Australian sport.'[5]

Brendan Schwab had set up PFA Management Ltd to run as a separate commercial arm of the players union, and alongside John Poulakakis, the son of a legendary South Melbourne Hellas coach, completely reimagined the national soccer league. They met secretly with the agents of change, including Nick Tana and Remo Nogarotto, and reached out to the players, both in the NSL and abroad. They noted happily that more Australians tuned in to watch the 2002 World Cup final than the AFL or rugby league grand finals. And then in 2002, an independent sports report noted that 44 per cent of Australians between the ages of 16 and 55 were interested in soccer. This gave the national league a potential market of six million people.

Like many reviews and reports before it, PFA Management Ltd's report recommended that the APL clubs be separated by district and geography, with three teams in Sydney, two teams in Melbourne, one team each in Adelaide, Brisbane and Perth, and two more from regional centres. Cutting the league down to just ten teams would lead to a 33 per cent job loss for the union's members, but this was written off as a necessary sacrifice.

These ten community-based franchises were the best chance of winning the hearts and minds of a new generation of soccer fans. 'The team brands will [...] establish strong and meaningful relationships with their respective local marketplaces,' read the report. 'Importantly, this will not be left to the discretion of the individual APL Team.'[6]

This was in direct response to the anarchy of the NSL and the political horse-trading that went on at Soccer Australia. Under the PFA model, a new direction would be set from the top, without favour to sectional interests or blocs. The days of the ethnic club were numbered. Soccer's great tribes became dead men walking.

★

'They knew the game had to change,' Remo Nogarotto once recalled. 'Whether that was from within or ultimately from outside, they knew. The only thing that stopped them was that weight of history. They carried the burden from people before them that had mortgaged properties; clubs that had been built around the need for migrants to coalesce around a common element. I don't think they wanted to be the guy who pulled the pin on all that history.'

One of the pre-eminent members of this old guard was Bob D'Ottavi, the president of Adelaide City. After taking over the club in 1998, D'Ottavi plunged millions of dollars of his own money into ensuring its survival in the NSL. He watched on as club stalwarts such as Alex Tobin and Damian Mori departed to rich, interstate rivals. And he threw open the gates in an attempt to bring the supporters back, but crowds barely rose above 3000.

Adelaide City was an old club on death row, and D'Ottavi was an elderly man with an overbearing style of ownership. In early 2002 he had tried to install club legends Sergio Melta and Carlo Talladira as coaches, while still demanding the final say on team selections. Both men refused any part of the arrangement. Another club legend, Charley Villani, resigned soon after, claiming boardroom interference in training and on match day. By the end of 2002, D'Ottavi had taken to coaching the side himself, while a committee of senior players ran the training sessions.

But while D'Ottavi maintained control over his club, he was powerless to influence the new corporate direction in which the game was heading. By April 2003, as rumours swirled about the future of Adelaide City, the federal government inquiry into the structure, governance and management of soccer in Australia was published. The Crawford Report drew upon eight months of investigation, more than 40 meetings with stakeholders and 200 submissions from the general public. The 88-page report contained a total of 53 recommendations, most notably for a new board at Soccer Australia and a new constitution. Nobody had a positive word to say about the state of soccer in Australia.

'The committee is of the view that the existing structure does not work,' said its author, David Crawford. 'It is overly complicated and simply does not make sense in today's corporate world.'[7]

While the existing board members were publicly ambushed, the report recommended that three men be installed as their interim replacements. They were John Singleton, a furiously Australian advertising mogul; Ron Walker, the head of Victorian major events; and Frank Lowy, who had been estranged from soccer for 15 years.

'I am prepared to be involved in an interim Soccer Australia board with the express purpose of driving through important changes within the sport,' announced Lowy. 'It is now up to the stakeholders of soccer in Australia to make a decision on whether they would wholeheartedly support the proposed changes and my involvement.'[8]

As Remo Nogarotto was chairman of Soccer Australia, all eyes were on him. At first he objected to the demands for him and his cohort to resign, labelling the report a 'nuclear holocaust'.[9] Then, after realising the magnitude of the opposition, he quietly relinquished his position.

But not everyone admitted defeat. Four of his fellow board members refused to budge. They were met with howls of anger from a soccer community itching for change. A group of ex-Socceroos captains even signed a letter calling on them to resign.

'A collection of bush lawyers and non-league businessmen have succeeded in defying a coalition of the Prime Minister, a major league businessman, the apparatus of government and an overwhelming tide of public opinion,' raged Michael Cockerill in the *Sydney Morning Herald*. 'It would be laughable if it weren't so embarrassing.'[10]

As these recalcitrant board members clung to their positions at Soccer Australia, D'Ottavi faced mutiny in Adelaide. He had earned the ire of the players union after publicly commenting 'you can't make a racehorse out of a donkey' about his goalkeeper.[11] Then he fell foul of his captain, Ante Kovacevic, who brought in the players union on a dispute about unpaid wages. Kovacevic was ostracised from training, left out of the last two games of the finals series, and by season's end he would depart the club altogether.

Adelaide City, which had been renamed Adelaide City Force, ended up missing the grand final by one game. Instead, Perth Glory hosted Sydney Olympic. In front of more than 38,000 spectators, the ex–Adelaide City striker Damian Mori scored Glory's winning goal. He became the first player to pass 200 national league goals and just the third player to appear in six grand finals. His goal secured Glory's first championship and, as if to prove the club's dominance, Mori and Bobby Despotovski finished first and second respectively in the league's goal-scoring charts. Mori was awarded the Golden Boot for the fifth time in his career and player of the season for the second time.

As the cold winds of change swirled from east to west, the last rites were read out for a broken-down, unpopular federation and a lonely, unsustainable club. Not long after the last board members exited Soccer Australia, allowing Frank Lowy to assume full control of the game's administration, D'Ottavi announced that he could no longer fund Adelaide City. He claimed to have poured $5 million of his own cash into the club and could afford no more.

By September 2003, after 27 seasons, 768 matches in the NSL and three championships, Adelaide City became the 29th club to exit the competition. City retreated to state league football for the first time since 1976. Club captain Aurelio Vidmar contemplated retirement, gun goal-scorer Carl Veart readied himself for life in the lower leagues, while D'Ottavi was left heartbroken.

'I have been putting money in for the last four years, and I just can't do it any more,' he said. 'This is a club with a long history – it's played more games than any other team in the competition – but no one has come forward. It's very obvious that they don't want the club.'[12]

Yet within a few weeks, a prominent local businessman named Gordon Pickard agreed to fund a new, federation-backed team to replace Adelaide City. Pickard was a child migrant from Manchester, a millionaire home-builder, and an agitator for change. 'Adelaide City is a spent force and I have no intention of throwing away good money after bad,' he told the *Advertiser.* 'South Australia must go with a brand new composite club with new colours and based on the Adelaide Crows [AFL] model.'[13]

Here was the saddest metaphor for the decline of soccer's great tribes. One of the most successful clubs in Australian history was suffocated and starved, and then thrown on the scrap heap by a quiet coalition of big business and the local federation. The grim irony was not lost on D'Ottavi, who left the NSL and never returned.

By 2003, Andrew Howe was a man in demand. He had been on the payroll of Soccer Australia since 1999, curating regular updates for each NSL round and a 'Did You Know?' segment for the organisation's media releases. In 2000, he had published his first NSL season guide and moved his huge database of statistics over to SBS. In 2001, Professional Footballers Australia had tasked him with working out the lifespan of a national league player, and by 2002 journalists began referring to him as 'the master statistician'.

Yet in nearly 15 years of religiously following the NSL, he still didn't have a team that he could truly call his own. He had loved watching the rise of the Croatian clubs of Sydney and Melbourne and was inspired by Perth Glory, but had never warmed to the teams in his adopted hometown.

When Gordon Pickard and the South Australian Soccer Federation unveiled 'Adelaide United', however, Howe immediately got involved. He contacted the club's media department and was placed in charge of producing the match-day program.

'I wouldn't say I was passionate about Adelaide City,' he recalled. 'I just followed them because they were Adelaide. At Adelaide United I loved putting bits of information about the game together in a magazine that I could craft myself. It was my heaviest involvement by far with a club, and with a really good bunch of people too.'

He became part of a new team that represented the best of South Australian soccer – the chairman was Basil Scarsella, a former head of Soccer Australia; the captain was Aurelio Vidmar, a former Socceroo and Adelaide City legend; and the coach was John Kosmina, arguably South Australia's greatest ever player.

Sixteen of the inaugural 24-man squad had played for Adelaide City at one point in their careers, and a supporter group was organised by Adam Butler, a former City fan. The players' names were Aloisi and Alagich; Budin and Bajic; Saric, Scarsella and Smeltz; Widera and Westervelt; Demourtzidis and Lozanovski; Vidmar and Veart and Valkanis; but Adelaide United buried soccer's ethnic identity in the red, yellow and gold colours of South Australia. The community radio stations were ordered to speak English, or not be involved at all.[14]

On the night of 17 October 2003, Adelaide United played its first match at Hindmarsh Stadium, the home of soccer in South Australia. As Howe marvelled at the mayhem at the turnstiles, United swept past the Brisbane Strikers to claim its first win.

Howe arrived home that night with a stack of gold coins and small bills. As he sifted through the cash, struck by the profits of Adelaide United's debut, he was overwhelmed by the magnitude of the occasion. The traditional ethnic clubs were now in the minority. He went to his study and typed out a final epitaph for the NSL.

The 1–0 win, he wrote, 'was just one of several factors which combined spectacularly to make Adelaide United's first ever national league match a resounding success'.

A club formed less than six weeks earlier created such hype that by early afternoon of the game, all 13,500 tickets allocated for pre-match sales were sold [...]

The sell-out crowd – soaked by the pre-match entertainment [...] perfect spring weather, a close match and three competition points – gives not just Adelaide United but the entire national league a much-needed and timely spurt of confidence. It is perhaps ironic that last Friday night's events in Adelaide came in the same week that the Australian Soccer Association announced the appointment of a task force to advise on a new domestic competition. Very early days notwithstanding, that a new team can generate such popularity will instil confidence in the sport's power-brokers and show potential investors that large-scale support for the domestic game does currently exist.[15]

Above all else, Adelaide United's success proved beyond doubt that soccer could simply do away with its pre-existing ethnic clubs, create new clubs in their place, and fans would come along in droves.

This was an important difference from Carlton or Northern Spirit, which had been forced to compete with traditional clubs in a congested marketplace, and Perth Glory, which was founded in a complete vacuum, without any local competition.

The NSL Task Force, which had been handpicked by Frank Lowy, was commissioned to replicate the Perth Glory and Adelaide United model across the country. The members were Johnny Warren, Jack Reilly, Charlie Yankos, Andrew Kemeny, Cheryl Bart, Remo Nogarotto and Brendan Schwab, with Stefan Kamasz as secretary. Between these men and one woman was more than a century of experience, either as players, lobbyists, media professionals or administrators. They met regularly, often at the Hakoah Club in Bondi, the place where Lowy had first given up on soccer in 1987.

By December, the final report of the NSL Task Force was launched by Lowy on the 23rd floor of his Westfield Tower in Sydney. The mood was buoyant but the findings were cataclysmic. The NSL clubs were chronically under-capitalised, with little funds to spend on marketing and promotions. The competition lacked appropriate television coverage and revenue, and relied on funding from the bottom up to survive. Incredibly, the clubs had collectively lost more than $50 million in just three seasons. The administration had also racked up a debt of more than $1 million to the Socceroos, which the players would forfeit to allow for reform.

The NSL, concluded the report, 'has proven to be remarkably resilient, although this largely appears to be as a result of the commitment and passion of club members and benefactors rather than through successful club business models'.[16]

The blueprint for change was almost identical to the Australian Premier League model developed by the players union. The new competition, Lowy promised, would comprise ten clubs drawn from Sydney, Melbourne, Adelaide, Perth, Brisbane and two other regions, with a budget of around $5 million per season.

Lowy did not surround himself with soccer people. Instead he assembled a team with a background in rugby union, horseracing, rugby league, motor-racing and other major sports. He wanted fresh eyes, new ideas and a clean break from a community that had burned him before. 'Above all,' once explained historian Roy Hay, 'he wanted a self-sustaining business model.'

Lowy was 73 years old, the patriarch of one of the richest families in Australia, said to be worth $3 billion, and had business and political links that stretched all over the world. He had more than 100 Westfield shopping centres across Australasia, Britain and the United States.

For the second time in less than three decades he was tasked with creating a national competition in a time of extreme crisis. At the launch of the Task Force report, one journalist even asked him to bankroll the entire league. Lowy flatly refused. His contribution would be sweat equity and profile, not hard cash.

Success has many fathers, and a gaggle of soccer fans, journalists and political lobbyists claimed credit for enticing Lowy back to soccer. As early as 2001, a council of reformers had visited his Westfield offices and pleaded for him to run their troubled sport. They included several journalists, ex-players Andy Harper and Robbie Slater, former Brisbane Strikers media manager and Socceroos team manager Bonita Mersiades, and Dr Mark Bowman, a lifelong fan. 'Something had to happen, because the game was going to die,' recalled Mersiades. 'There was no doubt about that.

Frank was obviously impressed with our group – not long after he offered me a job at Westfield.'

Lowy was the leader that everyone wanted. David Crawford had heard his name so many times during his inquiry that he recommended him for the position of chairman. At the 2003 NSL grand final, Perth Glory owner Nick Tana had distributed posters that read 'We Want Lowy' and flashed messages of support for Lowy across the big screen. Even Lowy's old nemesis Sir Arthur George, who had done more than anyone to drive him out of soccer back in the 1980s, wanted him to run the game. And the prime minister, John Howard, called Lowy personally. That, above all, had turned courtship into consummation.

'I resisted all the way until I realised I could tear up the rulebook and start with a new one,' Lowy would later recall in *A-League: The Inside Story of the Tumultuous First Decade*. 'When the prime minister asks you to do something, you don't like to refuse.'[17]

★

On the final weekend of February 2004, the final round of the final season of the NSL was played. In Sydney, a howling wind swept away the last Greek derby between South Melbourne and Sydney Olympic. In Melbourne, Sydney United and Melbourne Knights stood side by side, arm in arm, and farewelled top-flight soccer to the familiar, comforting chants of '*CRO-A-ZIA, CRO-A-ZIA, CRO-A-ZIA!*' Fittingly, both matches finished 0–0.

The Croatian clubs decided to go out in style. The fans turned up with Croatian flags, jerseys and hats, and as they entered the stadium, a few paused to inspect the Croatian-language books on sale. On half-way, a black flag with a giant 'U' slalomed through the sky, not far from the 'DEATH TO THE NSL' banner that hung ominously from a fence.

As the players lined up for kick-off, the Croatian national anthem was played over the loudspeakers, and the ground announcer referred to the teams as 'Melbourne Croatia' and 'Sydney Croatia'. Flares rained down on the pitch, engulfing the players in a hot, red blaze of nationalism, and after the final whistle the captains, Andrew Marth and Mark Rudan, were chaired from the field. The supporters danced to folk music from the old country and wiped away tears.

When asked by a journalist about the innumerable rule breaches, one club official just grinned and responded: 'What are they going to do – kick us out of the league?'[18]

Disliked by almost everybody, resistant to nearly every reform, these two Croatian clubs had been the bogeymen of the NSL for almost two decades. But no ethnic community ever produced finer footballers, and few clubs birthed more Socceroos. This was the end of the road for two clubs formed by generous, hardworking refugees and immigrants; clubs that did it their way to keep the flame burning in the darkest years of Australian soccer.

'I knew we had to cut ties,' Rudan once remembered. 'I became very emotional, just to think, I'm not going to see this again. That night I got hammered, and I got a bit emotional. What I grew up with, and what I became so proud of, was not going to be around anymore ...'

Unable to afford the cost of joining Frank Lowy's new corporate megalopolis, both Melbourne Knights and its neighbours South Melbourne were also refused entry to rejoin the Victorian Premier League. As they faced the horror of at least nine months of inactivity, their players departed and every revenue stream dried up. The rest of the soccer community watched on, stony-faced, as both clubs drowned in an ocean of debt.

South Melbourne, the most successful soccer club in Australian history, was forced to hold a 'Save Our South' rally. Hardly anyone turned up. In the end, it took two wealthy benefactors to rescue the club from certain death. 'We were underwhelmed by the number of people that came,' recalled the former South Melbourne CEO Peter Filopoulos. 'There was a lot of anger about the demise of the National Soccer League.'

The great tragedy of South Melbourne was that it had overinvested in the final years of the NSL, and was in too much debt to bid for a licence in Lowy's new competition. This was indeed a cruel and unusual period of suffering for Australian soccer's greatest clubs. Yet in their hour of need nobody spoke up on their behalf, and the overriding feeling was that their demise couldn't come quickly enough. There would be no grand farewells or lavish ceremonies. There was barely even a sheepish thank-you, goodbye and good luck.

Were these Croat or Greek or Italian clubs the true believers of Australian soccer? They had built the stadiums, produced the players, developed the coaches and invested their own money in ensuring the game's survival. Was Bob D'Ottavi a true believer, with his costly, old-fashioned dedication to his club and his game? Or was it Nick Tana, the visionary impresario who painted his beard in Perth Glory colours and sparked the imaginations of a generation of soccer fans? Or Frank Lowy, the millionaire messiah who returned to soccer only after being granted complete, unfettered power and a huge loan from the federal government?

Perhaps 'true believer' status belonged to Brendan Schwab, the lion-hearted lawyer who could have followed his father into AFL administration, but decided instead to protect and serve the interests of a group of unknown soccer players. Or did it belong to Michael Cockerill, the hard-as-nails journalist who travelled widely and was forced to constantly juggle soccer's competing interests and agendas?

Or Andrew Dettre, that romantic, forgotten old man who silently watched as all of his ideas were belatedly put into practice without proper credit or acknowledgement? He had to be a true believer.

And what of the Australian Women's Soccer Association, which had quietly built and supported the women's game in an atmosphere of disinterest and derision from the rest of the soccer community? Or the thousands of innocent bystanders who cut the oranges and put up the nets and coached the kids and paid Soccer Australia's extortionate levies? For those who bothered to ponder this question, there was no clear answer. In Australian soccer, one man's true believer is another man's apostate.

In the grey space between the end of the NSL and the start of a new competition, the fans, players, coaches, journalists and officials faced an uncertain, indeterminate break from top-flight soccer. Stefan Kamasz continued to write a five-year business plan for the new league, which was tentatively called 'New National Competition' or 'NNC'. Andrew Howe took up golf, and started assembling an encyclopaedia of Australian players, the likes of which had never been attempted before.

Many players went to Asia to find work, while many more dropped back to play in the state leagues. Damian Mori returned to Adelaide City, signed a five-year contract as player-coach and clocked on for work at Bob D'Ottavi's construction company.

Mori's strike partner, Bobby Despotovski, joined Inglewood United, a Western Australian state league side that had been founded in 1951 as Kiev Soccer Club. In October, he signed for Bonnyrigg White Eagles, a successful Serbian club in the NSW first division. Bonnyrigg agreed to fly him from Perth to Sydney every weekend, just to watch him play.

And on the morning of 6 November 2004, the former Socceroo Ray Richards rushed to the Royal Prince Alfred Hospital in Sydney. He and John Watkiss, another former Socceroo, sat on either side of Johnny Warren's bed. 'He was trying to get out,' remembered Richards. 'I put my arm on his, and stroked it with my other hand. I said, "Hey, Skip, we're here for you." And do you know, he laid back on the bed, and just died. Just like that – like he was waiting for me. I'll never forget it.'

John Norman Warren, soccer's truest believer, had finally succumbed to a year-long battle with cancer. He was 61 years old.

Warren had put his final years to good use. In 2002, with the help of Andy Harper and Josh Whittington, he wrote an 'incomplete biography' of his life in soccer. The title, *Sheilas, Wogs and Poofters*, had been rejected by several publishers before Random House finally agreed to it. He wrote that the title 'is a story of discrimination against the game and the individuals in it'.[19]

It sold well, and became the eternal bible for Australian soccer's devotees. To one lifelong fan, he signed it with the words, 'To another true believer'. To Senator Rod Kemp, the federal minister for sport who initiated the Crawford Report, he had scrawled: 'Rod, Let's make it happen.'

In 2003, he had been the most respected member of the Crawford Report committee and the NSL Task Force. He was the only individual in the land who could successfully negotiate the politics of soccer's various tribes. Remo Nogarotto, who knew Warren for decades and worked with him on the NSL Task Force, called him 'the most effective custodian of the game's conscience'.

In 2004, as cancer consumed his body and thinned his once thick, dark hair, he was awarded the FIFA Order of Merit. His name would ring out forever, alongside Franz Beckenbauer, Alfredo Di Stefano, Bobby Charlton, Johan Cruyff and Pele. It was Warren's most illustrious award in a swag of glittering prizes.

But he always remembered where he came from. When he was inducted into the Soccer Australia Hall of Fame, he thanked his mum, those unheralded players who came before him, his junior coaches, and said:

> I'm an Australian by accident, and I've mixed all my life with people who've chosen to be Australians. Who came here, and among other things, brought their passion for the greatest game in the world.
>
> I'd like to thank those Australians, the ethnic Australians if you like, who influenced my philosophy and gave me so much opportunity, whether at club level or national team level. Whether it was SBS ... or the ethnic press, who never get a mention around soccer, and do such a passionate job for the game.[20]

He got his 'Australian by accident' line from Alex Pongrass, the former St George-Budapest president who, along with Frank Lowy, had kick-started the NSL way back in 1975. Right to the end, Warren was a good listener. He was not a perfect man, his criticisms were not always fair, and he made life difficult for some. Nonetheless, soccer would never again see a man with such a generosity of spirit.

Two days after Warren's passing, Les Murray collected a bucket of ice, a bottle of scotch, a glass, and sat down to write. He had admired Warren from his days as a volunteer at St George–Budapest, commentated countless games with him since 1980, and travelled far and wide with him to bring the world back home via SBS. He had been there in Warren's final hours, not speaking, just silently holding his hand.

Murray wrote about Warren's devotion to soccer, the heartache it had caused for several women, and how the game made Warren question his own identity as an Australian. He noted that Warren had visited Brazil 28 times, and that he wished his fellow Australians would learn from their swagger on the soccer field.

The obituary was published by the *Daily Telegraph*. 'He was my mate,' concluded Murray, 'a brother whom I, the real "wog", found in the "wog" they labelled as such because of his association with people like me. Football and I will move on. But neither of us will ever be the same.'[21]

Warren was given a state funeral at the Sydney Town Hall – the first, some said, to be granted to a soccer player. But this wasn't quite right. Four years earlier, Johnny Warren's old mate Charles Perkins had also been farewelled in a state service at Town Hall. As Warren had once noted: 'Upon his death, Perkins was reported as being a great sportsman, not a great footballer. Even in eulogising this great Australian, remembering the sporting love of his life, soccer, seemed too difficult for some.'[22]

Steve Doszpot, who had worked with both Perkins and Warren at Canberra City, was the link between both men's funerals. At Perkins', he had been invited to eulogise the great Indigenous leader on behalf of the soccer community. It was the most difficult speech he ever delivered. 'One of the tragedies of life is that we don't tolerate the "Giants" amongst us,' he had told the congregation. 'We only recognise their greatness when they are gone.'[23]

Warren's funeral, held on 15 November 2004, was opened by Deryck Howell, the Archdeacon of South Sydney, before the grievers sang 'Abide with Me', by Henry Lyte. The tributes came from Johnny's nephew Jamie, George Harris, John Singleton and Les Murray. 'You told us so,' Murray kept repeating, listing all of Johnny's visions that had since transpired.

After Warren's death, one of his and Perkins' shared missions came true. The *Sydney Morning Herald* decreed that 'soccer' would no longer be used in the newspaper. The game would be called 'football'. It was the first newspaper in Australian history to make the change.

Warren's Socceroos teammates were his pallbearers. Attila Abonyi, who had roomed with Warren during the 1967 tour of Vietnam, told reporters that he was 'the true Aussie'.[24] Michael Cockerill, the journalist who had broken the news of Warren's cancer, wrote that 'professionally, I owe him everything'.[25] Everyone had a stake in this man. A huge crowd of mourners lined the streets, the Uruguayans and the Brazilians beat their drums, and a long banner read 'Goodbye Johnny. We Luv You. You Live in Our Hearts Forever.'

As old friends and complete strangers held back tears, many people came up to Andrew Dettre – who co-authored Johnny's first book back in 1974 – to say hello. Dettre was reunited with Mike Denton, a former teammate of Warren's at St George-Budapest. Dettre had brought Denton out from England in the late 1960s, around the same time that he had recruited the first Argentinian players, a pair of top-flight Yugoslavs, and Frank Arok.

The faith Dettre placed in Denton had changed his life: he married a local girl, settled down and became an Australian. 'Lovely boy, Denton,' Dettre would recall. 'When you have an episode like this, it makes it all worthwhile.'

Soccer entered its most exciting era without two of its greatest champions. Warren had spent most of his life fighting for the game's acceptance, and advocated Australia's immersion with Asia well before it became politically vogue. In a world where only soccer could make such vast connections, he was Australia's most visionary sportsperson.

His mate Charles Perkins had moved between soccer's ethnic clubs, the university, the Department of Aboriginal Affairs and the board-room of Canberra City in the NSL. He took on the racists and the xenophobes, defended soccer to the end, and fought valiantly for the cause of his people. He was the greatest Australian.

Together, they represented an eternal contribution from Australia's ethnic soccer clubs: Warren from the Hungarians; Perkins from the Croats and the Greeks. Both men respected the migrant communities, supported their right to exist in soccer, and were idolised in return.

That great migrant institution died with them.

'It was actually quite symbolic,' Doszpot later mused. 'Most of the ethnicity at the top level had already been eliminated. Charlie and Johnny signified the death of that era.'

★

On the sidelines of suburban soccer fields, on the internet forums and in the chatrooms, Australian fans debated the merits of the reformation. Most keenly anticipated the new competition, and hoped it would lead to a resurgence of interest in the local game. Others saw it as an attack on history and memory. The phrase 'ethnic cleansing' was used liberally and provocatively, and the supporters were divided into two camps that would become known as 'the bitters' and 'new dawners', 'old soccer' and 'new football'.

Some tried to paint the divide, such as it was, as 'wogs' versus 'skips' and ethnics against Anglos. This was terribly misleading. Soccer's transformation was built not on the exclusion of any individual but on a kind of conscious uncoupling from the ethnic blocs.

The idea was simple: the new franchises would be a privately subsidised, artificial shell – protected by the federation from organic inconveniences such as competition and relegation – under which the supporters could gradually create a new collective identity. As long as you left your history, your politics and your culture at the door, everyone was invited.

This was a crucial part of the game's survival as a commercial product. Almost every lesson of Australia's soccer history had essentially been a repetition of one uncomfortable truth: for as long as top-flight soccer included ethnic clubs, most Australians would not support it. The mainstream media would not support it. Corporate Australia would not support it. State and federal governments would not support it. The Anglo identity that underpins these institutions requires a system of total domination to feel comfortable, and so, in order to survive, soccer's national league needed to be rebuilt in the image of these uninvolved Australians.

Rather than celebrate and lionise the great and varied contributions of the ethnic clubs, however, the new guard at Football Federation Australia scorched the earth and wiped the NSL from the records, in the hope that it would soon fade from memory. In the minds of those who were making the cold, hard business decisions, the old world had to be destroyed to make way for the new. They knew that by doing so they would be setting new foundations for a silent majority of soccer supporters who had no love for or attachment to the NSL.

The man given the responsibility to light the bonfire was John O'Neill, a merchant banker and a rugby union man who admitted that he knew little about soccer but enough to blame 'the fiefdoms, the self-interest, the sectarianism' for 'holding the game back'.[26]

A negative film was wrapped around the pillars of structural reform. The game's arc was rewritten to cast yesterday as corrupt, ethnic and bad, and tomorrow as clean, mainstream and good. The narrative took hold. A newspaper slapped an article with the headline 'Australian Soccer Has a Vision and It's Not All Greek to Me'.[27] One journalist congratulated the new rulers for 'banishing the feeble ethnocentric fiefdoms' to the state leagues.[28] 'In come Rumble Stix and face-paint,' reported another, 'out go any re-enactments of the break-up of Yugoslavia.'[29]

At the last NSL grand final in 2004, which was fittingly won by Perth Glory in miserable, driving rain and in front of a banner that read 'DEATH TO THE NSL', John O'Neill likened a room full of NSL administrators to a scene in *The Godfather*.

Frank Lowy and O'Neill cherry-picked the findings of the players union and the NSL Task Force. The community-based franchises that had been advocated by the players union were suddenly ditched for corporate mega clubs, with Lowy now dismissing the Australian Premier League model as 'ill-conceived' and 'not in this world'.[30]

FFA ignored the Crawford Report's recommendation that the league be run as a separate entity, instead keeping it tightly controlled from head office. And instead of ten teams, the league would be cut to eight – just as it had been in rugby union's Super Eight competition. O'Neill credited the idea to John Singleton, a rugby man, who reasoned: 'You've got to Australianise the game. It can't be seen as a sport that's come from somewhere else. And to do that, we only want one team per city.'[31]

Brendan Schwab, who had been one of the favourites for the role of chief executive before O'Neill got the job, left soccer to work in a different union. For the first time in years, the PFA and the governing body failed to come to a collective bargaining agreement.

Nothing was sacred and nobody was immune from the shock therapy. The new league was shamelessly described in internal documents as a 'new mass entertainment product in the form of a national football competition'. The Australian Soccer Association was rebranded as Football Federation Australia, with Frank Lowy describing it as a 'symbolic move' and 'another small but important step on the journey away from old soccer and into new football'.[32]

SBS was held at arm's length by John O'Neill, who sold the A-League broadcast rights to Foxtel. The money invested by Foxtel was essential for the league's survival, but it also meant the games were hidden on pay television, out of the living rooms of most Australians. Les Murray wasn't happy about it, but he accepted that SBS had done its bit for soccer, and that it could not compete with the corporate dollar. But when he and Craig Foster were critical of the FFA on air, O'Neill would send long, angry emails in an attempt to bring SBS back to the party line.

The clubs selected for the new league were Perth Glory and Adelaide United, Melbourne Victory and Sydney FC, Central Coast Mariners and Newcastle Jets, New Zealand Knights and Queensland

Roar. From an economic and cultural perspective, the selection of most of these teams made sense: the traditional, ethnic clubs of these cities had either never existed or had long been absent from national level.

But in Sydney and Melbourne, where the last of the ethnic clubs clung to life, the slate was wiped clean, with just one franchise granted in each city. Melbourne Victory would play with a large 'V' on its jersey, in the style of an Australian Rules football jumper; while Sydney FC would be based in the east, away from soccer's multicultural heartland in the western suburbs. It was even suggested that the Sydney franchise be nicknamed the 'True Blues'.

The scale of this transformation can't be underestimated. In other parts of the world, when a new franchise replaces an historic community club, there are protests, fundraisers, feature articles in the newspaper, the works. Soccer's scorched-earth experiment would have been absolutely inconceivable, unworkable and unpopular in Australian Rules, rugby league, or any other soccer competition around the world.

But at the launch of the A-League it was rappers and street art and a slogan that said, 'It's football – but not as you know it.' When reporters asked the FFA marketing team about the edgy new commercial, which had nothing whatsoever to do with Australia's soccer heritage, they were told: 'We're trying to unveil a new culture.'[33]

Soccer would never be the same again. And people loved it.

Stefan Kamasz did not go to the A-League launch, despite having been the author of the competition's business plan. He didn't even get an invite. Kamasz had been wary of the 'old soccer, new football' dichotomy, but was resigned to its necessity. After all, he had been the secretary of the Task Force that had killed off the NSL, and he had spent months working on launching the A-League. For this he had been promised a role in the new competition, so he had gone on a short holiday to Greece to ready himself for the hard road ahead.

When he returned to work, however, he couldn't get inside his office. His personal assistant had been transferred to Matt Carroll, the new FFA head of operations. Kamasz was told that he was surplus to requirements. And with the stroke of a pen, 20 years of experience in managing a top-flight soccer competition were sacrificed for the dubious expertise of a former rugby union executive.

'I was devastated,' Kamasz later recalled. 'There was a cultural shift. I didn't feel part of new football. I felt alienated, like a lot of people.'

The Equal Opportunity Code, which had been pioneered by Francis Awaritefe and Brendan Schwab in the mid-1990s, was dropped, and the PFA's 'Living in Harmony Cup' was discontinued. All the youth development infrastructure, particularly the National Youth League, was abandoned along with the NSL.

In the pages of the *Sydney Morning Herald*, Michael Cockerill railed against the incendiary language, wrote against the purges, and continually raised concern at the lack of soccer knowledge inside the governing body. Most people, however, adopted a wait-and-see attitude. This new federation and its flagship competition had to succeed, whatever the cost.

'I've always found "old soccer, new football" an offensive marking line,' Remo Nogarotto would later concede. 'Had Johnny Warren been around, I don't think that would have been the case. There was never any conversation with Johnny about dispensing with the old guard. What you had to do was bring the traditional base of the game into a new model – you can't just dispense with them and call them "the great unwashed". I remember having a conversation with John O'Neill and Matt Carroll at the time [and] the line from head office was, "No, we need to demark ourselves clearly from what came before." I regret not being more forceful about that.'

★

As the bureaucrats and businessmen dreamed up new rivalries, old scores were settled in the forgotten stadiums of a discarded soccer culture. It had been 40 years since the infamous Anzac Day riot, 20 years since the Pratten Park riot, and almost on cue a dark carnival of violence broke out in Sydney and Melbourne. In the space of three months, three wild soccer riots would draw nationwide condemnation and bring a depressing end to 'old soccer'.

In March 2005, Sydney United played against Bonnyrigg White Eagles for the first time in more than two decades. United's King Tomislav Club was just a few kilometres away from Bonnyrigg's Serbian Sports Centre in Sydney's south-west, but the two sets of supporters had never maintained neighbourly relations. And although the wars in the Balkans had soothed since the 1990s, ethnic difference remained the overriding feature of the rivalry.

The match, which finished 2–1 to Bonnyrigg, was soundtracked by hand-to-hand battles in the terraces and followed by gunshots and a firebombed car. For the television cameras, John O'Neill said, 'There's no place for it in new football, that's old soccer,' and told the *Sydney Morning Herald*: 'It's now clear in my mind that the sooner the A-League comes along the better.'[34]

A few weeks later, a state league match between South Melbourne, formerly Hellas, and Preston Lions, formerly Makedonia, was interrupted by a pitch invasion. Mounted police were required to quell angry groups of supporters who hurled flares, darts and coins at one another. A section of South Melbourne fans unfurled a banner that read 'BULGARIANS GO HOME'. One fan even threw a trash can at a police horse.

But the carnage was not over. In May, Sydney United and Bonnyrigg White Eagles met again, this time on neutral turf at Parramatta Stadium. On the Orthodox Easter weekend, United lost 4–1 to Bonnyrigg against a backdrop of flares, violence and abuse. Outside the stadium a section of the Bonnyrigg supporters attacked the Sydney United bus with sticks and other projectiles, and as the media swarmed for footage one rioter yelled 'Go back to the A-League!'

In Melbourne's most popular tabloid newspaper, the *Herald Sun*, columnist Andrew Bolt pointed out with incredulity that most of the troublemakers were Australian-born. 'They are Australians, but the new breed for whom being Australian is not nearly enough,' he wrote. 'Meet the New Tribals – people who feel bigger by joining some ethnic, religious, political or social tribe that's at war with the society that shelters them.'[35] Piers Akerman echoed these sentiments in Sydney's *Daily Telegraph*, calling the riots 'another example of the failure of Australia's multicultural experiment'.[36]

The message from Akerman and Bolt, unvarnished though it may have been, had been the philosophical underpinning of 'old soccer, new football'.

In the end, the NSL would stand forever as Australia's first national football competition of any code, one of the first sporting competitions in the world to have a global recruitment program, and perhaps the most diverse sporting competition anywhere.

From the very beginning it had brought players from Europe, Asia, Africa, Oceania and the Americas to these shores, and included them in teams that had mostly been founded by European immigrants and refugees. And it was in the NSL that Charles Perkins gained the honour of being the first Indigenous man to become a president of an Australian sporting team on a national stage.

Both soccer and the broader Australian culture had moved on, however, and the NSL was now dead, killed by a lethal cocktail of mediocre governance, poor planning, occasionally riotous behaviour, collapsing balance sheets and the disinterest of a general public that had never been truly convinced that ethnic groups should have the right to run their own affairs. It was incredible that it had held on for as long as it did.

To a legion of new A-League supporters, the crowd trouble was seen as proof of the ethnic ghettos and the violence and the sectarianism that John O'Neill had warned them about. It didn't matter that the overwhelming majority were well-behaved, passionate soccer fans and loyal club volunteers. For years, these riots would be used as shorthand to explain the demise of the NSL, and to justify the exclusion of its pioneering clubs.

THE SUM OF ITS PARTS

2005–2006

Some men can only love
The country of their birth,
But some are not like that,
Their hearts have wider girth.

All trees have but one stem,
Yet some have many roots:
Don't judge them by their bark,
But judge them by their fruits.

David Martin
Roots, 1953[1]

At number 2A Norton Street, in the vibrant inner-Sydney suburb of Leichhardt, Joe and Franco Napoliello spent the 2004–05 off-season refurbishing one of the suburb's oldest cafes. Bar Sport had been serving espresso in Leichhardt since Rafaello Raffaelli, an artist from the north-east of Italy, opened it as Caffe Sport in 1956.

The cafe's popularity had precipitated the rise of several other espresso bars and joined the Italian-language newspaper, radio station, church and the APIA social club in transforming Leichhardt into

Australia's most recognised 'Little Italy'. Franco Napoliello had bought the business in 2001, and by 2004 Joe had come on board to make it a family enterprise. The brothers shared the cost and the labour to install a long bar, new furniture, a fresh coat of paint and their own menu. They kept the original floor and tried as best they could to update the place without changing its feel and its atmosphere.

Yet by 2005, the suburb's Italian flavour was steadily diminishing. The first generation of Italian migrants was getting old and the second and third generations were being replaced by an incursion of middle-class Anglo families. The APIA social club had collapsed in 1996, a twin disaster of assimilation and mismanagement, and its soccer team had been absent from the national league for more than two decades. The restaurants and the faces had changed, the kitschy Italian Forum down the road from Bar Sport never lived up to its promise, and over-zealous parking inspectors had killed off a lot of the late-night restaurant trade. Leichhardt was becoming a symbol of Italian life in Australia, but no longer its beating heart. Bar Sport was just one of many institutions imperilled by this demographic shift.

'Bar Sport allows me to indulge in a couple of things that I like in life,' Joe Napoliello once explained. 'First, I like being Italian. It allows me to keep the connection, from a language and cultural perspective. I love having conversations in Italian there. Second, it allows me to follow football, to talk about it all the time. And also it allows me to stay within my community, within the area that I grew up. People are their happiest if they live where they grew up. Cafes can be hard – the hours aren't always the best, but you can't have everything.'

Cafes are one of the pillars of Australian cultural life. In many ways they are the institution that soccer wanted to become: started by the European migrants in the 1950s, adopted by the Anglo-Australian sophisticates through the 1980s, domesticated during the 1990s to become an everyday activity in the 2000s.

By 2005, many Australian households had a stove-top moka pot or an espresso machine in the kitchen; an Australian had won the World Barista Championships; Coca-Cola Amatil had bought into the coffee business; and Vittoria Coffee, an Italo-Australian company, had won a swag of small business and multicultural awards. And 'flat white' – a distinctly Australian style of coffee that combined espresso with textured milk – made its first steps to becoming a genuine Australian cultural export. The Flat White Espresso Bar, tucked away in the narrow streets of Soho in London, was named best cafe of 2005 by the *Independent*. For Australians, coffee belonged to everyone.

While tea was Australia's safe and homely drink, coffee was the harbinger of public conversations, street theatre and lively exchange. Business meetings, first dates, big breakfasts, long lunches, interviews – all were held in the cafe. For many it was the sign of Australian sophistication and multiculturalism; to others it was the symbol of gentrification and pseudo-cosmopolitanism. The term 'latte-sipping leftie' or 'cafe crowd' became a favourite epithet thrown by conservatives at the progressives.

At Bar Sport, Italians would speak in their language to the Napoliello brothers, the Croatians and the Greeks and the Portuguese would argue about soccer, and the Anglos would laugh as they stumbled over their orders for *macchiato* or *sfogliatelle* or *focaccia*.

Joe Napoliello, with his fluent Italian and perfect English elocution, loved every minute of it. As he stood at the coffee machine, yelling across the cafe to a customer, his eyes would light up and he would throw his head back regularly to cackle at the debate. During his 34 years he had been back to Italy on six separate occasions, sometimes staying for months at a time, and falling madly in love with Juventus Football Club and the Italian national team. Napoliello plastered club stickers on the espresso machine, wrote the results of the Italian Serie A on the blackboard and made sure that soccer was always on the television.

The firstborn son of Rocco and Maria, Napoliello had arrived into the world in March 1971 and was given the name Giuseppe. As a kid his nickname was 'Pepe'; as an adult he became known simply as Joe. His parents came from Colliano, a rural village not far from Naples, and his ancestors were proud shepherds and entrepreneurial cheese-makers.

Rocco and Maria arrived in Australia in 1968, worked hard to save money to purchase a family home and a restaurant, and chose to live in Leichhardt to be close to other Italians. This decision meant Joe and Franco grew up in the shadow of Lambert Park, the home ground of APIA Leichhardt, and lived life in the rhythm of the hospitality business.

When Joe was eight years old, APIA Leichhardt entered the National Soccer League and his parents converted a Greek fish and chip shop into an Italian eatery called Il Pallone. The restaurant was just a few minutes' walk from Bar Sport, its name translated to 'the ball', and its logo was a man holding a soccer ball. The Napoliello brothers were destined to own Sydney's most prominent soccer cafe.

Bar Sport re-opened its doors to a steady stream of excited chatter about the A-League. A few customers expressed regret that the old NSL clubs were absent from the competition, but most looked forward, not back. The atmosphere was infectious.

On the first Saturday of August 2005, Joe Napoliello and one of his customers hopped in the car and drove to Gosford to watch a pre-season fixture between Queensland Roar and Sydney FC. More than 8000 supporters turned up, the match finished 3–0 to Sydney FC, and Napoliello ate dinner near the players in the Central Coast Leagues Club afterwards. It was a perfect evening.

'It felt very embryonic,' he later remembered. 'Finally I had a football club I could follow and go and watch. That's what you love – you want to go to the game, drink a beer and follow the team. For me, it was exciting.'

Mark Rudan, the former captain of Sydney United, was similarly enchanted by the possibility of the A-League. After spending the off-season in Malaysia, he had agreed to take a paycut in order to be a part of the new competition, in the hope that he would finally be involved in a championship-winning team. He joined a club that demanded glamour status in the new A-League.

At the time of Rudan's signing, Sydney FC was backed by Soccer NSW, the Lowy family, property developer Peter Turnbull and the

Hollywood actor Anthony LaPaglia. Lou Sticca, the former head of Carlton Soccer Club, signed the players, and the club officials decided to play its games at the Sydney Football Stadium in the inner-eastern suburbs. This decision caused Soccer NSW, based in the west, to immediately pull out of the arrangement. 'Sydney FC is no longer the people's team,' one insider told the *Sydney Morning Herald*. 'It may as well now be called Sydney City.'[2]

With the team dressed in sky blue, the Lowy family as backers and a base in the eastern suburbs, the suspicion that Sydney FC would be just a reformed Sydney City-Hakoah spread across town, from boardrooms to cafes to council grounds. Rudan's father, Luka, who had been a life-long Sydney United fan, refused to support Sydney FC on that basis. Rudan's explanations fell on deaf ears: he was arguing against decades of rivalry and tradition.

Before the first round of the A-League in late August 2005, in a *Sydney Morning Herald* column titled 'Come and Be the Children of the Revolution,' Rudan wrote:

> It's not out with the old and in with the new. It is about embracing those who have been through the dark times and welcoming those fans who love the world game but have never engaged in Australia's national competition.[3]

It was the latter group that turned out in record numbers. These previously unengaged soccer fans were attracted to the idea of a brand new club: a side that had a young, ambitious chief executive in Andy Harper, an internationally recognised coach in Pierre Littbarski, and Dwight Yorke as marquee player. Yorke, 33, had famously won the treble with Manchester United in 1999 and was the captain of Trinidad and Tobago. He was one of the coolest men in world football, with studded jewellery, a dazzling smile and a zest for Sydney's nightlife.

Before his death, Johnny Warren had warned that these marquee players would simply use the A-League as a glorified retirement home, but Yorke proved to be the gold standard. On one occasion, Rudan stayed out all night with him and went to training straight from the bar the following morning. Yorke put in the same effort as the rest of the players and finished the shift. 'The guy filled up pages in the entertainment section and the sports section,' Rudan later recalled.

It was perhaps fitting, then, that Dwight Yorke scored Sydney FC's first A-League goal. The match against Melbourne Victory finished 1–1, in front of a record crowd of more than 25,000 people. Yet the official number didn't include the thousands who flooded in as the gates were thrown open just before kick-off. Many, including Napoliello, estimated the crowd to be at least 30,000. It was a startling vote of confidence in Frank Lowy and John O'Neill's vision.

More than any other player, it was Yorke who achieved 'mainstream' credibility for Sydney FC and the A-League. He appealed primarily to the reserve army of supporters who would not watch the NSL but would regularly watch the English Premier League on television.

At Bar Sport, the first items of Sydney FC memorabilia began appearing – scarves on walls, stickers on furniture, hats on shelves. It sat neatly with the cafe's refurbishment and got people discussing local soccer again. One of the main talking points was the Cove, a motley crew of British ex-pats, unaligned soccer tragics and a few reformed NSL fans who took their name from Sydney Cove and set about designing banners, club merchandise, a website and a catalogue of chants and songs.

These chanting fans, who came to be known as 'active supporters', were the foot-soldiers in the Lowy–O'Neill revolution. Unknowingly, and almost overnight, they re-created the broad-based, active style of support pioneered by Canberra City back in the late 1970s.

Rudan became the the Cove's first hero, and Napoliello's favourite player. A hard man-stopper, ruggedly handsome, physically imposing and a natural leader, Rudan was reborn as a footballer at Sydney FC – his Croatian NSL identity buried beneath raucous chants of: 'Mark Rudan is a big blue man/Get past him if you fucking can!'

'I was captain of Sydney United in the last game of the NSL, and then captain of Sydney FC in the new era,' Rudan once explained. 'Sydney FC were one of the bigger clubs in the country, and only a year before I was captaining an ethnic side for the last ever time. I was loving life – I was representing the only club in Sydney. I'm a Sydney boy, and I knew there had to be a change. I just thought, "How good is this?" The fans accepted me. I'm not sure they knew too much about me, but the new era had started.'

★

In the week that followed the first round of the A-League, the media was called to assemble at a gleaming beachside resort in Bondi. Guus Hiddink, the Socceroos' ruddy-cheeked coach, sat beside Mark Viduka, his newly appointed captain.

Viduka was now a star of the English Premier League and an enigma for the national team. His Socceroos goal drought (just three goals in 28 appearances) was described by one journalist as 'legendary'.[4] But as the big striker smiled widely for the cameras, Hiddink described him as 'a strong, determined character and an exponent of how I see Australian football'.[5]

Next day, the Socceroos began their World Cup qualification campaign against the Solomon Islands. To the surprise of many, Hiddink left midfielder Mark Bresciano on the bench in favour of Jason Culina, a quietly spoken 24-year-old who had played just seven times for the national team.

After 20 minutes Culina opened the scoring with a thunderbolt strike from long range. Viduka followed Culina's goal with a double, including an extravagant bicycle kick that drew gasps from the crowd. The match finished 7–0 to the Socceroos. Hiddink's faith in the two men was rewarded. For as long as Hiddink was in charge, Viduka would be his captain and Culina would patrol the centre of midfield.

This was Hiddink's greatest quality as a coach. He assessed group dynamics quickly, deftly navigating the established interests and egos, and acted decisively on his instincts. Hiddink ran against the grain, and his decisions baffled supporters and the local media. One of his first acts as coach was to cancel a friendly match against Colombia and organise a training camp instead. He told the players to keep quiet unless absolutely necessary, explaining that Australians were 'some-times over-excited and too committed'.[6]

In a sporting culture built around the bloodbaths of rugby and the macho myth of heroic defeat, this was a revolutionary statement. Go to any park ground in Australia and you will find a group of possessed men frantically screaming at one another, stoically defending as if they are playing for the World Cup, and lunging into wild tackles. The most treasured Australian soccer player is the uncoordinated loser who puts in 100 per cent effort. Hiddink admired the 'never give up' attitude, but placed a higher premium on intelligence, creativity and style. And that's exactly why he favoured Culina and Viduka.

Hiddink was born in the Netherlands in 1946, the third of six boys, to a football-loving mother and a father who fought the Nazis in World War II. He began his managerial career at PSV Eindhoven in 1987, explored club coaching in Turkey and Spain, guided the Dutch national team to a World Cup semifinal in 1998, and then South Korea to fourth place in 2002. For this achievement, he received widespread acclaim, honorary Korean citizenship, his own private villa on a Korean island, and the nickname 'lucky Guus'.

By the time he took the Socceroos job in August 2005, he had returned to his roots at PSV Eindhoven. FFA chairman Frank Lowy gambled that he could manage the Socceroos on a part-time basis, and paid him handsomely for his services.

Hiddink was a tough operator, never friendly with his players, but at both club and international level he revolutionised Culina's career. Soon after he took over the Socceroos job, he signed him from FC Twente in the Netherlands to PSV Eindhoven.

Immediately he shifted Culina from his attacking position to the midfield, giving him the job as link man between the defence and the strikers. This position would define Culina's role in the Socceroos line-up for years to come.

In the 2005 Confederations Cup, before Guus Hiddink took over, the Socceroos had lost 4–3 to Germany, 4–2 to Argentina and 2–0 to

Tunisia. It was clear that the Australians had many capable individuals and a willingness to take the game to a more fancied opposition, but were weighed down by structural problems in defence. The Socceroos had conceded ten goals in three matches, double the number of any other team at the tournament. 'Guus has seen that we can hurt big teams, big nations,' explained Mark Viduka. 'Basically the only thing that was missing was organisation.'[7]

The efficiency introduced by Hiddink was matched by the professionalism of the front office. It had been just four years since the old Soccer Australia board had tried to save money by entering the Oceania Nations Cup with a third-string squad, but under Frank Lowy and John O'Neill there was a seismic shift in standards at Football Federation Australia. By November 2005 FFA had organised $12 million in corporate sponsorships from Nike, Westfield, Coca-Cola, National Australia Bank, Telstra and Hyundai. Qantas, the national airline, became the most important provider to the FFA war chest.

For a place in the 2006 World Cup, the Socceroos needed to beat Uruguay in a two-legged playoff. Four years earlier, Uruguay – a proud football nation of 3.3 million people and two World Cup titles – had beaten the Socceroos 3–0 at the Estadio Centenario, a cavernous open-air bowl in Montevideo.

But on 12 November 2005, La Celeste could only edge past the Socceroos 1–0, and the lion-hearted manner in which the players defended the last 15 minutes gave the Australians reason to believe. With just four days to recover for the deciding match, the Socceroos also had a decisive advantage on the return trip to Sydney. While the Uruguayans were left crammed in the back of economy class on a commercial flight, a Qantas 767 plane fit to hold 300 passengers was set aside for just 23 Australian players, the coaching staff and a few physiotherapists. It was re-fitted with Australian flags, massage tables and even an exercise bicycle.

After seven consecutive failed attempts to qualify for the World Cup, the mood in Sydney alternated between waves of genuine excitement and bouts of quiet trepidation. The tragedy of Iran 1997 still hurt, and the loss to Uruguay in 2001 was not long in the memory. But Tony Vidmar, who four years earlier had left the Estadio Centenario in tears, told reporters 'there's a confidence, there's an aura in the squad that says this is the time'.[8]

Two days before kick-off there were just 1000 tickets left for sale at the 82,000-capacity Telstra Stadium. A betting agency had the Socceroos as favourites to win the tie in 90 minutes, but with the vagaries of the away goals rule, the odds were even to qualify for the World Cup.

Guus Hiddink showed his team a promotional video with messages of support from Australian rugby, swimming and tennis legends, while Argentine legend Diego Maradona phoned Hiddink personally to wish him luck. After 31 years of pain and heartache, the 1974 Socceroos gathered in Sydney in anticipation of Australia's return to the World Cup. For Culina, a private message of support came from Marco van Basten, the coach of the Netherlands and his former mentor at Ajax Amsterdam.

On the morning of the game, 16 November 2005, Sydney's streets were filled with green and gold. Andrew Howe woke at his parents' place in the Sutherland Shire and ventured into the city, hoping for the best but fearing the worst.

Joe and Franco Napoliello closed Bar Sport early, which they never did, and travelled out to the stadium. Joe had bought tickets for 15 people, including his partner and his parents, whom he never took to soccer games.

Mark Rudan rejoined a crew of Sydney United old boys and headed to the stadium in a limousine. The NSW premier, Morris Iemma, predicted that Australia would win 2–0, and Prime Minister John Howard told the players they had '20 million very enthusiastic supporters' behind them.

The Uruguayan playmaker Alvaro Recoba tried to soften comments that he had made about La Celeste having a 'divine right' to play in the World Cup, while his coach, Jorge Fossati, said he didn't believe that the Australians had enough firepower to get past his men. And in the *Sydney Morning Herald*, Roy Masters, whose great-uncle Judy had captained the Australian team in the 1920s, before the great waves of European immigration, wrote: 'For too long the sport in Australia has been a kind of national orphanage, played by refugees from one disrupted country or another.'[9]

The blue-tracksuited Socceroos ran onto the pitch, and they were roundly and enthusiastically booed by the crowd. Mark Viduka's confused face flashed onto the big screen. As the Australian supporters realised their mistake, a paralytic pause filled the stadium, the last moment of quiet before a tidal wave of cheers enveloped the players.

In total, eight of those Socceroos in the starting XI were the sons of immigrant and refugee parents. These Socceroos were articulate, fluent in several languages, aware of the world around them and their place in it. They were not 'orphans'; they had hard-working parents, they had a thousand years of culture, and they had their own heroes from the NSL. They were the children of Australian soccer's first revolution.

There was the cheeky grin of Vince Grella, born in the south of Melbourne but based in the north of Italy; the charm of Lucas Neill, who had moved from Sydney's north shore to England at age 16 and returned sporting a soul patch and dimples like crevasses; Jason Culina, the product of three Croatian-Australian soccer clubs, with a no-nonsense buzz cut and a Dutch football philosophy; and Tim Cahill, the scrappy midfielder with an oversized jersey, shorts two sizes too big, and the unique honour of having represented both Samoa and Australia.

'It was a validation of Australia's policy,' explained Steve Doszpot, the former head of Soccer Canberra. 'Multiculturalism means different things to different people – to me, it means accepting people from other nations, but expecting those people to accept Australia as their home. I'm not sure soccer is accepted as a mainstream game – we're sort of tolerated at the national level when our results are good, but we're not given the undying passion that the Wallabies get, for example. Rugby league and union are accepted as Anglo-Saxon codes, and as Australian.'

Doszpot was at Telstra Stadium with his son, Adam. Behind them was a big banner that read 'Johnny, You Told Us So', and in front of them a tribute to Johnny Warren played on the big screen. Together the crowd sang 'You'll Never Walk Alone' through muffled tears.

Across the country, more than eight million Australians, a whopping 51 per cent of the population over the age of 14, tuned in to the SBS live broadcast. They listened to a united Australian crowd drown out the Uruguayan national anthem in boos and jeers, and sing 'Advance Australia Fair' with a gusto never heard before at a sporting event. Every Socceroos player slapped their hand over their heart, but none sang louder or more proudly than Mark Viduka. Head up, shoulders back, he belted out every last word. 'Eyes on the stars, feet on the ground,' proclaimed match commentator Simon Hill. 'Theodore Roosevelt's recipe for success has real resonance for Australia tonight.'

The Uruguayans won the first free-kick, the first corner-kick, and had the first attempt on goal. They protested that the ball wasn't inflated properly, and the crowd booed their every touch. The Socceroos needed just one goal but could not afford to concede – a 1–0 victory would mean extra time; a 1–1 draw would progress Uruguay to the World Cup instead of Australia.

After 27 minutes of cagey football, Alvaro Recoba broke away down the left side, and Tony Popovic interrupted his run by elbowing him firmly in the face. Recoba went down like he had been pole-axed, the referee brandished a yellow card in Popovic's face, and even Craig Foster – Australia's most patriotic commentator – said it was a 'blatant' foul. Popovic was lucky not to be sent off.

Five minutes later, Hiddink replaced Popovic with Harry Kewell. It was an early substitution and one that instantly changed the mood and the momentum. Kewell nonchalantly jogged onto the field, waving his arms about like a conductor who knew all the notes in advance. This was not a man accustomed to sitting on the reserves bench.

Within a few moments, Kewell collected the ball on the left flank, attracted a defender and back-heeled a pass to Scott Chipperfield.

Chipperfield passed it to Cahill, who shrugged off a heavy challenge and nudged a short pass in the direction of Viduka. With his back to goal, the big man delicately flicked it between his own legs and the legs of a Uruguayan defender.

The opportunity fell to Kewell, who had made the clever diagonal run inside towards goal. The crowd gasped, the voices of the commentators rose in anticipation, and Kewell fluffed his shot. Yet in the scramble, Mark Bresciano lashed the ball into the back of the net.

An entire nation burst into wild celebration. Nestled between his family, Joe Napoliello burst into a flood of tears.

'I've never seen anything like it and never will again,' he would later explain. 'The crowd got into it, and it's very rare that you see Australian crowds get into it together for the whole game. It didn't stop, and you just knew it was something special. And then Bresciano scored, and I cried. I'd worked myself up to the point where I thought we couldn't do it, and this was the realisation that we had a chance – it was possible to qualify for a World Cup. "Bresh" we always felt a great association with because he played in Italy and was a big star. I'm Italian, but I'm also Australian, and he's an Italo-Australian like me. That made me proud to be Australian.'

After 90 minutes the score remained 1–0, or 1–1 on aggregate. Thirty minutes of extra time ended scoreless; however, two extra-time substitutions proved crucial for the Socceroos. First, Guus Hiddink took off Mark Bresciano and replaced him with John Aloisi. Second, Brett Emerton went off injured and was replaced by Josip Skoko.

This unplanned change was the last of Hiddink's three substitutions, meaning the reserve goalkeeper, Zeljko Kalac, remained on the bench and Mark Schwarzer stayed on the field for the penalty shootout. 'We knew that if it went to extra time, Spida [Kalac] was coming on,' remembered Mark Rudan. 'If it went to penalties, he was in. If it wasn't for Brett Emerton coming off injured in extra time, he would have gone in for Schwarzer. Emerton, the fittest player, broke down with cramp. Sometimes football is just scripted in the stars.'

Australia's penalty takers were Harry Kewell, Lucas Neill, Tony Vidmar, Mark Viduka and John Aloisi. Their parents had come from the former Yugoslavia, from England and from Italy. They grew up in Sydney, Adelaide and Melbourne, and had plied their trade in England, Croatia, Scotland, the Netherlands, Belgium, Italy and Spain. None had played at a World Cup before, but collectively they possessed a world of experience.

Kewell placed the ball to the right of Uruguayan goalkeeper Fabian Carini, and Schwarzer saved the first Uruguayan penalty. 1–0 – advantage Australia. Neill went right as well, and Schwarzer narrowly missed the next attempt. 2–1. Again Vidmar went right, while Uruguayan Fabian Estoyanoff went high and to Schwarzer's left. 3–2. 'You must get this one,' said SBS commentator Craig Foster as Viduka strolled towards the penalty spot. Viduka went low and right, like the three Australians before him, but dragged the shot wide of the post. With two spot-kicks left for Uruguay and one for Australia, the Socceroos lost the advantage.

Uruguay's fourth penalty was taken by Marcelo Zalayeta, who placed his shot high and to Schwarzer's left. But the tall, 33-year-old son of German immigrants stuck up a strong left arm and parried it away. It was the greatest and most important save in Australian soccer history. In the SBS commentary box, Simon Hill, the nation's best commentator, was trying to negotiate his co-commentator's near emotional breakdown:

Hill: *If John Aloisi can score this goal, Australia will be there.*
Foster: *Are you sure?*
Hill: *I'm trying to do my maths ... I can hardly ...*
Foster: *... It's 4–2, it's 4–2, he wins it for us ... JOHN ...!*
Hill: *... Here's Aloisi for a place in the World Cup ...*
Foster: *JOHN ... YOU WIN IT FOR US ... YEEEEEEAAAAAAHHHH! JOHN! COOOOOME OOOOOONNN! GOOOO OOONN MYY SONNNN! GOLDEN BOOOOYYS! COME ON AUSTRALIAAAAAAAAAA!*

As Hill tried to continue the call, Foster yelled to the heavens for the guardian angel of Australian soccer: *JOHNNYYY WARRRREEEENNNNNNN!*

Almost exactly eight years prior, in the tragic World Cup qualifying loss to Iran, it had been Johnny Warren crying in the commentary box and Foster struggling through the postmortem on the field. Now the emotional link between Warren and Foster was complete. Foster's screams seared the message into the minds of millions of Australians watching from home – this victory was for Johnny Warren.

The Uruguayan novelist Eduardo Galeano once compared the goal to an orgasm, and for Australians Aloisi's goal was like making love to a long-lost partner and deciding afterwards that it was until death do us part. The ecstasy was tempered only by the deep, satisfying feeling of relief. Strangers were hugging and grown men crying into their Socceroos scarves and replica jerseys.

Aloisi took off his top and belted down the sideline, like a streaker trying to avoid security. He had first performed that iconic celebration as a child, inspired by a famous goal from Chris Kalantzis in the 1986 National Soccer League final. Back then, Kalantzis had taken off his shirt to celebrate, waved it around his head, and ran like a wild man down the sideline. The commentator Les Murray had yelled, 'Kalantzis scores! Kalantzis scores! And he strips for the occasion.'

'As a kid I used to love watching the national league, and my team was Adelaide City,' Aloisi later told Murray. 'We played Sydney Olympic that year in the [1986] final, and it was a two-legged affair which Adelaide City won. And the reason why that stuck with me was that I used to play out the back with my brother, and when I would score a goal, I would take off my top and I would say "Aloisi scores, Aloisi scores, and he strips for the occasion." I did it so often that it just became normal for me to take off my top.'[10]

Aloisi was the first Australian to play in the big three: the English Premier League, Spain's La Liga and the Italian Serie A. But like so many of his Socceroos teammates, he got his start as a skinny teenager in the NSL. During his debut game for Adelaide City, he had been heavily fouled and the match had ended in a wild pitch invasion. That penalty, that celebration, was the product of two decades of development. It was adopted by an Adelaide City junior from a Sydney Olympic player, and reproduced in the green and gold of the Socceroos. Australia's greatest sporting moment was inspired by and created in the NSL.

★

'In a multicultural nation in a fractured world, the Socceroos can bring together the sum of their parts,' concluded Michael Cockerill in his match report for the *Sydney Morning Herald*. 'Muslim, Catholic, Orthodox, Anglican. German, Lebanese, Polynesian, Croatian, Italian, Melanesian, Greek. It is a rich tapestry but last night they – and we – were one thing only. Australian.'[11]

In Melbourne, Andrew Bolt used the same ingredients to justify a totally different conclusion. He saw the Socceroos' achievement as proof of their assimilation, not the success of multiculturalism.

'[A] team of young Australians,' wrote Bolt in the *Herald Sun*, 'most from "ethnic" backgrounds, and several raised in our poorer suburbs, pulled on the gold strip and played not for some tribe, but for their country.' Yet he believed soccer's ethnic clubs were 'the worst of our multiculturalism', 'fortified against the assimilation we've always prized'.[12] This, he wrote, was the multiculturalism that divides.

The game was at a critical juncture – Football Federation Australia now had an historic opportunity to educate the new legion of fans about soccer's unique history and to extol the ethnic clubs' longstanding commitment to the Australian cause, their culture of volunteerism and their role in producing legions of Socceroos. Deep down, the old clubs and their fans knew that the A-League was a necessary step in the evolution of the game, and that their best days were over. 'All they want is recognition,' Mark Rudan later explained. 'Recognition that they existed, that they took some part in this game.'

Instead the FFA only looked forward, spoke only about 'new football', and in the vacuum Bolt's narrative grew into consensus. Few objections were raised. The majority of Australian soccer fans weren't in the mood to discuss the winners and losers of the game's impending boom. They wanted only to see unity.

For the first time in history the Australian national league was associated with a World Cup Socceroos side. The euphoria and the financial windfall of the achievement settled like fairy dust on the new A-League franchises, and made their forebears smaller and less relevant for the experience. The ethnic clubs were blamed for the problems of the past, written out of the success of the present and, as a result, a concert of opinion formed to justify their exclusion from the future.

The A-League immediately became associated with success, precipitating an unprecedented surge of corporate, media and spectator interest. And as the clock ticked over from 2005 to 2006, Australia was finally accepted as part of the Asian Football Confederation.

A new national league, qualifying for the World Cup and getting into Asia – this was the Frank Lowy trifecta. It seemed to justify all the collateral damage of an era that soccer fans would come to refer to as 'Year Zero'.

In Sydney, Rudan was amazed at the rapidity of soccer's transformation. Yet his father, Luka, remained unconvinced. Sydney United had been a centrepiece of the Rudan family – it connected the parents to their Croatian community and taught the children about the old country. When the A-League began, Mark's sister Mariana Rudan was a soccer presenter on SBS and he was captain of Sydney FC. But in the first season the siblings' father attended just two Sydney FC games: the first and the last. It took a lot to get him to the first game against Melbourne Victory, but as Sydney FC made the grand final against Central Coast Mariners, Luka happily went along with the entire family.

Steve Corica – a product of the Italo-Australian soccer community of Far North Queensland and a former Marconi player – scored the winning goal for Sydney FC in front of a sell-out crowd.

Sitting on the halfway line, Joe Napoliello was one of 42,000 spectators who celebrated another unforgettable moment. He had not been involved in a domestic championship-winning team since APIA

Leichhardt won the NSL in 1987. Back then he was 16 years old, still in school and uncertain of his future. Now, in 2006, he was involved in the family business, had seen his nation qualify for a World Cup and was expecting his first child. Sydney FC formed the last element in his hierarchy of needs.

On the field, as Mark Rudan deliriously celebrated his first championship, he looked over to find his father in the crowd. Luka smiled back at his son, and gave him a silent fist pump. 'I can't remember seeing that much emotion for a long time,' Rudan later explained. 'My mum told me later that they tried to eject him a number of times for smoking, and he wouldn't have a bar of it. When he got a tap on the shoulder from security he'd tell them to piss off.'

This was one of many atmospheric changes to Australian soccer. Instead of cevapi rolls and souvlaki at suburban, club-owned grounds, the A-League franchises rented large, smoke-free stadiums in the centre of the city and let private catering companies feed the fans. Only the Australian flag was allowed inside the ground, and all eight teams wore the same Reebok kit, just with different colours. Every form of diversity was tightly controlled. Napoliello noticed the most resistance from first- and second-generation Greeks and Croatians.

'I think the Italians adapted very quickly, and assimilated,' he said. 'That's very Italian. It probably comes down to the fact that because Italians have such a popular culture here, it's very relaxed – football isn't the only area where we can keep our culture going. It's not football or nothing. For the Croatians, they are a new country, they have to fight for their identity. And even the Greeks, although they have a culture here, it's not like the Italians. Their food isn't as much a part of Australian life, so to a certain degree they used football to hang on to their culture.'

The wholesale shift from ethnicity to geography disenfranchised many supporters, enfranchised thousands more, and created a new layer of uncertainty in the production line. The A-League sides did not have junior teams or a clubhouse or an army of youth coaches, but they did have large chequebooks and a stronghold over top-flight soccer.

Emboldened by that security, they were free to raid the old NSL sides for the best playing talent.

The A-League caused a huge shock to soccer's circadian rhythms. The traditional ethnic clubs had produced thousands of players from all walks of life, but often it was Croatian kids who came from the Croatian clubs, Greek kids from Greek clubs, Italian kids from the Italian clubs, and so on.

This process had caused some insecurity among the unaligned, but on the whole it had been an entirely natural and positive process for Australia's multicultural soccer community. The Socceroos class of 2006 wouldn't have existed without it. Mark Rudan and Mark Viduka – the captains of the A-League's first champions and the Socceroos – were both reared in this milieu.

'It was a natural progression,' once explained Jason Culina. 'Every Croatian in Melbourne would start off their football career there – it was a natural progression to go to the Melbourne Knights. I spoke to many ex-players who played at both NSL and A-League level who say the standard of play and players was better in the NSL. We didn't have the professionalism, the crowds, the stadiums, the TV coverage, that's what we didn't have. But nine out of ten people who experienced both the NSL and the A-League will tell you that the quality of play and players were better back then.'

As a child, Rudan could go to sleep in his Sydney Croatia jersey, dream of playing for them in the national league, and wake up to play for the junior side. The Australian Institute of Sport was his finishing school, and by the time he was ready to sign a professional contract he had the choice of four or five top-flight clubs in Sydney, and many more interstate. There was a straightforward, cradle-to-grave path for him to follow.

In the A-League, however, there was only one club servicing large populations in eight regions, seven if you excluded New Zealand Knights. This led to an enormous dearth in opportunity that had a seismic impact on a generation of soccer players. Many up-and-coming young men just got left behind in the corporate turn.

'That was the problem with starting a new competition and just eradicating everything that was there before,' Rudan once explained. 'All these NSL clubs had their own youth teams. There was a production line there: you went to a club at the age of eight at Sydney Croatia, knowing that your dream was to play for Sydney Croatia, not Australia. When the A-League started, there was no production, there was no youth system, no youth teams. There was no under-20s. I remember asking, "Where's the youth team? How are we going to start producing players? What's going to happen in ten years' time?"'

His calls were not heeded. The A-League sides were stocked mostly with older, established talent, not teenagers and young adults. Star players such as Tom Pondeljak, Sasho Petrovski, Ante Milicic, Michael Valkanis, Angelo Costanzo, Fernando Rech and Carl Veart had all been in their prime during the late 1990s and early 2000s. 'The old NSL, as a soccer spectacle, was a lot better than anyone ever wanted to give it credit for,' lamented one reporter.[13]

The best young player was Queensland Roar striker Alex Brosque, the 22-year-old son of Uruguayan parents and a product of Marconi in the last days of the NSL. He finished the season with eight goals and six assists, and was awarded the Golden Boot.

In the first season, Perth Glory lured Bobby Despotovski out of semi-retirement and re-signed Damian Mori on a short-term contract. Mori, 36, trained at Adelaide City during the week and then flew in on weekends for Glory games.

By the end of the season, the NSL's best strike partnership also finished as the A-League's best, scoring 15 goals between them despite their combined age of 72. Despotovski, 36, was awarded the Johnny Warren Medal for player of the year. At the A-League's first awards ceremony, he received his prize from FFA chief executive John O'Neill, who mispronounced his surname. O'Neill never did learn to speak with a soccer accent.

★

For more than half a century to 2006, soccer had assisted the integration of countless immigrants, provided a platform for the nation's greatest Indigenous leader, sent a national team into battle during the Vietnam War, and pioneered links with Asian nations and people during the time of the White Australia policy.

Soccer created Australia's first ever national league, one of the strongest players unions, adopted a wide-reaching Equal Opportunity Code, established the nation's first women's national league and conducted perhaps the most nuanced debate about the nature of citizenship and diversity in a multicultural society.

Yet it had done all of this in an environment of almost complete and utter disinterest. The intellectual class that puzzled over the Australian identity was drawn primarily from a white, male, Anglo-Australian set – the kind of people who had not dominated soccer's internal culture.

The Australian parliament, at least in terms of representation, had been one of the last vestiges of White Australia. The best-read Australian sportswriters came from cricket and Australian Rules. In 2001, when Black Inc. assembled the best Australian sportswriting of the previous 200 years, the editor of the anthology could not find room for a single article written about soccer. And of course, there were only one or two non-Anglo writers among the list.

This presented a perennial problem for soccer. The Anglo-Australian, regardless of talent or political persuasion, does not pursue a national narrative in which he or she is not at the centre of the conversation.

Soccer's heroes were the kinds of people that the nine-to-five socialists and the conservative intellectuals liked to talk and theorise about, but not actually listen to – wogs, blacks, reffos and immigrants. Many of soccer's great writers had learned English as a second language and were confined to small-circulation publications or the ethnic press. The two best reporters were Laurie Schwab, from *Soccer Action*, and Andrew Dettre, from *Soccer World* – both of whom arrived on migrant ships after World War II.

For more than 50 years many left-wing comrades, basket-weaving greenies and right-wing ranters alike cast occasional glances at soccer, scratched their heads and looked away. Its complexity was too confounding. There were too many shades of grey. Most of all, they couldn't simply waltz in and dominate. Those who maintained an interest in sport promptly returned to the monochrome worlds of cricket or AFL or rugby league. Regardless of their views on immigration or multiculturalism, most agreed that soccer was bad and divisive and needed to immediately become more 'Australian' – without ever explaining exactly what that meant.

'Johnny Warren always wanted Australians to follow the game and to like the game,' Les Murray once explained. 'While he respected the ethnic clubs, and certainly what they had contributed to the game, he wanted ultimately for all Australians to embrace the game. It's important we understand what he was on about – he wasn't just about promoting football for its own sake, he wanted to enrich his fellow Australians through football. He was a worldly guy – he saw that football was the universal language. If we wanted to be part of that world, we had to speak that language. That was his mission.'[14]

His wish came true in the summer of 2005 and carried on into the winter of 2006. John Aloisi's audacious spot-kick brought an abrupt end to soccer's half-century-old public crisis of confidence. Reams of newspaper copy were dedicated to the game, the airwaves danced with World Cup fever and the television screens filled with images of the Socceroos.

Fox Sports signed a $120 million broadcast deal with FFA to televise the A-League, while SBS secured the rights to the 2010 and 2014 World Cups and launched a reality show called *Nerds FC*. Australia Post released the first ever soccer-themed stamp. Tim Cahill was appointed 'the Weet-Bix Kid' and the Socceroos featured in an advertisement for the nation's favourite breakfast cereal.

The Victorian state government announced plans to build a lavish soccer stadium in the centre of Melbourne, and soccer officials started talking openly about converting Australian Rules and rugby fields to accommodate the participation boom. Books on Australian soccer were commissioned and published.

At Bar Sport, the first pieces of green and gold went up on the walls, joining the Italian, Juventus and Sydney FC memorabilia. And in the final week of May 2006, the Socceroos defeated Greece in front of 95,103 people at the Melbourne Cricket Ground.

'I didn't expect to see a second Greece here,' commented Greek striker Angelos Charisteas as thousands of Australians of Greek heritage flooded the streets in blue and white.[15] 'For cynics who say multiculturalism doesn't work,' wrote comedian Nick Giannopoulos, 'I hope this culturally integrated team of top players shuts you up forever.'[16]

Yet Andrew Bolt remained unconvinced. '[T]he raucous support so many Australians of Greek background gave the Greek soccer team last night should make us worry,' he wrote in the *Herald Sun*.

Why do so many men who were born here identify not with the Australian team, but its foreign opponent? This isn't our first warning – mild though it is – that we've failed to sell an image of Australia even the local-born thrill to. Ethnic identity still too often trumps our national one. Has the shame-Australia-shame movement gone too far? Has multiculturalism? After all, not every clash of loyalties involves just a game.[17]

For the first time in its history, middle Australia looked to soccer for proof of its identity. Its people used the game to dissect ideas of nationalism, the role of ethnicity in public life, and what it meant to be an Australian in a multicultural society. Andrew Dettre's great national question had gone mainstream.

Yet his three decades of literary and journalistic groundwork was long forgotten. *Soccer World* and *Soccer Action* yellowed in the storage units of state libraries, and in the living room cupboards of a few old men. And so the nation returned to square one, and old tropes resurfaced.

A cranky rump of Australians decided that soccer was either not necessary or a threat to their own sports. *Sunday Mail* columnist Kevin Naughton called the Socceroos 'a bunch of expatriates mixed in with a few locals' and said the game was 'not part of the Australian sporting fabric'.[18] Geoffrey Blainey worried that Australian Rules football – 'the spectacular game of our own, with its rich traditions' – would be swept away by soccer's surge in popularity.[19] John Birmingham, writing for the *Bulletin*, attributed soccer's large participation base to 'school-children and – more particularly – [...] their mothers', and blamed its lack of institutional power on the ethnic clubs' 'unfortunate histories as closed ethnic enclaves'.[20]

The resistance to soccer crossed class and political lines. Some of these words were written in jest, designed to provoke, but the language of their grievance relied on a familiar reference point: Australia was under threat from a foreign activity.

It had been proven time and time again that the FIFA World Cup was Australia's tournament, even when the Socceroos were not repre-sented. Yet for many Australians the tournament was a non-event for two major reasons. First, Australia had been involved just once since its inception in the 1930s. Second, Australia's lack of success in soccer had always been an uncomfortably accurate reflection of the nation's irrelevance to the rest of the world. Australians want to believe that they matter. And most of all, Australians want to see themselves as winners on the sporting field.

Soccer did not assuage these delusions of grandeur. 'Who cares if Senegal beat Uruguay?' dismissed Mike Carlton, a darling of the Australian left, in 2002.[21] In fact, most of the world did. At Bar Sport – the epicentre of Carlton's so-called 'Latte Triangle bounded by Balmain, Glebe and Leichhardt' – the 2002 World Cup had been a massive hit.

Australia never produced a world number one soccer player. It never produced a world-beating team, nor did it ever produce world-leading administrators. Australia is not in a position to change the rules of soccer, as it is with rugby league, Australian Rules football or even cricket, nor is it in a position to demand success.

At the 2006 World Cup, Australia was essentially a drop in the ocean, just one of 197 nations that attempted to qualify. It is cliche to say that FIFA has more members than the United Nations, but it is inescapably true. The World Cup was beyond Australia's control – all that it could offer the tournament was its humble participation. And for a young and frantically insecure country, this was never going to be enough.

★

The Coalition government had spent the ten years to 2006 demonising refugees as 'boat people', fighting against the so-called 'black armband' view of Australian history and against the republican movement. Prime Minister John Howard threatened schools with funding cuts if they did not fly the Australian flag, and poured money and energy into transforming Anzac Day from a quiet, sombre reflection to a chest-beating, militaristic occasion.

Despite many opinion polls that indicated public support for multiculturalism, Howard had never been comfortable with the term, and many feared that the idea was disintegrating. An ugly race riot on the beaches of Cronulla had strengthened these fears and provided fuel for multiculturalism's opponents. Howard, wrote historian Robert Manne, 'saw multiculturalism as a project for demeaning the achievements of the British settlers and turning Australia into a nation of tribes'.[22]

The Socceroos waded directly into this febrile political atmosphere. Not long after the team qualified for the World Cup, Peter Costello, the weak-chinned treasurer of Australia, lashed out at what he labelled 'mushy, misguided multiculturalism'. In an address to the Sydney Institute, he said:

> I was reminded of this recently when watching the Socceroos play in the World Cup qualifier against Uruguay. A television commentator was moving amongst the crowd that was lining up to come into the ground. He came across an elderly woman with a heavy accent. He asked her where she came from, and she replied, 'I come from

Uruguay to Australia twenty years ago.' The reporter said, 'So you're barracking for Uruguay.' The woman was outraged. 'No!' she yelled back at him. 'I go for Australia!' and looked incensed that he would think otherwise. Whether she went on to say Australia is my country I can't be sure but that is what she meant.

If you loved Uruguay, wanted to speak Spanish, loved Uruguayan food, culture and political institutions, you would not mark out Australia as the place to pursue these passions. The fact that you have moved to Australia says that there is something about Australia that you want to embrace that you do not find in your country of birth.[23]

This national question – *who do you support?* – became the over-arching discussion point of the 2006 World Cup. Many people spoke of their relief at not needing to support a 'second team' any longer, but for thousands of Australians the question was impossible to resolve.

The Socceroos were drawn in Group F with Croatia, Brazil and Japan, each nation representing a step in the development of the Australian game. Croatia reflected Australian soccer's European soul; Brazil were Johnny Warren's great love and the benchmark in world football; and Japan were representative of Australia's Asian future. The three nations were each ranked in the top 25 in the world. Australia was ranked number 42.

Mostly, Australians watch the world's biggest sporting event from the privacy of their home, in the early hours of the morning, mediated through bleary eyes and SBS. This is tradition. In 2006, however, thousands of Australian fans descended on the German streets of Kaiserslautern, Berlin and Stuttgart. Even *The Footy Show*, an unreconstructed Anglo asylum of dimwitted rugby league and Australian Rules presenters, travelled to Germany to broadcast a 'Soccer Spectacular'. Unsurprisingly, one of its hosts ended up in a pub brawl.

The first two matches announced the arrival of the Socceroos as a genuine threat. Against Japan they clawed their way back from 1–0 down to win 3–1; against Brazil they played without trepidation and lost 2–0. Guus Hiddink expertly rotated his team selection and managed the playing formation and the substitutions. The midfield combination of Vince Grella and Jason Culina reached its peak; Brett Emerton, Luke Wilkshire, Mile Sterjovski and Scott Chipperfield tore ferociously up and down the flanks; while Lucas Neill, Tony Popovic and Craig Moore defended valiantly at the back.

Mark Bresciano and Mark Viduka combined effortlessly in attack and Harry Kewell was a constant threat going forward. Tim Cahill, the 26-year-old Weet-Bix Kid, became the first Australian to score at a World Cup. At 1–0 down against Japan after 53 minutes, he came off the bench, levelled the score on 84 minutes, and then put the Socceroos 2–1 ahead after 89 minutes. The match finished 3–1 after John Aloisi scored in added time.

Cahill had represented Samoa at the age of 14, was offered the chance to play for Ireland in the 2002 World Cup thanks to his Irish heritage, and was only able to play for Australia after FIFA changed its eligibility rules in 2003. 'I tried to bring him up the Samoan way,' his mother, Sisifo, once said.[24]

'The kid who fought for nine years for the right to wear the green and gold produced his finest moment on a football field, and probably the greatest moment of his life,' wrote Michael Cockerill in his match report. 'Two goals, inside the last ten minutes, turned the match upside down.'[25]

For a place in the quarterfinals the Socceroos needed to get past Croatia. On the streets of Germany, people began wrapping Croatian scarves over Australian jerseys, and waving Socceroos flags above Croatian hats. In the Socceroos' 23-man squad there were seven Australians of Croatian parentage: Zeljko Kalac, Ante Covic, Tony Popovic, Jason Culina, Josip Skoko, Mark Viduka, and Mark Bresciano, who was born to a Croatian mother and an Italian father. In the Croatian team were three Australians: Joey Didulica, Ante Seric and Joe Simunic. In total, Croatian-Australians made up more than 20 per cent of the two squads. Some called it 'Croatia A versus Croatia B'. Culina's father,

Branko, supported the Socceroos and countered, 'No, we are playing Australia B.'[26]

Some households were divided. In Sydney, Mark Rudan's parents supported Croatia while he supported the Socceroos. 'I watch them, and I think, *We all grew up the same way*,' Rudan once said of the Croatian Socceroos. 'We all had the same parenting, we had the same type of culture, we had the same upbringing.'

The match was a willing, sometimes spiteful occasion. The Croatian team, nicknamed Vatreni ('the fiery ones'), went ahead after just two minutes. Viduka committed a foul on the edge of the penalty area, and Kalac – selected in goals ahead of Mark Schwarzer – fumbled the resulting free-kick and let the ball dribble into the Australian net.

But Viduka was in inspired form. Up front he wrestled with the Croatia centre-back and fellow Melbourne Knights alumnus, Joe Simunic, who growled and scrapped and rugby tackled him to the ground. Australia equalised via a Craig Moore penalty just before half-time.

The Croats had already accumulated two yellow cards, and in the second half came out even more aggressive. Niko Kovac scored early for Croatia to make it 2–1. In response, Guus Hiddink sent on John Aloisi, Bresciano and beanpole striker Josh Kennedy.

Again his substitutions paid off. With just 13 minutes left, Bresciano swung a deep cross in the direction of Kennedy. It was Aloisi who jumped the highest, however, and he flicked the ball down into the six-yard box. Dialling in on goal was Harry Kewell. Putting aside injury concerns that had plagued him all tournament, Kewell crashed the ball into the Croatian goal. 2–2. If the Socceroos could hold on to that scoreline, they were through to the next round, and Croatia would be out.

Australia did hold on, and in the final moment of the game Tim Cahill even had a goal disallowed. In the carnage and the confusion, Simunic continued to berate the referee, even though he had already earned two yellow cards, and should have been sent from the field. When the English referee, Graham Poll, finally sent him off, Simunic became the first player since Socceroo Ray Richards in 1974 to receive three yellow cards in one game.

Poll was pilloried around the world for his mistake. The *Guardian* even headlined its match report: 'Poll Loses the Plot'. Unknowingly, however, he had provided the most poignant conclusion to the most poignant of matches. 'I cannot fully understand why I got it wrong and why I failed to send off Simunic,' wrote Poll in his autobiography. 'Aussie Joe certainly speaks with a broad Australian accent. Maybe, just maybe, that is where the confusion set in.'[27]

In the stadium, Socceroos fans showered each other in beer, threw inflatable kangaroos at each other and sang 'Down Under' by Men at Work and AC/DC's 'You Shook Me All Night Long'. In cities around Australia, they partied as the sun rose. Joe Napoliello laughed and cheered and marvelled at Australia's win. Bar Sport had its greatest ever day of trading: both Italy and Australia were through to the round of 16. In the celebration, however, he couldn't help but notice some anger among the Croatian supporters.

'Guys would be talking to me on the side because they didn't want anyone to hear, saying: "Who are these Australians, they know nothing about football – they have given nothing to our game",' recalled Napoliello. 'It was a very interesting moment. These were friends of mine, they were really upset. The Croatians have produced for this country the most amazing footballers – the best. Their clubs had been wiped clean, and Australia had used their players.'

For three days after 23 June, the news media converged upon Bar Sport. Cameras clicked, boom microphones dangled, lights shone in customers' faces, dictaphones and notepads were shoved in front of mouths. Australia had drawn Italy in the round of 16. One reporter called Leichhardt 'Ground Zero', and Joe Napoliello was asked the same question that had been asked of the Greeks and the Croatians: *Who do you support?*

Napoliello fended them off with a cheeky grin and a sparkle in his eye. He told reporters it would be a 'win-win', posed for the *Sun-Herald* with Franco in Socceroos and Italian jerseys, and predicted: 'If Australia win then I think Leichhardt is going to see its biggest night ever.'[28]

He pointed to his chest, and explained that it had been Franco's idea to create special World Cup T-shirts. Some were printed in blue, others in gold, but on every shirt there was the Australian flag with the Union Jack replaced by the Italian tricolour. On the back were the dates and times of every Italian and Australian group game.

Reporters whizzed around the country to quiz every prominent Italo-Australian on where their loyalties lay. ABC presenter Virginia Trioli. NSW premier Morris Iemma. Comedians Santo Cilauro and Vince Sorrenti. Sports minister Sandra Nori. Melbourne-based Italian senator Nino Randazzo. Even the furniture king, Mr Grand Sale himself: Franco Cozzo.

'I always said, "First half Australia, second half Italy,"' recalled Napoliello. 'It's a veiled threat, but I took it in jest and tried to joke about it. I understand why they ask it, I understand the context, but it's not a fair question to ask. It was hard to not only watch the Italians. Emotionally you can't switch off – you're emotionally connected to that team.'

The reporters only needed to look to the team sheet for evidence of loyalty. Vince Grella. Mark Bresciano. John Aloisi. Jason Culina. Tony Popovic. Josip Skoko. Mark Viduka. Stan Lazaridis. Ante Covic. Zeljko Kalac. Ten of the 23 Socceroos came from the Italian, Croatian and Greek communities.

And if you were to include Harry Kewell, Mark Schwarzer, Mile Sterjovski, Brett Emerton, Michael Beauchamp, Archie Thompson and Tim Cahill – each of whom played for one of Marconi, Sydney United or Sydney Olympic at some point in their career – the number rose to 17 of 23. Almost 75 per cent of the Socceroos' golden generation had come from, or been influenced by, these three ethnic communities and their soccer clubs.

Yet the argument prosecuted by Andrew Bolt and many others within the soccer community was that the Australian team was greater than the sum of its parts. Moreover, they believed that the parts – the ethnic clubs and communities – were at best no longer necessary and at worst an idle threat. Australia needed to hear the ethnic communities reconfirm their loyalty to the national cause. It needed them to say it out loud. And even when the majority performed this bizarre ritual, for many, it was still never going to be enough.

Ironically, in the years to come it would be those diverse parts that would be excluded. The ethnic clubs would languish in the state leagues, while the AIS, which had played an enormous role in developing many of the Socceroos, would be sidelined by the FFA and replaced by new people, new philosophies and new curriculums. The 2006 FIFA World Cup marked Australian soccer's final transition from the old ways to a brand new culture.

Australia played a good game against Italy. With Harry Kewell out injured, however, the team lacked penetration up front. The Italian defenders dealt with wave after wave of attacks with relative ease, even after Italian defender Marco Materazzi was sent off with more than half an hour left on the clock.

Australia simply could not score. And, for the first time, Guus Hiddink got his substitutions wrong. Always the gambler, he sent on Aloisi with just nine minutes to play, and decided to wait until extra time to make the next two changes. Italian coach Marcello Lippi took off striker Alessandro Del Piero, brought on Francesco Totti, and in the final play of the match the Italians swept down the exposed left flank. As Fabio Grosso swanned into the penalty area and readied himself to shoot, Lucas Neill slid along the turf and upended him. Penalty.

Totti stepped up and, with the last play of the match, sent the kick past Schwarzer. Australia's World Cup dream was over. At Bar Sport, Joe Napoliello once again celebrated long and loud. Italy was through to the quarterfinal.

'I don't get it,' wrote Andrew Bolt in the *Herald Sun*.

Australia gets beaten with the last kick of its World Cup game against Italy – an outrageous penalty – and thousands of Australians roar with joy. Yes, I call them Australians, since most were born right here. Shouldn't that mean something? But these cheerers actually see themselves more as Italians. Or, in the polite camouflage, 'Italian-Australians'. Did you see the pictures from Sydney's Norton St – the Italian heart of our most ethnically torn city – when the ball fizzed past Mark Schwarzer's despairing glove? As many as 8000 people, many in Italy's blue shirts, screamed, clapped, sang, danced, lit flares, honked car horns and set off fireworks.[29]

★

In the days after the round of 16 match, the anger towards the Italians reached its climax. Socceroos fans felt robbed. Many Australians labelled the Italians 'cheats' and circulated hoax videos of the Italian team practising diving routines. One journalist laughably recommended that FIFA introduce a sin-bin rule and many more suggested that the rules be changed. Malcolm Knox, a senior sportswriter for the *Sydney Morning Herald*, decided that the unmanly, foreign practice of diving was the root of the game's problems in Australia.

Joe Napoliello believed that Lucas Neill had fouled Fabio Grosso. He also felt that the Socceroos had been tactically naive. And he was certain that the Italians had deserved their victory. The passage of time would prove him correct. Yet for the rest of the year he would cop the full force of Australia's furious indignation. As Italy trounced Ukraine in the quarterfinal and defeated Germany to qualify for the final, he tried to keep his cool with a few irate customers who continued to deride the 'cheating Italians'. Napoliello explained to them that although he too was sad to see the Socceroos go out, controversy and tragedy are just part of the drama of the World Cup.

The stress of this debate, however, was soon dwarfed by the stress of the World Cup final. Zinedine Zidane scored for France after just seven minutes, before Marco Materazzi equalised for Italy. During extra time, Zidane headbutted Materazzi in the chest, knocking him to the ground and immediately stopping play. The referee sent Zidane off and, in the resulting penalty shootout, Grosso scored his spot-kick to deliver Italy its fourth World Cup.

The sun rose over Norton Street, Leichhardt, illuminating a long stretch of blue. Red flares burst into the sky as whistles and chants for '*IT-AL-IA!*' rang in the morning.

After a short conference, the Napoliello brothers decided to close Bar Sport and join the throng on the main street. Joe stood back, smiled, and watched as a coffin draped with the French flag was passed over the crowd. A reporter asked one of the pallbearers what they would have done if Italy had lost. 'It was never going to happen, mate,' came the response.[30]

The afterparty dominated the rest of the month. Tim Cahill and Lucas Neill jetted back to Sydney to thank the Australian supporters. 'Never in the time I've covered sport have I come across a team that made me feel as good as this soccer team,' concluded Rebecca Wilson, a rugby league journalist.[31]

Tony Wilson, an ex-AFL player who had travelled to Germany, put the final touches on a new book titled *Australia United*. Part tour guide, part diary, it described blow by blow the highs and lows of the experience. In the chapter about Australia's gut-wrenching loss to Italy, he commented: 'I find it difficult to understand why second-generation Australians would have supported Italy, but don't want to put that argument too forcefully for fear of agreeing with Andrew Bolt – the Melbourne *Herald Sun*'s Viceroy of Vitriol.'[32]

By the end of July, Suzy Canelas, Napoliello's partner, was heavily pregnant with their first child. The family was on cloud nine – the business was booming in the afterglow of the World Cup, Leichhardt was still celebrating Italy's victory, and Joe was readying himself for season two of the A-League. It had been a perfect 12 months.

Francesca Napoliello came into the world on the second day of August 2006. During labour, Suzy wore an Italian World Cup champions' shirt.

'My daughter Francesca was born one month after the World Cup,' Napoliello later explained. 'Suzy was pregnant through all the games. When we went to do the scans I spoke to the nurse. Francesca was born in a record birth year. Baby boom. I asked the nurse what it could be attributed to, and she said a lot of the time it could be traced back to some sort of happy event that's occurred. I did my numbers – we conceived in November of 2005. I said to the nurse: "That was when the Socceroos qualified for the World Cup.'"

JUST ANOTHER PAGE

2007–2014

I remember as a youngster traveling to grounds like Schintler Reserve, home of Footscray JUST, Olympic Village, home of Heidelberg Alexander, Connor Reserve, home of Preston Makedonia and Olympic Park, where Juventus used to play. These arenas held some memorable clashes between our team Hellas and their respective sides [...] I know these memories will be passed down to my children, to show them how our game has developed and also to make sure that these great Clubs and players are not forgotten [...]

Every time I drive past a now derelict Schintler Reserve, I get shivers. When I watch the Premier League and see Heidelberg and Preston play in front of 500 supporters, it makes me sick to my stomach. It is then I realize that I don't one day want to be talking to my children about a Club that no longer exists, or is a pale shadow of its former self. I remember those Clubs and they were all GREAT CLUBS, and I'm sure they all felt as indestructible as we do now. Yes, we've managed to survive whilst others have fallen, but survival is no longer enough. We must prosper and stay ahead of everyone else in order to ensure our future [...]

Don't let this great Club become just another page in Soccer's history.

Ange Postecoglou
Our Legacy, 1997[1]

Ange Postecoglou was an enthusiastic supporter of 'new football' and also one of its first victims. In November 2006, as the nation nursed a World Cup hangover, Postecoglou took the Australian under-20 team to the AFC Youth Championship in India. After losing to China in the group stage, the Young Socceroos were knocked out by South Korea in the quarterfinal. It was not the introduction that Australia had expected from the Asian Football Confederation.

'We have no reserves competition, no second-tier league where these kids can play week in and week out against men, alongside A-League players who have not made the first team at their clubs,' Postecoglou reasoned. 'Back in the days of the old NSL there were a lot more teams, and a lot of the best kids got the chance to play senior footy at 16 or 17. By the time you got to an under-20 World Cup they might have had 30 or 40 games in the NSL.'[2]

During the first season of the A-League, of all the players who had made at least one appearance, only 35 per cent were aged 23 or younger. It was the lowest rate of young players in the national competition for more than a decade. During the final season of the NSL, in 2003–04, the rate had been 48 per cent. In 1994–95, the season when most of the Socceroos' golden generation ventured into the NSL as youngsters, the rate had been 50 per cent.

Yet Postecoglou's warning was not well received. He was invited to explain himself further on SBS's Sunday-afternoon program *The World Game*. Craig Foster called for him to resign, Postecoglou refused, and the interview descended into an angry 12-minute argument. A news agenda was set. Not about the lack of opportunity for young players in the A-League, however, but about the personality clash between Foster and Postecoglou.

Born in Greece in 1965, Ange Postecoglou had seen it all as a supporter, as a ballboy, as a player and as a coach. When Ange was nine, his father, Jim, signed him up to play soccer at South Melbourne Hellas. He did not leave for 25 years.

In 1984 he made his NSL debut, in 1991 he was Ferenc Puskas' championship-winning captain, and in 1994 he was assistant coach to

Frank Arok during the final game at Middle Park. Between 1997 and 1999, he guided South Melbourne to back-to-back titles, and in 2000 he took his boyhood club to the Club World Championship in Brazil. In 2002, he was named captain of South Melbourne's team of the century.

'It was all part of my dad's plan,' he once said. 'He came from a foreign country, he didn't know the culture of the place, he didn't understand a lot of the things that happened here, and he wanted me to have the same values as him. At South he knew who my friends were going to be and what my values were going to be. It went beyond football. That place moulded me as a person.'

George Vasilopoulos, the former South Melbourne president, was the first person to have confidence in him as a coach, predicting back in 1998 that he would one day coach Australia. Yet by the time the NSL was euthanised in 2004, Postecoglou was in charge of the Australian under-17 team, known as the Joeys, as well as the under-20 team, known as the Young Socceroos, and he had growing concerns about the future of his club. Just prior to the Save Our South rally in 2004, he penned a column for the Melbourne *Herald Sun*.

> My club may not exist in three weeks' time and I find it hard to comprehend [...] The dreamer in me wants to take to the streets and protest along with thousands of others and somehow save the club. However, another side of me thinks differently. My passion for the club does not match the passion for my sport. I love the game and want it to prosper [...] All I say to those who will pave the road ahead is to not ignore our past [...] The greatness of the sport is always measured by its champions. Soccer should not ignore this lesson.[3]

By the second season, dubbed 'A-League Version 2' by Football Federation Australia, Ange Postecoglou could see the enormous success of soccer's reformation. He saw Melbourne Victory draw an average crowd of more than 14,000 people, despite finishing second-last on the competition ladder. He witnessed the first Melbourne–Sydney derby of season two attract just under 40,000 people to Telstra Dome in Melbourne. Many of the Victory fans were converts from South Melbourne, including the former assistant editor of *Studs Up*, Harry Georgiadis, who became a member from the first day of the A-League. In Melbourne Victory, Postecoglou could see the development of the A-League's first superclub.

Paul Mavroudis, a 23-year-old South Melbourne supporter, was moving in the other direction. He had been to each of Melbourne Victory's pre-season games in 2005, as well as every home game of season one. Like many South Melbourne supporters he had been ready to give the new franchise a chance.

But while most stayed and became passionate Victory fans, Mavroudis decided that the A-League was not for him. It was not Australian soccer as he knew it. The gallows humour had been replaced by hardcore supporter groups who took things way too seriously, the standard was not what he had hoped for and, most of all, South Melbourne was not, and could not, be involved.

He returned to the eternal winter of state league soccer. It was a decision that would invite ridicule, contempt and constant investigation from friends and colleagues. 'While in the majority of the rest of the soccer world, not having your team in the top-flight is reason enough not to take an interest,' he once lamented, 'the peculiar situation of Australian soccer means that this position makes you come across as a recalcitrant.'[4]

Mavroudis was born into a Greek family from Melbourne's western suburbs in July 1983. His father followed Heidelberg and his mother had no interest in soccer at all. He inherited his auburn hair and his name from a grandfather who had died fighting for the communists in the Greek Civil War.

He was always an unusual kid. With his thick glasses and pale skin, he wasn't a typical 'wog boy' or Aussie. He studied literature at university, read voraciously, and became an avid contributor to the 'bitter' versus 'new dawn' debate, an incredibly niche online version of the 'old soccer, new football' split. It happened mostly in internet chatrooms and SBS's *The World Game* forums. As all of the mainstream media and most of the soccer journalists were spruiking the A-League, it became the only outlet for the supporters left on the wrong side of history.

Andrew Howe's season guide – once a dense, historical reference book of statistics – was a testament to this new reality. Howe had the entire history of the NSL at his fingertips, personally collated over a 15-year period, yet as dictated by the FFA the guide for 2006–07 showed only the previous season of history.

This meant that Damian Mori, who scored 225 goals in the NSL and seven in the A-League's first season, was now listed as having scored just seven goals. Clint Bolton's 98 clean sheets as a goalkeeper were whittled down to five. There was no interest in Alex Tobin's 522 appearances in the NSL. Those who played in the NSL but not the A-League, such as Bob Catlin, Sergio Melta, Paul Trimboli, Mark Viduka, Francis Awaritefe, Dez Marton, Gary Cole and Rod Brown, were simply scrubbed from the record. The four NSL titles that Postecoglou had won with South Melbourne – two as a player, two as a coach – were nowhere to be seen.

The intent might have been harmless but the result was insidious. Season guides are created specifically for the purpose of informing journalists and commentators, who in turn educate supporters through newspaper articles and broadcasts. Statistics, often seen as the niche domain of dateless wonders and hopeless nostalgics, are in fact the life-blood of all sport. If it was no longer important to recognise the statistical achievements of the NSL, then why bother collating them at all for the A-League?

The truth was that in the early days of 'new football', some stats, some clubs and some players were more important than others. The *2006–07 A-League Season Guide* was like the Holy Bible without the Old Testament.

Yet in the enormous effort to reboot and rebuild soccer, these types of omissions were considered trifling matters. Supporters like Paul Mavroudis were considered collateral damage, their memories irrelevant. There were huge amounts of money being thrown around in an expensive, growth-oriented competition, and there was a new cadre of supporters to be won over.

The future of the A-League was of paramount importance, not the preservation of the past. And on the evidence of the previous 18 months, the FFA had been given no indication that supporters wanted to know of anything that occurred before 2005. The A-League demographic skewed young, middle-class, aspirational and entrepreneurial. Indeed if the A-League had proven anything, it was that you could forget about history, occasionally dance on the graves of the old clubs, and that this would actually *encourage* more fans to be involved. The past had become a vanquished, foreign country.

Melbourne Victory played the role of coloniser-in-chief. At one club function, a Victory staff member was reported to have said 'the days of wogball and pumpkin seed eaters are gone'.[5]

The club's brainchild was Tony Ising, a brilliant marketing man who told the press that the Victory would transcend old rivalries and allow all the ethnic groups to sit side by side, arm in arm, watching a new type of club in modern, peaceful surrounds.

'We are moving towards all-seater stadiums and away from standing room,' Ising explained in 2006.

> This is all about supporter comfort and safety. We are moving unashamedly to a family friendly environment. We are seeing women and children attending games in unprecedented numbers, and the club will act against anyone who threatens this trend [...] We are the EMBODIMENT – the quintessential MANIFESTATION – of Modern Football.[6]

The Melbourne Victory squad was built by the coach, Ernie Merrick, a monotone Scot who had coached in the NSL and had just finished his tenure at the Victorian Institute of Sport, and the football operations manager, Gary Cole, the ex–Heidelberg United striker. Many of the players in the second season were Victorian born or bred: Danny Allsopp, Adrian Leijer, Vince Lia, Michael Theoklitos, Daniel Piorkowski, Rodrigo Vargas, Kristian Sarkies. Ex–South Melbourne player Steve Panopoulos recommended to the club three Brazilians – Alessandro, Claudinho and Fred.

The two stars, however, were Archie Thompson, a 26-year-old fringe Socceroo who had once entered *The Guinness Book of Records* for scoring 13 goals in an international match; and Kevin Muscat, a veteran of three Victorian NSL clubs who was often described as 'the most hated man in football' for his antics in the English second division. It was the ideal blend of hardworking locals, high-quality foreign imports and repatriated Socceroos.

By season's end, Melbourne Victory finished on 45 points, 12 clear of its nearest challenger, Adelaide United. In the grand final, held on Saturday 18 February 2007, Victory smashed Adelaide 6–0. The combination of Fred and Thompson tore mercilessly through Adelaide's defence, Thompson alone scored five, and on the winners podium Muscat specifically congratulated the supporters.

Like the Cove in Sydney, the Squadron in Newcastle, the Den in Brisbane and the Red Army in Adelaide, many Melbourne Victory fans organised themselves into a large, active supporter group called the Blue and White Brigade. Many were recent converts, while some others had supported one of the 12 Victorian clubs in the NSL.

In total, more than 400,000 people clicked through the turnstiles at Victory home games at Olympic Park or the Telstra Dome, at an electrifying average of 31,374 people per game. In the 28 seasons of the NSL, the crowd for a regular season match had never risen above 20,000 people. Even during the heyday of Perth Glory in the late 1990s, the highest average season attendance was less than 15,000 people. Something truly special was happening. Ange Postecoglou, who was now jobless after being sacked as coach of the Joeys and the Young Socceroos, wrote that Victory home games were 'the best sporting atmosphere in the country'.[7]

★

The pacification of Sydney and Melbourne, the two biggest, richest and most politically volatile cities in the country, was a critical milestone in the reformation of Australian soccer. During the three decades of the national league, these cities had fielded a total of 24 clubs under a variety of guises, representing the full spectrum of the soccer community without ever attracting city-wide support. Together, Sydney FC and Melbourne Victory accounted for 25 per cent of the A-League competition, 42 per cent of its total attendances and 100 per cent of championships, helping to bring an unprecedented wave of attention to the domestic game. Soccer, noted the *Age* during Victory's all-conquering second season, 'never again will be out of sight and out of mind'.[8]

For as long as there had been a national league in Australia there had been arguments about its structure, its presentation, and its relationship to the state federations and to the grassroots participants. The mind-boggling success of the A-League's first two seasons, as well as the entry into Asia and the 2006 World Cup campaign, allowed FFA to fasten a tight lid over these skirmishes. The executive had unprecedented authority, more government support than ever before and a largely pliant base of constituents. Success drove criticism underground, behind closed doors, heard only in frantic whispers from the sides of mouths and from miserable corners of the internet. No Australian soccer organisation was ever so popular – or so powerful – as the FFA was in mid-2007.

This concentration of power at FFA helped to engender a new culture of dependency. Where soccer clubs once lived and died by the spirit of their community and their members, now they were little more than privatised avenues of weekend entertainment.

'There isn't the passion that surrounded the old ethnic clubs,' Les Murray once explained. 'We all did massive amounts of volunteer work. Our passion was driven by the need to get more Australians to embrace the game – we worked our fingers to the bone for this noble cause. There's not much of that in the A-League. There are some volunteers, but in the NSL days almost everyone was a volunteer. Even the CEO wasn't paid on some occasions. It was based on volunteerism. People just wanted to be part of it.'

With a privatised ownership structure and tight restrictions over what the franchises could and could not do, owners and supporters learned to look to FFA for everything: television rights, sponsorship guidelines, ownership issues, revenue, the works. If Melbourne Knights or Marconi or Sydney Olympic had hit a financial crisis in the old national league, where there had been no money and precious little corporate support, it would have been the responsibility of their communities to bail them out. Family homes would be mortgaged, loans would be refinanced, working bees would be organised, new investors found and fundraisers held.

One of Andrew Howe's favourite memories from the NSL was standing among Sydney Olympic supporters on the hill at St George Stadium, watching old Greek men stuffing wads of cash in a large bucket with 'Scott Ollerenshaw' written on the front in Greek. That money went to the club office, which had used it to sign the young attacker.

This culture of community self-sufficiency well and truly died in the A-League. When Nick Tana handed back the ownership licence of Perth Glory after the first season, for example, the FFA took over the running of the club and the search for a new owner. And although the Crawford Report had recommended that the national league be run as a separate entity from the governing body, the FFA steadfastly refused to let go of its most precious asset. To borrow a line from historian WK Hancock, the Australian soccer community came to look upon the FFA as a vast public utility, whose duty it was to provide the greatest happiness for the greatest number.

The positive aspect of this structural change, however, was that it allowed FFA to set strategic direction from on high, something that had been sorely lacking from previous administrations. There were equalisation measures such as the salary cap, which kept the competition as fair as possible and reined in spending, and tight controls on marketing and promotions. The overriding goal for FFA was to destroy the old structures, build an entirely new foundation for soccer and, as Frank Lowy had once said, 'organise the game from the bottom to the top in a homogenous way'.[9]

On the first day of November 2007 – roughly halfway through the third A-League season – FFA announced its $10 million National Football Development Plan. With funds drawn from government grants, from its own coffers and from an increase in the participation levy, the review focused on the education of local coaches and players, the creation of a youth league and a national women's league, and a plan for developing and identifying talented players in regional areas and Indigenous communities.

Investment in Indigenous communities was long overdue. For decades, the pioneering legacy of Charles Perkins, John Moriarty and Gordon Briscoe had been effectively wasted. Soccer journalists would routinely implore the governing bodies to invest in Indigenous development programs, only for their calls to fall on deaf ears. As a consequence there had only been a few Indigenous players in the NSL.

Perhaps the best-known Indigenous player who crossed over from 'old soccer' to 'new football' was Jade North. Born to a white mother and an Indigenous father in Taree, a small town two hours north of Newcastle, North spent his childhood with his mother in Queensland and New Zealand, and didn't identify as Indigenous until he was an adult. By 2007, North was 25 years old, with a partner and a newborn baby. He had reunited with his father, replaced his trademark flying dreadlocks with a smarter short-back-and-sides haircut, and assumed the captaincy of Newcastle Jets. This made him the first ever Indigenous captain of an A-League side.

Led by rookie coach Gary van Egmond, the nucleus of the Jets squad came mostly from Sydney: goalkeeper Ante Covic, defender Andrew Durante, midfielder Matt Thompson, wing-back Tarek Elrich, striker Mark Bridge, and the Griffiths brothers Joel and Adam. The imports were Mario Jardel, a chronically overweight Brazilian, Korean young-ster Song Jin-Hyung and Brazilian playmaker Denni, while Stuart

Musialik, James Holland, Jobe Wheelhouse and Troy Hearfield joined North to form a local contingent.

Since Federation in 1901, Newcastle, a working-class city built around the heavy industries of coal and steel, had always voted Labor. In December 2007, the Labor government swept to office after 11 years of conservative rule. Newly elected prime minister Kevin Rudd had run a campaign of fairness in the workplace, action on climate change and education, and reconciliation with Indigenous people. The soccer players union gave him unqualified support, releasing a statement that said Rudd would embrace the multiculturalism of the game, and pitch in $32 million to help build grassroots soccer. 'Our colonial past,' read the PFA statement, 'has little relevance to this future.'[10]

The national apology to the Stolen Generations of Indigenous children was one of the first election promises fulfilled by the Labor government. For Jade North, who had spent half his life covering up his Indigenous identity, the apology had both practical and symbolic influence. On his father's side, he had learned of uncles and aunties who had been taken away as children and raised by white people, and by living in Newcastle he had begun to learn more about the Biripi nation to which he belonged.

His family would travel down to games to watch him play and he would travel up to visit them in Taree. He had tattooed the word 'Biripi' on his left forearm, both to make his family proud and also to show an example for Indigenous kids. 'Today is going to turn things around and make every Aboriginal in Australia come out and say we're proud to be a black man walking on this country,' North told the *Daily Telegraph* after Rudd's apology.[11]

That weekend, North led Newcastle Jets to a 3–2 victory over Queensland Roar, booking a place in the grand final against the Central Coast Mariners. It was a new frontier – the first grand final to be contested by two clubs from regional centres. The game was shifted to the 45,000-capacity Sydney Football Stadium, forcing both sets of supporters to travel down the F3 highway.

The day before the game, North brought the squad together at the hotel in Coogee and asked each player to say a few words about what winning a grand final would mean to them. North spoke last. He began by telling his teammates that they deserved to win as a collective. Then he spoke himself: he wanted to be the first Indigenous man to lift that trophy.

For three decades, Newcastle had played under different guises – KB United in the 1970s, Rosebud in the 1980s, Breakers in the 1990s, United in the early 2000s – and yet had never managed to win a premiership or a grand final.

That all changed on the afternoon of Sunday 24 February 2008 when Mark Bridge scored the only goal of the match to secure a 1–0 win. North became the first Indigenous captain to win a national league title, and as he held the trophy aloft the word 'Biripi' was in full view on his forearm. 'I've won a few championships,' he told reporters, 'but this is the most special by far.'[12]

Despite the ongoing financial losses, the ownership drama at Perth Glory and the collapse of New Zealand Knights, which was replaced by Wellington Phoenix in 2007, Football Federation Australia pressed ahead with its development agenda. Not long after Newcastle Jets won the 2008 grand final, FFA announced the establishment of a national youth league and a national women's competition.

At the launch of the W-League, eight clubs were announced for the first season: Adelaide United, Queensland Roar, Canberra United, Central Coast Mariners, Newcastle Jets, Sydney FC, Melbourne Victory and Perth Glory. 'Women's sport has not received the profile it deserves and I and the Rudd government are working to change that,' declared Kate Ellis, the federal minister for sport, at the launch. 'They should be celebrated as the household names they deserve to be.'[13]

At the grassroots, soccer boasted more registered female participants than any other team sport except netball, while at the top level the Matildas had qualified for the quarterfinals of the 2007 Women's World Cup.

Yet the crucial link between grassroots and national team had not been available to women since the collapse of the Women's National Soccer League in 2004. Some players were forced to drop back to the state leagues, others went abroad to play in the USA or Sweden, while Melissa Barbieri, the Matildas goalkeeper, made history in 2007 by competing with the men in the Victorian Premier League. Clearly the women's game was in desperate need of attention and investment.

In this context, the creation of the W-League resolved a long history of distrust and detachment between women's and men's soccer. The Australian Women's Soccer Association had remained separate from the Australian Soccer Federation for nearly three decades from 1974, and there had never been any institutional will by the NSL sides to be involved in the WNSL. So although most of the W-League sides were run by state federations and institutes, the fact that they now shared a brand and an identity with the A-League clubs was considered a significant breakthrough. By having integrated men's, youth and women's teams at club and national level, soccer was the first code of football to achieve full inclusivity.

Yet for decades an element within women's soccer had argued *against* integration with the men's game. It was a feminist argument grounded in the notion of self-determination and community empowerment: if women had separate structures, they would not need to fight for resources and attention with men. The integrationists, meanwhile, took the view that unification with men would bring greater access to funding and support.

Heather Reid, the CEO of Capital Football and Canberra United, always sat somewhere in between these two schools of thought. When the W-League kicked off, so did Canberra United. While most of the A-League owners and chief executives were largely uninterested in the fate of their W-League sides, Reid was able to devote ample time and energy into building Canberra United into the first W-League 'superclub'. She was able to secure relatively lucrative sponsorships with a trade union and the local electricity and water company, and developed good relations with the local media.

'I wouldn't say I was glad that we didn't have an A-League team,' Reid would later explain, 'but it gave us more leverage talking to the government and to sponsors by not having another team in the summer space. We don't have a competitor.'

This unique focus on women's soccer immediately made Reid a target for acrimony and abuse. Many of the men in Canberra blamed her for prioritising women's soccer over everything else, and accused her of not doing enough to bring Canberra an A-League team. Reid's response was always the same: it was an issue of money, not gender. While the budget to run a W-League club was just $300,000 per season, FFA required private owners and around $8 million to consider giving Canberra an A-League licence.

Yet by mid-November the success of Canberra United became a lobbying tool in the push to bring the A-League to Canberra. To its first home game, Canberra United drew more than 1500 people, which set an early attendance benchmark. This prompted the '2k for the 22nd' campaign to get 2000 supporters to the second home game on 22 November.

Throughout the first season, Canberra United and Newcastle Jets boasted the best attendances in the W-League, while Queensland Roar took out the premiership. In the inaugural grand final, held in Brisbane in front of nearly 5000 people, Queensland Roar beat Canberra United 2–0. It was not a fully professional league, and many of the players were paid a pittance or played at their own cost. Yet for the first time in history, the national governing body had taken steps to ensure gender equity in Australian soccer.

By the end of season two of the W-League, the Australian women's team would defeat Vietnam, South Korea, Japan and North Korea to win Australia's first ever Asian Cup. The Matildas had played for W-League clubs Canberra United, Sydney FC, Melbourne Victory, Newcastle Jets, Central Coast Mariners and Perth Glory in the lead-up to the tournament.

'It gave the players years of intensive competition,' explained Reid. 'It was a surprise to me – going into Asia was a concern from the women's point of view, because the women's game is so strong in Asia. There was a concern that we would get swamped, so winning was very significant.'

★

In the first mission statement adopted by Football Federation Australia, there was a commitment to foster a 'unifying new football culture which embraces success, diversity, professionalism, integrity and the universal appeal of the game'.

It could be argued that by 2009 this aim had been achieved. FFA claimed that participation had increased by more than 50 per cent since 2001; there were seven fully professional, well-supported Australian clubs in the A-League, as well as an integrated W-League and National Youth League, a more unified corporate and governance structure across the states and territories, a national technical director, a program to develop the game in regional centres, and a five-year collective bargaining agreement with Professional Footballers Australia. The only significant omissions were Western Sydney, which was the multicultural heartland of Australian soccer, and the once-mighty ethnic clubs.

South Melbourne fan Paul Mavroudis had started writing a blog, *South of the Border*, to document life below the A-League. It was a good time to start writing on the internet. Many A-League supporters began their own websites, as well as their own fan forums. Social media sites such as Facebook and Twitter allowed writers to build an online readership at relatively low cost, and blogging had become a serious alternative to mainstream news.

Mavroudis wrote once a week, usually on a Sunday or Monday, to wrap up South Melbourne's latest match and perhaps to provide comment on the issues of the day. His writing is sharp, funny and insightful. Like Andrew Dettre, he is the great curmudgeon, exploring his own misery with verve, humour and the occasional retreat into fiction and poetry. And when Ange Postecoglou got a coaching job in Greece, Mavroudis set up an 'Ange-watch' to keep tabs on his club's favourite son. He is nothing if not loyal.

'No matter how well you do at a lower level, you're stuck in this no-man's-land,' he once explained. 'A team like South Melbourne, when it was founded, was not founded for second-tier football. In 1959, the Victorian league was the best you could do. But after that we got to the National Soccer League, and that's the pinnacle of what you could achieve. It wasn't built like other suburban Greek teams to be just at a lower level, a more social thing. In a way that's what a lot of my writing tries to address – what it's like to be a South Melbourne fan in the exile years, in the exodus.'[14]

Herein lies the irony of Australian soccer's great leap forward: while the game itself catapulted into the mainstream, its pioneer clubs actually retreated further into the margins, watched only by the last remnants of their immediate communities.

For Mavroudis, this exclusion was a betrayal of Australia's pluralistic, multicultural soccer community. The ethnicity that once defined the Australian game had been repackaged to fit corporate sensibilities; national flags were carried onto the field by sweet school children on federation-sanctioned Harmony Days, but disallowed from the hands of the supporter on the terraces. It was, as Mavroudis observed, the logical endpoint of the view that 'multiculturalism means everyone acting the same, just eating different food'.[15]

And the violence, which had been forever associated with the unruly ethnics of the NSL, did not stop. There were fights at A-League games too, mostly between the self-described 'ultras' supporter groups of Sydney FC and Melbourne Victory, yet that too was always reported with gratuitous reference to 'the old NSL' and clips of the riots in 1985 and 2005. This narrative destroyed the capacity for a club such as South Melbourne to redefine itself in the modern era.

But it was a gilded age for soccer, the biggest boom of interest since the migrant ships unloaded their human cargo to the soccer fields back in the 1950s and 1960s, and by the fourth season of the A-League, expansion had become the hottest topic in the game.

Confident after several years of unimaginable success, the FFA had developed an insatiable appetite for growth. Chairman Frank Lowy decided to bid for the right to host the World Cup in either 2018 or 2022, while the FFA fielded interest in the A-League from consortia in Western Sydney, the South Coast of NSW, Canberra, Tasmania, Melbourne, Townsville and the Gold Coast. The last two were the first to receive a green light to enter the A-League in 2010–11, leaving the FFA with ten teams.

Placing new teams in Melbourne and Sydney, however, became a philosophical question as well as a logistical one. The success of the A-League had been predicated on artificial insemination, but in the two biggest cities there were still highly ambitious ex-NSL clubs that wanted to be part of the new world order.

One of the most talked-about bids was from a consortium known as 'Southern Cross FC'. Yet although it had the public backing of South Melbourne, the most successful soccer club in Australian history, as well as SBS commentator Les Murray, FFA chose instead to go with a different Melbourne bid led by horseracing identity Peter Sidwell. The franchise would be kitted in red and white, play out of the new rectangular stadium at Docklands and be known as 'Melbourne Heart'.

'It was really obvious to me as someone who came from a wog background that there was a lot of anti-wog feeling among the FFA executive,' recalled Bonita Mersiades, who joined FFA in 2007. 'They were mostly from white, Anglo-Saxon backgrounds. When South Melbourne was bidding for the A-League, they were looking for the second Melbourne team. The tone was, "We keep South Melbourne out. We don't want South Melbourne in there." Why not? I don't have to answer that – they were Greek.'

This desire to replace traditional clubs with sanitised franchises and new money owners was best typified by the inclusion of Gold Coast United, a corporate wonder-club bankrolled by Clive Palmer, the richest man in Queensland. With hair dyed jet black to cover the grey, large shirts that barely stretched over his huge belly, and more interest in his own profile than in soccer, Palmer shamelessly told reporters that his team would fly around the country in a private jet, and that Gold Coast United would fill the stadium every week and win the competition undefeated at its first attempt. He signed Miron Bleiberg, the former Queensland Roar coach, and brought Jason Culina home to captain the side.

Meanwhile in Townsville, 1500 kilometres north of the Gold Coast, North Queensland Fury was funded by Don Matheson, a golf course developer who was haemorrhaging money. Matheson appointed the ex–Glasgow Rangers player Ian Ferguson as coach, signed the former Liverpool and England striker Robbie Fowler as marquee player and promised to make North Queensland a destination club for Indigenous players.

The expansion of the A-League and the success of the W-League were soon overshadowed by Lowy's ambitious World Cup bid. After months of research and a total cost of $45 million to the taxpayer, the FFA presented its 'bid book' to FIFA. It was a gamble of incredibly high stakes: succeed and a wave of corporate and media support would wash over the A-League and the W-League; fail and the FFA would face an acrimonious, uncertain future.

But Lowy, the King Midas of Australian soccer, was confident. He was still incredibly popular among the rank and file of A-League supporters and, nearing 80 years of age, wanted to provide one final legacy for a game he had loved since he was a child.

And then, after nearly six happy years of good fortune, everything went wrong.

First, North Queensland Fury had to be bailed out by FFA after losing millions in its first season. Then it was reported that Gold Coast United was also on the brink of collapse after it too lost a small fortune. Then Archie Fraser quit his job as head of the A-League, and in South Africa the Socceroos were humiliated 4–0 in their opening match of the 2010 World Cup against Germany. Without Mark Viduka leading the line up front, the Australians started the match without a recognised centre forward, and after a draw with Ghana and a win over Serbia, they were eliminated at the group stage.

On SBS, Craig Foster led a stinging attack on the outgoing Socceroos coach Pim Verbeek, while Harry Kewell and *Sydney Morning Herald* journalist Michael Cockerill got into a very public argument over Cockerill's reportage. Many fans and commentators questioned the lack of regeneration in a squad that had an average age of 28. The extended honeymoon period from the 2006 World Cup was officially over.

It would be the last World Cup for Mark Schwarzer, Lucas Neill, Jason Culina, Craig Moore, Vince Grella, Brett Emerton, Luke Wilkshire and Harry Kewell. 'The Golden Generation will steadily recede from view,' predicted one reporter. 'They gave football in this country an identity and an increasing appeal. They have served their sport well.'[16]

So began the most intense period of scrutiny and acrimony for FFA. As the World Cup drew to a close, investigative reporters Nick McKenzie and Richard Baker at the *Age* published explosive allegations of 'secret millions' of taxpayers' money spent by FFA on lobbying for the right to host the World Cup. The A-League began the 2010–11 season against a backdrop of plummeting crowds, huge financial losses and little exposure. The FFA was forced to support Adelaide United, previously one of the model franchises, as well as North Queensland Fury and Brisbane Roar. The glowing headlines grew darker and journalists began to question whether the A-League would collapse entirely.

Leading the pack, as usual, was Michael Cockerill. Between August and September 2010, he penned searching investigations for the *Sydney Morning Herald* into the relationship between the governing body and supporters, as well as articles about the fickleness of A-League fans and about the development of young players. He even called for Frank Lowy to underwrite the entire competition.

Cockerill's investigation spurred Andrew Dettre, who had been absent from soccer journalism for two decades, back to his study. He had seen the NSL go through similar growing pains in the early 1980s, surviving only due to the hard yakka and undying passion of the ethnic communities. In a letter to the *Sydney Morning Herald*, Dettre wrote that Australia was the only country that had 'four different football codes competing for talent, venues, media space and crowd support'. This, he wrote, was a 'fundamental problem'.

Pointing to the facilities that had been built by the ethnic communities, Dettre mused that it might have been 'a mistake to indirectly chase away the migrant support'. 'Where,' he asked, 'is the clubhouse and football stadium of Sydney FC?'[17]

Those facilities – St George Stadium, Knights Stadium, Marconi Stadium, Bob Jane Stadium, Edensor Park – were still there, but they lay abandoned in the summer and were frequented by just a few hundred fans in the winter. The foundation clubs had lost their supporters, profile and sponsors, and were rapidly losing their ambition and their hope. On the Melbourne Victory forum, Paul Mavroudis wrote an epitaph for the game he loved.

'The game has come along in leaps and bounds in many ways,' he wrote.

> Better stadiums, better conditions for players, more media. But it's not my game – in much the same way that previously, people who felt (rightly or wrongly) that the game wasn't theirs, now feel a sense of ownership over it. It's not the game that I grew up with – with all the negative and positive things that came with it. There is no timetable for reconciliation. There's no need for it. The changes that have been enacted have been done so forcefully, that there's no turning back, really. It's a different culture, a different environment, tapping into something broader in society.[18]

Despite the tens of millions of dollars spent on soccer since 2005, new facilities did not spring up at Sydney FC or any of the other A-League clubs around the country. None of them set down roots or fortified their existence with bricks and mortar. They were rent-seekers, the private plaything of millionaires like Clive Palmer or Nick Bianco or Don Matheson, without direct ties or obligations to the community.

So when the going got tough due to the global financial crisis that began in 2008, perhaps it should have been no surprise that many owners simply walked away from the game. Frustrated by the uncertainty, but with no recourse to get involved and help the franchises stay afloat, supporters routinely turned on the FFA and demanded that it find them new sugar daddies. Spin-the-rolodex and find me a new millionaire: the national league had become entirely dependent on the corporate socialism of the FFA.

By the end of 2010, the FFA had stripped Con Constantine of his ownership licence at Newcastle Jets, handing it over to mining magnate Nathan Tinkler; killed off plans for a new franchise in Western Sydney; and failed in its attempt to host the 2022 World Cup. After millions of taxpayer dollars, two years of work and a newspaper investigation into claims of improper conduct by FFA, Australia received just one vote.

★

Running against the grain of the A-League's first recession was Ange Postecoglou. He had started his A-League coaching career in October 2009, in the middle of the fifth season, following the dismissal of Frank Farina from Brisbane Roar. His first move was to cut several players from the squad, including veterans Craig Moore, Charlie Miller, Danny Tiatto and Bob Malcolm.

The decision was not well received. Some people, including Tiatto and Farina, publicly questioned the direction of the club. When Brisbane finished ninth on the ladder, many more thought Postecoglou had gone mad.

From the moment he was sacked from the national youth teams in 2007, Postecoglou had more or less disappeared from Australia's collective memory. Only Paul Mavroudis at *South of the Border* updated his readers on Postecoglou's progress. Apart from that, his triumphs with South Melbourne Hellas as a player and a coach were considered ancient history.

In the intervening years between 2007 and 2009 he had coached in Greece, at Whittlesea Zebras in the Victorian Premier League, and worked part-time on the Fox Sports A-League broadcast. But the new Brisbane Roar coach was best known for his on-air argument with Foster back in 2006. Few people believed in him. '[H]e's offering nothing new,' wrote one pundit. 'His name is old soccer.'[19]

Things were trending downward for Australian coaches. When Vitezslav Lavicka led Sydney FC to the 2009–10 A-League title but missed out on winning coach of the season, Craig Foster called it a 'fitting disgrace', blaming the other A-League coaches for not understanding the way Lavicka worked.[20]

At the beginning of the 2010–11 season, five of the A-League clubs were led by Czechs, Dutchmen and a New Zealander, leaving just five head coaching positions for Australians. Since 2005, Postecoglou had been campaigning for A-League coaches to give young players an opportunity. For a lot longer he had been waiting for the cultural cringe towards Australian coaches to end. The 2010–11 season was his chance to convert theory into practice.

Under Postecoglou, eight players, including top scorer Sergio van Dijk, left Brisbane in the off-season. Twelve players were signed, five under the age of 25, forming the third-youngest team in the competition. Matt Smith and Shane Stefanutto were pinched from North Queensland Fury, former Melbourne Victory goalkeeper Michael Theoklitos arrived after an ill-fated stint in England, and striker Jean Carlos Solorzano was recruited from Costa Rica. The most important arrival, however, was Thomas Broich: a 29-year-old wandering midfielder who had once been tipped as the next big thing in German football. Nicknamed 'Mozart' for his taste for classical music, Broich was the commissar of Postecoglou's stylistic revolution.

After four rounds – two wins, two draws – Postecoglou explained his philosophy in one of his regular columns for Brisbane's *Sunday Mail*. Commenting on the need for regeneration under the new Socceroos boss, Holger Osieck, he noted: 'The most critical element in a player's development at any level is opportunity.'[21]

His A-League team was proof of commitment to that vision. Previously unheralded centre-backs Smith and Milan Susak were flanked by Ivan Franjic and Stefanutto; the all-Australian midfield of

Matt McKay, Mitch Nichols and Erik Paartalu were instructed to keep possession and play the ball along the ground; his forwards Broich and Kosta Barbarouses and Solorzano were explosive in an attacking front three. There were no marquee players or golden generation Socceroos. No A-League coach had ever combined such a high degree of experimentation with such resounding success.

By mid-season, as floods tore through South East Queensland, causing nearly $3 billion worth of damage, affecting thousands of homes and forcing Brisbane Roar away from its home ground, Postecoglou's team had lost just one match and were seven points clear at the top of the A-League ladder. In January 2011, Brisbane broke APIA Leichhardt's old record of 22 undefeated games, and in mid-February, after a winning a Queensland derby 4–0 against Gold Coast United, it was handed the Premiers Plate. By qualifying for the grand final, Brisbane Roar brought soccer's showpiece event to Queensland for the first time since 1997.

After 90 minutes, in front of a record crowd of 50,168 people at Suncorp Stadium, the scores remained locked at 0–0. The first half of extra time saw Central Coast Mariners go two ahead, seemingly putting the result beyond doubt. But in the second half, Henrique – Postecoglou's mid-season signing – pulled one back for Brisbane. And in the final play of the match, Paartalu – a former Postecoglou pupil from the national youth teams – nodded home a powerful header from a corner. 2–2.

In the penalty shootout, Franjic, Paartalu, McKay and Henrique each converted their spot-kick for Brisbane to win its first national league title. Brisbane Roar won the double and the fair play award. Paartalu was awarded goal of the year, Theoklitos goalkeeper of the year, Postecoglou coach of the year.

'We started as a team most people picked to finish fairly low down the ladder and ended as champions of the highest order,' Postecoglou wrote for the *Sunday Mail*. 'What I have enjoyed as much as anything has been the journey rather than the end result.'[22]

Ange Postecoglou liberated the imagination of the Australian soccer community, and showed how its teams could win with style. He waded through the jungle to hack out a clear path for young Australian players and coaches to follow. More than any other individual, he got Australians thinking about the future of the domestic game.

Yet the echoes of history reverberated through him. The Postecoglou revival was like rediscovering a long-lost species of native vegetation: where did he sprout from? How did he survive? Why had we forgotten about him for so long? Brisbane Roar's success got people thinking back to APIA Leichhardt's undefeated streak in 1987, and to Brisbane Strikers' first national title in 1997. Some compared him to Zoran Matic, the long-forgotten coach of Adelaide City, and even Craig Foster said that he 'couldn't be more pleased' for Postecoglou's success.[23]

Yet Postecoglou was only just getting started. Next season, he added Besart Berisha, an angry Albanian striker, to the finesse of Thomas Broich. He lost McKay, Solorzano, Susak and Barbarouses, but recruited Jack Hingert from the Victorian Premier League, Matt Jurman from Sydney FC, Issey Nakajima-Farran from Canada and signed Sayed Mohammad Adnan, a 28-year-old political refugee from Bahrain, from the local Brisbane competition.

The on-field reshuffle was complemented by huge changes off the field. The Bakrie Group – an Indonesian conglomerate with a huge bank balance and a questionable human rights record – took a 70 per cent stake in Brisbane Roar, with the remaining 30 per cent retained by FFA. This meant that four A-League clubs were owned by big miners: the Bakries at Brisbane, Nathan Tinkler at Newcastle Jets, Clive Palmer at Gold Coast United and Tony Sage at Perth Glory.

But the sale of Brisbane Roar to the Bakrie family marked the first time a club was sold to Asian investors and, considering Australia's ongoing integration with the region, it was a landmark moment in the game. Within five years, one-third of the Australian A-League clubs would be owned by investors from Asia.

This privatisation of Australian soccer undoubtedly brought fabulous wealth to the national league, helped secure better wages and conditions for players, and brought a large swathe of new supporters to the games. Even in 2010–11, the worst season of the A-League, the average crowd was double that of the average at the end of the NSL.

The best way to imagine the cultural changes that ensued was as gentrification: the game remained the same, was played in the same cities, but it was relocated away from the suburban grounds, pumped full of new money and injected with a large dose of middle-class families. When some supporters lamented the fact that the ethnic networks and the idiosyncrasies had been lost, people just shrugged their shoulders and said house prices had become too expensive but there was nothing anybody could do about it.

Despite soccer's rapid commercialisation, and perhaps because of it, people from all backgrounds formed new friendships, hated new rivals, cried, laughed, sang, chanted, made love, experienced ecstasy and heartbreak and, most of all, had fun.

Thousands of lives were imbued with greater meaning and a sense of intense belonging. Marriages between supporters who had met at A-League grounds were celebrated. Babies were born into those supporter groups. Club logos that had not existed only a few years beforehand were tattooed onto body parts. Essentially the A-League was the combination of soccer and multiculturalism as middle Australia had always wanted it: without ethnic chants, flags or teams; without ethnic blocs, politics or tension; with fewer displays of violence, confusion and corruption; and with more women and children.

The A-League was built to transcend grassroots soccer as it existed at the turn of the 21st century, not to reflect it. It was the world that former Soccer Australia boss David Hill had wanted but could not find; the world that Canberra City, Newcastle KB United, Perth Glory, Brisbane Strikers, Carlton, Northern Spirit, Parramatta Power and Adelaide United had promised but could not deliver within the structure of the NSL. Without promotion and relegation or the inclusion of any of the old clubs, the league acted as a membrane that kept the game's less attractive features concealed. It operated as a kind of benevolent cartel, hermetically sealed off from the complicated and politically volatile reality of the Australian soccer community.

'The new league was imposed on the sport, rather then melding with it,' Foster once wrote, 'and the game was treated with contempt. Plenty of owners lost money because of those oversights.'[24]

This disconnect between the grassroots and the A-League's corporate wonderland was illustrated when the Townsville soccer community was unable to raise the $1.5 million needed to save North Queensland Fury. The club folded.

'I think they [FFA] were so focused on the World Cup bid that they neglected their own backyard,' concluded Fury chief executive Rabieh Krayem on *Four Corners*.[25]

Aware of the growing anger among A-League supporters, as well as increased discontent among the owners, FFA spent big on an advertising campaign called 'We Are Football'. New websites for A-League teams, television commercials, even an FFA-funded sticker campaign. It seemed to strike a chord.

'The best thing that has come out of FFA is "We Are Football",' explained Canberra United CEO Heather Reid. 'Those three words can be said in so many different ways, but we're sending a message to the other football codes – *We* are football. Or we *are* football. Or we are *football*.'

Just a few hours after being involved in the filming of the 'We Are Football' ad, however, Newcastle Jets coach Branko Culina was sacked and his son, Jason – whom he had signed from Gold Coast United in the off-season – had his contract terminated.

On the Gold Coast, Clive Palmer slashed his club's operating budget and refused to lift a controversial 'crowd cap' that saved him money on stadium costs. And the Smith Review into the sustainability of Australian soccer, which had been commissioned by the federal government, found that A-League clubs were losing $20–25 million per year and urgently needed to connect with the game's large participant base.

Yet through the drama, Brisbane Roar continued their undefeated streak: 1–0 against the Central Coast Mariners, 2–0 over Sydney FC, 3–0 against Gold Coast United, 7–1 against Adelaide United. By Round 7, Postecoglou's team came back from a 1–0 half-time deficit to beat Newcastle Jets 2–1. This brought Brisbane level with the Eastern Suburbs rugby league club's record of 35 consecutive undefeated matches.

But Eastern Suburbs' record had been set in the 1930s, during the days of amateur, state-based competition. Nothing like this had ever been achieved since the advent of professional, national league sport. 'During that run we have scored in every game,' noted Postecoglou. 'No-one has kept us at zero.'[26]

In Round 8, Brisbane Roar's demolition of Perth Glory was both fitting and comprehensive. On Saturday 26 November 2011, in front of nearly 20,000 people at Suncorp Stadium, new imports Berisha and Nakajima-Farran scored two each within the first half. The match ended 4–0. Brisbane Roar was officially the best club side, in any sport, in Australian history. By season's end, it would win a dramatic grand final in Brisbane.

'Statistically, Brisbane Roar's 36-game undefeated streak in 2010–11 was huge,' explained FFA statistician Andrew Howe. 'It smashed the previous record of 22 games by more than 50 per cent, which is all the more remarkable in the salary-cap era of the A-League, as the cap somewhat "equalises" the competition, unlike the NSL years.'

Yet as Brisbane Roar soared, its neighbour Gold Coast United sank further into crisis, and Clive Palmer's actions became increasingly erratic. He sacked German midfielder Peter Perchtold for refusing to have his contract shortened by a season, and then refused to pay him compensation. He forced coach Miron Bleiberg to appoint a 17-year-old as captain, fired Bleiberg for criticising this decision, and called the A-League 'a joke' and soccer 'a hopeless game'.[27] And when sanctioned by FFA, he sent the team onto the field with jerseys adorned with the words 'FREEDOM OF SPEECH'.

Frank Lowy called Palmer's actions 'illogical' and 'confusing' and revoked the club's licence.[28] With both North Queensland Fury and Gold Coast United now dead, A-League expansion had been an embarrassing, expensive failure.

'Some of the owners were in it for the wrong reasons,' recalled Jason Culina. 'They were not passionate people and they did not love the game like the people that ran Sydney United or Marconi or South Melbourne or Melbourne Knights. They are different people – they love the game and want to be involved. Now clubs are created and run without as much passion, without the love and knowledge of the game. The people that matter, the ones that know the game, are not necessarily involved. They need to be – they were the ones that for generations built the game up to what it is today. You do things better when you do have the love and passion for it. I don't think any kind of TV deal or sponsorship or any kind of stadium can replace that passion and love for the game.'

★

The autumn of 2012 brought important structural and personnel changes to Australian soccer. After winning two championships with Brisbane Roar, Ange Postecoglou moved back to his hometown to coach Melbourne Victory. FFA released its National Competitions Review, recommending a new second-tier of state league soccer, and Frank Lowy descended into a war of words with Nathan Tinkler, who threatened to hand back the Newcastle Jets ownership licence. And out of the ashes of Gold Coast United emerged a new franchise in Western Sydney, paid for by a grant from the Gillard Labor government and operated by the FFA.

The challenge was enormous. The new franchise, initially labelled #NewSydneyClub on social media, needed to negotiate the various politics and loyalties of the Western Sydney soccer community, the errors of two failed expansion projects and the competition of 12 other professional football clubs in the Sydney area, including the new Greater Western Sydney Giants AFL side. 'If FFA stuffs this up,' warned Les Murray, '[...] the damage to the game's image may be terminal.'[29]

The first appointment was chief executive Lyall Gorman, a Bankstown boy, a foundation owner of the Central Coast Mariners and a former head of the A-League. He conducted fan forums in Mount Pritchard, Parramatta, Rooty Hill, Penrith, Castle Hill, Campbelltown and Bankstown, asking for input from regular supporters, ex-Socceroos, local politicians, and heads of local federations and state league clubs. Everything from the club name, colours, logo, values, culture, home ground and playing style was up for debate.

By May, Tony Popovic and Ante Milicic – both products of Western Sydney – had been installed as head coach and assistant coach, while Ron Corry, a former Socceroo, became the first goalkeeper coach. In June, Aaron Mooy, Tarek Elrich and Kwabena Appiah-Kubi, each raised in the western suburbs, were the first players signed. And the club was unveiled as the Western Sydney Wanderers, with a black and red hooped jersey, a traditional logo and an appeal to history.

'You may know that in 1880, not far from here, the first game of football was played in New South Wales,' read the club's press release.

> The King's School played a team known as the Wanderers. That was 132 years ago, but there's been a constant presence ever since – football has been a part of the fabric of western Sydney. We feel a huge responsibility with the new club to honour the history and build on the legacy. That's why we will we call the Western Sydney Wanderers FC the 'NEWEST, OLDEST CLUB IN AUSTRALIAN FOOTBALL'.[30]

For Sydney FC, which had tried and failed to engage the west for eight seasons, the introduction of the Wanderers presented both danger and opportunity. On the one hand, the new franchise threatened to eat into its supporter base; on the other, it gave Sydney FC an opportunity to solidify a clearer identity.

Over the course of its short history, Sydney FC had gone from Bling FC, with Dwight Yorke as a marquee player, to a hard-working, no-name team of triers. It had churned through five coaches in eight seasons and several chief executives. Its attendances had steadily declined, from an average of nearly 20,000 fans in season one to less than 12,000 by 2012. In a city of four million, one club could not be all things to all people. Even in its own internal corporate strategy, the club described itself as 'Australian football's greatest opportunity [and] its greatest risk', and admitted that it was 'being squeezed in all directions'.

As the Wanderers started to sign players and recruit new supporters, Sydney FC was cutting costs and trying to stabilise the club. With Gary Cole as football director and Ian Crook as head coach, it was in the process of building a squad that would play, as the football department had indicated, 'a possession-based, high-intensity attacking game'.

Yet by September, just four weeks before the start of the new season, everything changed with the arrival of the 37-year-old Italian super-star Alessandro Del Piero. At his welcome at Sydney Airport, Del Piero was swamped by a crush of happy Juventus and Sydney FC supporters.

At Bar Sport in Leichhardt, customers wore their Juventus jerseys, and the words 'Alex Del Piero, 2012' were pressed into wet cement outside the entrance. The *Sydney Morning Herald* printed the back page in pink newsprint and completely in Italian, with the headline '*La Gazzetta Del Piero*', a tribute to the famous Italian sports daily, *La Gazzetta dello Sport*. Even rugby league writer Roy Masters' article carried an Italian headline.

Overnight, bookmakers slashed the odds of Sydney FC winning the title. Newcastle Jets promptly lured former England international Emile Heskey to Australia, while the Western Sydney Wanderers signed Japanese star Shinji Ono. Instantly the A-League regained its mojo.

'The media up until that point had been fairly negative,' remembered player agent Lou Sticca, who orchestrated both Del Piero's and Ono's deals. 'We'd lost two clubs in the Gold Coast and Townsville. The Western Sydney Wanderers had just been admitted to the competition, and in their first couple of practice games there had been flares and fights at a couple of grounds. There was a huge level of negativity, [but] the capture of Del Piero plotted a different course for the A-League. It made a lot of clubs react. Del Piero and Ono were sensational for the league and sensational for the city. They were almost a perfect fit, you know you've got Alessandro and the Bling FC, and then you've got Shinji and the new hard-working, passionate, supporter-driven club in Western Sydney. You almost couldn't pick a better duo to hit the league at the same time.'

On a wet and gloomy Saturday night, in Round 1 of the eighth season of the A-League, Western Sydney Wanderers played its first match against the Central Coast Mariners. Parramatta Stadium was only half-full, and the game finished 0–0, but the atmosphere was electric. Traffic in Parramatta was brought to a standstill as hundreds of chanting supporters marched through the streets, assembled in the bay at the northern end of the ground, and unveiled a large banner that read 'Football Comes Home'.

The Red and Black Bloc were exactly what a supporter group should be: loud, rough around the edges, genuinely multicultural, and with a self-righteous theatricality that would invite ridicule and intense hate. They quickly became the most recognisable feature of the A-League.

Coach Tony Popovic harvested old hands in the service of the A-League's newest franchise. The 14-man squad for the Wanderers' debut featured nine locals and five foreigners. Apart from Ono, none of them were stars. In fact most of the squad were cast-offs and rejects from the other clubs. They were Wanderers by name and Wanderers by nature. Five of them, including Popovic, had previously played for crosstown rivals Sydney FC. In its 2012 recruitment strategy, Sydney FC had described Mark Bridge as a 'spectator', noting that the supporters 'give him a hard time' and that 'both Mark and Sydney FC may benefit from a move'.

Raised in St Clair, in an unfashionable housing estate at the foot of the Blue Mountains, Bridge was reborn at the Western Sydney Wanderers. He played his heart out, and penned a weekly column for the *Penrith Press* newspaper. 'This is the area I'm from,' he told his readers. 'I have wanted to represent it for so long.'[31]

Bridge scored the Wanderers' first A-League goal, its first goal at Parramatta Stadium and the club's first hat-trick. From there, the Wanderers won 12 of its remaining 15 matches, including a record ten-game winning streak. In Round 26, when the Wanderers beat Newcastle Jets 3–0 to secure the premiership, Bridge scored two goals. And at the club's first awards night, he was named player of the season.

The fundamental question of the A-League's first decade was this: how could an elite-level franchise with no history and no culture faithfully represent regions with deeply embedded traditions, rivalries and characters? That aim had arguably been realised in Adelaide and Perth during the NSL, and in Newcastle and the Central Coast in the first seasons of the A-League.

But in Sydney, Melbourne and Brisbane the franchises did not reflect a true sense of place. Even at Melbourne Victory, the league's best-supported side, it was difficult to know exactly what the club said about its city.

At the Western Sydney Wanderers the resolution arrived almost instantly. The supporters proudly waved placards embossed with the various postcodes of Western Sydney, nurtured a deep distaste for the FFA and for Sydney FC – which they labelled 'East Sydney FC' – and when the Red and Black Bloc asked, 'Who do you sing for?', the entire crowd bellowed back, 'We sing for Wanderers'. Matches and merchandise sold out. The Parliamentary Friends of the Western Sydney Wanderers was formed in the NSW Legislative Assembly. And in an essay for the *Griffith Review*, one writer used the club as the central theme to explain the rise of Western Sydney as an influential economic, social and political region.[32] Even after only one season, nothing said Western Sydney quite like the Wanderers.

By sharp contrast, Sydney FC remained as unstable and direction-less as ever. Unable to adapt to the Alessandro Del Piero show, Ian Crook stepped down as head coach after just six rounds. He was soon followed by football director Gary Cole, who was relieved of his duties, and Frank Farina was appointed head coach.

Despite the dysfunction, the budding rivalry with the Wanderers re-energised many supporters and drove up television ratings and attendances. For the first time in ten years, the A-League had found a structure that seemed to work.

After three matches, the Sydney derby became one of the fiercest rivalries in Australian sport, stalemated at one win for Sydney FC, one for the Wanderers and one draw. It has the potential to be the defining rivalry of 21st-century Australian club sport. It taps into the east–west Sydney rivalry, certainly the most intense geographic split in Australia, better than any other game. As Andrew Dettre had predicted back in 1977: 'Sydney can and it will support two [...] teams – but only if those two teams belong to much larger and broader groups than hitherto and through their neutral name, organisation and composition, also appeal to the average, uninvolved Australian.'[33]

At the end of season 2012–13, Clint Bolton retired from professional soccer. He had played for the Brisbane Strikers, Sydney Olympic and Parramatta Power in the NSL, and Sydney FC and Melbourne Heart in the A-League. After 11 seasons of 'old soccer' and eight seasons of 'new football', he had played 479 national league matches and been part of four championship-winning teams. But the game had changed, and at 37 years of age his body had started to break down. He had lost the enjoyment.

'The NSL had culture, there was history,' he once explained. 'It's something we're trying to build now. Twenty or 30 years down the track, we might have that with the A-League clubs. At Sydney Olympic I felt part of something bigger than the football team. There was no money, and they were under-resourced, and it was never a good business model. It's sad, because there were so many good things about the NSL. I loved it. The A-League certainly hasn't captured what the NSL had in that regard, definitely not. And who knows if it ever will? The Wanderers home matches are as close to the NSL as I've felt – there's a real sense that this is bigger than the football.'

★

Australia qualified for the 2014 World Cup, but only just. After a torrid qualification campaign, the Socceroos needed two wins in its final three games in June 2013. It drew 1–1 with Japan in Saitama, thrashed Jordan 4–0 in Melbourne and scraped past Iraq 1–0 in Sydney.

By October, however, the Socceroos were beaten 6–0 in a friendly against Brazil, and then by the same score against France. The squad was in a serious state of paralysis, ground down by the weight of reputation and in desperate need of generational change. Holger Osieck was promptly sacked as coach.

The move from Brisbane to Melbourne had been good for Ange Postecoglou. He penned columns for the *Age* newspaper, appeared regularly on the ABC's *Offsiders* program and cultivated relationships with influential sports commentators, furthering his own stature not just as a participant but as a powerful spokesperson for Australian soccer.

A few days after the loss to France, he used his regular column in the *Age* to write what many believed to be an open application letter. 'There needs to be a cultural shift so we understand once again the essence of our national shirt,' he wrote, calling for an end to 'self-interest' and for Australians to lift their expectations of the Socceroos. 'The national team is there to sell hope,' he wrote, 'not to dampen dreams.'[34]

He got the job five days later, granted a five-year contract to reinvigorate the squad and to make Australia the number-one side in Asia. His redemption was complete.

And for the first time since 1974, the Socceroos would be guided to a World Cup by an Australian.

Everybody loved and claimed a piece of him, and the Melbourne Victory supporters farewelled him as one of their own. At *South of the Border* – the only place that kept tabs on Postecoglou during his exile in 2007 to 2009 – Paul Mavroudis posted an old photo of him with a youthful moustache, standing with the rest of South Melbourne Hellas' 1984 championship-winning team.

It had been a rough few years for Australia's most successful soccer club. All the hallmarks of collapse that had made Postecoglou 'sick to my stomach' back in 1997 had now arrived upon South Melbourne. Crowds had dropped into the hundreds. The intimacy of Bob Jane Stadium, which had been renamed Lakeside Stadium, was destroyed by an athletics track that separated supporters from the field. And for the first time in decades, there was no social club at which the fans could coalesce.

South Melbourne had become, as Postecoglou had once feared, 'a pale shadow of its former self'.

Out of desperation, the club had launched its own television show, boasted that it would play in an Asian super league, and tried to get into the A-League via several Trojan Horse campaigns. First it was Southern Cross FC, then it was rumoured that South would take over the Central Coast Mariners, and when Melbourne Heart proved to be a terrible experiment there was even talk of 'South Melbourne Heart'. Nothing worked. For the club's remaining supporters like Mavroudis, the A-League – which for tens of thousands of young Australians was a great awakening – had been the great interruption.

In the end, the Postecoglou revival would be the most fitting moment of the first decade of the A-League: a project that set about destroying all the old structures and institutions, while also re-organising the individuals into new teams, new loyalties and a new culture. When asked, Postecoglou still spoke lovingly about South Melbourne Hellas, but now it was in past tense, as just another page in soccer's history. There was no redemption story for South Melbourne Hellas to match that of its favourite son.

THE WAY WE ORGANISE OURSELVES

Epilogue

I haven't come
to praise ethnicity
nor to bury it.
Just to say
that you can't bury
the shadows
of the living.

Pino Bosi
Who Is Afraid of the Ethnic Wolf?, 1986[1]

My first contact with Andrew Dettre came in the autumn of 2013. I had, over a period of more than 12 months, devoured most of his journalism in old copies of the *Soccer World* newspaper. His writing struck me as both visionary and tragic. Why was I only just learning about the origins of summer soccer, for example, or his call for two superteams in Sydney, or his advocacy for Asian integration and an Australian Institute of Sport, or his nuanced arguments about the nature of Australian multiculturalism?

More importantly, why was I only just learning about Andrew Dettre? This man should be a hero to the soccer community.

Although more than three decades old, his work seemed to have enormous relevance to the era of soccer in which I was living in and trying to articulate through my writing. From the moment I read his work, I had wanted to meet him. I sent off an email, asking if we could arrange an interview for a profile that I had planned for the *Guardian*. Within two hours, he had responded. Yes, he was happy to meet.

Five days later, I received another email from Andrew. He had decided not to go ahead with the project. He was concerned that the subject would be 'so vast that it would require almost an entire biography to deal with and this, I am sure, isn't your aim'.[2]

Two months passed before I received another email from Andrew. He had changed his mind. I was told to come to his house on Tuesday 10 September, at 11 am. And so I did.

In the corner of the living room I noticed a bookshelf stuffed with literature on European history and soccer. At the top of the pile I glimpsed a biography of Karl Marx. Later, Andrew would open the cupboard beside the bookshelf to reveal stacks of old bound copies of *Soccer World*. He would also present me with a signed copy of one of his own books, *How to Play Winning Soccer*.

We chatted for more than an hour. When I brought up his final article for *Soccer Action*, which had concluded with the lines 'Soccer, as I said, will survive. But for me it will not be the same', I asked whether he still felt the same way.

'I do,' he said. 'I really do. When you get old, you are resentful of youth ... You are aware of your mortality, which at the age of 22 you're not. At the age of 22 I skipped away from Hungary, never to return to see my parents again, for political reasons ... The communists. I didn't think what would happen to me at 30 or 50 or 80 or 87. It's not resentment but a sad admission of defeat that your best days are over, you're not going to repeat the huge adventures that you had in publishing and in newspapers and book writing.

'At the same time, honestly, I feel very proud to have done what I've done. I didn't get rich, I didn't get famous, but I enjoyed myself ... I love journalism, I love writing, I'm in love with the English language – to me, there is nothing else in life. I didn't want to be a bank manager, I didn't want to be a politician, I didn't want to be a merchant or entrepreneur or chef. This is it. I am glad I was enabled to do what I did. And now, at 87, I don't want to start again, I don't want to renew old contacts. As they say in Hungary, "a stuffed cabbage doesn't taste any good when you heat it up for the second time".'

For the next two years, I would revisit Andrew to learn more and dig deeper into the archive of his writing, to the point that I decided that his life did require a biography. But it needed to be about much more than him – the story of Andrew Dettre is, in so many ways, the story of Australian soccer.

That spring Leopold Baumgartner passed away, aged 81. Few people in the modern era remembered his name or his achievements, or why he was so important in the development of Australian soccer. Yet perhaps more than any other individual, it was Baumgartner in the late 1950s and early 1960s who symbolised soccer's entrepreneurialism, its confidence, its style and its modernisation. He was the Alessandro Del Piero of his time, except he stayed in Australia, and in his retirement he spent his time coaching at the Coffs Coast Tigers and Sawtell Scorpions.

During his career he had transformed from an Austrian to an Australian, and inspired thousands of youngsters both as a player and as a coach. One of those players was Attila Abonyi, with whom he became great friends in his twilight years. They lived not far from one another in Coffs Harbour, and at Leo's funeral Atti was one of the few soccer people in attendance.

'I never told Leo this, but he's always been my hero,' Abonyi later told me. 'I still can't believe that he became such a good friend of mine. I would never have dreamt it. I used to respect him so much as a player.'

Four weeks later, Football Federation Australia celebrated the 'Summer of Football'. With a hashtag #SummerFootball and an extravagant launch at Sydney's Bondi Beach, the FFA presented Alessandro Del Piero to the cameras and listed the statistics on its website. 'Prior to this season,' it boasted, '107 matches had been played across the traditional Christmas and New Year summer football period.'[3]

The article praised Brisbane Roar and Melbourne Victory for 'the most summer football wins', and the Western Sydney Wanderers for not having lost a game during the period. There was no mention of Andrew Dettre. No mention of his decade-long struggle to have the NSL season switched from winter to summer. No mention of the 336 NSL games that had been played in that 'traditional' Christmas and New Year period.

Andrew showed no resentment at this glaring omission from history, but there was recognition of the irony. 'What matters,' he once told me, 'is that it works.'

Whichever way you look at it, the story of soccer in Australia is not a happy one. It is as a vast mess of shattered dreams, colonised tribes and forgotten heroes, splayed out like a Jackson Pollock painting across the landscape of Australian history. It is a story that haunts rather than comforts. 'There are a lot of broken people in the game,' Michael Cockerill once said. 'Yet it's still the sport with the most blue sky in Australia. Even after everything, it's still only scratched the surface.'

Not far from Sydney Airport, on the banks of the Cooks River, is St George Stadium, the saddest monument to the tragedy of soccer in Australia. Built specifically for the NSL, it opened in 1978, hosting its first Socceroos match in 1984, and its final national league game in 1994.

For years the stadium has been sinking into a state of severe disrepair, covered in pigeon shit and graffiti. The 'Pongrass Stand' sign is cracked and weeds have repossessed the concrete terraces. It is now a dilapidated, condemned wreck. St George Saints still play there, but to anyone with a sense of history it is a macabre scene. Once the pride of the Sydney soccer community, the grandstand is now a safety hazard, fenced off by barbed wire.

In the A-League, there isn't a single club that plays out of a stadium that it can call its own, and there isn't a single club that was there at the beginning of the soccer revolution of the 1950s. Many of the original clubs have simply collapsed. Many more have been forced over the years to take on different names and guises, rendering them almost unrecognisable. In 40 years of national league soccer, some 52 clubs have come and gone. No wonder the game has existed in a hypochondriac state for so long: that is a story of sheer survival, not triumph.

Fading with the pioneer clubs are real people. In Melbourne, Paul Mavroudis, author of the *South of the Border* blog, is slowly losing his sight. He is in and out of meetings with eye specialists, forever trying to avoid the horror of complete blindness. He doesn't like to talk about it, but he no longer takes it for granted that his faculties will survive long enough for him to enjoy soccer and reading, his two lifelong passions. And it is fair to say that, apart from South Melbourne, he has grown increasingly detached from the game he loves. Friends worry that his world is getting smaller. Even he admits that the circumstances of South Melbourne's decline have made him more introverted.

'The position of chief unofficial cultural surveyor of the South Melbourne Hellas exodus years,' he once wrote, 'is possibly a fate worse than the exodus itself.'[4]

Life in the shadow of the great soccer boom has not been kind to the game's true believers. The radical idea once proposed by soccer was not that Australians would accept individuals of different ethnic and cultural backgrounds, but that they would accept those individuals as communities, and join those communities to make their clubs popular and successful.

It has become fashionable to blame the ethnic clubs themselves for not opening their doors enough to a wide cross-section of the population, a view that in some cases has merit. Still, look at the fate of St George, a club that did more than any other to encourage its local district to be involved; a club that, in the space of three decades, built an accessible stadium and junior scheme and social club that all Australians could enjoy. It made absolutely no difference.

Rather than bring the ethnic clubs along on the journey into the brave new world, the success of the A-League has pushed them further into a corner. It has brought on the death of an idea, even if it hasn't yet totally killed off its incarnation. It's not only the economics that excludes South Melbourne and the other ethnic clubs – it's their identity. The ethnicity that provided these clubs a foundation has been both the key to their survival and the cause of their decline. South Melbourne supporters no longer see theirs as a 'Greek club', but almost all of the board members are of Greek background, as are most of the remaining supporters. Sadly, the only way South Melbourne might be able to get into the A-League is by removing themselves from this history and heritage.

We must remember that the A-League was built so that the reserve army of soccer fans no longer had to watch these ethnic clubs play. The game was reconstructed to enfranchise the uninvolved Australians, and exclude people like Mavroudis. We forget this too readily. We forget that the A-League was a state of mind before it became reality; the Promised Land of soccer without its soul, without the ethnic clubs; soccer re-calibrated and reformed to look and feel similar to Australian Rules football or rugby league or rugby union.

By his association with South Melbourne, Mavroudis has been marginalised, told repeatedly to assimilate and to stop living in the past. South Melbourne, the most successful club in the history of the game, has been erased from soccer's present and, since its demotion to the state leagues, has been slowly erased from memory. This, according to Mavroudis, is purgatory.

★

In the 2013–14 Australian Bureau of Statistics survey of participation in sport and recreation, soccer was listed as having 438,800 participants over the age of 15. If you include indoor soccer in the total, the number rises to more than 650,000.[5] That is nearly triple the number of people listed as playing Australian Rules football, and more than triple the number of people playing rugby union and rugby league combined. If you combine the participants of cricket and Australian Rules football – both of which lovingly refer to themselves as 'the national game' – there were still more Australians involved in soccer.

There is nothing new or remarkable about these statistics. Since at least the 1990s, soccer has been Australia's sport of choice. It is unlikely that the game's stranglehold over the hearts and minds of ordinary people will ever cease. The struggle for soccer in Australia has been to organise these participants for commercial ends; to turn players into spectators, and spectators into captains of industry, political leaders and influencers in popular culture.

Soccer in Australia has been, and will always remain, the game of tomorrow. Gough Whitlam recognised this back in 1966, in his article for the *Sun*, when he placed the game alongside issues of national identity, Indigenous disadvantage, free education and immersion with Asia. Countless players, coaches, journalists and officials have realised it since.

There will forever be a swirl of competing interests, agendas and possibilities available to soccer, yet it is also true that the game has never been comfortable in its own skin. Perhaps this has been best illustrated by the three chief executives who presided over the first decade of the A-League. First, it was John O'Neill, a rugby union man. Then it was Ben Buckley, an ex-AFL administrator. Then it was David Gallop, the former rugby league CEO.

Since the introduction of the Western Sydney Wanderers, there has been a growing sense that Australian soccer needs to reconcile the present with the past. There have been symbolic gestures, such as greater recognition of the 1974 Socceroos; or the 'Wanderers' name; or the white socks worn by the Socceroos at the 2014 World Cup: a throwback to the 1974 kit. Having Ange Postecoglou at the helm of the national team at the World Cup was also a significant symbolic moment that brought together the previous 40 years of national league soccer.

On a more practical level, there is the FFA Cup. Launched in February 2014 at the Rockdale Ilinden Club in Sydney's south, the tournament was designed to be Australia's version of the FA Cup: a knockout competition that would draw A-League franchises against suburban teams, bush clubs and ex-NSL giants. The shape of the trophy was designed off the old Australia Cup, the one that Attila Abonyi once held aloft in 1967.

In a column published on the FFA website, Andrew Howe wrote: 'The FFA Cup is a long-awaited tournament and while in one sense it's a new competition, in another it is carrying on a tradition that started in Australia more than fifty years ago.'[6]

Indeed the philosophy inherent in the FFA Cup is inclusivity: Gallop generously called the state league clubs 'the engine room of Australian soccer', and offered an opportunity for them to be part of the national stage once a year, if they're good enough to qualify. What it unwittingly brought forward, however, was the rise of two arguments that had been buried for ten years like a skeleton in the cupboards of Australian soccer history: ethnicity, and promotion and relegation.

Just days before the FFA Cup launch, the governing body announced the introduction of the National Club Identity Policy (NCIP), which prevents clubs from creating names or logos that 'carry any ethnic, national, political, racial or religious connotations either in isolation or combination'.[7]

So the earth is now being sown with salt. This policy is not directed at the A-League – it is aimed at little state league and community clubs. It seeks to whitewash the game at every level, to ensure that there will be no explicit signs of the game's ethnic base at any point in the future. Once at the vanguard of Australian multiculturalism, soccer has now internalised all the hate directed at it for doing so and finally adopted a policy of assimilation. That grand, hopelessly idealistic view that soccer could provide liberation and space for migrant and ethnic communities, and in the process change Australia for the better, is withering.

The justification that Gallop gave for the NCIP – 'the way we organise ourselves' – is one of two eternal lines that he has delivered during his reign at FFA. The other, which he used during the launch of the National Premier Leagues, is that soccer 'faces a burden of opportunity'.

These two lines speak directly to the challenges facing soccer in this country. They have a much deeper resonance than perhaps even he realises. After all the skulduggery and xenophobia from the rival football code, and the historic resistance of a hostile media establishment – not to mention the game's own history of petty feuding and cannibalism – soccer is still the only Australian sport that can galvanise every possible ethnic, regional, metropolitan, gender and political group from Perth to Sydney, Darwin to Adelaide, Cairns to Hobart.

It will always be the code of football with the most potential to provide equal opportunity for both men and women and to truly connect us to our Asian neighbours, and to the rest of the world. It is this burden of opportunity that has, for more than four decades, raised questions about the way we organise ourselves as a soccer community.

Professional soccer in Australia will always be retarded by three major factors. The first is the tyranny of distance. The second is the sparseness of the population relative to the size of the country. The third is the presence of three other major codes of football, each of which competes for market share, for supporters and for sponsorship dollars. Each of these factors has contributed to the demise of soccer in its traditional form and the rise of the mongrel version of soccer that we now see in the A-League. The entire history of the game in this country has been about resolving the tension between the traditions of soccer and the desires of the Australian commercial marketplace.

If top-flight soccer had never been interrupted by commercialism, and still existed in its original form, then it would be played in the winter, in state leagues, with a system of promotion and relegation, with member-owned teams adorned with names like Croatia and Hellas and Azzurri, without a finals series, without a salary cap or foreign quotas, in front of perhaps a few thousand diehard supporters.

The success of the A-League has been realised by transcending every single one of these factors. It is one of the few competitions in world football to be played in summer. One of the few competitions to determine the champion by a grand final rather than the league table. One of the few to have stringent equalisation measures, such as a salary cap. It sits alongside the Indian Super League or Major League Soccer in the USA in creating new and modern ways of organising the game for commercial ends.

In the space of less than 40 years, the national league has been transformed from a traditional, community-owned asset to an entirely private enterprise. Few other sports have made such a ruthless transition from community to corporate, and in material terms there is still little that connects the A-League to the rest of the soccer community. The thousands of supporters have no recourse in the running of the club, no social clubs at which they can meet and – unless they have their own private fortune to waste – no way of owning any part of the enterprise. The A-League franchises are ostensibly rent-seekers, benefiting enormously from the wealth created by others, without any obligation to put anything back into the community.

And yet, after decades of trying to find the right formula, strangely enough this is the structure upon which top-flight soccer has finally flourished in Australia.

Despite these incontrovertible lessons of history, the introduction of the FFA Cup quickly led to a demand for a system of promotion and relegation to the A-League. This demand would come from many of the soccer journalists, spectators and, especially, the exiled former NSL clubs.

The proponents have argued that it will achieve several aims: one, that it will provide more opportunity for players; two, that it will bring Australia in line with the rest of the world; three, that it will encourage reconciliation between the clubs of 'old soccer' and 'new football'; four, that it will energise the grassroots game; and five, that it will provide a unique difference to the closed football leagues of rugby union, rugby league and the AFL.

It is hard to find fault in any of these claims, but what is rarely mentioned is that the history of promotion and relegation in Australia is not good. In the NSL it was mostly a managed process, with clubs such as Canberra, Newcastle, Wollongong and South Melbourne all deemed too important to be relegated, at least at one point in time.

When it did exist in its traditional form, promotion and relegation brought absolute chaos and instability to the league.

Many reviews and reports recommended its abolition, such as in 1981, when the ASF Marketing Report noted that it 'is simply not a practical system in the 1980s for a sport that wishes to develop nationally'.[8] When that advice was ignored, the 1980s proceeded as the most democratic and open decade in national league history. It was also the decade when attendances dipped as low as the hundreds and soccer all but died as a commercial product.

The Bradley Report's recommendations in 1990 were, for many people, a statement of the bleeding obvious: promotion and relegation brought a cluster of teams from the rich, populous cities of Sydney and Melbourne at the expense of a true national spread, and that it 'had the effect of teams concentrating their time and resources on the field and neglecting such areas as the development of facilities and their spectator base'.[9]

The report commissioned by Professional Footballers Australia in 2002 recommended clubs be included on the basis of market share and geographic spread, which implicitly excludes the meritocracy and the unknown of promotion and relegation. The NSL Task Force, which delivered its report in 2003, made it explicitly clear that 'the optimum number of clubs will be determined by market forces and the capacity of the key markets to support a team that meets the necessary criteria and benchmarks', and that investors would have 'certainty of tenure in the early seasons of the League and not be subject to a system of promotion and relegation'.[10]

Promotion and relegation is the fairest and most democratic feature of soccer, and that is exactly why it is unlikely to work in Australia. Nowhere else in the world has such a perfect storm of problems that would prevent a successful implementation. Few countries have equalisation measures such as the salary cap, which in the event of promotion and relegation would have to be immediately scrapped. No country has so many other professional codes of football to compete with, along with such huge distances and such a small population base.

No other country has such enormous and unresolved questions around the identity of its best lower-league clubs. No other game in Australia has been so transformed by the mercenary demands of modern sport. Soccer is now in the era of showbiz.

The entire industry of professional sport in Australia will continue to be governed not by fairness or tradition or merit, but by the promise of huge television rights deals and corporate sponsorship. The successful negotiation of these deals rests upon the league being strategically spread across the country and, most of all, being stable from year to year. Promotion and relegation would imperil each of these fundamental requirements.

Most of all, promotion and relegation would challenge the economic, conceptual, social and cultural foundations that helped create the A-League. It would bring an end to the cartel. Melbourne Victory, for example, would have to confront the prospect of being relegated to a second division, replaced by a real club like Adelaide City, or Bonnyrigg White Eagles, or Floreat Athena, or South Melbourne.

Perhaps the economic conditions have changed since the 1980s, but the fundamental principle hasn't: promotion and relegation would break the protective membrane and reintroduce structural diversity to a community that loathes it. There is a huge difference between getting the uninvolved Australians to eat souvlaki once a year at an FFA Cup game and getting them to accept an ethnic-backed club as a legitimate partner in soccer's future.

More than anything else, soccer has been the lamentable proof that most Australians like multiculturalism without politics, without culture, without self-determination, without dual identities and without any threats to the existing structure of things.

To try and reverse-engineer promotion and relegation into the competition would return soccer to its role of trying to change Australian culture, rather than simply fitting in. And for the past couple of decades, there has been no greater desire in Australian soccer than to fit in. As Paul Mavroudis once put it: 'What I loved about soccer is that it never did what it was told. The thing I loved is the thing they killed.'

★

For years, Paul Mavroudis and Roy Hay both sat on the history committee of Football Federation Victoria. Mostly they get along. More recently, however, Mavroudis and Hay have had blistering arguments over the direction that Australian soccer has taken. To Mavroudis, soccer is in danger of selling its soul. To Hay, the FFA's attempts to domesticate the game are in keeping with a school of thought that stretches back to the 1880s, when the Scots were told not to establish their own clubs and to assimilate into the district structure. Hay's most powerful argument is that soccer's popularity, for the first time in its history, is not being driven by immigration.

The opportunity for newer migrants from Asia and Africa to create their own soccer teams has shrunk rapidly over the past few decades. Once upon a time, a community of immigrants could set up a club in the state leagues at little or no cost, without junior sides, without restrictions on their collective identity or their ambition. That is how the great migrant clubs all started in the postwar period. Yet it is no longer possible under the current FFA structure.

Soccer is now a middle-class, aspirational game with high registration fees and relatively large barriers to entry. As a result, there have been very few Asian or African faces in the starting XIs or on the boards of A-League franchises, in the state and national federations, or in positions in the media. The argument prosecuted by many people within soccer is that these new migrants simply don't care enough to force their way in, as the European migrants did back in the 1950s and 1960s.

I am not so sure.

Two events that occurred in the space of three months gave me pause for thought. Between November 2014 and February 2015, the Western Sydney Wanderers became the first Australian club side to win the Asian Football Confederation Champions League (ACL), and the Socceroos won the Asian Cup on home soil. It meant that Australia, as Ange Postecoglou later reflected, was 'the first-ever country to simultaneously hold the Asian club and national team titles'.[11]

What struck me most was not the achievement but what happened behind the scenes. As the Western Sydney Wanderers made the ACL final, held over two legs in Saudi Arabia and Australia, I began to think we were approaching an historic Asian moment.

For the next two months I wrote articles about the history of Australia's engagement with Asia through soccer; about Iranian-Australian women using soccer to protest against the Iranian government; about the need for designated Asian visa players in the A-League; about the formation of the Palestinian Community Association Futsal League, and an Australian–Lebanese soccer association.

I wrote about the work of the Asian Cup Local Organising Committee in engaging with Australia's Asian communities; about a group of Korean-Australians using soccer to raise awareness of Korean reunification; and about a mini Asian Cup conducted by the Western Sydney Wanderers.

I went on Al Jazeera to speak about the history of the game to a reporter who was asking himself the same question as I was: if the European communities drove Australian soccer during the 20th century, does that same drive and spirit exist in the Asian communities that will likely define 21st-century Australia?

It was the most enjoyable few months I have spent as a soccer journalist. I was fortunate to be there among the thousands of Western Sydney Wanderers fans on the streets of Parramatta, at the bustling intersection of Centenary Square, watching Wanderers goalkeeper Ante Covic avoid the glare of lasers and wave after wave of Al-Hilal's attacks in the ACL final. The 1–0 victory on aggregate was the greatest moment in the Wanderers' short history, and the finest moment in the history of Australian club soccer.

It struck me that the Western Sydney Wanderers, in the lead-up to the final, beat club sides from Japan, China and South Korea – nations that, in 2014, were three of Australia's top trading partners. But more profound was the fact that as the Wanderers went on its incredible run of victories, the club reached out to Asian communities in its local area and invited them to play a part on game day.

'If we played a Japanese team then we've worked with the Japanese, if we played a Korean team then we work with the Koreans,' the

Wanderers' former community, pathways and football development manager, Tim Thorne, told me. 'What we've found is that the
Wanderers unites these guys. I asked a Saudi Arabian guy, just out of
interest, who he's supporting and he said, "We're Wanderers."'

One week after the final, the Western Sydney Wanderers held a mini
Asian Cup at Marconi Stadium in Fairfield. With the assistance of
Club Marconi, the Asian Cup Local Organising Committee and
Red Elephant Projects, a multicultural marketing firm from Sydney,
16 local men's teams representing Bahrain, China, Hong Kong, Iran,
Iraq, India, Indonesia, Japan, Lebanon, Nepal, Oman, the Philippines,
Saudi Arabia, South Korea, Vietnam and the NSW Police contested
the week-long tournament.

It was, for me, the most startling sporting vision of Australia's pivot
from Europe to Asia. Where once Italians were a major demographic
group in Fairfield, the 2011 census found that the biggest overseas-born
population came from Iraq. And on fields built by Italian migrants back
in the 1950s and 1960s, the Iraq team beat a team representing Bahrain
but filled mostly with Iraqi players, 6–1. This grassroots Iraq team did
so in front of a bigger crowd than Marconi has drawn in years.

In truth, the Western Sydney Wanderers' mini Asian Cup was just
the tip of the iceberg. By 2015, there existed ethnic soccer associations for Chinese, Nepalese, Bangladeshi, Assyrian, Ethiopian, Somali,
Indonesian, Filipino, Afghani, South Sudanese, Egyptian, Korean,
Japanese, Palestinian, Lebanese, Fijian, Burmese, Thai, Vietnamese
and Iranian communities. There are also associations of Chaldean,
Mandaean, Oromo, Chin, Karen and Sikh people.

Most of these associations are small, existing in loose fragments,
organised independently and without support from the state and
national federations. They play together for the same reasons as the
Scots did back in the early 1900s, and as the European communities
have since the postwar period: community, family, self-determination,
cultural survival and, most of all, fun.

Some, like the Palestinian Community Association Futsal League, were created in almost exactly the same fashion as the ethnic clubs of a bygone era, complete with team names that connect the players to their heritage and their culture. And this is the uncomfortable counter-argument to those who say that the Asian communities don't care enough about the game to upset the applecart: the structure of Australian soccer no longer exists to support the ambitions of immigrant communities. This has been the silent cost of the quest to domesticate soccer.

I talk about this often with Patrick Skene, who runs multicultural programs for Red Elephant Projects across all sports, including the A-League. He looks at the game with fresh eyes, and sees huge untapped potential in the newer immigrant groups.

'Soccer is the only sport in this country, really, where people have teams that reflect their ancestral identity,' he explained. 'That's very challenging for Australians. Soccer is at the absolute core of the broader success of the Italian, Greek and Croatian communities. The fact is they stayed together, they stayed strong through soccer, they solidified as a voting and economic bloc, and it underpinned the extraordinary success of their communities. Everybody looks to the clubs and their leaders as the dual-identity role models that we want the other communities to follow, and to remove football – which was the key tool to keep these communities together – is a tragic and fatal mistake that could impact social inclusion. It seems counter-intuitive, but people become Australians faster if they are given the space for their heritage to be positively acknowledged.'

Less than three weeks after the Western Sydney Wanderers' mini Asian Cup, with just days to go before the 2015 Asian Cup, the Palestinian national team played a friendly match against a Malaysian club side. The game was not promoted or advertised to the public. Technically, it was played behind closed doors at Marconi Stadium. But many local Palestinians squeezed their way in, dressed in *keffiyeh* and holding Palestinian flags.

Ayman Mosleh, a young father of two from Sydney's south-west, showed me his trunk full of half-and-half Palestine–Australia jerseys.

'I made over 4000 of them,' he explained. 'I got the idea from the Croatians and Italians in Australia during the World Cup in 2006.'

Just days before the friendly match, Australia had been one of just two countries to veto a United Nations resolution on Palestinian statehood. As I continued to Melbourne for the group stages of the Asian Cup, I met Mohammad Othman and Zaid Jubran, two young men involved in the Palestinian Community Association Futsal League. Their parents hold Jordanian passports courtesy of Jordan's annexation of the West Bank between 1948 and 1967. They are Kuwaiti by birth, Jordanian by documentation, Australian by location, but always Palestinian.

These are familiar anxieties. The Croatians, perhaps the single most important ethnic group in the history of Australian soccer, dealt with them for years in the national league as their homeland struggled for independence from Yugoslavia.

The Asian Cup, however, was the first time in a decade that Australian soccer faced these questions head on, allowing Australians of every colour and creed to work through their own national questions in full and public view. Thousands of spectators from the Asian communities emerged in the stadiums, bearing national flags and religious symbols. It was exhilarating and inspiring – a clear and positive picture of Australia's so-called 'Asian century'.

'Where are these people during the A-League season?' some asked on social media. 'How did they get them to show up?' The answer was in the preparation. Red Elephant Projects, along with the Asian Cup Local Organising Committee, developed community ambassador programs, targeted marketing campaigns and pre-tournament ticket sales driven by leaders of all the different ethnic groups. The communities felt a sense of ownership of Australia's tournament.

By the end of the tournament, Skene surveyed the 280 community ambassadors from the 31 Asian communities engaged by the Asian Cup. A whopping 92 per cent of the ambassadors said that they felt *more* Australian by representing and supporting their ancestral country.

For the Socceroos, Massimo Luongo – Ange Postecoglou's handpicked midfield man – started every game. He played with a grin and a wink, looking always to pass forward, running cleverly into space. He scored with both his feet and his head, and linked well with Tim Cahill, undoubtedly Australia's most important player.

Like countless Australian soccer players before him, Luongo comes from impeccable migrant stock. Born to a father of Italian heritage and an Indonesian mother, he was one of only two Asian faces in the Socceroos squad. He is the personification of Australia's Eurasian future. Luongo provided the assist for Australia's first goal in the Asian Cup. He scored the second. In the semifinal, he was awarded man of the match.

On the last day of January 2015, the Socceroos faced Korea Republic in the final. Korea was the one team that had beaten Australia throughout the tournament and, with several thousand local fans in attendance, was also very well supported. In the stands, a sea of red lapped against the wall of green and gold. Those who couldn't get tickets flooded into Korean restaurants around Sydney, divided over a familiar national question: *who to support?* Korea or Australia?

One Korean man, who runs an ethnic soccer association in Melbourne, told me that he would support Korea, but his children would support Australia. It was the ultimate finale to a revelatory few months. It proved that Australia's newer migrants – Palestinians, Iranians, Iraqis, Koreans, Chinese – do speak with a soccer accent. The question is whether the rest of the soccer community has the capacity to truly listen and to support their ambitions, whatever they might be.

In the final, the Socceroos went ahead just before half-time thanks to Luongo. It was an individual goal: a delightful right-foot touch to bring the ball under control, a left-foot touch to take him away from his marker, and then a right-foot thunderbolt that sailed past the keeper from 25 yards out. On the bench, Postecoglou thrust both arms in the air and beamed proudly. Hold on for another 45 minutes, and Australia would be Asian champions.

In the final minute of the match, moments after Postecoglou had desperately signalled for the crowd to lift, disaster struck. Korea's star winger Son Heung-min scored the equaliser. The final whistle blew for full-time, leaving Postecoglou shaking his head in despair on the bench.

Yet in extra time, as the legs began to tire, Tomi Juric picked up possession on the right flank. Closely marked by Korean defenders, twice Juric fell as he struggled to maintain control of the ball. As he regained his footing, he back-heeled the ball through the legs of a defender, ran into the penalty box and slid a neat pass across the face of goal. James Troisi's confident finish sent the stadium into raptures. Champions of Asia.

Luongo was named player of the tournament; Mat Ryan was awarded best goalkeeper. Australia won the fair play award, and Ange Postecoglou was later named the best coach in Asia.

In the press conference after the match he spoke confidently of the achievement. One comment stood out from all the others.

'I really believed this was important from the moment I took the job that we shed ourselves of this inferiority complex that Australian footballers can only do certain things and play a certain way,' said Postecoglou. 'We've done this with myself as an Australian coach, all the backroom staff are Australian coaches, Australian staff, and Australian players. You know, I said from day one: we won't take a backward step to anyone.'[12]

The spellbinding success of the Western Sydney Wanderers and the Socceroos, in the space of just three months, created perfect conditions for another soccer boom. In the months after the Asian Cup victory, Football Federation Victoria would report a surge in participation, with soccer overtaking netball as the most popular sport for girls for the first time. Soccer would overtake swimming as the most popular sport for children. Yet success imbued the game with something that can't be measured by attendances, statistics or participation rates – and that is confidence.

In the decade between 2005 and 2015, Australian soccer managed to completely transform itself from a niche, third-tier competition to a commercially viable and mainstream league. It was able to create a women's league within the structure of the A-League, which, with the right investment, has endless possibilities for the future. It was able to join the Asian Football Confederation, and the Socceroos and the Matildas were both able to win an Asian Cup.

For those teenagers and young adults, including myself, targeted by Football Federation Australia in 2005, the only experience we know is of success. We are only vaguely aware of the heartbreak and the missed opportunities that soccer had to endure for most of the 20th century. And perhaps that is a good thing. Why would we burden the future generations with the past?

There is a tendency to try and flatten history, to draw a line from point to point, to try and assimilate each of the constituent parts of the past into a coherent whole. That is almost impossible to do with the history of Australian soccer. Every ethnic, gender and political group has experienced the game in different ways, with different meanings attached to its events, and different ideas about how it should be administered in the future. The history of soccer is a wonderful, stressful, genuinely Australian and ultimately confusing mess.

It is also true, however, that the culture and organisation of top-flight soccer has fundamentally changed. I am an historian, not a fortune-teller, but it seems to me that the history of the game, interesting and rich as it was, won't be particularly necessary for its future. As blogger Adam Woolcock once wrote: 'The truly unique thing about Australian soccer fans is that they're one of the few groups to despise the history of their own sport.'[13]

You can add to that perhaps the biggest group of all: those who find the whole thing a total mystery. Most of the children, teenagers and young adults who are now growing up with an A-League side know the National Soccer League only as an abstraction, as a flash of memory or as an ornament on the wall.

They might find it interesting to read about, but unlike the other sports it will be difficult for them to truly feel it, or to link back to it in any tangible way. The institutions that facilitate this memory – the clubs – are no longer part of the atmosphere of professional soccer. Think of clubs like Collingwood in the AFL or South Sydney Rabbitohs in the NRL, or even Manchester United in the English Premier League. Clubs like these have gone through huge changes over the last three decades, but still the names are the same, the colours are the same, the culture is still there in the DNA of their sport. You can't make that claim about Australian soccer.

In time, the great players, coaches, journalists, commentators and volunteers will likely be recognised in some kind of soccer museum. In Andrew Howe's season guides, the NSL statistics will continue to gradually merge with those of the A-League. Perhaps one or two sides from soccer's lower tiers will be able to reconstitute themselves as A-League franchises.

Yet it is also likely that for the foreseeable future the A-League will continue its ascendancy as a closed shop, emboldened by its own success, protected from promotion and relegation, strengthened by massive television-rights deals, and, in turn, it will create its own history and its own traditions.

The *tabula rasa* granted to that young demographic of supporters in 2005 will continue to provide a space for A-League supporters to create a new world of their own. There are so many possibilities for expansion in the future: south and south-west Sydney, perhaps, the western or southern suburbs of Melbourne, Wollongong, Canberra, Fremantle, Townsville, Cairns, Geelong, Auckland, maybe even second teams in Adelaide, Brisbane and Perth, and one in Tasmania.

The great clubs of the past will likely remain in the purgatory of lower-league soccer. The circumstances of their shared experience may be smaller than those of the A-League, much less celebrated and in some quarters detested and misunderstood, but they were no less profound.

'The NSL was so much fun,' once remembered Paul Mavroudis. 'It didn't feel like anything else in Australia. That was obviously a hindrance in commercial terms, but it was part of the loose-cannon irreverence of the competition.'

For better or worse, this is how the process of gentrification works. The new takes on bits and pieces of the old, leaves a few fragments of its facade, all the while losing the characters, the charm, the spirit, the corruption, the scum, the villainy, the chaos and the warts-and-all diversity. But just as there were never enough supporters on the terraces of NSL grounds, there will never be a big enough market for the requisite club histories, biographies, documentaries and coffee table books needed to fill in the gaps of soccer's unique and multicultural history.

That hagiography will instead be written about the soccer that middle Australia actually watches: the A-League. For the clubs of soccer's most multicultural period, as Les Murray once foretold, 'their mementos will be the plaques in their honour in community halls. Some will live on as State league or amateur clubs, playing in stadiums built with unselfish passion for a more extravagant future, with a handful of ageing fans, out of sentimental duty, watching them.'[14]

In future soccer will probably sell its multicultural credentials through targeted advertising campaigns and photo opportunities and occasional coaching clinics with the Asian, Arab and African communities. Once or twice a year it will celebrate its ethnic past at FFA Cup games.

But the days of a truly pluralistic, multicultural national league – in which the clubs could be drawn from a variety of different communities, in which foreign languages could be heard from the terraces, in which rivalries could stretch far back into history, in which clubs could literally reconfigure how Australia might look – are over. That period was far too chaotic, too prone to cycles of boom and bust, and, ultimately, too democratic to fit into the commercial demands of sport in the 21st century.

The social, economic and cultural conditions that gave rise to that type of soccer are simply not there anymore; the migration patterns have changed, for one thing, and member-owned clubs have been rendered almost obsolete by the corporate imperative of modern sport. People are also more transient and time-poor than ever before.

Still, we should remember that era well, not least because it reared the individuals who were so crucial in creating the foundations of 'new football'. And we should always remember that through the darkest period, through the era of uncertainty from the 1970s to the 1990s, it was the ethnic communities and their clubs that kept the game alive. Perhaps, as Sophocles decreed, 'One must wait until the evening to see how splendid the day has been.'

The effects of this demographic and cultural shift are difficult to predict. Australia will always be a multicultural country, but it is also true that the Anglo-Australian population will probably always be the largest, the most privileged and the most un-integrative ethnic group. Since the advent of the A-League, the Anglos feel a sense of ownership over top-flight soccer and its clubs more than any time since the 1940s.

This is the most powerful, if unspoken, force in Australian society. Nothing else like it gets the wheels of the media, business and politics turning. But as new waves of immigrants and refugees continue to arrive on these shores, we should hope that in the future there emerges a Les Murray from the Assyrian community, or a Frank Lowy from the Chinese community, a Mark Viduka from the Koreans, a Remo Nogarotto from the Filipinos, a Kimon Taliadoros from the Indians or an Andrew Dettre among the Somalis. We should hope that Australian soccer still has the capacity to play the role for Indigenous people that it once did for Charles Perkins. We should hope that a successful new youth development system can be created to give rise to another golden generation of players. And we should hope that the future of Australian soccer is female – there is so much untapped energy and potential in the women's game.

If in the decades to come the newer migrant communities have not taken over leadership positions in soccer, and it is predominantly Anglo males running the show, then we will know that soccer has lost its most important social dividend. But at least then, at long last, soccer will finally be able to say that it is just another Australian sport.

★

On a mild April afternoon, three months after the 2015 Asian Cup final, Paul Mavroudis stood waiting for the No. 1 tram to take him to Lakeside Stadium, the home of South Melbourne Hellas.

It was a familiar trip: metro train from the western suburbs, a short walk to the tram stop, and then on in the direction of South Melbourne beach. Surrounding him on all sides was the iconography of a city: Flinders Street station, the Yarra River, Federation Square. People swarmed in all directions. This, after all, was the heart of Melbourne on a Saturday afternoon.

Long ago Mavroudis had stopped searching for fellow South fans making the pilgrimage. But as he fiddled with his glasses, a tram worker spotted his blue beanie with the club logo, and asked who South were up against.

'Croatia,' responded Mavroudis, using the old parlance.

'What kind of crowd will there be?'

'Probably 1000,' said Mavroudis, 'maybe 1500.'

The worker looked shocked. 'But we used to get 8000 for this game.'

Perplexed, Mavroudis established that this man was in fact a South Melbourne Hellas fan in self-imposed exile, one of the thousands of NSL regulars who had drifted away from his club. Despair and fury ran through Mavroudis – how could he explain, without losing his composure and his dignity, why Hellas was no longer the club of this man's memory? How do you explain the problem to the problem itself?

As Mavroudis mumbled a feeble explanation, trying as always to be fair and even-handed, the tram crawled to a halt in front of him. 'Happy Easter,' the tram worker offered, recognising the upcoming Greek Orthodox celebrations. When Mavroudis said he wouldn't be attending the church service, the man asked, 'Why not?'

'I'm not a believer,' said Mavroudis, stepping onto the tram.

The lapsed Hellas fan shook his head. 'You should go anyway.'

ACKNOWLEDGEMENTS

Thanks to Mum and Dad and my brother, Jack, who have always supported me. Thanks also to Andrew Dettre and Steve Dettre. I remain lost in admiration for Andrew's work, and the opportunity to meet him and tell his story was a personal highlight.

To Ben Williams and Asami Ako; Pave and Katarina Jusup; Andrew and Vaniece Howe; Dom Bossi, Tom Mortimer and Kieren Fairbairn, thanks for the spare rooms, couches and terrific company. Much of this book was written in Bar Sport in Leichhardt, in the company of Joe and Frank Napoliello. Thank you both for the long chats and the best coffee in Sydney.

For friendship, support and inspiration thanks to Jesse Walker, Anna Millan, Axel Williams, Hannah Burnett, Patrick Skene, Brad Cooke, Scott McIntyre, Elia Santoro, Bonita Mersiades, Richard Parkin, Di Popic, Aristea Kaydos-Nitis, Stuart Randall, Tracey Holmes, Andrew McMillen, Sarah Conte, Mohammad Othman, Sterling and Amy McQuire, Ian Syson, Paul Mavroudis, Roy Hay, Shaun Mooney, Vince Rugari, Mario De Vecchi, John Bomben, Francis Awaritefe, Nick Tsiaras and Kimon Taliadoros.

Professionally I owe an enormous debt of gratitude to Tom Lutz and Mike Hytner from the *Guardian*. Thanks also to Alexandra Payne from UQP, who believed in and championed this book before a single word had been written, and to Rebecca Starford and Ian See, who brought it to fruition.

Thank you to everyone who agreed to be interviewed – your time and energy are greatly appreciated.

ENDNOTES

PART I: THE NATIONAL INTEREST

The World Is for Them: *Introduction*

1   'Marconi', *Soccer Action*, 13 March 1985.
2   πO, *Fitzroy: The Biography*, Collective Press, Melbourne, 2015.

They Speak with a Soccer Accent: *1950–1966*

1   'The Gospel According to Trevor Jones', *Soccer Mirror*, 3 October 1953.
2   Andrew Dettre, *The First 15 Years of St George-Budapest (1957–1972)*, Atlas Printery, Sydney, 1973.
3   'New Arrivals in Fisticuff Soccer', *Sporting Globe*, 12 April 1950.
4   'When in Rome', *Argus*, 11 October 1951.
5   'Soccer Victory Shock to National Code', *Argus*, 24 February 1954.
6   'Broken Glass Found on 3 Soccer Grounds', *Mail*, 18 July 1953.
7   'Editorial: At War with a Sadist', *Soccer Mirror*, 25 July 1953.
8   'After the Kick-off Today We Enter a Time of Crisis', *Argus*, 17 April 1954.
9   The NSW Federation of Soccer Clubs, 'Resolution', 5 January 1957.
10 'A Soccer Fan's Forgotten Dream: The William Kennard Cup', *Australian Society for Sports History Bulletin*, no. 24, June 1996.
11 'Sir William Walkley Steps Down', *Sydney Morning Herald*, 23 September 1967.
12 Lex Marinos, *Blood and Circuses: An Irresponsible Memoir*, Allen & Unwin, Sydney, 2014.
13 'Grand Final Crowd Australian Record', *Soccer World*, 8 October 1959.
14 'An Appreciation – and a Plea', *Soccer and Other Sports*, 12 July 1958.
15 'Have Your Say', *Soccer World*, 5 August 1960.
16 'One of the Weird Mob', *Soccer World*, 7 March 1958.
17 'From the Sidelines', *Soccer World*, 17 February 1960.

18   Pierre Lanfanchi, Christiane Eisenberg, Tony Mason & Alfred Wahl, *One Hundred Years of Football: The FIFA Centennial Book*, Weidenfeld and Nicolson, London, 2004.

19   'We Need a "Super League!"', *Sport*, September 1962.

20   'What of the Schools? Boys Have a Right to Play Soccer if They Want To', *Soccer News*, 7 May 1960.

21   'A Real Australian Boy Makes Good', *Soccer News*, 1 October 1960.

22   'Black in a White World', *Sun*, 8 June 1968.

23   Charles Perkins, *A Bastard like Me*, Ure Smith, Sydney, 1975.

24   Rachel Perkins, Ivan Sen & John Williams, *Fire Talker: The Life and Times of Charles Perkins*, television documentary, ABC TV, Sydney, 2010.

25   '*Soccer Year Book*'s Player of the Year … 1960', *The South Australian Soccer Year Book*, South Australian Soccer Federation, Adelaide, 1961.

26   'Star Parade: Johnny Wong – Polonia N.S.', *Soccer World*, 16 June 1961.

27   'From the Sidelines', *Soccer World*, 17 February 1960.

28   'Editorial: Another First', *Soccer World*, 2 March 1962.

29   'Australian Star Parade: C. Perkins – Pan Hellenic', *Soccer World*, 2 March 1962.

30   'Soccer Featured in Aust. Novel', *Soccer World*, 21 September 1962.

31   'Language of the Future?', *Soccer World*, 28 September 1962.

32   'Australian Soccer Lost Its Inspired Leader', *Soccer World*, 22 February 1963.

33   'Budapest Had the Wong-complex during Big Game', *Soccer World*, 25 September 1964.

34   'Domain Plea for Aim of United Mankind', *Sydney Morning Herald*, 26 April 1965.

35   'He Only Wanted to Talk', *Daily Telegraph*, 29 April 1965.

36   'Soccer Brawls', *Daily Telegraph*, 26 April 1965.

37   'Soccer Riots Must End', *Sydney Morning Herald*, 26 April 1965.

38   'Open Letter to a Young Player: Goalkeepers May Be Crazy, but They're Human', *Soccer World*, 18 June 1965.

39   'Readers Letters', *Soccer World*, 18 June 1965.

40   'Editorial – Tell Him, Luv, Don't Show Him', *Soccer World*, 10 July 1964.

41   'Fresh Blood in APIA Will Have Benefits', *Soccer World*, 24 September 1965.

42   Donald Horne, *The Lucky Country: Australia in the Sixties*, Penguin, Melbourne, 1964.

43   'Of Friends and Matches', *Soccer World*, 12 November 1965.

44   'We Must Swallow These Bitter Pills, but They're Not All Poison', *Soccer World*, 3 December 1965.

45   'What Will Lou Do with New "Freedom"?', *Soccer World*, 26 November 1965.

46   'Immigration Says Star Must Leave', *Sydney Morning Herald*, 17 December 1965.

47   'Wong Still Hopes He Can Stay', *Canberra Times*, 24 December 1965.

48   'Mass Exodus of Players from Sydney Clubs Could Be Blessing', *Soccer World*, 21 January 1966.

49   'Leo's Exit Spells End of Our Greatest Era', *Soccer World*, 25 February 1966.

50   ibid.

It's Time: *1967–1976*

1   Ray Richards, *The Birth of the Socceroos*. Reproduced with permission of the author.

2   'Hungarian Athletes Decide to Seek Asylum', *Daily Telegraph*, 3 December 1956.

3   'Many Fresh Talents in Asia-bound Side', *Soccer World*, 27 October 1967.

4   'Asian Tour Certain to Foster Goodwill', *Leader*, 18 October 1967.

5   'Saigon Mission May Start a New Asian Policy', *Soccer World*, 27 October 1967.

6   Frank Kunz, *The Hungarians in Australia*, Australasian Educa Press, Melbourne, 1985.

7   'Frankly, We're Upset About …', *Soccer World*, 23 January 1970.

8   'Japan Wants Return Visit', *Soccer World*, 26 March 1971.

9   'St George Tour Big Milestone', *Soccer World*, 2 April 1971.

10   'ASF Chief Promises Peaceful Changes in Policy', *Soccer World*, 19 November 1971.

11   'My Mission to China', *Sunday Australian*, 4 July 1971.

12   'ASF Chief Promises Peaceful Changes in Policy'.

13   'Emus It Is – They Can Run and Kick', *Daily Mirror*, 8 December 1967.

14   'Australian Players Rose to Great Heights against Pele', *Soccer World*, 23 June 1972.

15   'Theme Is Unity, Says Whitlam', *Age*, 21 December 1972.

16   'Life in Australia … 20 Years from Now', *Sun*, 22 June 1966.

17   'Slow Boat to China May Pick Up Speed', *Soccer World*, 19 January 1973.

18   'Club Patrol', *Soccer World*, 2 March 1973.

19   AJ Grassby, *A Multi-cultural Society for the Future*, Australian Government Publishing Service, Canberra, 1973.

20   'Soccer Struggle Over – Australia in Last 16', *Sydney Morning Herald*, 14 November 1973.

21   'Parliament Hails Our Triumphant Socceroos', *Soccer World*, 23 November 1973.

22   'Rale Still Bitter about Soccer Knight', *Soccer World*, April 1982.

23   ibid.

24   'Anthem of Discord', *Age*, 22 April 1974.

25   'Editorial – We've Got a Winning Team', *Soccer World*, 10 May 1974.

26   'Rale Still Bitter about Soccer Knight'.

27   Sir Arthur George, Soccer Australia Hall of Fame acceptance speech, 1999. https://www.youtube.com/watch?v=7P1GBPIfoJg

28   '"We're All Australians" – Rale Rasic', *Soccer World*, 26 April 1974.

29   'A Soccer Ballad: Garbo Street Drop-outs', *Soccer World*, 15 March 1974.

30   'Not Disgraced', *Sydney Morning Herald*, 16 June 1974.

31   'World Cup Diary', *Soccer World*, 12 July 1974.

32   'Where Do We Go from Here?', *Sydney Morning Herald*, 28 June 1974.

33   'A Glimpse of the Future', *Soccer World*, 5 July 1974.

34   'Soccer "Threat" – Barassi', *Soccer World*, 6 September 1974.
35   'Schaefer Starred in Classic Grand Final', *Soccer World*, 4 October 1974.
36   'Epitome of a Sportsman', *Sydney Morning Herald*, 30 September 1974.
37   Frank Stewart, address to the inaugural dinner of the Australian Sports Council, 28 August 1974.
38   Andrew Dettre, *The First 15 Years of St George-Budapest (1957–1972)*.
39   'Anglomania Prevails – Rasic Dumped', *Soccer World*, 29 August 1975.
40   'Migrant Policy Must Be Fully Reversed', *Soccer World*, 26 March 1976.
41   'Smalltalk', *Soccer World*, 9 April 1976.
42   'Editorial – How We Must Hate Ourselves', *Soccer World*, 16 April 1976.
43   'Rale Still Bitter about Soccer Knight'.
44   'Startalk', *Soccer Action*, 28 July 1976.

A Golden Opportunity: *1977–1979*

1   Pino Bosi, *Who Is Afraid of the Ethnic Wolf?*, Kurunda Films and Publications, Sydney, 1986.
2   Gordon Sheldon & Jan Neil, *Canberra: Dream to Reality*, Mullaya Publications, Melbourne, 1975.
3   'All Roads Led to Canberra', *Soccer World*, 30 October 1980.
4   Jerzy Zubrzycki, address to the inaugural meeting of the Australian Ethnic Affairs Council, 23 March 1977. http://www.multiculturalaustralia.edu.au/doc/zubrzycki_3.pdf
5   Australian Ethnic Affairs Council, *Australia as a Multicultural Society – Submission to the Australian Population and Immigration Council on the Green Paper 'Immigration Policies and Australia's Population'*, Australian Government Publishing Service, Canberra, 1977.
6   'Smalltalk', *Soccer World*, 27 April 1978.
7   Australian Soccer Federation minutes, obtained from Roy Hay.
8   'Canberra's Chance to Be True Soccer City', *Soccer World*, 18 March 1977.
9   'Why I Won't Play Again', *Canberra Times*, 7 April 1977.
10   'Leg Injury Puts Pillans in Doubt', *Advertiser*, 4 April 1977.
11   'Philips League Goes On in "War-time" Conditions', *Soccer World*, 13 May 1977.
12   'Only Stars Can Get Fans Back', *Soccer World*, 20 May 1977.
13   Nick Hornby, *Fever Pitch*, Gollancz, London, 1992.
14   Patrick Mangan, *Offsider: A Memoir*, Victory Books, Melbourne, 2010.
15   'It's Not You, David, It's the Gimmick', *Age*, 23 November 2012.
16   'Alston May Yet Play for City', *Canberra Times*, 30 June 1977.
17   'Alston Waits for a Telephone Call', *Canberra Times*, 25 August 1977.
18   'Canberra', *Soccer World*, 29 July 1977.
19   'Superb Display, Precious Win', *Soccer World*, 29 July 1977.
20   'Canberra Brought Breath of Fresh Air', *Soccer World*, 2 December 1977.
21   'A Toast to City's "Success"', *Canberra Times*, 28 July 1977.

22 'Only New Methods Can Revive Sydney Soccer', *Soccer World*, 25 November 1977.

23 'Sydney Can't Support These Five PSL Clubs', *Soccer World*, 16 September 1977.

24 'Transferred Playboy Considers Marriage', *Soccer Action*, 10 March 1976.

25 'Blackmail: Soccer Player Gets 18 Months', *Age*, 23 March 1978.

26 'Welcome', *Canberra Soccer News*, 1 April 1978.

27 'How Well Is Canberra City Doing?', *Canberra Times*, 5 May 1977.

28 'Many Happy Returns Canberra–tra–tra–tra', *Canberra Soccer News*, 20 May 1978.

29 'Newcastle Has a City behind It', *Soccer World*, 20 July 1978.

30 'Philips Chief Predicts: PSL Boom in 1979', *Soccer World*, 8 March 1979.

31 'Q'land Country Comes to Life', *Soccer World*, 19 April 1979.

32 'Rudi Gutendorf in Conversation', *Canberra Soccer News*, 7 April 1979.

33 Review of Post-arrival Programs and Services for Migrants, *Migrant Services and Programs*, Australian Government Publishing Service, Canberra, 1978.

34 ibid.

35 'Saints Hit Rock Bottom', *Soccer World*, 27 September 1979.

36 'Prime Ministers Cup on Sunday', *Soccer World*, 14 September 1978.

37 'Supporters Corner', *Canberra City Soccer News*, 19 August 1979.

We Took Their Name and Their Game: *1980–1982*

1 'Comment', *Soccer World*, 15 January 1982.

2 'Bid to Form $2m Super Team', *Soccer World*, 13 September 1979; 'Lowy Set to Back Our Own "Cosmos"', *Soccer World*, 4 October 1979.

3 'Can We Imitate or Emulate America?', *Soccer World*, 21 February 1979.

4 'Warmer Days for Soccer', *Sydney Morning Herald*, 21 July 1980.

5 ibid.

6 'Summer Soccer Gets Big Vote', *Soccer World*, 28 August 1980.

7 'From the Press Box', *Soccer World*, 9 October 1980.

8 ibid.

9 'From the Press Box', *Soccer World*, 21 August 1980.

10 'ASF Chief Slams "Biased" Networks', *Soccer World*, 25 September 1980.

11 'From the Press Box', *Soccer World*, 15 January 1981.

12 'The TV View ...', *Sydney Morning Herald*, 27 October 1980.

13 *Daily Telegraph*, 24 October 1980.

14 'Olympic Have High Hopes for '77 Season', *Soccer World*, 10 September 1976.

15 'We Can Make It to the Top – Charlton', *Soccer World*, 17 July 1970.

16 'Grassby's Warning', *Soccer World*, 30 August 1979.

17 'Views on NL and the Rest', *Soccer World*, 2 April 1965.

18 'Soccer Move on Names', *Sun-Herald*, 3 December 1978.

19 'Ethnic Club Affairs Need Some Revision', *Soccer World*, 10 April 1970.

20 'From the Press Box', *Soccer World*, 26 February 1981.
21 *Considerations Related to the Future of the Philips Soccer League of Australia*, ASF Marketing, Sydney, 1981.
22 Australian Bureau of Statistics, *Year Book Australia: No. 67, 1983*, ABS, Canberra, 1983. http://www.ausstats.abs.gov.au/ausstats/free.nsf/0/BA850 6A2EE8CA2B9CA257AF70012D231/$File/13010_1983_bk67.pdf
23 *Considerations Related to the Future of the Philips Soccer League of Australia*.
24 ibid.
25 ibid.
26 ibid.
27 'Editorial', *Australian Soccer Weekly*, 20 October 1981.
28 'Now It's Sydney Surfers: Again They Want to Change the Name of Hakoah's Soccer XI', *Jewish Times*, 18 September 1980.
29 'A Sad Thing Happened on the Way Out ...', *Soccer World*, 30 August 1979.
30 'Hakoah Chief Warns of Gloomy Future of Australian Soccer', *Jewish Times*, 21 February 1980.
31 'Caesar Slays All the Brutuses but It's Nothing Really Serious', *Soccer World*, February 1982.
32 '"Hendo's" Dream Turned Sour', *Australian Soccer Weekly*, 30 March 1982.

They're Our Fucking Wogs: *1983–1985*

1 David Martin, *Foreigners*, Rigby, Sydney, 1981.
2 'Why Sydney FC v Western Sydney Wanderers Is the Derby the City Has Been Crying Out For', *Sydney Morning Herald*, 23 October 2015.
3 'Operation Rescue About to Start Again ...', *Soccer World*, February 1982.
4 'Saints Have a Do-or-die Feeling', *Sydney Morning Herald*, 2 October 1982.
5 'Marton Goals Give Title to the Saints', *Leader*, 6 October 1982.
6 'This Wasn't What You Could Call a Vintage Year', *Soccer World*, October 1982.
7 'PSL '82 review', *Soccer World*, October 1982.
8 'Dez's Magic Does Trick', *Daily Telegraph*, 24 October 1983.
9 Ivan Nimac, *More than the Game: 50 Years of Sydney United*, Sydney United Football Club, Sydney, 2008.
10 'Syd. Croatia Arrives – At Long, Long Last', *Soccer Action*, 1 February 1984.
11 'NSL Must Take Some Blame for United's Downfall', *Newcastle Herald*, 5 April 1984.
12 'KB United', *Newcastle Herald*, 8 April 1984.
13 'Heroic Act at Middle Park: Davidson Saved by Fan', *Soccer Action*, 18 April 1984.
14 'Footscray Kiosk Set Alight', *Soccer Action*, 16 May 1984.
15 '"Croatia" nije klub za Rozica', *Spremnost Hrvatski Vjesnik*, 4 September 1984. Translation thanks to Dario Brentin.

16   'Nedvojbena steta svima', *Spremnost Hrvatski Vjesnik*, 4 September 1984. Translation thanks to Dario Brentin.
17   'Bungle Puts Rozic Out of Action', *Soccer Action*, 5 September 1984.
18   Geoffrey Blainey, *All for Australia*, Methuen Haynes, Sydney, 1984.
19   'Soccer's Anguish', *Sun-Herald*, 14 July 1985.
20   'Political Muscle Needed to Fight Anti-soccer Bigotry', *Soccer Action*, 8 August 1984.
21   'Nick Carle, Go for the Oscar', *SBS The World Game*, 13 October 2006. http://theworldgame.sbs.com.au/blog/2006/10/13/nick-carle-go-oscar
22   Roy Hay, personal email to Joe Gorman.
23   Les Murray, *By the Balls: Memoir of a Football Tragic*, Random House, Sydney, 2006.
24   'Letters to the Editor', *Geelong Advertiser*, 10 June 1985.
25   'Soccer Riot Madness', *Daily Telegraph*, 8 July 1985.
26   'Soccer: Ban the Thugs!', *Sun*, 8 July 1985.
27   'Make Oz Soccer-free', *Sun*, 17 July 1985.
28   'Anatomy of a Riot', *Soccer Action*, 17 July 1985.
29   'Lamington Lads Are Bound for Europe's Best Pitches', *Geelong Advertiser*, 11 October 1985.
30   'Farewell Dez Marton', *Soccer House Journal*, September 1985.
31   Letter from Alex Ferguson to Roy Hay, 14 November 1985. Personal collection of Roy Hay.
32   Craig Johnston and Neil Jameson, *Walk Alone: The Craig Johnston Story*, Collins, Sydney, 1989.
33   'How the Socceroos Missed the Best', *Bulletin*, 3 December 1985.
34   'Arok Continues to Push for Sydney', *Age*, 12 November 1985.
35   'Just like Paradise, Say Scots', *Australian*, 3 December 1985.
36   'Socceroos Draw – Bye, Bye, Mexico', *Sun*, 5 December 1985.
37   'Well Done, Australia the Brave', *Australian*, 5 December 1985.
38   'Scottish Goalie Foils Socceroos', *Age*, 5 December 1985; 'Local Fans Given a Night to Remember', *Sydney Morning Herald*, 5 December 1985.
39   'Blast from the Past and a Personal Story', *Goal Weekly*, 25 February 2008.

The Final Winter: *1986–1989*

1   'Readers Write', *Jewish Times*, 23 April 1987.
2   'An Airlift to Rival Buljevic, Zoraja?', *Soccer Action*, 12 February 1986.
3   'PAOK Offer Tempts "Seki" but He's Here till September', *Soccer Action*, 2 April 1986.
4   'Nikitovic Saves Four Penalties; Fan Punches Referee', *Soccer Action*, 26 March 1986.
5   ibid.
6   'Seki's JUST Best Yet!', *Soccer Action*, 28 May 1986.
7   'Hakoah Club Board of Directors Election', *Jewish Times*, 26 March 1987.

8   'Readers Write', *Jewish Times*, 7 May 1987.
9   'It's Time to Gird Loins and Drop "Dinki-di" Names', *Soccer Action*, 28 January 1987.
10   'Readers Write', *Jewish Times*, 19 March 1987.
11   *Jewish Times*, 9 April 1987.
12   'An Open Letter to Frank Lowy', *Jewish Times*, 9 April 1987.
13   'Readers Write', *Jewish Times*, 23 April 1987.
14   'Readers Write', *Jewish Times*, 26 March 1987.
15   Johnny Warren, Andy Harper & Josh Whittington, *Sheilas, Wogs and Poofters: An Incomplete Biography of Johnny Warren and Soccer in Australia*, Random House, Sydney, 2002.
16   'A True Club Med in Our Midst', *Soccer Action*, 25 February 1987.
17   'The End of an Era', unpublished column. Reproduced with the permission of Andrew Dettre.
18   'No Need to Purify Soccer', *Sydney Morning Herald*, 24 December 1987.
19   Jacquie Atallah, Ross Clelland & Gary Martin, *Sport 88: A Guide to Bicentennial Sport and Recreation*, Australian Bicentennial Authority, Special Events Section, Sydney, 1988.
20   'We Can Beat the World's Best, Says Arok', *Sydney Morning Herald*, 5 July 1988.
21   'Don't Cry for Us, Argentina', *Sydney Morning Herald*, 15 July 1988.
22   'Brazil's Cup, but Glory Is Shared', *Age*, 18 July 1988.
23   'Olympic on Top but Crowd Hits Bottom', *Sydney Morning Herald*, 20 July 1988.
24   'Readers Opinions', *Australian Soccer Weekly*, 15 July 1987.

PART II: THE UNINVOLVED AUSTRALIANS

For the Homeland: *1990–1995*

1   Konstandina Dounis, 'Soccer at Middle Park', *Poems for My Mother*, Olive Grove Publishing, Melbourne, 1999.
2   'Broadening the Horizons Would Be a Capital Idea', *Sydney Morning Herald*, 14 October 1989.
3   Graham Bradley, *Report to the Australian Soccer Federation on the Structure and Organisation of Australian Soccer*, Australian Soccer Federation, Sydney, 1990.
4   'Bradley Leaves Vital Questions Wide Open', *Australian Soccer Weekly*, 13 June 1990.
5   Graham Bradley, *Report to the Australian Soccer Federation on the Structure and Organisation of Australian Soccer*.
6   'It's a Big Blunder', *Australian Soccer Weekly*, 28 May 1991.
7   'Players the Victim of Price Spiral', *Australian*, 7 December 1989.
8   'Soccer's Slave Trade', *Inside Sport*, October 1993.

9   'The Rise and Rise of Francis', *Soccer Australia*, September–October 1993.

10   'Letters to the Editor', *Australian and British Soccer Weekly*, 22 November 1994.

11   'Viduka Loss Will Hurt: Bazic', *Australian and British Soccer Weekly*, 28 March 1995.

12   'What a Knight for Viduka', *Australian and British Soccer Weekly*, 2 May 1995.

13   Mark Viduka, pre-match interview with SBS, 7 May 1995. https://www.youtube.com/watch?v=bL5oySt96B0.

14   'Tudjman Asks Croats to Return', *Australian*, 20 June 1995.

15   Paul Keating, speech at luncheon in honour of Franjo Tudjman, President of Croatia, 20 June 1995. http://pmtranscripts.pmc.gov.au/release/transcript-9640

16   ibid.

17   'Croatian Leader's Visit Raises Risk of Violence: Serbs', *Australian*, 24–25 June 1995.

18   'Postcard from Zagreb', *Age*, 17 November 1995.

19   ibid.

20   ibid.

A Generosity of Spirit: *1996–1998*

1   'Soccer Must Change to Grow', *Sydney Morning Herald*, 21 August 1996.

2   'Australian Soccer Shattered', *Australian and British Soccer Weekly*, 17 January 1995.

3   Parliament of Australia, *Soccer: A Report from the Senate Environment, Recreation, Communications and the Arts References Committee: First Report*, (J Coulter, chair), Parl. Paper 119, Canberra, 1995. *Second Report*, (M Lees, chair), Parl. Paper 14, Canberra, 1996.

4   'Hill Doing It His Way', *Daily Telegraph*, 12 February 1996.

5   'Quotes of 1995', *Australian and British Soccer Weekly*, 2 January 1996.

6   'National Soccer Summit Melbourne – May 19–21', *Studs Up*, June–July 1995.

7   'Old Habits Die Hard in Soccer's Top Division', *Australian*, 18 November 1995.

8   Judith Brett, *Quarterly Essay 19: Relaxed & Comfortable: The Liberal Party's Australia*, Black Inc., Melbourne, 2005.

9   'Hanson Still Dividing Liberals', *Age*, 2 September 2003.

10   Steve Waugh, *Out of My Comfort Zone: The Autobiography*, Penguin, Melbourne, 2005.

11   'Editorial', *Australian and British Soccer Weekly*, 15 August 1995.

12   Australian Bureau of Statistics, *Sport and Recreation: A Statistical Overview*, ABS, Canberra, 1997. http://www.ausstats.abs.gov.au/ausstats/subscriber.nsf/0/C2507089DB64417ECA256AFB007B7BE5/$File/41560.pdf

13   '"Ethnic" Threat Splits Clubs', *Sydney Morning Herald*, 15 August 1996.

14   'Broaden Our Appeal', *Daily Telegraph*, 16 August 1996.

15   'Cursed by Ethnic Angst', *Daily Telegraph*, 16 August 1996.

16   'Hill's "Ethnic" Plan Is Wrong', *Sydney Morning Herald*, 20 August 1996. On 14 September, the newspaper issued a statement that said it 'did not intend to convey' any suggestion that David Hill was racist.

17   'Soccer Must Change to Grow', *Sydney Morning Herald*, 21 August 1996.

18   'Mike Rann Joins the Debate: Open Letter to David Hill', *Australian and British Soccer Weekly*, 27 August 1996.

19   'NSW MP – Morris Iemma Calls for Soccer "Super League"', *Australian and British Soccer Weekly*, 3 September 1996.

20   'Letters to the Editor', *Australian and British Soccer Weekly*, 10 September 1996.

21   'Dear Studs Up', *Studs Up*, November–December 1996.

22   'Letters to the Editor', *Australian and British Soccer Weekly*, 17 December 1996; '(Psst)', *Age*, 15 December 1996.

23   'Heartland', *Sydney Morning Herald*, 14 December 1996.

24   '1996 – Not a Year to Remember', *Studs Up*, January 1997.

25   'Glory Days', *Sydney Morning Herald*, 31 December 1996.

26   Braham Dabscheck, 'Moving beyond Ethnicity: Soccer's Evolutionary Progress', in Bob Stewart (ed.), *The Games Are Not the Same: The Political Economy of Football in Australia*, Melbourne University Press, Melbourne, 2007.

27   'Hill in Socceroo Pay Ultimatum', *Sydney Morning Herald*, 10 April 1997.

28   ibid.

29   'Warriors Fall Foul of the Collywobbles', *Age*, 30 March 1997.

30   'Confusion Reigns in Our League of Nations: Four Diverse Soccer Devotees Search for the Answers in the Great Australian "Ethnic" Debate', *Sydney Morning Herald*, 22 August 1996.

31   'Ultimatum Time: Soccer Violence', *Sydney Morning Herald*, 20 May 1997.

32   ibid.

33   'Soccer Sinking into an Ethnic Quagmire', *Courier-Mail*, 22 May 1997.

34   'Soccer Goals', *Sunday Mail*, 18 May 1997.

35   'United's Fans Told to Behave for Final', *Courier-Mail*, 22 May 1997.

36   'Greatest Day in History of Australian Soccer', *Courier-Mail*, 26 May 1997; 'A Win for Multi-ethnic Harmony', *Australian*, 26 May 1997; 'Dawn of a New Age', *Studs Up*, May 1997.

37   'Win for Soccer', *Sydney Morning Herald*, 27 May 1997.

38   'Brawl Lesson', *Sydney Morning Herald*, 4 June 1997.

39   'No Fuss Foster', *Sydney Morning Herald*, 1 July 1997.

40   'Injury Won't Stop MCG Dream Date', *Australian*, 26 November 1997.

41   'Bowled Over at the "G"', *Herald Sun*, 29 November 1997.

42   'The Dream Is Dead', *Age*, 30 November 1997.

43   'Studs Up Needs YOU!', *Studs Up*, December 1997–January 1998.

44   Robbie Slater & Matthew Hall, *Robbie Slater: The Hard Way*, HarperCollins, Sydney, 1999.

45   'Clash That Almost Destroyed Socceroos', *Daily Telegraph*, 22 January 2012.

The Sons of Immigrants: *1999–2002*

1 'Migrant Clubs' Myopic View Paves Way for NSL Revolution', *Australian and British Soccer Weekly*, 2 February 1999.
2 'Dear Studs Up', *Studs Up*, February 1999.
3 'Migrant Clubs' Myopic View Paves Way for NSL Revolution'.
4 'Moss Written into Spirit World', *Sydney Morning Herald*, 23 September 1998.
5 'New Club Idea Foolish, Says Makris', *Advertiser*, 19 March 1999.
6 Kevin Christopher, *The Un-official Beginners Guide to the History of the Australian National Soccer League*, Studs Up, Melbourne, 1999.
7 'The Studs Up Report on the International Soccer Expo', *Studs Up*, July 1999.
8 'Players' Initiative Sows Seeds for Full-scale Revolution', *Sydney Morning Herald*, 27 December 2000.
9 'Collingwood's Captain a Leader Twice Over', *Age*, 7 October 1996.
10 'Soccer Can't Afford Its Balkan Wars', *Australian*, 11 May 2001.
11 'West Assault on the "Cold Hole of Hell"', *Age*, 9 January 1999.
12 'Muslims Threaten to Sue over Soccer Salute', *Age*, 17 May 2001.
13 'Serb Salute Puts Glory Striker in Hot Seat', *Herald Sun*, 9 May 2001.
14 'Despotovski Defends Salute', *Australian*, 9 May 2001.
15 'Time NSL Embraced Its Multiculturalism', *Sydney Morning Herald*, 19 May 2001.
16 'And Finally ...', *Studs Up*, March 2000.
17 'Australian Media Takes Its Eye off the Ball', *Australian*, 27 June 2002.
18 'A Patriot Shame – No Green and Gold Jumper Generates Less Passion', *Sunday Telegraph*, 21 July 2002.

Death to the NSL: *2003–2004*

1 Loukas Founten, *A Decade United: A 10-year History of the Adelaide United Football Club*, Loukas Founten, Adelaide, 2015.
2 'Labbozzetta "Smelled a Rat" in Days before Coup', *Australian*, 7 August 2001.
3 'Interview – Former Prime Minister John Howard', *Leopold Method*, 9 January 2015. http://leopoldmethod.com.au/interview-former-prime-minister-john-howard/
4 'Stokes Okayed Rugby Bid Leak', *Australian*, 11 October 2005.
5 *Australian Premier League: For the Fans*, PFA Management Ltd, Melbourne, 2002.
6 ibid.
7 'Board Asked to Quit', *Herald Sun*, 8 April 2003.
8 'Report Calls for Soccer Board to Go', *Age*, 8 April 2003.
9 'Soccer Australia Faces Its Most Crucial Moment – Remo's in the Hot Seat', *Daily Telegraph*, 2 May 2003.
10 'Time for Howard and Blatter to Act', *Sydney Morning Herald*, 2 July 2003.

11   'Godley Quits after "Donkey" Remark', *Sunday Mail*, 9 February 2003.

12   'Adelaide Quits NSL as Bid to Find a White Knight Fails', *Age*, 1 September 2003.

13   'No Bail-out by Pickard', *Sunday Mail*, 31 August 2003.

14   'Australia United for Its Brilliant Soccer Goal', *Age*, 1 November 2003.

15   'Match Reports', *Adelaide United Football Club*, Sports Information Services, Adelaide, 2003.

16   Australian Soccer Association, *Report of the NSL Task Force into the Structure of a New National Soccer League Competition*, ASA, Sydney, 2003.

17   John Stensholt & Shaun Mooney, *A-League: The Inside Story of the Tumultuous First Decade*, Black Inc., Melbourne, 2015.

18   'Once a Knight Not Enough for Croats', *Age*, 1 March 2004.

19   Johnny Warren, Andy Harper & Josh Whittington, *Sheilas, Wogs and Poofters*.

20   Johnny Warren, Soccer Australia Hall of Fame acceptance speech, 1999. https://www.youtube.com/watch?v=yB0wrU2tWOA

21   'Top Player, Great Friend', *Daily Telegraph*, 8 November 2004.

22   Johnny Warren, Andy Harper & Josh Whittington, *Sheilas, Wogs and Poofters*.

23   'Buried History: Aboriginal Leader Charles Perkins Was a Pioneering Soccer Star', *Sydney Morning Herald*, 16 October 2015.

24   'Club Farewells Saint Johnny', *Sunday Telegraph*, 14 November 2004.

25   'A Unifying Force for His Beloved Football', *Sydney Morning Herald*, 8 November 2004.

26   'O'Neill Believes Soccer Has the Right to Dream', *Age*, 4 June 2004.

27   'Australian Soccer Has a Vision and It's Not All Greek to Me', *Sydney Morning Herald*, 27 March 2004.

28   'Too Long a Wait to See Soccer's Brave New World – NSL GRAND FINAL 2004: GO THE POWER', *Sunday Telegraph*, 4 April 2004.

29   'Is Australian Football Worth the Hype?', *When Saturday Comes*, November 2005.

30   'Talkin 'Bout a Revolution', *Sydney Morning Herald*, 24 July 2004.

31   John O'Neill, *It's Only a Game: A Life in Sport*, Random House, Sydney, 2007.

32   'Soccer's Australian Name Change', *Sydney Morning Herald*, 16 December 2004.

33   'Soccer Ads Aim to Net Hip Youth', *Australian*, 4 August 2005.

34   'Clubs Face Fan Lockout after Brawl', *Sydney Morning Herald*, 15 March 2005.

35   'New Tribes Grow in Cultural Desert', *Herald Sun*, 20 April 2005.

36   'Australia Is an Oasis of Calm: Don't Pollute It', *Daily Telegraph*, 5 May 2005.

The Sum of Its Parts: *2005–2006*

1   David Martin, 'Roots', *From Life: Selected Poems of David Martin*, Current Book Distributors, Sydney, 1953.

2   'NSW "Cut Ties" with New Club over Lowy"', *Sydney Morning Herald*, 12 December 2004.

3   'Come and Be the Children of the Revolution', *Sydney Morning Herald*, 26 August 2005.
4   'Viduka Aims to Reopen His Socceroos Account', *Sydney Morning Herald*, 9 June 2005.
5   'Viduka Rewarded with Captaincy', *Age*, 3 September 2005.
6   'Calm before the Storm', *SBS The World Game*, 8 November 2005. http://theworldgame.sbs.com.au/article/2005/11/08/calm-storm
7   'Viduka Laments Last Campaign', *SBS The World Game*, 11 November 2005. http://theworldgame.sbs.com.au/article/2005/11/11/viduka-laments-last-campaign
8   'Vidmar: This Is Our Time', *SBS The World Game*, 11 November 2005. http://theworldgame.sbs.com.au/article/2005/11/13/vidmar-our-time
9   'It's Time for Cinderella to Go to the Ball', *Sydney Morning Herald*, 16 November 2005.
10 *Shootout*, television program, Fox Sports, Sydney, 9 November 2014. https://www.youtube.com/watch?v=CraKfRrN6yM
11 'At Last, the End of the Darkness ... This One's for You, Johnny', *Sydney Morning Herald*, 17 November 2005.
12 'We're All Winners', *Herald Sun*, 18 November 2005.
13 'The Not-so-bad Old Days', *Age*, 18 December 2005.
14 *Shootout*, television program, 9 November 2014.
15 'Melbourne "Second Greece"', *Sydney Morning Herald*, 21 May 2006.
16 'Wogball, the Beautiful Game of Aussie Heroes', *Sydney Morning Herald*, 25 May 2006.
17 'Shame Game Gets a Kick', *Herald Sun*, 26 May 2006.
18 'World Game Needs a Little Respect to Win Us Over', *Sunday Mail*, 27 November 2005.
19 'Why I Fear for Our Own Beautiful Game', *Age*, 19 November 2005.
20 'Is Australia Ready for a New National Game? No', *Bulletin*, 20 June 2006.
21 'OK, Someone's Got to Say It: I'm Sick of Soccer', *Sydney Morning Herald*, 29 June 2002.
22 'Little America: How John Howard Has Changed Australia', *Monthly*, March 2006.
23 Peter Costello, 'Worth Promoting, Worth Defending: Australian Citizenship, What It Means and How to Nurture It', address to the Sydney Institute, 23 February 2006. http://www.petercostello.com.au/speeches/2006/2111-worth-promoting-worth-defending-australian-citizenship what it means and-how-to-nurture-it-address-to-the-sydney-institute-sydney
24 'The Ties That Bind', *Sydney Morning Herald*, 2 April 2005.
25 'Fairytale Finale Allows Australia to Live the Dream', *Age*, 13 June 2006.
26 'Croatian Community's Proud Role in Australian Soccer Still Reaping Rewards', *Sydney Morning Herald*, 31 May 2014.
27 Graham Poll, *Seeing Red*, HarperCollins, London, 2007.
28 'Leichhardt Ground Zero for Australia–Italy Clash', *AAP*, 25 June 2006; 'Australia–Italy Clash Win-win for Italian Community', *AAP*, 23 June 2006.

29   'Joy at Our Loss', *Herald Sun*, 28 June 2006.
30   'Australian-Italians Celebrate Fourth World Cup', *AAP*, 10 July 2006.
31   'Roos Epitomise the All-Australian Boy', *Advertiser*, 8 July 2006.
32   Tony Wilson, *Australia United*, Geoff Slattery Publishing, Melbourne, 2006.

Just Another Page: *2007–2014*

1   'Our Legacy', *Inside Lakeside*, vol. 1, no. 2, 26 October 1997.
2   'Troubled Youth?', *Sunday Age*, 19 November 2006.
3   'Don't Ignore Our Past', *Herald Sun*, 1 April 2004.
4   'FFA's Whole of Football Extravaganza – Melbourne Edition', *South of the Border – a South Melbourne Hellas Blog*, 5 December 2014. https://south melbournefc.blogspot.com.au/2014/12/ffas-whole-of-football-extravanganza.html
5   'Krncevic's Corner', *Goal! Weekly*, vol. 1, no. 20, 13 July 2005.
6   Tony Ising, post on *MelbourneVictory.net*, 18 April 2006. http://www.melbournevictory.net/archive/index.php/t-12305.html
7   'Troublemakers Will Not Stop Us This Time', *Herald Sun*, 14 December 2006.
8   'Football's Changing Landscape', *Age*, 28 February 2007.
9   'Lowy to Shake Up Game at the Top', *Daily Telegraph*, 15 May 2007.
10   'Labor Nets Player Backing', *Age*, 24 November 2007.
11   'North Says Apology Was a Proud Moment – Today Is Going to Turn Things Around', *Daily Telegraph*, 14 February 2008.
12   'A-League Grand Final What They Said', *Newcastle Herald*, 25 February 2008.
13   'Canberra's Best Players on National Stage', *Canberra Times*, 29 July 2008.
14   'Episode 8 – Paul Mavroudis', *Behind the Game*, podcast episode. http://www.behindthegame.com.au/blogs/podcast/17592585-episode-8-paul-mavroudis-south-melbourne-hellas
15   'It Does My Head In / What Happened to the Bigger Picture?', *South of the Border*, 26 May 2009. https://southmelbournefc.blogspot.com.au/2009/05/it-does-my-head-in-what-happened-to.html
16   'Cheers Pim, You Served Us Well', *ABC The Drum*, 25 June 2010. http://www.abc.net.au/news/2010-06-25/cheers-pim-you-served-us-well/880916
17   'There Must Be a Market for the A-League', *Sydney Morning Herald*, 18 September 2010.
18   'In Summary …', *South of the Border*, 8 April 2010. https://southmelbournefc.blogspot.com.au/2010/04/in-summary.html
19   'Old Hands Won't Win New Fans', *SBS The Finktank*, 14 October 2009. http://www.sbs.com.au/blogarticle/113701/Old-hands-won-t-win-new-fans/blog/The-Finktank
20   'Lavicka Loss a Fitting Disgrace', *Sydney Morning Herald*, 21 February 2010.
21   'Osieck Must Gamble on Youth', *Sunday Mail*, 12 September 2010.

22 'I Never Lost Sight of Goal at Hand', *Sunday Mail*, 20 March 2011.

23 'With Ange, It's Not Personal', *SBS The World Game*, 27 October 2010. http://theworldgame.sbs.com.au/blog/2010/10/27/ange-its-not-personal

24 'Del Piero in the Right Place at Magically the Right Time', *Sydney Morning Herald*, 21 October 2012.

25 'Own Goal', *Four Corners*, television program, ABC TV, Sydney, 12 September 2011.

26 'Roar Savour Scoring Record amid Streak', *AAP*, 20 November 2011.

27 'A Hopeless Game – Clive's Stunning Broadside for His "Insignificant" Club', *Sunday Mail*, 19 February 2012.

28 'Lowy Says Gold Coast a "Spectacular Failure"', *Geelong Advertiser*, 29 February 2012.

29 'How the West Can Be Won', *SBS The World Game*, 7 April 2012. http://theworldgame.sbs.com.au/blog/2012/04/07/how-west-can-be-won

30 'The Newest, Oldest Club in Australian Football', media release, Western Sydney Wanderers, Sydney, 27 June 2012. http://www.wswanderersfc.com.au/article/the-newest-oldest-club-in-australian-football/bzqc7yjk6iio14c1gi2rcmc9m

31 'Proud to Stand Up for West', *Penrith Press*, 19 October 2012.

32 'How the Westies Won', *Griffith Review 41: Now We Are Ten*, June 2013.

33 'Sydney Can't Support These Five PSL Clubs', *Soccer World*, 16 September 1977.

34 'Socceroos Have Lost Their Way', *Age*, 18 October 2013.

The Way We Organise Ourselves: *Epilogue*

1 Pino Bosi, *Who Is Afraid of the Ethnic Wolf?*

2 Andrew Dettre, personal email to Joe Gorman, 2013.

3 'Summer of Football: The Stats', media release, Football Federation Australia, Sydney, 25 December 2013. http://www.footballaustralia.com.au/article/summer-football-the-stats/pj7biefn5ddq1akwnynjiaigi

4 'Ten Years Gone', *South of the Border*, 17 November 2015. https://south-melbournefc.blogspot.com.au/2015/11/ten-years-gone.html

5 Australian Bureau of Statistics, *Participation in Sport and Physical Recreation, Australia, 2013–14*, ABS, Canberra, 2015. http://www.abs.gov.au/AUSSTATS/abs@.nsf/Lookup/4177.0Main+Features12013-14?OpenDocument

6 'FFA Cup a New Old Tradition', media release, Football Federation Australia, Sydney, 1 March 2014. http://www.footballaustralia.com.au/article/ffa-cup-a-new-old-tradition/khp5b1id8pfi1pig6bjm7seb9

7 'FFA Announces National Club Identity Policy', media release, Football Federation Australia, Sydney, 26 June 2014. http://www.footballaustralia.com.au/article/ffa-announces-national-club-identity-policy/159tpdfz6wrja164o95ot6xc9u

8 *Considerations Related to the Future of the Philips Soccer League of Australia.*

9   Graham Bradley, *Report to the Australian Soccer Federation on the Structure and Organisation of Australian Soccer.*

10   Australian Soccer Association, *Report of the NSL Task Force into the Structure of a New National Soccer League Competition.*

11   Ange Postecoglou & Andy Harper, *Changing the Game: Football in Australia through My Eyes*, Penguin Random House, Melbourne, 2016.

12   'The Socceroos: Champions of Asia and Plucky Australian Underdogs No More', *Guardian Australia*, 2 February 2015.

13   'In Defence of "Old Soccer"', *South of the Border*, 29 October 2013. https://southmelbournefc.blogspot.com.au/2013/10/in-defence-of-old-soccer.html

14   'Migrant Clubs' Myopic View Paves Way for NSL Revolution', *Australian and British Soccer Weekly*, 2 February 1999.

INDEX